THE SYNTAX OF RELATIVE CLAUSES

LINGUISTIK AKTUELL/LINGUISTICS TODAY

Linguistik Aktuell/Linguistics Today (LA) provides a platform for original monograph studies into synchronic and diachronic linguistics. Studies in LA confront empirical and theoretical problems as these are currently discussed in syntax, semantics, morphology, phonology, and systematic pragmatics with the aim to establish robust empirical generalizations within a universalistic perspective.

Series Editor

Werner Abraham
Germanistisch Instituut
Rijksuniversiteit Groningen
Oude Kijk in 't Jatstraat 26
9765 EK Groningen
The Netherlands
E-mail: Abraham@let.rug.nl

Advisory Editorial Board

Guglielmo Cinque (University of Venice)
Günther Grewendorf (J.W. Goethe-University, Frankfurt)
Liliane Haegeman (University of Lille)
Hubert Haider (University of Salzburg)
Christer Platzack (University of Lund)
Ian Roberts (University of Stuttgart)
Ken Safir (Rutgers University, New Brunswick NJ)
Höskuldur Thráinsson (University of Iceland, Reykjavik)
Lisa deMena Travis (McGill University)
Sten Vikner (University of Stuttgart)
C. Jan-Wouter Zwart (University of Groningen)

Volume 32
Artemis Alexiadou, Paul Law, André Meinunger and Chris Wilder (eds.)
The Syntax of Relative Clauses

THE SYNTAX OF RELATIVE CLAUSES

ARTEMIS ALEXIADOU
PAUL LAW
ANDRÉ MEINUNGER
CHRIS WILDER

Zentrum für Allgemeine Sprachwissenschaft, Berlin

JOHN BENJAMINS PUBLISHING COMPANY
AMSTERDAM / PHILADELPHIA

The paper used in this publication meets the minimum requirements of American National Standard for Information Sciences — Permanence of Paper for Printed Library Materials, ANSI Z39.48-1984.

Library of Congress Cataloging-in-Publication Data

The syntax of relative clauses / Artemis Alexiadou ... [et al.].
    p.   cm. -- (Linguistik aktuell / Linguistics today, ISSN 0166-0829; v. 32)
   Includes bibliographical references and indexes.
    1. Grammar, Comparative and general--Relative clauses. I. Alexiadou, Artemis.
  II. Linguistik aktuell ; Bd. 32.
P297.S96   2000
415--dc21   99-462049
ISBN 90 272 2753 5 (eur) / 1 55619 916 3 (us) (Hb; alk. paper)

© 2000 – John Benjamins B.V.
No part of this book may be reproduced in any form, by print, photoprint, microfilm, or any other means, without written permission from the publisher.

John Benjamins Publishing Co. · P.O.Box 75577 · 1070 an Amsterdam · The Netherlands
John Benjamins North America · P.O.Box 27519 · Philadelphia PA 19118-0519 · USA

Table of Contents

Introduction *Artemis Alexiadou, Paul Law, André Meinunger and Chris Wilder*	1
Some Issues in the Syntax of Relative Determiners *Valentina Bianchi*	53
Type-Resolution in Relative Constructions: Featural marking and dependency encoding *Alexander Grosu*	83
Some Syntactic and Morphological Properties of Relative Clauses in Turkish *Jaklin Kornfilt*	121
On Relative Clauses and the DP/PP Adjunction Asymmetry *Paul Law*	161
Relative Asymmetries and Hindi Correlatives *Anoop Mahajan*	201
An Antisymmetry Analysis of Japanese Relative Clauses *Keiko S. Murasugi*	231
A Complement-of-N^0 Account of Restrictive and Non-Restrictive Relatives: The case of Swedish *Christer Platzack*	265
Some Consequences of the Complement Analysis for Relative Clauses, Demonstratives and the Wrong Adjectives *Cristina Schmitt*	309
A Head Raising Analysis of Relative Clauses in Dutch *Jan-Wouter Zwart*	349

Name Index	387
Subject Index	389

Introduction*

Artemis Alexiadou, Paul Law,
André Meinunger and Chris Wilder
ZAS Berlin

This volume presents a cross-section of recent generative research into the syntax of relative clause constructions. Interest in this topic has been revitalized by Kayne's recent proposal to handle relative clauses in terms of determiner complementation and raising of the relativized nominal (Kayne 1994: ch. 8). Most of the papers collected here react in some way to Kayne's ideas. With this in mind, Part I of this introduction centres on a discussion of these proposals, their background and motivations, arguments for and against.[1] In Part II, we introduce each of the papers, positioning them in the wider theoretical context.

Part I. The theoretical context

1. Relative clauses: two approaches

Advances in syntactic research of the past decades, leading to the minimalist program, are due largely to the investigation of complex structures arising

---

* This volume has its origins in a conference on Relative Clauses, organized by the editors and hosted by the Zentrum für Allgemeine Sprachwissenschaft (ZAS) in Berlin in November 1996. The papers by Bianchi, Mahajan, Murasugi, Platzack, Schmitt and Zwart derive from presentations at that conference. We take this opportunity to thank all the speakers and everyone else who participated in making that event a success. The conference itself was made possible by the generous assistance of the Deutsche Forschungsgemeinschaft (ZAS, Berlin), and of the Max-Planck-Gesellschaft (Arbeitsgruppe Strukturelle Grammatik, Berlin). We are indebted to Manfred Bierwisch and Ewald Lang for encouragement and support. Special thanks to Marcel den Dikken, Hans-Martin Gärtner, Eric Haeberli, and Gereon Müller for assistance with the manuscripts; and to Christine Maaßen for indispensable help in preparing the text for publication. Finally, we thank Werner Abraham for agreeing to include the volume in the Linguistik Aktuell series.

through 'canonical complementation', whereby a clause (or other extended projection) functions as the complement of a higher lexical predicate. The most studied simple and complex structures are, respectively, the simple clause (CP), with its internal processes of phrasal (A-/A'-) and head movement; and verb-clausal complement structures, with associated interclausal processes such as Raising, Exceptional Case Marking and Restructuring. Less progress has been made in understanding complex structures which do not arise through canonical complementation, as Chomsky (1995: 382, fn.22) notes: "... we still have no good phrase structure theory for such simple matters as attributive adjectives, relative clauses, and adjuncts of many different types".

An important subclass of complex constructions involves finite subordinate clauses that show properties (1)–(2):

(1)　'Noncanonical complementation':
　　　the clause is not an argument of a lexical predicate.

(2)　'Noncanonical *wh*-movement': the clause contains a *wh*-dependency which
　　　a.　is not associated with interrogative semantics.
　　　b.　serves to link a position inside the clause and an item outside that clause.

The best studied case of (1)–(2) cross-linguistically is the relative clause (RC) construction, in which the clause is embedded inside a nominal expression (DP) which it modifies:

(3)　a.　[the book [which John has read]]
　　　b.　[das Buch,　　　[das　　　　Hans gelesen hat]]　[German]
　　　　　the　book-NEUT.SG　REL-NEUT.SG Hans read　　has
　　　　　'the book which Hans read'

The fronted relative pronoun (*which/das*) in the RC heads an internal *wh*-dependency of a noncanonical type (not associated with interrogative semantics). The pronoun enters an external dependency with the containing noun phrase (*the book.../das Buch...*), reflected by morphosyntactic agreement between the head noun (*book/Buch*) and the pronoun (*which* vs. **who/das* vs. *den [MASC.SG], *die [FEM.SG], etc.). This dependency is instrumental in determining the construction's interpretation — in (3), restrictive modification by the RC.[2]

Properties (1) and (2) define two basic issues in the syntax of relative clauses: (a) the structural relation of the clause to the DP containing it — whether the clause is a complement or an adjunct, and where it is located; (b) the nature of the relation between the *wh*-dependency and the head noun — whether the noun is generated outside the clause, or originates from inside the clause. (1)–(2) are common to (virtually) all proposals. However, there are two competing approaches to relative clause syntax which diverge according to their view on the syntactic expression of each relation.

The semantic distinction between a complement and a relative clause, respectively 'argument' and 'modifier' of the head noun, is generally assumed to be encoded in the syntactic configuration. The argument relation is encoded as sisterhood — in (4a), the clause is sister to the lexical head N^0 ('canonical' complementation):

(4)   [$_{DP}$ the [$_{NP}$ claim [$_{CP}$ that John left]]]

The view on (1) that was standard in work of the 1980's and early 1990's is that the modification relation is encoded structurally via adjunction of the clause to a higher projection of the modified head. In (5), the RC is a sister of a higher projection of NP/DP to which it is adjoined:

(5)   [$_{DP}$ the [$_{NP}$ [$_{NP}$ claim$_j$] [$_{CP}$ OP$_j$ (that) John made t_j]]]

On (2), the standard view is that the N-head is base-generated outside CP, and is linked to the *wh*-dependency in CP by an interpretive (predication, binding or 'construal') relation (Chomsky 1977; Safir 1986; Browning 1991). The *wh*-movement dependency may be headed by a *wh*-pronoun (3a), a [–wh] pronoun (as in German (3b)), or a null operator (5). The standard view is summarized in (6):

(6)   a.   *Adjunction hypothesis*
              Relative clauses are adjoined to NP
       b.   *Base-generated head hypothesis*
              The head noun of a relative clause is base-generated outside that clause.

Alternatives to both hypotheses have existed for a long time. On (1), an early proposal was that relative clauses are sisters (complements) to determiners (Smith 1969). In the framework of the time, the determiner was a daughter of NP and left sister of the head noun. The surface 'head N-RC' order was analysed as the product of a movement rule extraposing the clause in NP — schematically:

(7)   a.   [$_{NP}$ [$_{Det}$ the + S] N]   →   b.   [$_{NP}$ [$_{Det}$ the] N S]

On (2), according to the 'head-raising' ('promotion') hypothesis (Vergnaud 1974), the external N-head originates inside CP, and so is directly linked with a CP-internal position by syntactic movement. These alternatives are summarized in (8):

(8) a. *Determiner Complement hypothesis*
 The relative clause is syntactic complement of the determiner head of DP.
 b. *Head-raising hypothesis*
 The noun phrase raises from inside the relative clause

The alternatives in (6) and (8) are independent of one another. Smith's version of (8a) is proposed in conjunction with (6b); (8b) is logically compatible with (6a). Moreover, the raising hypothesis is compatible with a landing site for the noun phrase outside of the relative clause, as in Vergnaud's version of (8b).

Developments in X'-theory and the introduction of the DP-hypothesis have altered background assumptions about constituent structure within which proposals are framed. In the context of current models, Kayne (1994) proposes that both alternatives (8) to the standard approach (6) are correct. Given the binary branching hypothesis, this has the unorthodox consequence that the head noun phrase in (3) cannot be the complement of D, even in derived structure. In Kayne's variant of the 'head raising' hypothesis (8b), the head noun raises to the specifier of the complement of D (i.e. SpecCP):

(9) a. [$_{DP}$ the [$_{CP}$ that John made [$_{DP}$ claim]]]]
 b. [$_{DP}$ the [$_{CP}$ [$_{DPj}$ claim] that John made t_j]]]

Examples with relative pronouns (analysed as transitive determiners) have a more complex derivation, involving an initial step in which the NP complement of D raises to SpecDP:

(10) a. [$_{DP}$ the [$_{CP}$ that John made [$_{DP}$ which [$_{NP}$ claim]]]]]
 b. [$_{DP}$ the [$_{CP}$ that John made [$_{DP}$ [$_{NPj}$ claim] which t_j]]]]
 c. [$_{DP}$ the [$_{CP}$ [$_{DP}$ [$_{NPj}$ claim] which t_j]$_k$ C^0 John made t_k]]]

From the standpoint of the state of research of the early 1990's, each of the approaches (6) and (8) has its specific problems, which, moreover, appear to a large extent to be complementary, the weakness of one approach being the strength of the other.

1.1 *Adjunction to external head*

1.1.1 *Constituency*
The adjunction hypothesis rests on the assumption that the semantic distinction between a complement and a relative clause is encoded in the syntactic configuration — sisterhood to head (complement) vs. adjunction to a higher projection (modifier relation):

(11) a. [$_{DP}$ the [$_{NP}$ claim [$_{CP}$ that John left]]]
 b. [$_{DP}$ the [$_{NP}$ [$_{NP}$ claim] [$_{CP}$ that John made]]]

While there is no consensus about the adjunction site of relative clauses (N', NP, D', DP are all suggested in the literature; cf. Browning 1991: 56), under the DP-hypothesis various considerations converge on NP for restrictive relative clauses at least. If maximal projections may only adjoin to maximal projections (Chomsky 1986), then only NP and DP are available. A restrictive relative is interpreted within the scope of the determiner, most clearly when this is a quantifier, as in (12). Assuming semantic scope reflects c-command, then restrictive relatives cannot be adjoined to DP:

(12) a. every girl that Mary saw
 b. $\forall_x$ [girl(x) ∧ Mary saw(x)]

Appositives (ARCs) differ in not being interpreted within the scope of the determiner. Jackendoff (1977) proposed that the restrictive/non-restrictive distinction is reflected configurationally, non-restrictives being adjoined higher than restrictives; Demirdache (1991) suggests specifically that non-restrictives are DP-adjuncts.

The analysis (11b) fulfills basic requirements in capturing surface distribution and 'constituency facts'. The DP (D^0+NP) exists as a constituent independently of the 'optional' adjunct. The string corresponding to CP correctly appears right-peripherally and forms a constituent that can be displaced from DP (via extraposition).

Questions about the adjunction analysis arise when comparatives, equatives and degree constructions are considered.

(13) a. more books [than John can read]
 b. as many books [as John can read]
 c. too many books [for John to read]

The bracketed clauses in (13) are very similar to RCs. The whole construction functions externally as a DP. The degree word (*-er*, *as*, *too*) in combination with a cardinal determiner (*many*) functions like a determiner, governing N and heading the construction (Corver 1990). Syntactically the clause displays internal *wh*-movement. Semantically, too, the clause is like a restrictive relative in that it is interpreted in the scope of the determiner. The positioning of the clause is identical to that of an RC; it appears right-peripherally in DP or may undergo extraposition. To analyse the clauses in (13) as adjuncts to NP seems equally motivated, except that the selection of the clause by the degree word fails to be captured. The optimal expression of selection relations is in terms of a head directly selecting its complement; it is conceptually unattractive to have a head select an adjunct to its complement. Such considerations give rise to analyses similar to the determiner complement analysis with extraposition in (7) above (cf. Bresnan 1979):

(14)   a.   [$_{NP}$ [$_{Det}$ Deg + S] N]   →   b.   [$_{NP}$ [$_{Det}$ Deg] N S]

While right-adjunction may be the correct surface analysis, for both degree complement clauses and relatives, this does not entail that the adjunction structure is base-generated. For the constructions in (13), the selection relation suggests this is not so. Since it is known independently that RRCs are susceptible to extraposition in the same way as comparative clauses, surface order is no compelling argument for base-generating RRCs in right-adjoined position.

1.1.2 *Null operators and connectivity*

Internal *wh*-movement in relative clauses (15a) differs in crucial ways from interrogative *wh*-movement in argument clauses (15b) or in root clauses. There is no morphosyntactic or referential dependency between the *wh*-phrase and the containing DP in (15b); the clause itself satisfies requirements of the argument position of the lexical head (N = *question*) which selects it.

(15)   a.   the claim [which John made _]
        b.   the question (of) [which claim John made _]

The *wh*-pronoun in the RC (15a) displays agreement with the N-head of NP/DP (see above). Its interpretive function is to establish a link between the head NP/DP and some position within CP (via the trace it binds), on the basis of which the semantic modification of the nominal by the RC arises.[3]

Unlike interrogative *wh*-forms, relative pronouns need not be realized in English and many other languages. The early analysis whereby a *wh*-word is moved and subsequently deleted, was replaced by the 'null operator' hypothesis (Chomsky 1980: 1981) — in (16) it is assumed that a null operator is fronted:

(16)   the claim [OP that John made _]

Chomsky (1977) demonstrated that a range of constructions involving such a dependency between a gap in a dependent clause and an external 'head' show diagnostics of A'-movement (*wh*-movement) (on (17ii), cf. Chomsky 1982; Browning 1991):[4]

(17) the dependency between gap and head is (a) governed by Subjacency (i.e. shows the full range of island effects also observed in interrogative *wh*-movement), and (b) licenses parasitic gaps, like interrogative *wh*-movement

Given (17), the base-generated external head hypothesis makes the assumption of a null/deleted element in (16) necessary.

The 'base generated external head' hypothesis raises questions about the proper treatment of connectivity (reconstruction) effects. A reflexive contained in the 'external head' may be interpreted as dependent on a subject commanding the gap (Higgins 1979; Barss 1986). They thus differ from interrogatives, where connectivity effects show up inside the moved phrase:

(18) a. the picture of *himself* [OP$_j$] that *John* painted t_j
b. [which picture of *himself*]$_j$ did *John* buy t_j?

Chomsky's (1993) account of reconstruction effects in terms of movement chains predicts reconstruction effects will arise only under displacement via movement. However, under the standard approach to RCs, reference to displacement under movement alone is insufficient to account for the syntactic basis of connectivity. 'Reconstruction' of the operator into its trace position in (18a) will not account for binding of the anaphor, since it is not part of the operator (rather, the anaphor is linked to the operator by being contained in a phrase that functions as external 'head').

The head raising analysis on the other hand allows a direct assimilation of (18a) and (18b), since in that analysis, the head does form part of a chain extending into the c-command domain of the antecedent of the anaphor:

(19) the [picture of *himself*]$_j$ that *John* painted t_j

Thus, to the extent that the copy-theory of reconstruction is correct, connectivity effects between the head and items inside the RC provides an argument favouring the head-raising approach.

The null operator thus plays a crucial role in the 'external head' analysis of these constructions. The place of this element in the Government-Binding typology of empty NPs remained unclear during the 1980's (Chomsky 1981 suggests PRO; Browning 1991 suggests *pro*). In the context of Chomsky's (1993) proposal to treat traces as a phonologically silent copies of their moved antecedents, the status of the null operator is questioned anew. Should OP be considered a pronominal element (a phonologically null 'intransitive' D^0)? Or a deleted copy of the external head which binds it? The latter possibility would suggest a copy-based approach to connectivity effects in (18a); the movement chain would contain 'copies' of the reflexive (cf. Munn 1994). However, the basic issue remains — the external head is not part of the movement chain.

1.2 Determiner complementation and head raising

1.2.1 Selection effects

Arguments for alternatives to the standard adjunction analysis of relative clauses have generally taken the form of showing selection of the relative clause by the determiner. Such cases include German *derjenige* 'the (very)', which requires the presence of a relative clause, but not of N/NP:

(20) derjenige (Mann) *(der dort sitzt)
the+that man who there sits
'the very man(/person/one) who is sitting there'

Other cases in which a combination of a noun with an (in)definite article require a relative clause also suggest a close dependency between the relative clause and the (in)definiteness of the determiner (Smith 1969; Stockwell et al 1973):

(21) a. She is that kind of person
b. She is the kind of person *(that is always helpful)
(22) a. He did it in that way
b. He did it in a way *(that annoyed me)

However, what such data suggest is some kind of interpretive dependency between determiners and RCs; it is not clear *a priori* that a syntactic selection relation is involved. No specific relation between specific determiners and complementizers such as found in degree constructions (*more-than* etc.) is evident (but see Section 1.2.3 below).

1.2.2 Binding and scope reconstruction

A second class of arguments speak against the 'base-generated external head' hypothesis and for the existence of a movement chain between the head noun and the trace position in the relative clause (the head-raising/promotion analysis of Vergnaud 1974).

The main such argument is that the head raising analysis permits connectivity effects in relatives to be assimilated to those of canonical *wh*-movement, both now internal to a movement dependency. It also permits the assumption of a null operator to be given up; but leaves the role of overt relative pronouns in need of clarification.

Chomsky's (1993) 'copy-trace' analysis of anaphor reconstruction facts in relative clauses is straightforward in a generalized head-raising analysis. The head NP in restrictive relatives displays the full range of BT-reconstruction facts (cf. 'multiple binding possibilities' in (23b) discussed in Barss 1986):

(23) a. the portrait of himself$_j$ that John$_j$ painted. [BT Principle A]
 b. the portrait of himself$_{j/k}$ that Bill$_k$ said that [BT Principle A]
 John$_j$ painted.
 c. *the portrait of him$_j$ that John$_j$ painted. [BT Principle B]
 d. the portrait of him$_j$ that John$_j$ thinks that [BT Principle B]
 Mary painted
 e. *$^?$the portrait of John$_j$ that he$_j$ (thinks that [BT Principle C]
 Mary) painted

These facts indicate that copies of the head are present in the movement chain inside the RC (however, Platzack, this volume, casts doubt on the cross-linguistic validity of this paradigm).

Further evidence for head-reconstruction comes from facts about pronominal variables and scope. A pronoun in the head position can be interpreted as a variable bound by a QNP inside the RC (24), and a quantifier in the head position may have narrow scope with respect to a quantifier in the RC (25) (Bianchi 1995: 123–4):

(24) The [period of his$_j$ life] [about which nobody$_j$ speaks t] is adolescence.
(25) I telephoned the [two patients] [that every doctor will [$\forall > 2$]
 examine t]
(26) I telephoned two [patients] [that every doctor will [*$\forall > 2$]
 examine t]

If *two* can be part of the raised head when an external overt determiner is present (25), but is itself the external determiner in (26), then the inverse scope reading can be attributed to reconstruction of the raised head into the scope of *every N*.

A priori, it is also possible that scope reversal is due to raising of *every N* out of the relative clause to a position where it takes scope over the head, as in May's (1985) 'inverse linking' cases:

(27) Two senators from every city$_j$ will represent it$_j$ at the [$\forall > 2$]
 convention.

Such an approach may be plausible for cases like (28), where a pronoun outside a DP may be bound by the RC-internal QNP (Arnim von Stechow, p.c.).

However, examples where this is possible are generally copula sentences, not the case in (25).

(28) The period of his$_j$ life about which nobody$_j$ speaks willingly is his$_j$ adolescence.

Connectivity effects in copula constructions (including pseudoclefts) have been argued to be a different phenomenon to those found in A′-movement constructions (Barss 1986). It is not reasonable to suppose that the clefted XP is generated in the position of the *wh*-trace inside the *wh*-CP in (29a), since the same connectivity effects show up in non-clefted 'equational' copula sentences in which there is no *wh*-trace into which that XP can be reconstructed (29b):

(29) a. *What he$_j$ claimed was that John$_j$ was innocent
 b. *His$_j$ claim was that John$_j$ was innocent

There is a lively controversy currently under way over the correctness of the copy-based approach to connectivity, with doubts being expressed especially on the basis of facts such as (28)–(29) (cf. Heycock & Kroch 1996; Boskovic 1997; Sharvit 1997; Den Dikken et al. 1998 for recent contributions). It suffices to note here that the strength of the connectivity argument for head-raising in RCs depends not least on the outcome of that debate.

1.2.3 *(In)definiteness of trace*

The lack of definiteness effects on the trace of *wh*-movement in relative clause with definite heads (tested by relativization of the subject of *there*-constructions) has also been identified as a problem for the base-generated external head hypothesis (Carlson 1977; Heim 1987; Browning 1991). The trace of interrogative *wh*-movement appears to inherit definiteness of the moved *wh*-phrase (Heim 1987):

(30) a. *How many people* will there be __ in the room?
 b. **Which three people* will there will be __ in the room

The gap in a relative clause may occur in a position barring definite DP, despite the 'head' DP being definite, indicating that it is not a definite DP that is interpreted in the position of the gap:

(31) a. *There were *the men* in the garden
 b. *The men* that there were __ in the garden

Browning (1991), assuming an external head/adjunction analysis, sees in such examples evidence for adjunction to NP, claiming that the relative operator-variable chain is construed with the NP (not marked for definiteness) rather than the containing DP.

Carlson (1977) makes a case for a raising analysis on the basis of similar data. He observes that definiteness effects are often reversed by the addition of relative clauses. Abstract mass nouns generally resist 'strong' determiners (definites, universal quantifiers), as in (32). However, adding a relative clause reverses judgements — a strong determiner is required (33):

(32) a. Americans exhibit much/some/little courage in such situations
 b. ??Americans exhibit the/any/all courage in such situations

(33) a. ??Americans exhibit much/some/little courage *that is required* in such situations
 b. Americans exhibit the/any/all courage *that is required* in such situations

Similar reversal holds in the case of (31): relative clauses containing 'indefinite trace' resist attachment to nominal heads with weak determiners:

(34) ??Some/three/few men that there were in the garden ...

Carlson distinguishes a third type of relative clause — Amount Relatives, alongside the two classes (Restrictives and Appositives) traditionally recognized. He proposes that while restrictives are compatible with cardinal (weak) determiner or strong determiners, amount relatives are compatible with (selected by) a strong determiner only (33).

It is proposed that the relativized NP in Amount Relatives contains a phonetically null indefinite determiner AMOUNT designating a quantity or amount, equivalent to overt *much/many* (and related to the zero determiner involved in comparatives). Assuming that this determiner is reconstructed into the trace position inside the relative yields a plausible representation for interpretation (crucially, the external strong determiner is not reconstructed):

(35) the$_x$ [[x AMOUNT courage] is required]   [cf. (33b)]

The restriction of relatives with 'indefinite' trace to relatives headed by strong determiners suggests that such relatives are generally Amount Relatives.

This analysis thus provides two arguments against the standard analysis, at least for Amount Relatives, one favouring a determiner complementation analysis — selection of relative clause type by a class of determiners; and one favouring head-raising (we return to these facts in Section 3.5 below; see also Schmitt, this volume, for discussion).

1.2.4 *Idioms*

Perhaps the most well-known argument against the assumption of base-generated external heads concerns idiom expressions (Schachter 1973; Vergnaud 1974):

(36) a. How much headway did they make?
 b. *The headway was insufficient
 c. The headway that we made was insufficient
 d. *We made the headway that was insufficient

The standard assumption is that nominal parts of an idiom expression (*headway*) must be generated as the complement of the verb of the expression (*make*), and cannot be generated independently, hence the illformedness of (36b). Displacement of an idiom N from its verb arises from movement of the nominal away from its verb (36a). The base-generated head hypothesis requires that in RCs, the nominal can be generated independently, while under the head-raising hypothesis, the idiom N head of the relative has raised from the object position of *made* in the relative clause, allowing (36c) to be assimilated to (36a).

The contrast (36c) vs (36d) (Carlson 1977) is particularly suggestive. Not only may the idiom chunk be licensed internal to the relative clause and not externally (36c), it appears that it must be licensed internally — if it is not, the example is bad despite being licensed externally.

However, on closer inspection the evidence from idioms turns out to be equivocal. On the one hand, in cases involving idiom chunk displacement that support head-raising, i.e. those where the head NP must be licensed inside the relative (36), the displaced noun is an abstract mass noun, so that such constructions count as Amount Relatives. Thus, arguments for a head-raising analysis of Amount relatives might suffice to account for those data, without reference to the idiom status of the head noun. On the other hand, cases exist in which the idiom is not licensed in the RC (McCawley 1981):

(37) a. John pulled the strings that got Bill his job
 b. *The strings/Strings got Bill his job

Such facts raise new questions concerning how the relative clause is interpreted; and more generally, the status of idiom chunk displacement as an argument for reconstruction.[5]

1.2.5. Head internal relatives

Cross-linguistically, the determiner-complementation hypothesis derives support from the existence of internally headed relative clauses (IHRCs) in languages such as Japanese, Quechua and Lakhota.

The nominal head of the relative clause is contained within it, rather than external to it. The clause itself joins with a determiner to form a constituent that functions externally as a DP, indicating a relative clause that is complement to

D (Lakhota example from Williamson 1987):

(38) [$_{DP}$ [$_{CP}$ Mary [$_{DP}$ owiza wa] kage] ki] he ophewathu
      Mary   quilt a   make the I-buy
      'I bought the quilt that Mary made'

The internal DP in this construction must be indefinite even if, as in (38), reference is to a definite entity ('the quilt...'), indicating that the noun is construed with respect to the upper determiner, definite in (38).

Under the base-generated external head hypothesis, the existence of constructions like (38) is mysterious. Adopting a head raising approach permits them to be analyzed as an ordinary relative construction in which head-raising takes place after S-structure. Head-internal and head-external relatives can then be viewed as instances of essentially the same construction. Languages with head-internal relatives can be related to those with head-external relatives via an overt/covert movement parameter, paralleling the result established for interrogative *wh*-movement (Huang 1982).

1.3 *Coordination: a problem for both approaches*

Problems for both approaches arises with respect to two sets of coordination facts — multiply-headed RRCs (Link's (1984) 'hydras'); and relative clauses taking split antecedents (Perlmutter & Ross 1970).

From the point of view of the adjunction/external head approach, the 'hydra' in (39) appears to underly contradictory requirements. The plural relative modifies the plural conjunction of singular DPs, which seems to require a DP-adjunction analysis (39b). If the RC were adjoined to NP inside the second DP, then it would be contained in one of the DP conjuncts, i.e. inside the constituent it modifies. On the other hand, scope requirements dictate NP-adjunction (39c). That such relative clauses can be restrictive modifiers of the conjoined DP is clear from (40):

(39) a. the man and the woman who were arrested
     b. [$_{DP-PL}$ [$_{DP-PL}$ DP$_{SG}$ and DP$_{SG}$] [$_{RC}$ who$_{PL}$ ...]]
     c. [$_{DP-PL}$ [$_{DP-SG}$ the [NP *RC*]] and [$_{DP-SG}$ the [NP *RC*]]
(40) a. every man and every woman who was arrested
     b. $\forall_x$ [(man(x) ∨ woman(x)) ∧ was-arrested(x)]

The RC in (39a) or (40a) cannot be simultaneously c-commanded by both determiners, without recourse to additional assumptions (such as across-the-board raising). Such examples pose as much a problem for the syntax and semantics of coordination as of relative clauses; but they serve to show that the adjunction analysis is by no means straightforwardly correct.

The problem raised for the adjunction analysis by (39)–(40) applies in equal measure to the determiner complementation analysis, which also has the RC c-commanded by the determiner. Such examples pose an additional problem for the head-raising analysis. Interpretation indicates a coordinated head (as does agreement in the RC in (39)). If the determiners (*the*, *every*) are external to the raised head, then these examples appear to involve a discontinuous raised head (*man* ... *woman*).

A similar issue is raised, only in a more extreme form, by the existence of relative clauses taking split antecedents (Perlmutter & Ross 1970). In (41), a plural RC appears at the edge of conjoined main clauses, modifying two singular 'heads', one in each clause:

(41) John saw *a man* and Mary saw *a woman*
      [who were wanted by the police].

Such examples were used to argue against the original head-raising approach to relative constructions (Andrews 1975); this is one argument that Kayne (1994) does not address. While it is feasible for an RC to be linked to multiple antecedents by a rule of construal, as in the standard approach, to claim that they are linked by a movement dependency is problematic. It seems rather far-fetched to suppose that the antecedents in (41) could have originated inside the relative clause (say, as a conjoined DP) to then be split and distributed across two clausal conjuncts after raising (a kind of 'reverse' Across-The-Board raising).[6]

1.4 *Summary*

The considerations just reviewed give an idea of the major lines of argument for and against the two approaches (6) and (8) to RCs. The raising hypothesis leads to the expectation that we should find connectivity effects, i.e. syntactic interactions between subconstituents of the head nominal and subconstituents of the RC, not predicted by the external head hypothesis. The determiner complementation hypothesis leads to the expectation of syntactically controlled selection effects between determiner and complementizer, not expected under the adjunction hypothesis. In addition, the head raising analysis makes available a natural way of integrating the account of IHRCs, not available under the external head hypothesis.

In Section 2. we examine Kayne's specific approach in more detail, concentrating on restrictive relatives of English. In Section 3, we present a more fine-grained classification of RC types (drawing on Grosu & Landman 1998), pointing to new issues they raise, and reassessing some of the points raised in Sections 1–2.

2. Kayne's proposal

As mentioned above, Kayne's specific variant of the head raising hypothesis (1994: ch. 8) has the head noun raise to the specifier of the CP complement of D, while examples with relative pronouns involving an initial step in which the NP complement of D raises to SpecDP (cf. (9) and (10), repeated here):

(42) a. [$_{DP}$ the [$_{CP}$ that John made [claim]]]]   [= 9]
     b. [$_{DP}$ the [$_{CP}$ [claim]$_j$ that John made t_j]]]
(43) a. [$_{DP}$ the [$_{CP}$ C^0 John made [$_{DP}$ which [$_{NP}$ claim]]]]   [= 10]
     b. [$_{DP}$ the [$_{CP}$ C^0 John made [$_{DP}$ [$_{NPj}$ claim] which t_j]]]
     c. [$_{DP}$ the [$_{CP}$ [$_{DPk}$ [$_{NPj}$ claim] which t_j] C^0 John made t_k]]]

The derivations of more complex examples with pied-piping and/or stacking are composed of these two processes.

2.1 *Linear order and hierarchy*

Kayne's proposal is developed in the context of his Antisymmetry hypothesis concerning the relation of hierarchical structure and linear order, which claims that hierarchical structure fully determines linear order as in (44), according to the Linear Correspondence Axiom (LCA):

(44)   For any two non-terminals X, Y, if X asymmetrically c-commands Y, then all terminals x dominated by X precede all terminals y dominated by Y

One consequence of the LCA is that right-adjunction is prohibited. Since Y adjoined to X asymmetrically c-commands X, the terminals of Y may only precede those of X in the string. The adjunction analysis is thus excluded for postnominal relatives (as in English), where the RC follows the rest of the DP it is supposed to be adjoined to. The D-CP complementation analysis is consistent with the LCA; D precedes its complement CP, whose daughters it asymmetrically c-commands.

The main conceptual motivation for the proposal therefore hinges on the fact that it enables a restrictive theory of phrase structure and of the order-hierarchy relation to be upheld; but even if that theory proves not to be correct, the approach to RCs may well be, and it certainly merits consideration independently of the LCA.

2.2 Other advantages

The proposal inherits specific advantages of the determiner complementation and head-raising hypotheses discussed above. Supposing the determiner complementation hypothesis to be correct, the analysis (42) provides a structure in which D selects CP directly, thus avoiding the extension of selection to adjuncts, while preserving binary branching. The head-raising analysis is able to capture connectivity effects within a restrictive (copy theory) approach — reconstruction effects can be attributed to movement chain formation in relatives, as in interrogatives. A basis is also provided for capturing the facts of § 1.2.3 — the definiteness of the trace in the RC is linked to the definiteness of the raised NP/DP, not to that of the external determiner. We return to these cases, and to the possibility for an integrated approach to externally headed RCs and IHRCs (and other RC types) in Section 3.[7]

2.3 Problems

The D-CP + head-raising approach faces basic issues of descriptive adequacy having to do with the unorthodox constituency it imposes on the head-relative nexus, of which we mention a few here (cf. Borsley 1997 for more extensive discussion).

2.3.1 The nature of the raised constituent

A descriptive issue arising immediately concerns what constituents may raise to SpecCP. The raised consituent in (42) is a bare count noun *claim*. It is well-known that English singular count nouns may not occur without an overt determiner in other contexts:

(45) John made *(the/a) claim

As pointed out by Borsley (1997: 631 ff.), several generalizations converge on the conclusion that the trace of the relativized element (at least where it corresponds to an argument inside the RC) is not a 'bare' NP but a DP. This suggests that the raised element in RCs lacking a relative pronoun is actually a DP, with covert D. In other words, the null operator of the standard approach (Section 1.1.2) reappears in this analysis in the form of an abstract D.

Questions arise concerning the first step in the derivation of RCs with a relative pronoun, i.e. raising of NP to SpecDP, cf. (43). While such processes may be attested outside relative constructions in other languages (all languages with DP-final D^0, in Kayne's approach), it is not motivated elsewhere in the grammar of English.

Part of the motivation for taking the head NP to form a constituent with the relative pronoun in SpecCP comes from some recalcitrant facts about relative pronouns in Romance. In Italian (46) and French, while relative pronouns are used in RCs when prepositions are pied-piped (46a), they cannot be used for relativization of direct objects (46b):

(46) a. la persona {*cui / che} Bill ha visto   [Italian]
         the person {*who / that} B. has seen
         'the person who Bill has seen'
     b. la persona con cui Bill ha parlato
         the person with whom B. has spoken
         'the person with whom B. has spoken'

An obvious line on (46a) would be to invoke an "avoid (relative) pronoun" principle (cf. Chomsky 1981), with the overt pronoun forced if pied-piping occurs. Kayne (1994: 88f) rejects this on the basis of (47), which suggests the correct generalization to be that a relative pronoun is possible only if the phrase moved is a PP (i.e. not if pied-piped in a DP).

(47) a. *l'homme la femme de qui tu as insulté   [French]
         the-man the wife of who you have insulted
         'the man whose wife you have insulted'
     b. l'homme avec la femme de qui tu t'es disputé
         the-man with the wife of whom you argued
         'the man with whose wife you argued'
     c. [$_{DP}$ le [$_{CP}$ [$_{PPk}$ [homme]$_j$ [avec [la femme de [qui t_j]]]] C^0 [$_{IP}$ ... t_k ...]]]

If, as in the analysis (43) above, the head must occupy the highest specifier of the phrase moved to SpecCP, then the head in (46b) and (47b) is in SpecPP (47c). (46a) and (47a) are accounted for if French/Italian D does not tolerate NP in its specifier. English differs from French/Italian in that in the former, SpecDP is available as a landing site for the head NP as in (43), as well as SpecPP.

Crucially, if there were a landing site for the raised NP outside of CP, say a functional specifier between D and CP, this account of the contrast would be lost. On the other hand, the assumption that the head NP and the XP containing the relative pronoun form a surface constituent, gives rise to conflicts with the constituency indicated by extraposition (cf. Section 2.3.3 below), which would be avoided if it were assumed that the NP raises out of CP, leaving (the phrase containing) the relative pronoun inside CP. A number of proposals are to be found in this volume that reject the assumption that the head and the (XP containing the) relative pronoun form a constituent in surface structure. Kayne's proposal relies on there being 'no extra space' between the external D and the IP of the RC for the head and the relative pronoun — i.e. both must 'fit into' the single specifier of CP. Bianchi (this volume) and Zwart (this volume) each argue for a 'split CP', with different C-heads providing extra such specifier positions.

Another question is raised by the fact that a contrast like the one in (46)–(47) also appears in English infinitival relatives:

(48) a. the person {*who/Ø} to see
 b. the person with whom to speak
 c. *the person {whose mother/the mother of whom} to see
 d. the person {$^?$to whose mother/$^{??}$to the mother of whom} to speak

The contrast (48c) vs. (48d) suggests strongly that this is the same fact as found in Romance finite RCs; yet here, an account in terms of D not tolerating NP in its specifier is of no help, as this would lose the account of the contrasts in finite RCs.

Law (this volume) takes a different tack on the paradigm (48), seeking to relate it specifically to the finite/non-finite distinction; though his proposal too leaves open the generalization to Romance finite RCs.

Such facts are just the tip of an iceberg of complex, cross-linguistically varying, and apparently syntactically determined patterns in the realization of relative pronouns and complementizers in RCs, on which little progress seems to have been made beyond the 'filters' account of Chomsky & Lasnik (1977) (but see Section 3.4 below).

2.3.2 *Morphology*

Generally, a noun shows Case-agreement with the determiner with which it forms a constituent/extended projection. In the analysis (42), the head noun, being raised, does not form a constituent with the external determiner, but may form a constituent with an internal relative pronoun/determiner with which it raises, as in (43). Yet in German and other languages with relevant morphology, the head N of a relative construction consistently bears the Case of the external determiner rather than of the internal relative pronoun.

(49) der   Junge   (/*Jungen), den   wir kennen
      the-NOM boy-NOM   (/*boy-ACC) who-ACC   we know
      'the boy who we know'

This situation is *prima facie* more compatible with the constituency induced by the standard (adjunction) analysis, in which the N-head forms a constituent (extended projection) with the external determiner and never with the relative pronoun (50a). In the standard analysis, this relation between the head NP and the external D is reflected already in the base structure. In the D-CP analysis, the clausal complement of D supplies D with its NP argument during the derivation. Kayne (1994: 88) suggests that the D-NP relation is reflected at logical form by incorporation of N^0 (head of the raised NP) into D (50b):

(50) a. $[_{DP}$ D $[_{NP}$ N] $[_{CP}$ (Rel) ... t ... $_{CP}]$ $_{DP}]$
      b. $[_{DP}$ N_j +D $[_{CP}$ $[_{Spec}$ t_{Nj} (+Rel)$]_k$ C $[_{IP}$ ... t_k ...]]]

This proposal may provide the basis for an account of the Case agreement facts, assuming this agreement is determined by LF-configuration. Cf. Bianchi (1995, this volume) for further discussion.

2.3.3 Constituency and extraposition

The derivations of more complex examples with pied-piping yield structures in which the relative pronoun (or a constituent containing the relative pronoun) form a constituent with the raised head, in stark constrast with the constituency imposed in standard adjunction analyses. (51a) exemplifies the standard analysis, (51b), the Kaynian analysis:

(51) a. $[_{DP}$ the [*boy*] $[_{CP}$ $[_{PP}$ with [*whose* mother]] C^0 $[_{IP}$ I spoke t_{PP}]]], ..
      b. $[_{DP}$ the $[_{CP}$ $[_{PP}$ *boy*$_j$ [with [[*who* t_j] 's mother]] C^0 $[_{IP}$ I spoke t_{PP}]]], ..

Crucially, the string *boy with whose mother* forms a constituent within CP in (51b).

When a relative clause is extraposed, the string D+N becomes separated from the remainder of the construction:

(52) a. we will discuss *the claim* tomorrow *that John made yesterday*
      b. we will see *the boy* tomorrow *with whose mother I spoke*

The extraposition facts appear straightforwardly compatible with the right-adjunction hypothesis, since the displaced string always corresponds to a maximal constituent (CP), a suitable target for movement.

In combination with the assumption that movement is always to a c-commanding position, the LCA has the consequence that a moved constituent always precedes its trace, i.e. there is only movement to the left. Not only is the right-adjunction analysis of relatives inconsistent with the LCA, so also is the view in which extraposed relative clauses are moved from inside DP, a case of apparent rightward movement, in conflict with the LCA.

Independently of the question of direction of movement, Kayne's analysis provides the 'wrong' constituency for extraposition phenomena. Assuming that the clausal constituent *that John made yesterday* in (52a) is displaced by movement, its status as a submaximal constituent is problematic. In (52b), the displaced string *with whose mother I spoke* does not form a constituent at all (cf. (51b)).[8] See Kayne (1994: ch. 9), Wilder (1995), and Mahajan (this volume) for further discussion.

3. A more fine-grained typology

The discussion of the two approaches in the previous sections concentrated largely on one type of RC, namely restricted relatives with external heads. Once other RC-types found across languages (or even within one language) are taken into consideration, questions concerning the pros and cons of each approach arise in more detailed form, i.e. separately for each type, and with respect to the relations and distinctions between the various types.[9]

3.1 *Relative clause construction types*

The standard typology of relative clause types distinguishes headed relative constructions from non-headed relatives, i.e. free relatives (FRs). In fact, in most currrent accounts (see below), FRs are internally headed, in the sense that the noun contained in the fronted *wh*-phrase, which plays a similar role to the external noun in headed relatives, is generated, and situated at surface structure, within the clause.

Languages like Japanese, Lakhota and Quechua (Cole et al. 1982; Cole 1987; Williamson 1987) have internally headed relative constructions of a different type (cf. § 3.3 above). The nominal head is superficially contained within a clause, in construction with a determiner (in languages with overt determiners), that functions as an argument of the higher clause.

In South Asian languages, e.g. Hindi, Marathi, the form of RCs — known as 'correlatives' — is rather different again. The head is contained inside the

clause, and is related to a pronoun or other expression in the containing sentence
(here: *vah* 'he') (Andrews 1975; Lehmann 1984: 133; Srivastav 1991):

(53) [Jo larkaa mere paas rahtaa hai], vah meraa chotaa   [Hindi]
     REL boy me near living is he my small
     bjaaii hai.
     brother is
     'The boy who lives near me is my small brother.'

Among the headed relatives, restrictive relatives are distinguished from non-restrictive (appositive) relatives. The semantic distinction (restrictive vs. non-restrictive modification) is reflected in differing syntactic properties in different languages.

Carlson's (1977) proposal to distinguish a third class of externally headed RCs (his 'Amount Relatives') is taken up by Grosu & Landman (1998), who identify this class as Degree relatives (DegRCs). Reassessing Carlson's proposal, they argue that DegRCs form one instantiation of a wider class of RCs, characterized by an interpretive operation of 'maximalization' (hence 'maximalizing relative clauses' or MaxRCs). Along with DegRCs, the class of MaxRCs includes free relatives, Srivastav's (1991) correlatives, and certain internally headed relative constructions.

The Grosu-Landman typology can be summarized as follows:

(54) a. ARCs
     b. RRCs
     c. MaxRCs (DegRCs, FRs, correlatives)

As they observe, left-to-right order can be construed as reflecting the degree to which the RC is essential to the meaning of the phrase it is in construction with (ARCs being non-essential, MaxRCs being essential). It also corresponds roughly with the evidence for the head being interpreted within the clause: in ARCs, there is less evidence that the external head should be interpreted within the RC, than in RRCs; while MaxRCs appear to require this. However, the language-type parameter (internal/external head) appears to cut across the classes.

In the following sections, we briefly examine each of these types, commenting on their relevance for the issues raised in Sections 1–2.

3.2 *Free relatives*

FRs are to be distinguished from headed relatives on the one hand, and interrogative complements on the other:

(55) a. John liked [what(ever) I cooked]   [FR]
    b. John liked [the thing(s) [which I had   [headed relative]
       had cooked]]
    c. John wondered [what I had cooked]   [interrogative]

While the FR in (53a) behaves interpretively like the headed relative (53b), its internal syntax is more akin to that of (53c). Overt *wh*-phrases are obligatory in both questions and FRs but not in headed relatives; and the set of fronted *wh*-phrases permitted in FRs is largely identical to those found in questions, the main difference being the occurrence of *-ever* forms in the former but not the latter (other languages, e.g. Bulgarian, Greek, also have specialized pronouns for FRs). Hence, interrogatives and FRs can be assumed to have a common syntactic core, a CP whose head contains a [+wh]-feature, triggering movement of a *wh*-phrase to its specifier:[10]

(56) $[_{CP}\ wh\text{-}XP_j\ [C^0_{+wh}\ [_{IP}\ \ldots\ t_j\ \ldots]]]$

With respect to external syntax, FRs fulfill a range of functions, including those of AP-predicate, PP-complement, and sentential adjunct:[11]

(57) a. John will grow [$_{FR}$ however tall his father did]   [=AP]
    b. John never puts his socks [$_{FR}$ where he should]   [=PP]
    c. [Whatever you say], he won't move.   [=adjunct-CP]

Keeping to the case of FRs in argument position (55a), the interpretive difference between the interrogative and the FR can be attributed to the fact that the former is a bare CP, licensed as a clausal interrogative complement, while the FR is a CP contained in a DP-projection, hence externally licensed as a DP-argument.

Distributional arguments show that FRs are DPs rather than bare *wh*-CPs (the latter tested for by *whether*). Though *wh*-CPs occur in many positions where DPs are licensed, there are some DP-positions that do not tolerate bare *wh*-CPs. One is the subject position under an inverted aux; another is the goal argument position of double-object verbs:

(58) a. Does what you ordered taste good?
    b. *?Does whether he'll fail seem obvious?
(59) a. He gave whoever she named a kiss
    b. *He V [whether I failed] DP

FRs also license Antecedent Contained Deletions, impossible in complement CPs, which is accounted for if FRs (as quantificational NPs/DPs) undergo QR, but complement CPs do not:

(60) a. Sue [$_{VP1}$ kisses [who Mary does [$_{VP2}$ e]]
         [ok if VP1 antecedes VP2]
     b. Sue [$_{VP1}$ wonders [who Mary does [$_{VP2}$ e]]
         [*if VP1 antecedes VP2]

There has been much discussion about what the head of the construction is. Early proposals to take the *wh*-phrase as the head (61a) (Bresnan & Grimshaw 1978) can be rejected on the basis that the *wh*-phrase has moved, and moved items do not project (Chomsky 1995). Most authors agree that the *wh*-phrase occupies SpecCP, as in other constructions. The issue then turns on whether FRs are 'headless' NPs (61b), or contain an abstract head (61c) (Groos & van Riemsdijk 1981), with the latter obviously favoured on conceptual (X-theoretic) grounds (cf. Grosu 1995). In terms of the DP analysis, FRs may be taken to be CP complements to a phonetically zero D^0 — (61c) is replaced by (62):[12]

(61) a.

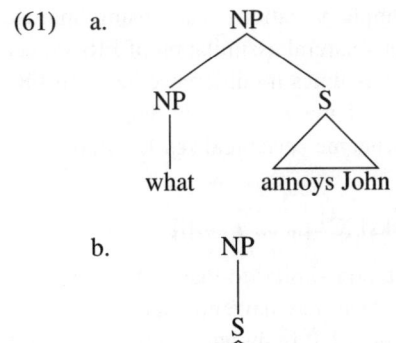

b.

c.

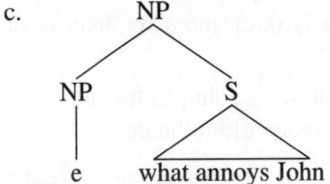

(62)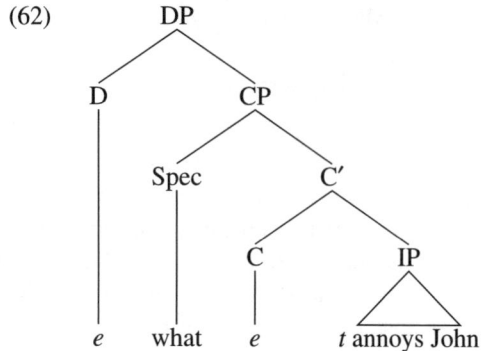

Clearly, if (62) is along the right lines, then under the standard (external head / adjunction) approach to headed RCs, FRs and RRCs are structurally rather different creatures. The determiner complementation / head-raising approach to headed RCs, on the other hand, permits a natural assimilation of FRs (under this analysis) to headed RCs. Kayne (1994) assumes no difference between FRs and other relatives, treating both as CPs complements of D^0. In the case of FRs, he suggests (1994: 125&154) that the morpheme *-ever* realizes D^0, into which the *wh*-word incorporates:

(63) $[_{DP}$ what$_k$+ever $[_{CP}$ $[t_k$ books$]_j$ C^0 $[_{IP}$ ... t_j ...]]]

FRs in DP-position receive an interpretation similar to that of a singular definite or a universally quantified DP, cf. (64). That they have no reading similar to that of a nonspecific indefinite / weak existential DP is shown also by the violation of the definiteness restriction induced in (65):[13]

(64) a. What is annoying John is annoying Mary
      b. ≠Something which is annoying John is annoying Mary
      c. =The thing(s) which is (are) annoying John is (are) annoying Mary

(65) a. *There is [what is annoying John] in this film.
      b. *There is [what you ordered] on the desk.

Jacobson (1995) proposes to explain the definite/universal reading of FRs in terms of 'maximalization' in their interpretation (cf. also Rullmann 1995). Grosu & Landman (1998) subsume FRs under their class MaxRC — see below.

Given the analysis (62), it is tempting to attribute the definite reading of FRs to properties of the abstract external determiner, with the universal reading licensed when D is realized by *-ever*, in the spirit of Larson (1987).[14]

The incorporation of the *wh*-form into the external determiner proposed by Kayne is also of relevance in accounting for matching effects. While in ordinary relative clauses, prepositions may pied-pipe with the relative pronoun, in FRs this is only possible if the preposition is also required in the external context (on this case, see Larson 1987; Grosu 1996). (66) requires the FR to function as a PP (adverbial). (67) requires the FR function as NP(DP), barring pied-piping of the preposition:

(66) a. I will live [$_{PP}$ in whatever town you live]
 b. *I will live [$_{PP}$ whatever town you live in]

(67) a. *John loves [$_{NP}$ in whatever town you live]
 b. John loves [$_{NP}$ whatever town you live in]

However, some languages (Romance, Greek, Bulgarian) allow non-matching FRs in non-subcategorized positions (topic, dislocation and subject positions), unlike English (modulo the cases mentioned in note 10):

(68) a. M' opjon vgo ekso tha ehi aftokinito
 with whoever-ACC go-1SG out FUT have-3SG car [Greek]
 'Whoever I go out with will have a car'
 b. *With whoever I go out will have a car

Alexiadou & Varlokosta (1996) argue that such 'nonmatching' FRs are actually CPs in nonargument positions linked to a null subject in the matrix, so that the issue of 'matching' does not arise.

Better-studied languages do not allow relativization of more than one constituent within one relative clause. Rudin (1986: ch. 6) describes a multiply-headed FR construction of Bulgarian:

(69) Na kogo kakvoto (/kojato sapka) mu haresva, da [Bulgarian]
 to whom what /which hat him pleases PRT
 go nosi.
 it wear-3SG.
 [Lit: 'Whoever likes whatever (/whichever hat), let him wear it']

Though multiple *wh*-movement suggests a link with *wh*-questions, the form of the second relative pronoun, suffixed with the definite morpheme (*-to*) precludes analysis of the clause as an interrogative (cf. English *-ever*). Rather, (69) instantiates a form of correlative construction, as described by Srivastav (1991) for Hindi (Izvorski 1996).

3.3 Correlatives

With respect to the descriptive typology of relative clause constructions, Hindi (along with related S. Asian languages) occupies a special place. The relativized noun may appear in construction with the external determiner or with the relative pronoun inside the relative clause; and in either combination, the relative clause may appear in construction with the determiner, or dislocated from it, either to the right (postposed) or to the left (preposed) — schematically:

(70)   a.   [$_{RC}$ ... *wh*-(+N) ...] ... Det(+N) ...   preposed RC
       b.   ... Det(+N) [$_{RC}$ ... *wh*-(+N) ...] ...   'normal' RC
           (adjacent to Det(+N))
       c.   ... Det(+N) ... [$_{RC}$ ... *wh*-(+N) ...]   postposed RC

These options leads to a plethora of possible surface realizations (see Mahajan, this volume).

In the typology offered by Srivastav (1991), the 'correlative' construction with preposed relative clause (71a) is syntactically distinct from the other two.[15] In the former, the RC is generated as an adjunct to the main clause, and is related to its 'correlate' by binding; in other words, RC and correlate do not form a constituent at any point in the syntactic derivation in (70a), while in the (70b–c), they do, (70c) being related to (70b) via rightward movement of the RC away from the determiner.

Srivastav identifies and analyzes several properties distinguishing correlatives from the other types, among which the fact that the possibility for 'multiple relativization' in the pattern (69) is available only to correlatives; and that with correlatives, the 'correlate' is restricted to strong determiners / definite pronouns. She proposes that the RC in the correlative is interpreted as a quantificational expression which binds the correlate; and attributes the restrictions on the nature of the correlate to conditions on what expressions can function as variables.

Grosu & Landman (1998) follow Srivastav's syntactic analysis, but argue for a somewhat different approach to the interpretation of correlatives; in particular, they argue on the basis of the determiner restrictions on the correlate, that the RC and the correlate must be interpreted 'as a unit'.

Mahajan (this volume) argues for a different, uniform syntactic approach in which correlatives are derived from the same (single constituent) source as 'normal' and 'postposed' RCs.

3.4 Internally headed relative clauses

As noted above, FRs in familiar European languages can be regarded as a form of IHRC; as can, too, Hindi RCs and correlatives (at least those taking the option of realizing the head noun inside the *wh*-phrase — see above).

Genuine IHRCs, i.e. constructions in which the head N appears inside the clause not in construction with a relative (or *wh*-) pronoun, appear to be restricted to languages with prenominal relative clauses (Cole 1987). Kayne (1994: 92 ff.) exploits this ordering correlation within the LCA framework to suggest that IHRCs have essentially the same (D-CP) structure as English RCs, with head raising to SpecCP. The sole difference between prenominal and postnominal RCs is claimed to be overt raising in the former of the IP of the RC to SpecDP.

As suggested above, if head-raising is covert in such languages, the internal-external head difference follows; however, the restriction to prenominal RCs would not. Instead, Kayne suggests that head-raising is overt in all cases, with internal-headedness arising from a copy-deletion option made available by overt IP-raising.[16] An RC of the form (71a) has a surface structure like (71b) with at least three copies of the head N present (two indicated, one in the trace of IP). The option to delete the copy in SpecCP rather than its 'trace' in IP (71c), and its restriction to the case where IP has raised, is attributed to a condition on copy-deletion (72):

(71) a. ... head N ... D
 b. [$_{DP}$ [$_{IP}$ ... [head N] ...] D [$_{CP}$ head N [C t_{IP}]]]
 c. [$_{DP}$ [$_{IP}$ ... [head N] ...] D [$_{CP}$ head N [C t_{IP}]]]

(72) A given chain link c_k can license PF deletion of another link c_l only if c_l does not c-command c_k.

The distinction between prenominal and postnominal RCs seems to partially determine further properties. Kayne (1994: 93–95) collects a series of cross-linguistic generalizations about the properties of pre-N relatives:[17]

(73) a. Pre-N relatives lack relative pronouns (Downing 1978: 392–4; Keenan 1985: 149)
 b. Pre-N relatives never display a complementizer that is identical to the normal complementizer of sentential complementation. (Keenan 1985: 160)
 c. Pre-N relatives contain verbs with non-finite/participial morphology (Keenan 1985: 160)

On (73b), the ordinary declarative C^0 found in post-N relatives (English *that*,

French *que*) is not found in pre-N relatives. Kayne derives this from his claim that since the final NP is stranded in SpecCP, the preposed relative can be maximally IP, hence cannot contain C^0. Some relevant Turkish facts are discussed by Kornfilt (this volume).

3.5 *Degree relatives*

In Carlson's (1977) analysis (see Section 1.2.3), RCs of the type (74a) involve abstraction over degrees or amounts rather than individuals, being interpreted as (74b). The degradedness of (74c) is attributed to the relative pronoun *which* abstracting over individuals (Heim 1987), while the NP associate in the *there*-construction is existentially bound inside IP (cf. Milsark 1977), leading to vacuous abstraction (74d):

(74)   a.   the wine that there was in the bottle
           b. $\lambda d\ [\exists x:\ d\text{-much wine}(x) \wedge \text{in-bottle}(x)]$.
           c.   *?the wine which there was in the bottle
           d. $\lambda x:\ \exists x\ [\textit{in-bottle}(x)]$.

If abstraction in DegRCs is not over individuals but over degrees, then interpretation via set-intersection, as for restrictive RCs, cannot be correct; rather, the head NP is interpreted inside the CP, as a restriction on the degree variable. This suggests strongly that the RC contains a silent copy of the external head NP, as predicted by a head-raising analysis under the copy-theory of movement.

The fact that DegRCs require an external D that is definite or universal was stipulated by Carlson as a selectional property of those determiners (and if correct, provides a direct argument for determiner complementation):

(75)   a.   {the / those / all / every / any} girl(s) that there were _ in the garden ...
           b.   *{some / several / three / few / no / most} girl(s) that there were _ in the garden ...

However, this analysis is revised by Grosu & Landman (1998), who propose that the restrictions on the external determiner in DegRCs can be explained a consequence of their status as maximalizing relatives.

3.6 *Determiner restrictions and maximalization*

Maximality is central to the meaning of the definite determiner (Link 1983). Given a concept of 'individual' covering plural entities (sums of atomic entities) as well as atomic entities, the 'universal meaning' of plural definites and the 'uniqueness' of singular definites follows from assuming that the determiner picks out the unique *maximal* individual satisfying the description introduced by the NP.

Several researchers have argued that maximality also plays a crucial role in the semantics of constructions involving *wh*-movement, including FRs (Jacobson 1995; Rullmann 1995).[18] Thus, while it is natural to assume that a *wh*-CP denotes a set, e.g. the set of things Mary ordered in (76), the meaning of the FR indicates that one member — the maximal member — of that set is singled out in interpretation.

(76)   John ate [what Mary ordered]

The FR obtains a universal reading, just in case there was a plurality of things Mary ordered; and a singular (definite) reading otherwise.

Grosu & Landman argue that degree RCs are also subject to maximalization, and that the determiner restrictions can be related to this. More specifically, the maximalized CP is compatible only with determiners that "preserve max [=the cardinality of the set obtained by maximalization of CP] into the quantification", i.e. do not single out subsets of the set obtained by the maximalization. The max-preserving determiners have the intersective property (77):

(77)   'D N *be* A' is true iff max(N) = max(N) $\cap$ max(A);

For instance, *the/those/all apples are red* is true iff max(apples) = max(apples) $\cap$ max (red things), which is not so for *some/no/most/... apples are red*.

If this is correct, then Carlson's determiner restrictions can be used as a diagnostic for the presence of a 'maximalized relative CP'. When external determiners are restricted to the class (75a), or an RC lacking overt external D is subject to universal or definite interpretation, it can be concluded that the CP-denotation is subject to maximalization. Other cases include FRs, Hindi correlatives, and IHRCs in Quechua (Cole 1987), and in Japanese, which Grosu & Landman claim (following Watanabe's 1991 analysis of them as covert free relatives) are also confined to universal or definite interpretation.

Murasugi (this volume) argues that Japanese IHRCs are not RCs at all, but adjuncts to the matrix clause, binding an external DP in the matrix. If so, then the fact that they show signs of being maximalizing CPs suggests a resemblance to Hindi correlative constructions that deserves examination.

The class of maximalizing CPs also coincides with another property of degree RCs identified by Carlson, i.e. that unlike restrictives, these RCs do not stack:

(78) *the men that there are in the garden that there were in the house.

There are IHRCs — Lakhota (Williamson 1987) — that permit indefinite as well as definite NP-interpretations; significantly, Lakhota IHRCs also seem to permit stacking, suggesting that they are like ordinary restrictive RCs.

In the maximalizing RCs discussed by Grosu & Landman, the 'head NP' is interpreted internal to the RC. The only superfically head-external members of the group are the degree RCs, whose external head is argued to be interpreted inside CP. There are other cases of headed RCs that display Carlson's determiner restrictions, which seem not to belong to the class of DegRCs. One case is Rothstein's (1995) 'adverbial NP-quantifiers over events' (79); Schmitt (1996a, b) discusses more cases, including secondary predicate DPs (80):

(79) I regretted it ...
{every / the / both / *most / *no / *some} time(s) I had dinner with him.

(80) John painted their house ...
{every / the / both / *most / *no / *some} colours that his girlfriend liked.

The role that maximalisation plays in the description of the meaning of the constructions mentioned is relatively clear: there is less clarity about its source; e.g. whether there is a syntactic correlate. Grosu & Landman merely stipulate that maximality is applied in the interpretation of the CPs in question. It also an open question whether and how maximality in RCs is related to maximality in comparatives and in interrogatives.

3.7 Appositive relative clauses

Appositives relatives generally take the form of RRCs; the semantic distinction (restrictive vs. non-restrictive modification) is reflected syntactically to differing extents and in different ways in different languages. In English, the distinction manifests itself in the following properties (Carlson 1977):[19]

(81) a. Appositives are separated from their head by an intonational break
b. Appositives must contain a *wh*-pronoun, whereas restrictives may lack a relative pronoun, being introduced by *that* or a zero complementizer.
c. Appositives, unlike restrictives, may modify (bare) names.

d. Appositives may not attach to certain quantified heads.
e. Appositives may not stack, unlike restrictives.[20]
f. Appositives occur DP-finally (i.e. following all restrictive post-N modifiers).

(82) a. *Any lion, which eats small mammals, is cowardly [ARC]
b. Any lion that eats small mammals is cowardly [RRC]

(83) a. The tiger that I saw that I wanted to buy was expensive.
b. The tiger, which was 5 weeks old, *(and) which was fed twice a day, ate only fish.

Other languages make further distinctions, such as Greek, in which a resumptive clitic pronoun is obligatory in appositives, but not in restrictives. On the other hand, the distinctions in (81) do not hold generally: e.g. (81b) does not hold in Italian; and Swedish uses the same special complementizer in ARCs and RRCs (Platzack, this volume). Even (81a) fails to hold in many languages (Keenan 1985; Kayne 1994: 111).

Further properties to be explained include the fact that ARCs may generally not extrapose, cf. (84a). Extraposition appears marginally possible, but only with presentative focus on the antecedent (84b):[21]

(84) a. *John *arrived*, who happens to be an expert in aerodynamics.
b. ??*John* arrived, who happens to be an expert in aerodynamics.

Both the standard and the Kaynian approaches have problems in accounting for the properties of ARCs.

Consider first the head-raising approach. In generalizing the head-raising analysis of RRCs to ARCs, Kayne attributes special properties of ARCs to covert raising of the IP of the RC to the specifier of DP, i.e. out of the restriction of D:

(85) the Greeks (,) who are industrious
a. [$_{DP}$ the [$_{CP}$ [Greeks(+who)]$_j$ C^0 [$_{IP}$ t_j are industrious]]] [RRC]
b. [$_{DP}$ [$_{IP}$ t_j are industrious] [the [$_{CP}$ [Greeks(+who)]$_j$ t_{IP}]] [ARC]

Three problems arise which are specific to the head-raising operation itself (we return to other problematic properties of ARCs below). Firstly, in contrast to RRCs, there is no evidence for head reconstruction in ARCs (see Bianchi 1995: 109–130, in disagreement with Kayne 1994: 112–3). Apart from some marginal cases of anaphor reconstruction, none of the evidence discussed in Section 1.2.2. yields positive results in ARCs:

(86) a. *John took advantage, which Peter also took of Mary, of Bill.
b. *?That portrait of himself$_j$, which John$_j$ painted last year, is expensive.
c. That portrait of him$_j$, which John$_j$ painted last year, is expensive.
d. That portrait of John$_j$, which he$_j$ (thinks Mary) painted last year, is expensive.
e. *That phase of his$_j$ career, in which every linguist$_j$ works hard, is difficult.
f. I called those two patients, who every doctor will examine.
[*∀>2]

The second problem concerns the fact that the *wh*-phrase of an ARC may contain its own head-NP (87).[22]

(87) ?*War and Peace*, which novel Peter read while he was in Scotland, ...

Thirdly, a head-raising approach appears unworkable for ARCs that take a clause or a predicate as antecedent:

(88) a. [John has left], which we are glad about.   [CP]
b. John has [left], which Mary hasn't.   [VP]
c. John is [stupid/in trouble], which Mary isn't.   [AP/PP]

The first problem is admittedly not fatal. Head-raising only opens the possibility for reconstruction from the head, it does not force it. The facts in (86) would be consistent with generalized head-raising, if independent principles ensure that the head cannot reconstruct in appositives (cf. Bianchi 1995: ch. IV on this point). However, the lack of head-reconstruction is equally compatible with an alternative in which the external head is not raised.

Examples like (87) in which the relative pronoun takes a nominal of its own distinct from the external head appear to be directly incompatible with head-raising, requiring at least the possibility for an alternative source for ARCs.[23]

The third problem is also very acute. As Borsley (1997) points out, the head-raising approach to sentential and predicate ARCs implies that the relative determiner (*which*) can take not only clausal complements, but also non-nominal predicative constituents (AP, PP; VP). A conceivable way to avoid this consequence would be to postulate that an abstract nominal functions as complement to *which*, mediating the relation with the raised clausal or predicative 'head', along the following lines.

On the head-raising analysis, (88a) might be derived as in (89). The bracketed constituent starts as complement to an abstract N *fact*, with the ARC forming the root clause. CP2 then raises to the specifier of *which* within the DP, which itself raises to the specifier of the root clause (cf. also Kayne 1994: 164, fn. 71):

(89) a. [$_{CP_1}$ we are glad about [$_{DP}$ which (*fact*) [$_{CP2}$ (*that*) John has left]]]
 b. [$_{CP_1}$ [$_{DP}$ [$_{CP_2}$ (*that*) John has left] which (*fact*) t_{CP_2}] we are glad about t_{DP}]

The analysis has two potential gains. Treating the relative as the root and the bracketed constituent as embedded predicts that only the relative is accessible to tag-formation, which generally cannot access embedded clauses (90). It also follows that an ARC may not cooccur with a root question or imperative (91):

(90) a. John has left, which is unfortunate, isn't it? / *hasn't he?,
 b. Mary met someone who was unlucky, didn't she? / *wasn't he?
 c. John believes that this is unfortunate, doesn't he? / *isn't it?

(91) a. *Has John left, which is unfortunate?
 b. *Leave, which we are glad about!

However, it remains doubtful whether such an approach is tenable. There seems no reasonable extension of the approach in (89) to cases in which predicates are relativized (88b,c). Also, there are ARCs that can take embedded clauses as antecedents (92):

(92) a. Mary believes that John has left, which would be unfortunate (if it were true)
 b. If John has left, which would be unfortunate, then we must stay.

A more promising alternative might then be to take *which* in the ARC to be an intransitive pronoun not related to its antecedent via head-raising, and its link to the head as involving intersentential anaphora as in (93) (see Sells 1985):

(93) a. [John has left]$_i$. We are glad about that$_i$
 b. John is [stupid]$_i$. Mary (is a lot of things but she) isn't that$_i$.

The facts about tag-formation and the blocking of ARCs in questions and imperatives would then await alternative explanations.

The paradox of ARCs, which has yet to be satisfactorily explained (cf. Grosu, this volume) is that, despite the fact that it must be strictly adjacent to its 'head' DP/CP/predicate, (however deeply embedded), subconstituents of an ARC are barred from entering grammatical dependencies with material from the clause containing them. A pronoun cannot be bound as a variable by a QNP outside the

RC (Jackendoff 1977); a polarity item cannot be licensed from outside; and parasitic gaps are not licensed from outside (Safir 1986):

(94) a. *Everyone$_j$ likes Mary, who he$_j$ met at school.
 b. *John didn't like Bill, who anyone met.
 c. *A man who Bill, who knows pg, admires t, came in.
 d. A man who everyone who knows pg, admires t, came in.

The only c-command diagnostic to which ARCs are sensitive is obviation (Principle C), which however holds of coordination and parataxis as well. In (95b), it is doubtful whether the obivation effect is due to c-command of the name by the pronoun:

(95) a. *He$_j$ met Mary, who John$_j$ went to school with
 b. *He$_j$ met Mary; (and) John$_j$ went to school with her.

Previous approaches seek to capture such facts by putting the ARC beyond the reach of the matrix, either configurationally, i.e. at the root (Emonds 1979; McCawley 1982), or in terms of derivational level (LF′, beyond LF — Safir 1986; in 'discourse' — Fabb 1990). These approaches then resort explicitly or implicitly to extra mechanisms to account for placement facts (cf. Emonds' parenthetical placement rule, McCawley's 'crossing branches') that stand in need of independent motivation.

There is reason to suppose that progress on the syntax of ARCs will depend on a deeper understanding of the interface between discourse mechanisms and syntax proper, as implied by Safir's and Fabb's proposals (cf. also Grosu & Landman 1998). If ARCs are a form of parataxis, not syntactically integrated into the host sentence, then by usual assumptions, the ARC does not enter syntactic relations with the host sentences (dominance, c-command, etc.). It would follow that the relation between head and relative pronoun is not grammatically determined (head-raising or syntactic binding).

The head-relative pronoun relation cannot be explained in terms of simple coreference either. As well as the cases with predicate/clausal antecedents, there are cases like (96) (Sells 1985), where the antecedent of an ARC is scope-dependent, hence does not refer.

(96) Every Korean$_j$ owns a donkey, which he$_j$ keeps in a shed

Notice also that in this case, bound variable anaphora into the ARC *is* possible. Sells argues that the relative pronoun of ARCs takes a discourse referent (in the sense of Kamp 1984) as its antecedent.[24]

Part II. The papers

Bianchi's contribution discusses three phenomena which appear to be problematic for the standard (adjunction) analysis of relative clauses. These are: (a) correlatives found for instance in Latin or Hindi; (b) case attraction phenomena found in Latin, Ancient Greek, Old English and Old High German; and (c) 'inverse' attraction, as attested in Latin and Old High German. She argues that these are straightforwardly accounted for under the raising analysis of relative clauses proposed by Kayne (1994), given a number of elaborations of his system.

Correlative structures consist of two clauses, the main clause and a dependent clause, which contain two constitutents interpreted as coreferent (*quibus.. isdem..*):

(1) quibus diebus Cumae liberatae sunt obsidione [Latin]
which days C. released was from the siege
isdem diebus T. Sempronius prospere pugnat
the same days T. S. wins a victory
'T.S. won a victory in the same days in which Cuma was released from the siege'

Bianchi observes that in both correlatives and headed relatives the same relative morpheme is used, e.g. *quis*, in Latin. This coincidence is not expected from the perspective of the adjunction analysis of relative clauses, under which the relative morpheme introducing headed relatives is an independent pronoun anaphoric to the antecedent NP, while the relative morpheme introducing the dependent clause in the correlative structure is a determiner selecting the 'head' noun. Further, the adjunction analysis cannot explain the diachronic link that has been established between the two structures without invoking major reanalyses of the construction.

'Case attraction' refers to the phenomenon in which a relative pronoun bearing structural Case is attracted to the case of the head NP:

(2) notante iudice quo nosti [Latin]
judging the judge.ABL who.ABL you know
'judging the judge whom you know'

Any analysis of this construction would have to assume some sort of accessibility of the specifier of the relative CP, so that the relative DP can exchange morphosyntactic information with the external head. Case attraction raises a problem for the adjunction analysis in which the relative CP is a barrier: the agreement between the head and the relative DP necessarily crosses this barrier. A related phenomenon is inverse attraction, in which the head noun is attracted to the case of the relative pronoun:

(3) urbem quam statuo vestra est   [Latin]
     city.ACC which.ACC I found yours is [NOM → ACC]
     'the city which I found is yours'

If the relative head is generated outside the relative clause, it is quite unclear how it comes to agree with the relative noun.

To account for these crosslinguistic patterns of relativization, Bianchi, adapting Kayne's (1994) raising analysis, proposes that the relative determiner, taking the head noun as its complement, raises to SpecCP, and the head noun subsequently raises to SpecDP. Bianchi explicitly suggests that the relation between the external D and the NP qualifies as a proper checking configuration (cf. Chomsky 1995: 172–73, Manzini 1994) and that the raising of the internal head to SpecCP is triggered by the need for the [+N] categorial feature of the external D to be checked (see Zwart, this volume, for a different view). Since the NP head appears in the minimal domain of the external determiner, it receives its case feature from it via agreement copying mechanisms in the morphological component (à la Halle & Marantz 1993).

Under this analysis, it can be assumed that the relative D is also governed by the external D; thus it can be involved in the process of morphological agreement. In the case of inverse attraction, the head noun simply bears the case assigned to it inside the relative clause. However, in cases in which the head noun and the relative determiner bear different morphological cases, the proposed analysis would not work. For this case, Bianchi argues that the relative D is not in the minimal domain of the external D, but rather occupies a specifier position below SpecCP which is outside the minimal domain of the external D. Evidence that more than one specifier position is involved in relativization (following the spirit of Rizzi's split C hypothesis) comes from cases where postposition of the relative determiner is possible (e.g. Latin, where other elements may intervene between the head and the relative determiner).

From the perspective of the raising analysis, correlative clauses and headed relatives actually involve the same element which is a determiner selecting the NP head. The difference between the two is that the head in the headed relatives moves to the left of the relative D to establish a checking relation with the external D. Moreover, the raising analysis permits a straightforward analysis of the diachronic link between the two structures: the introduction of an external D selecting the CP is the crucial step in the development from correlatives to headed relatives.

Grosu's paper addresses basic questions of typology (not intended here in the sense of a survey of cross-language variation, though that aspect too forms part of Grosu's concerns). To what extent do RC constructions form a coherent class? What subtypes are there? What are their properties, how are they to be explained? Grosu presents Grosu & Landman's (1998) (=GL) 'fine-grained typology' of RC constructions (see Part I, Section 3. above), detailing their semantic properties. Submitting the major accounts of relative clause syntax (including Kayne 1994) to critical inspection in the light of GL's results, Grosu proceeds to argue for certain general conclusions concerning their syntactic basis.

As discussed above, GL identified alongside restrictives and appositives a third class of maximalizing RCs (MaxRC), encompassing Degree RCs, FRs, correlatives, and some IHRCs. This class displays two restrictions setting them off from RRCs: (a) inability to stack; and (b) the 'determiner restriction' property. GL argue (a)–(b) to be due to an abstract maximalizing operator applying in the interpretation of this class of RCs. Alongside ARCs, RRCs, and MaxRC, Grosu points out further minor types, e.g. the existentially interpreted irrealis *wh*-CPs found e.g. in Romance and Slavic (cf. also Izvorski 1997).

In this paper, Grosu is concerned with the proper syntactic account of the three major types of RCs. His main argument is that the typology emerging from GL requires a feature-based approach (where feature combinations directly determine logical type). Any search for a purely configurational account of RC-types would be 'quixotic', doomed to fail.

All three classes, he proposes, share a feature [REL] in C^0 of an RC. The semantic import of [REL] is to require (a) that CP include at least one unbound variable; and (b) that this variable match (be 'consonant' with) the syntactic category and logical type of the phrase containing the RC.[25]

MaxRCs differ from ARCs and RRCs in having a [MAX] feature in C^0 (this stipulation is made in the absence of an independent explanation for the source of the 'max'-operator). Most accounts of the distinction ARC vs RRC hold that no further feature is necessary, configurational properties suffice. Grosu provides convincing arguments against this view; concluding that an additional feature is needed. In doing so, he reviews major accounts of ARCs, evaluating 'antisymmetric' proposals (Kayne 1994; Bianchi 1995) against earlier accounts (Jackendoff 1977; Emonds 1979; McCawley 1982; Safir 1986).

Having argued that featural (rather than purely configurational) distinctions underlie the semantically distinct types of RC, Grosu proceeds to examine the role of the syntactic operations in determining other major properties of RCs, focussing on operator-variable and other dependencies. Grosu tentatively concludes that arguments for the head-raising approach to dependency-creation in RCs outweigh those against, though a final judgement awaits resolution of the many aspects of the issue — e.g. the treatment of Link's (1984) 'hydras' under head-raising — that are still open.

Kornfilt considers three types of RCs in Turkish, arguing (contra existing 'phrasal' analyses) that they are indeed clauses and involve A′-movement. Kornfilt shows that they exhibit the same subjacency effects that are observed in RCs in languages like English.

Her main proposal concerns the distributions of the nominalized morphologies appearing in these constructions in Turkish, which she relates to a generalized binding condition B. In particular, she proposes that the nominalizer *-DIK*, which carries agreement morphology, identifies a phonetically null pronoun, in contrast with the nominalizer *-(y)AN*, which does not carry agreement morphology and therefore cannot identify a phonetically null pronoun. Assuming that a phonetically null pronoun must be present when it is identified (cf. Jaeggli 1984), Kornfilt can explain why the nominalizer *-(y)AN* must be present when a local subject is relativized, as the agreement morphology on the nominalizer *-DIK* would require the presence of a phonetically null pronoun, which would then be bound by either an empty operator or the head of the relative clause, in violation of the generalized binding condition B.

Turkish allows extraction out of a subject in RCs, which like the last type must carry the nominalizer *-(y)AN*, not the nominalizer *-DIK*. Kornfilt suggests that in these cases, the larger subject out of which a subconstituent has been extracted moves to the specifier of a TopP projection that appears between a CP and an AgrSP. It is the movement to SpecTopP that allows for a unified account for the distribution of the nominalizers.

Kornfilt also claims that the distribution of the nominalizers in a phrase is extracted out of a subjectless clause falls under the same account for the last two types as well. Suppose the empty operator in SpecCP agrees with the C, which governs SpecIP and transmits its index to it. Now, if the nominalizer *-(y)AN* is used, the agreement morphology it carries would require that a phonetically null pronoun be present in SpecIP, which would then be bound by the empty operator in SpecCP bearing the same index. This representation would yield a strong crossover violation, since the empty operator locally A′-binds both the pronoun in SpecIP and its trace in argument position.

Law argues that the curious ban on a bare *wh*-phrase in non-finite RCs (cf. *the man about whom to talk* vs **the man who(m) to talk about*) is due to two independent factors. One is that the category of the non-finite RC is not an IP, and the other is the more restricted distribution of DPs in comparison with PP, the distributional difference between the two bearing on their different Case properties. He argues that if movement is indeed subject to Emonds' (1976) Structure-Preserving Constraint according to which a category may move to a position only if a phrase of the same category can be independently generated in that position, then the fact that a PP, but not an DP, may adjoin to a non-finite RC follows directly, since PPs, like other categories that are not constrained by Case theory, have a less restricted distribution than DPs.

As noted in Part I (Section 3.3), Hindi RCs permit the relativized noun to appear in construction with the external determiner or with the relative pronoun inside the relative clause; with the RC appearing in construction with the determiner, or dislocated from it (postposed or preposed). **Mahajan** takes issue with Srivastav's (1991) proposal that the 'correlative' construction (4a) is syntactically distinct from the other two:

(4) a. [$_{RC}$ ... *wh*-(+N) ...] ... Det(+N)   preposed RC
     b. ... Det(+N) [$_{RC}$ ... *wh*-(+N) ...] ...   'normal' RC (adjacent to Det(+N))
     c. Det(+N) ... [$_{RC}$ ... *wh*-(+N) ...]   postposed RC

Mahajan shows how the head-raising hypothesis in conjunction with the copy-and-deletion theory of movement provides an interesting new route to a unified analysis of all three constructions in terms of movement. Mahajan's aim is to show that with these tools, two language-specific properties of Hindi — (a) the possibility for *wh*-in situ, and (b) the possibility for (definite or 'strong') DPs to scramble — are sufficient to account for the manifold attested permutations of determiner, head noun and RC. A key innovation in the account is the exploitation of the possibility for phonological deletion to apply to *parts* of copies generated by movement (instead of to a *whole* copy, as in 'standard' trace-gap creation). Thus, it is suggested that the preposed RC (4a) is the surface manifestation of applying scrambling to the DP containing the RC, and deleting part of the moved copy as well as (the complementary) part of the trace copy:

(5) a. *scrambling*
     [$_{DP}$ **Det(+N)** [$_{RC}$ ... ***wh*-(+N)** ...]] ... [$_{DP\text{-Trace}}$ Det(+N) [$_{RC}$ ... *wh*-(+N) ...]]
     b. *deletion*
     [~~Det(+N)~~ [$_{RC}$ ... *wh*-(+N) ...]] ... [Det(+N) [$_{RC}$ ... ~~*wh*-(+N)~~ ...]]

This analysis derives interesting support from the account its provides for the determiner restriction on the correlate in preposed RCs, namely, that the construction is only possible with DPs headed by determiners that independently permit scrambling. This represents a dramatically different alternative to the account of the 'determiner restriction' of Srivastav (1991), and Grosu & Landman (1998). (There is one asymmetry between (4a) and (4b,c) — the restriction of multiply headed RCs to the former — which Mahajan leaves aside. A syntactic approach which successfully integrates this property and explains the asymmetry is still outstanding.)

Mahajan also demonstrates how this simple idea, in conjunction with certain plausible hypotheses concerning restrictions governing 'partial deletion' in copies, can be exploited to account for additional aspects of the maze of surface manifestations of Hindi RCs. The discussion concentrates on (a) options in the placement of the head noun (inside or outside the RC); (b) the possibility for the head noun to be 'spelled out' in two places; (c) the restriction of this option to pre- and postposed RCs.

Many details of this approach remain to be explored and better established.[26] Mahajan's main point is that, once UG is assumed to provide the tools (movement, copy-and-deletion, and more specifically, the head-raising derivation for RCs), then a unified analysis of the three manifiestations (4a-c) of Hindi RCs is to be preferred on conceptual grounds alone — regardless of the difficulties involved in accounting for the empirical details.

As is well-known from previous work (e.g. Kuno 1973; Perlmutter 1972 and Hoji 1985) the lack of subjacency and reconstruction/connectivity effects in Japanese RCs show that these constructions do not and in fact cannot involve movement of a (relative) operator. **Murasugi** proposes to derive this non-movement property of Japanese RCs as a consequence of Kayne's (1994) analysis of N-final RCs. More specifically, she tentatively suggests that in Japanese the head N is base-generated in the specifier of the CP complement of D, and the IP complement of C containing a phonetically null pronoun in argument position moves to the left of D.

Japanese also has a type of RC in which the head of the RC is apparently in argument position in the RC. Murasugi argues that the distribution of particle *no* shows that what appears to be a internally headed RC is in fact a sentential adjunct; the apparent head of the RC is in argument position within the RC, and the RC itself modifies a phonetically null pronoun in the matrix clause. As independent evidence, she brings facts about the occurrence of *tokoro* 'place' after internally headed RCs and adverbial clauses to bear on the sentential adjunct status of the head-internal RC.

Murasugi argues that the universal D-CP structure as Kayne proposes for RCs has much redundancy, and may be problematic for the distribution of the particle *no* in adult and child grammars. She suggests to link the structure of RCs in adult grammar to that of pure complex NPs in that they both involve DPs with leftward movement to SpecDP of the IP-complement of N. The presence of *no* in child RCs now follows directly on the assumption that Japanese children initially take the unmarked D-CP structure for RCs and generate the particle *no* in COMP. The structure of pure complex NPs is later chosen for RCs when children receive examples of pure complex NPs without *no* and thus cease to generate *no* in COMP.

In his study of Swedish RCs, **Platzack**, while sympathetic to the LCA approach to syntax in general, casts doubts on Kayne's analysis of RCs. The validity of the reconstruction argument for head raising (provided by English examples like (6)) is called into question by its failure to account for the non-licensing of the Swedish possessive reflexive *sin* in examples like (7).

(6)   the picture of himself$_i$ that John$_i$ found on the table

(7)   *var   la   du   [brevet   frå   sin$_i$ lärare
       where put you letter-the from POS-REFL teacher
       som   Sara$_i$ fick igår]?
       which S.   got yesterday?
       'where did you put the letter from her teacher which Sara got yesterday?'

Platzack proposes to abandon the head-raising approach for an alternative LCA-compatible version of the external head hypothesis, in which RRC's are generated as a sister not of D but of N, as in (8) (for *mannen(,) som...*, Engl.: 'the man that...'):

(8)   [$_{DP}$ D^0 [$_{NP}$ [$_{N_0}$ mannen] [$_{CP}$ [$_{DP}$ OP$_i$] [$_{C'}$ [$_{C_0}$ som] [$_{AgrSP}$ ... t_i ...]]]]
       (RRC)

(9)   [$_{DP}$ D^0 [$_{NP}$ [$_{DP}$ mannen] [$_{N'}$ [$_{N_0}$ Ø] [$_{CP}$ [$_{DP}$ OP$_i$] [$_{C'}$ [$_{C_0}$ som] [$_{AgrSP}$ ... t_i ...]]]]

He further proposes that ARCs involve essentially the same structure, in which the RC is complement to a null N; the head being a DP in SpecNP (9). The 'base structure' (9) however does not reflect surface order in ARCs; drawing on agreement facts, Platzack argues that the uppermost D^0 in appositive relatives overtly attracts the complementizer *som*. The head-complementizer order results from raising of the head (a full DP) to the uppermost SpecDP.

(10)   [$_{DP}$ mannen$_i$ [D^0+[$_{C_0}$ som]$_j$] [$_{NP}$ t_i [$_{N'}$ Ø $_{N_0}$ [$_{CP}$ OP$_i$ [$_{C'}$ t_j [$_{AgrSP}$...t_i...]]]]

This analysis draws support from extraction facts. Swedish RRCs allow for extraction whereas ARCs do not, an asymmetry attributed to the presence vs. absence of a SpecDP escape hatch.

Platzack claims further support from two problems for the head raising approach (cf. Part I, Section 2.3.) which vanish under the 'sister-to-N' analysis: the Case problem and pied-piping facts. Additional advantages concern agreement facts in Swedish predicative constructions, aspectual phenomena (linked to the theory advocated in Schmitt, this volume), and extraposition and stacking facts. A comparison of ARCs with left dislocation constructions reveals similarities such as intonational and scope properties, which, it is argued, can be traced back to structural similarities under the analysis (9).

Schmitt is concerned with one of the well-known arguments for the determiner complementation/head raising analysis (cf. Part I, Section 1.2 above): why in some constructions nominals are unacceptable with the definite article, but improve to full grammaticality when a relative clause is added. As well as classic examples involving proper nouns and idioms, Schmitt considers *type of* expressions (11) and measure constructions (12).

(11)   a.   *I bought the type of bread.
            b.   I bought the type of bread you like.
(12)   a.   *Maria weighs the 45 kilos.
            b.   Maria weighs the 45 kilos Susana would love to weigh.

Schmitt's core proposal she calls 'Determiner Transparency' (DT), by which a definite nominal enriched with a (restrictive) relative clause functions like an indefinite with respect to the external context. Such indefinite behavior is argued to be due to the fact that the definite article takes something else other than the nominal projection as its complement, freeing up the raised head (itself an indefinite). That indefinite may then satisfy indefiniteness requirements of the relevant external context. Schmitt suggests a configuration for RRCs as in (13), whereby the head is a NumP occupying the specifier of AgrP outside the RC proper:

(13)   [$_{DP}$ the [$_{AgrP}$ NumP(='head') [$_{Agr'}$ [*that*+Agr] [$_{CP}$ ...]]]]

This instantiates a more general configuration (14):

(14)   [$_{DP}$ the [$_{AgrP}$ NumP [$_{Agr'}$ Agr XP]]]

If XP in (14) is able to satisfy requirements of the external definite determiner, then the head (NumP) is free to act as an indefinite. Schmitt proposes that a definite D must be licensed by a 'potentially referential' expression. This may, but need not, be a common noun like *book, garden, knowledge*; finite (tensed) clauses may also fulfill this role (given that the event time counts as a referential anchor). On the other hand, nominals such as idiom parts, *type of*-expressions or measure phrases, which are inherently non-referential, cannot satisfy the requirements of the definite D. Schmitt further examines the status of APs and demonstratives as instances of XP in (15); adjectives like *wrong* (but not *big* or *yellow*) and demonstratives also license a definite *type of* construction:

(15) a. I bought the wrong type of house.
b. *I bought the big type of house.
c. I bought this type of house.

Another striking example of DT concerns the role of RCs in determining aspectual interpretations of the containing VP, illustrated with respect to Brazilian Portuguese. In combination with an eventive verb, a definite object triggers a terminative reading. A definite with an RC is ambiguous — (16) has a durative as well as a terminative reading.

(16) Pedro [matou [os coelhos que comiam suas plantas]] por dos anos/
P. killed the rabbits that ate his plants for two years
em uma hora
in one hour
'P. killed the rabbits that ate his plants for two years in one hour'

Schmitt suggests that the durative interpretation is made available by Case-driven raising of the head NumP (the bare plural *coelhos*) to move out of DP to the matrix AgrO, where it affects the aspect calculation (in the sense of Verkuyl 1993) just like an ordinary bare plural.

Zwart discusses the properties of relative clauses in Dutch and dialects of Dutch in the light of Kayne's raising analysis and Bianchi's 'split CP' hypothesis for relativization. The paper pays special attention to the morphology and the syntax of the elements appearing in the left periphery of the relative clauses in Dutch. Building on Hoekstra (1993) (see also Müller & Sternefeld 1993), Zwart assumes that the structure of CP in Germanic consists of three layers of complementizer phrases. According to Zwart, these three layers also show up in relative constructions in (dialects of) Dutch. Zwart proposes that CP2 and CP3 provide landing sites for the interrogative and the demonstrative relative pronoun respectively. Following Bianchi, he argues that the head noun ultimately raises out of the projection hosting the relative determiner in CP2 or CP3 to the specifier position of CP1, the highest layer. Zwart presents two further arguments in favor of the view that the head of the relative is raised to a higher layer within CP. The cases discussed are extraposition in Dutch, analysed as an instance of leftward movement, and relative constructions with *amba* in Kiswahili.

Zwart argues that further movement of the head noun to SpecCP1 is semantically motivated. It is trigerred by the need to create a configuration in which the head noun and the relative clause are interpreted as independent constituents much like in the adjunction analysis. CP1 is the functional projection which actually expresses the relation of restriction that is characteristic of relative clauses. In this respect, CP1 differs from CP2 and CP3 which attract elements to their specifier positions for purely morphological reasons.

Notes

1. Part I draws on Wilder et al. (1995, 1997).
2. Other cases of noncanonical *wh*-dependencies include those in (i)–(iii):
   - (i) What John claims (annoys me)   [free relative]
   - (ii) What John claimed was that I annoyed him [pseudocleft]
   - (iii) It was John that claimed this.   [cleft]

   Interpretively, these constructions differ from relative clauses, which typically function as nominal modifiers. Free relatives refer independently, pseudo-clefts have been argued to function as the predicate of an external subject (Williams 1983), clefting serves to focus a constituent of the clefted clause. Non-canonical A′-dependencies also arise in 'null operator constructions' such as purpose clauses; on which see e.g. Chomsky (1977), Browning (1991), Jones (1991). Apart from free relatives, these will not be discussed here.
3. The function of the relative pronoun is usually construed as that of a λ-abstractor.
4. As well as finite relatives, these include infinitival relatives, clefts, comparatives and other degree constructions, *tough*-infinitives and purpose clauses.
5. Example (37a) appears to be interpreted as if the RC modifies the whole idiom VP, cf. the paraphrase in (i):
   - (i) Pulling (those) strings got Bill his job.
   - (ii) Sue has *met Mary*, which Fred hasn't.

   Thus, (37a) appears, semantically, to involve a restrictive modification of a VP. Perhaps this case forms a restrictive counterpart of appositive RCs taking VP-antecedents (ii) discussed in Section 3.7.
6. See Moltmann (1992) for further discussion; she analyzes these cases in a 'three-dimensional' theory of coordinate structures.
7. Further advantages of the proposal, not discussed here, are to be found in the new insights it affords into the syntax of DP-modification in general. The determiner complementation hypothesis opens the way to a unified approach to RCs, reduced relatives and other modifiers not available under standard approaches. For discussion of Kayne's (1994: ch. 8) proposals on adjectival and genitival modifiers, see Alexiadou & Wilder (1998).
8. Borsley (1997) raises a similar objection concerning the nonconstituent status imposed by Kayne's analysis on the conjuncts in examples like (i):
   - (i) the picture which Bill liked and which Mary hated
9. Descriptive and typological groundwork can be found i.a. in Peranteau et al. (1972); Andrews

(1975); Keenan & Comrie (1977); Downing (1978); Lehmann (1984); Keenan (1985); and, for Romance and Germanic, Smits (1989).

10. There are other differences between interrogatives and FRs, having to do with more restricted options for pied-piping in the latter. Thus, FRs in DP-positions do not tolerate pied-piped prepositions or *wh*-possessors:
    (i)   *John liked with what I cooked
    (ii) *John liked whoever's book it was that he found.
    (iii) *Whoever's beer I stole can have it back

    On PP cases, cf. Bresnan & Grimshaw (1978); Grosu (1995). On (iii), see Jacobson (1995), who gives it a single *?* with the reading 'the person whose beer I stole…'. Both restrictions are presumably explained by reference to the factors underlying matching restrictions on FR's in DP-position. Neither restriction holds absolutely in English for FRs that do not occupy argument positions (but see Kayne 1994: 155); cf. the 'concessive' FRs in (iv)–(v), which are arguably bare CPs in adjoined position:
    (iv) In whatever state he is, don't let him in.
    (v) Whoever's beer (it was that) I stole, he can have it back.

11. The *wh*-CP in the specificational pseudocleft construction (i) identified in Higgins (1979) is a special case on which no consensus obtains. Notice that *-ever* is not permitted (Iatridou & Varlokosta 1996). Williams (1983) argues that the *wh*-CP is an FR that acts as a predicate of the matrix copula clause; Den Dikken et al (1998) argue that is more closely akin to a *wh*-question, at least in a subclass of cases:
    (i) what(*-ever) John is is angry

12. See Rooryck (1994) for a different proposal, which analyses FRs as bare CPs, like interrogatives.

13. There is a class of apparent counterexamples to this generalization, e.g. (i).
    (i) There are [*what seem to be* German tourists] lying on the lawn.

    See Wilder (1998), where it is argued that the italicized string in (i) is actually a species of parenthetical.

14. There is debate over whether a quantificational reading is only licensed by the presence of *-ever*. Jacobson's (1995) examples (i)–(ii) are intended to demonstrate the contrary; see also Grosu (1996). But Iatridou & Varklokosta (1996) argue that *-ever* indeed induces a quantificational reading, and that the effect of singular specific reference in (i) arises through presupposition.
    (i) Everyone who went to [whatever movie the Ritz is now showing] said it is boring.
        =*definite singular* (=the movie showing at the Ritz)
    (ii) Do [what they tell you].
        = *universal* (do everything they tell you)

    For yet another view, see Dayal (1997).

15. The term 'correlative' is often applied to the postposed RCs as well as the preposed RCs. We keep to Srivastav's usage here.

16. This suggestion conflicts with what Mahajan (this volume) reports for Hindi. Kayne suggests that in English FRs, the noun does not raise (out of it base-position in the fronted *wh*-phrase) since the relative pronoun (*wh*-pronoun) itself raises to the external D. Hindi postnominal RCs can involve *wh*-phrases in situ, i.e. with no sign of overt raising of either the head NP or the

wh-determiner to SpecCP or to the external D.
17. The properties (73) are shared with reduced relatives (pre-N or post-N) in English, Germanic and Romance, which suggests there is a common basis. To (73) we can add (i), not mentioned by Kayne:
   (i)   Pre-N relatives do not extrapose from DP

   It appears that (i) holds for Japanese and Korean, at least. The generalisation extends to other DP-internal clause types. If complements to N precede N, they do not extrapose. For an account compatible with the LCA framework, see Wilder (1995).
18. Others listed by Grosu & Landman include comparatives (von Stechow 1984; Rullmann 1995), wh-questions (Rullmann 1995), correlatives (Dayal 1995), and internally headed relative constructions in some languages.
19. The semantic distinction also applies to other modifiers, such as attributive adjectives, where the distinction is reflected (if at all) only in intonation (Kayne 1994: 111).
20. A DP may be modified by more than one ARC if these are conjoined (83b), but ARCs seem unable to recursively modify a single DP. Grosu (this volume) suggests that ARCs may in fact stack, a judgement we do not share.
21. Fabb (1990: 70) observes that when the head DP of an ARC is moved, the ARC must be stranded, claiming this as support for a constituent structure in which the maximal projection of the moved wh-phrase does not contain the ARC:
   (i)   Who did we teach [e], some of whom were deaf, French?
   (ii) *Who, some of whom were deaf, did we teach [e] French?

   However, (i) is dubious at best; and other examples display the opposite behaviour:
   (iii) *Whose son did you teach [e], who was deaf, French?
   (iv) Whose son, who was deaf, did you teach [e] French?
22. Cf. Fabb (1990: 72). Kayne's comment (1994: 165) is that "it is not clear what to make of" examples of type (87), which are "rather artificial".
23. The uniform head-raising approach might be defended in the face of examples like (87), if it could be shown that the external head in such cases is a raised *out* of the NP complement of *which*. Thus in (87), perhaps the external head is an apposition to the noun in the wh-phrase, as in (i):
   (i)   [the novel *War and Peace*], Peter read while ...
24. There are links to be explored between ARCs and German 'V2-relative clauses' like (i)–(ii), studied in Gärtner (1996).
   (i)   Es gibt Sachen, die   darf's nicht geben.
         It give things them may-it not   give
         'There are things that shouldn't exist' / 'Some things just shouldn't be'
   (ii) Jeder Mensch$_j$ hat einen Freund$_k$, dem$_k$ vertraut er$_j$ alles   an
         every person   has a   friend,   him   entrusts he everything PRT
         'Everybody has a friend who he confides everthing to'

   Though the second clause displays V2, generally taken to mark root status, it is interpreted much like a relative clause modifying a noun in the first (notice that the first clause in (i), taken without the second, would be semantically empty). The construction underlies an adajcency restriction reminiscent of ARCs, and further restrictions besides (e.g. the modified N must be a non-negated indefinite). Notice that the scope dependence of the indefinite in (ii) gives rise to cross-sentential variable binding, similar to that in (96). Gärtner argues that in this construction, too, the antecedence relation from 'head' (*Sachen / einen Freund*) to d-pronoun (*die / dem*) is established at the level of discourse representations.

25. The proposal is by no means uncontroversial; see Wiltschko 1995 for an extended argument that there is no 'construction-specific' feature [REL] characterizing RCs.
26. One wonders, for example, what would explain the difference between Hindi, which allows (4a), and German, which does not, though German, too, is a scrambling language.

References

Alexiadou, A. & S. Varlokosta (1996). The Syntactic and Semantic Properties of Free Relatives in Modern Greek. *ZAS Papers in Linguistics* 5: 1–31.
Alexiadou, A. & C. Wilder (eds.) (1998). *Possessors, Predicates and Movement in the DP*. Amsterdam: John Benjamins.
Andrews, A. (1985). *Studies in the Syntax of Relative and Comparative Clauses*. New York: Garland [Doctoral Dissertation, MIT, 1975].
Barss, A. (1986). *Chains and Anaphoric Dependence: On Reconstruction and its Implications*. Doctoral Dissertation, MIT.
Bianchi. V. (1995). *Consequences of Antisymmetry for the Syntax of Headed Relative Clauses*. Doctoral Dissertation, Scuola Normale Superiore, Pisa.
Borsley, R. (1997). Relative Clauses and the Theory of Phrase Structure. *Linguistic Inquiry* 28: 629–647.
Boskovic, Z. (1997). Pseudoclefts. *Studia Linguistica* 51: 235–277.
Bresnan, J. (1979). *Theory of Complementation in English Syntax*. New York: Garland. [Doctoral Dissertation, MIT, 1972]
Bresnan, J. & J. Grimshaw (1978). The Syntax of Free Relatives in English. *Linguistic Inquiry* 9: 331–391.
Browning, M. (1991). *Null Operator Constructions*. New York: Garland [Doctoral Dissertation, MIT, 1987].
Carlson, G. (1977). Amount Relatives. *Language* 53: 520–542.
Chomsky, N. (1977). On Wh-Movement. *Formal Syntax*, edited by P. Culicover, T. Wasow & A. Akmajian, 71–132. New York: Academic Press.
Chomsky, N. (1980). On Binding. *Linguistic Inquiry* 11: 1–46.
Chomsky, N. (1981). *Lectures on Government and Binding*. Dordrecht: Foris.
Chomsky, N. (1982). *Some Concepts and Consequences of the Theory of Government and Binding*. Cambridge, Mass.: MIT Press.
Chomsky, N. (1986). *Barriers*. Cambridge, Mass.: MIT Press.
Chomsky, N. (1993). A Minimalist Program for Linguistic Theory. *The View From Building 20*, edited by K. Hale & S. Keyser, 1–52. Cambridge, Mass.: MIT Press.
Chomsky, N. (1995). *The Minimalist Program*. Cambridge, Mass.: MIT Press.
Chomsky, N. & H. Lasnik (1977). Filters and Control. *Linguistic Inquiry* 8: 425–504.

Cole, P. (1987). The Structure of Internally Headed Relative Clauses. *Natural Language and Linguistic Theory* 5: 277–302.
Cole, P., W. Harbert & G. Hermon (1982). Headless relative clauses in Quechua. *International Journal of American Linguistics* 48: 113–124.
Corver, N. (1990). *The Syntax of Left Branch Extractions*. Doctoral Dissertation, Tilburg University.
Dayal, V. (1995). Quantification in Correlatives. *Quantification in Natural Languages* Vol. 1, edited by E. Bach, E. Jelinek, A. Kratzer & B. Partee, 179–205. Dordrecht: Kluwer.
Dayal, V. (1997). *Free Relatives and* ever: *identity and free choice readings*. Manuscript, Rutgers (to appear in the proceedings of SALT VII).
Demirdache, H. (1991). *Resumptive chains in restrictive relatives, appositives and dislocation structures*. Doctoral Dissertation, MIT.
Den Dikken, M., A. Meinunger & C. Wilder (1998). Pseudoclefts and Ellipsis. *ZAS Papers in Linguistics* 10: 21–70.
Downing, B. (1978). Some Universals of Relative Clause Structure. *Universals of Human Language*. Vol. 4 *Syntax*, edited by J. Greenberg, 375–418. Stanford University Press.
Emonds, J. (1976). *A transformational approach to English syntax*. New York: Academic Press.
Emonds, J. (1979). Appositive Relatives Have No Properties. *Linguistic Inquiry* 10: 211–243.
Fabb, N. (1990). The difference between English restrictive and non-restrictive relative clauses. *Journal of Linguistics* 26: 57–78.
Gärtner, H.-M. (1996). *Are there V2-Relatives in German?* Manuscript, Max-Planck-Gesellschaft, Berlin.
Groos, A & H. Van Riemsdijk (1981). Matching Effects in Free Relatives: A Parameter of Core Grammar. *Theory of Markedness in Generative Grammar: Proceedings of the 1979 Glow Conference*, edited by A. Belletti, L. Brandi & L. Rizzi, 171–216. Pisa: Scuola Normale Superiore.
Grosu, A. (1995). *Three studies in Locality and Case*. London: Routledge.
Grosu, A. (1996). The proper analysis of "missing-P" free relative constructions: a reply to Larson. *Linguistic Inquiry* 27: 257–293.
Grosu, A. & F. Landman (1998). Strange Relatives of the Third Kind. *Natural Language Semantics* 6: 125–170.
Halle, M. & A. Marantz (1993). Distributed Morphology and the Pieces of Inflection. *The View From Building 20*, edited by K. Hale & S. Keyser, 116–176. Cambridge, Mass.: MIT Press.
Heim, I. (1987). Where does the Definiteness Restriction Apply? *The Representation of (In)definiteness*, edited by E. Reuland & A. ter Meulen, 21–42. Cambridge, Mass.: MIT Press.
Heycock, C. & A. Kroch (1996). *Pseudocleft Connectivity: Implications for the LF Interface*. Manuscript, Univ. of Edinburgh & Univ. of Pennsylvania.

Higgins, F. R. (1979). *The pseudocleft construction in English.* New York: Garland [Doctoral Dissertation, MIT, 1973].

Hoekstra, E. (1993). Dialectal Variation inside CP as Parametric Variation. *Dialektsyntax* [Linguistische Berichte Sonderheft 5], edited by W. Abraham & J. Bayer, 161–179. Opladen: Westdeutscher Verlag.

Hoji, H. (1985). *Logical form constraints and configurational structures in Japanese.* Doctoral Dissertation, University of Washington.

Huang, C.-T. J. (1982). *Logical Relations in Chinese and the Theory of Grammar.* Doctoral Dissertation, MIT.

Iatridou, S. & S. Varlokosta. (1996). A crosslinguistic perspective on pseudoclefts. *NELS 26*, edited by K. Kusomoto, 117–131. Amherst: GSLA.

Izvorski, R. (1996). The syntax and semantics of correlative proforms. *NELS 26*, edited by K. Kusomoto, 133–147. Amherst: GSLA.

Izvorski, R. (1997). *Non-indicative* Wh-*complements of existential and possessive predicates.* To appear in the proceedings of NELS 28.

Jacobson, P. (1995). On the Quantificational Force of English Free Relatives. *Quantification in Natural Languages.* Vol. 2, edited by E. Bach, E. Jelinek, A. Kratzer & B. Partee, 451–486. Dordrecht: Kluwer.

Jackendoff, R. (1977). *X-bar Syntax: a Study of Phrase Structure.* Cambridge, Mass.: MIT Press.

Jaeggli, O. (1984). Subject extraction and the null subject parameter. *NELS 14.* 132–153.

Jones, C. (1991). *Purpose Clauses: Syntax, Thematics and Semantics of English Purpose Constructions.* Dordrecht: Kluwer.

Kamp, H. (1984). A Theory of Truth and Semantic Representation. *Truth, Interpretation and Information*, edited by J. Groenendijk, T. Janssen & M. Stokhof, 1–41. Dordrecht: Foris.

Kayne, R. (1994). *The Antisymmetry of Syntax.* Cambridge, Mass.: MIT Press.

Keenan, E. (1985). Relative Clauses. *Language Typology and Syntactic Description.* Vol. 2, *Complex Constructions*, edited by T. Shopen, 141–170. Cambridge: CUP.

Keenan, E. & B. Comrie (1977). Noun Phrase Accessibility and Universal Grammar. *Linguistic Inquiry* 8: 63–99.

Kuno, S. (1973). *The structure of the Japanese language.* Cambridge, Mass.: MIT Press.

Larson, R. (1987). 'Missing Prepositions' and the Analysis of English Free Relatives. *Linguistic Inquiry* 18: 239–266.

Lehmann, C. (1984). *Der Relativsatz.* Tübingen: Gunter Narr.

Link, G. (1983). The logical analysis of plurals and mass terms. *Meaning, Use and Interpretation of Language*, edited by R. Bäuerle, C. Schwarze & A. von Stechow, 302–323. Berlin: De Gruyter.

Link, G. (1984). Hydras. On the logic of Relative Constructions with Multiple Heads. *Varieties of Formal Semantics*, edited by F. Landman & F. Veltman, 245–257. Dordrecht: Foris.

Manzini, M.-R. (1994). Syntactic Dependencies and their Properties: a note on strong islands. *UCL Working Papers in Linguistics* 6: 205–218.

May, R. (1985). *Logical Form: Its Structure and Derivation.* Cambridge, Mass.: MIT Press.
McCawley, J. (1981). The Syntax and Semantics of English Relative Clauses. *Lingua* 53: 99–149.
McCawley, J. (1982). Parentheticals and Discontinuous Constituent Structure. *Linguistic Inquiry* 13: 91–106.
Milsark, G. (1977). Towards an explanation of certain peculiarities of the existential construction in English. *Linguistic Analysis* 3: 1–29.
Moltmann, F. (1992). *Coordination and Comparatives.* Doctoral Dissertation, MIT.
Müller, G. & W. Sternefeld. (1993). Improper Movement and Unambiguous Binding, *Linguistic Inquiry* 24: 461–507.
Munn, A. (1994). A Minimalist account of reconstruction asymmetries. *NELS* 24, 397–410.
Peranteau, P. M., J. N. Levi & G. C. Phares (eds.) (1972). *The Chicago Which Hunt. Papers from the Relative Clause Festival.* Chicago: CLS.
Perlmutter, D. (1972). Evidence for shadow pronouns in French relativization. *The Chicago Which Hunt. Papers from the Relative Clause Festival*, edited by P. M. Peranteau, J. N. Levi & G. C. Phares, 73–105. Chicago: CLS.
Perlmutter, D. & J. Ross (1970). Relative Clauses with Split Antecedents. *Linguistic Inquiry* 1: 350.
Rooryck, J. (1994). Generalized Transformations and the *Wh*-cycle: Free Relatives as bare *Wh*-CPs. *Minimalism and Kayne's Antisymmetry Hypothesis* [Groninger Arbeiten zur Germanistischen Linguistik 37], edited by C. J.-W. Zwart, 195–208. University of Groningen.
Rothstein, S. (1995). Adverbial quantification over events. *Natural Language Semantics* 3: 1–31.
Rudin, C. (1986). *Aspects of Bulgarian Syntax: Complementizers and* WH *Constructions.* Columbus, Ohio: Slavica.
Rullmann, H. (1995). *Maximality in the Semantics of* WH-*Constructions.* Doctoral Dissertation, University of Massachusetts, Amherst.
Safir, K. (1986). Relative Clauses in a Theory of Binding and Levels. *Linguistic Inquiry* 17: 663–689
Schachter, P. (1973). Focus and Relativization. *Language* 49: 19–46.
Schmitt, C. (1996a). *Aspect and the syntax of noun phrases.* Doctoral Dissertation, University of Maryland.
Schmitt, C. (1996b). Licensing Definite Determiners. *ZAS Papers in Linguistics* 5: 104–118.
Sells, P. (1985). *Restrictive and Non-Restrictive Modification.* CSLI Report No. CSLI-85-28. Stanford, Calif.
Sharvit, Y. (1997). *A semantic approach to connectedness in specificational pseudoclefts.* Manuscript, University of Pennsylvania.

Smith, C. (1969). Determiners and Relative Clauses in a Generative Grammar of English. *Modern Studies in English*, edited by D.Reibel & S.Schane, 247–263. Englewood Cliffs: Prentice-Hall.
Smits, R. (1989). *Eurogrammar: the relative and cleft constructions of the Germanic and Romance languages.* Dordrecht: Foris.
Srivastav, V. (1991). The Syntax and Semantics of Correlatives. *Natural Language and Linguistic Theory* 9: 637–686.
Stechow, A. von (1984). Comparing Semantic Theories of Comparison. *Journal of Semantics* 3. 1–77.
Stockwell, R., P. Schachter & B. Partee 1973. *The Major Syntactic Structures of English.* New York: Holt, Rinehart & Winston.
Vergnaud, R. (1974). *French Relative Clauses.* Doctoral Dissertation, MIT [Revised version (1985), *Dépendances et niveaux de représentation en syntaxe.* Amsterdam: John Benjamins].
Verkuyl, H. (1993). *A theory of aspectuality.* Cambridge: CUP.
Watanabe, A. (1991). *Wh*-in situ, Subjacency and Chain Formation. *MIT Occasional Papers in Linguistics* 2.
Wilder, C. (1995). Rightward movement as leftward deletion. *Extraction and Extraposition in German*, edited by U. Lutz and J. Pafel, 273–309. Amsterdam: John Benjamins.
Wilder, C. (1998). Transparent Free Relatives. *ZAS Papers in Linguistics* 10: 191–199.
Wilder, C., A. Alexiadou, P. Law & A. Meinunger. (1995). *The Syntax of Non-canonical Complementation.* [Project proposal]. Manuscript, ZAS Berlin.
Wilder, C., A. Alexiadou, P. Law & A. Meinunger. (1997). Untitled excerpt from project application. Manuscript, ZAS Berlin.
Williams, E. (1983). Syntactic vs. Semantic Categories. *Linguistics & Philosophy* 6: 423–446.
Williamson, J. (1987). An indefiniteness restriction for relative clauses in Lakhota. *The Representation of (In)definiteness*, edited by E. Reuland & A. ter Meulen, 168–190. Cambridge Mass.: MIT Press.
Wiltschko, M. (1995) *On relative pronouns.* Manuscript, University of Vienna/University of British Columbia.

Some Issues in the Syntax of Relative Determiners

Valentina Bianchi
Scuola Normale Superiore, Pisa

1. Introduction

The standard analysis of relative clauses in the Principles and Parameters framework takes them to be CPs right-adjoined to a nominal constituent that they modify, e.g. NP for a restrictive relative:

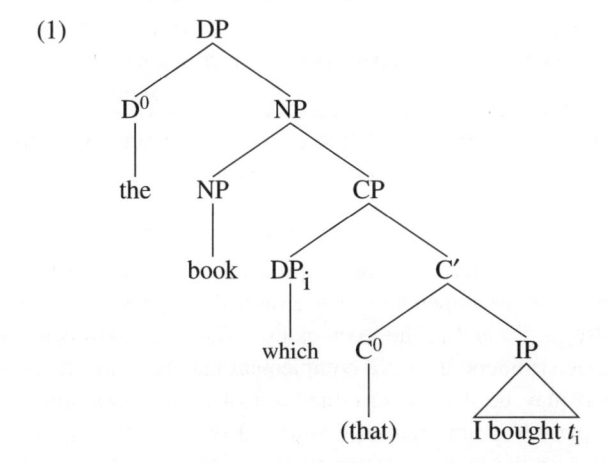

(1)
```
           DP
          /  \
         D⁰   NP
         |   /  \
        the NP   CP
            |   /  \
          book DPᵢ  C'
               |   /  \
            which C⁰  IP
                  |   /\
               (that) I bought tᵢ
```

The CP contains a relative DP operator, either overt or null, which raises to SpecCP, leaving a trace behind; this operator turns the CP into a predicative expression. Furthermore, it is standardly assumed that the operator is linked to the NP 'head' by some sort of anaphoric or binding relation.[1]

In this paper, I wish to discuss some data from Latin, Ancient Greek, Old English and Old High German which appear problematic for the 'adjunction' analysis in (1). After a presentation of the relevant data in Section 2, in Section 3

I shall review an alternative approach to relative clauses, namely the 'raising' analysis proposed by Kayne (1994: Ch. 8), and in Section 4 I shall show how this approach can provide a more satisfactory account for the problematic data of Section 2.

2. The data

2.1 *Correlative clauses*

The correlative structure constitutes a normal relativization strategy in various Indo-European languages, including Hindi, Latin, Sanskrit and Old English (cf. Downing 1978: 399–405; Haudry 1973; Hock 1988; Keenan 1985; Srivastav 1991; Dayal 1995). The structure is exemplified by the following Latin example:

(2)   [$_{CP}$ [$_{DP}$ *Quibus* [$_{NP}$ diebus]]$_i$ Cumae liberatae sunt obsidione],
           which   days-ABL Cuma   released   was from the siege
       [[isdem   diebus]$_i$ ... Tib. Sempronius ... prospere pugnat]
        the same days-ABL ... T.S.   ... wins a victory
       'T.S. won a victory in the same days in which Cuma was released
       from the siege'   [Livius 23, 37, 10]

Descriptively, the structure is composed of two clauses, the main clause and a dependent clause which appears at the left or right margin of the main clause. The dependent clause and the main clause contain two constituents which are interpreted as (roughly) coreferent:[2] they will be called the relative and correlative element respectively. The relative element (*quibus diebus* in (2)) is usually fronted at the beginning of the dependent clause, and the correlative element (*isdem diebus*) may also be fronted in the main clause. The two constituents are introduced by specific determiners; their NP complement may be realised in both clauses, as in (2), or it may be deleted in either one of them. Assuming with Srivastav (1991) that the dependent clause is adjoined to the main clause, the schematic representation of the correlative structure is (3):

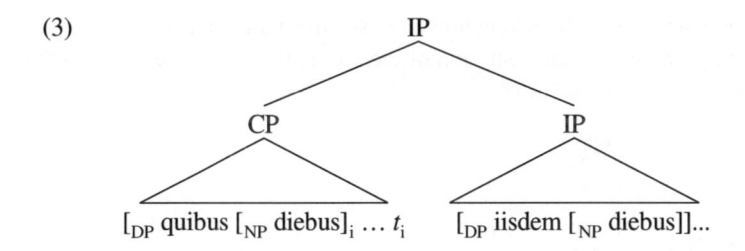

(3)
```
                    IP
                   /  \
                  CP   IP
                 /\    /\
```
[_DP_ quibus [_NP_ diebus]]$_i$ ... t_i [_DP_ iisdem [_NP_ diebus]]...

Up to now, the correlative structure seems to be unrelated to the headed relative clause of the type exemplified in (1). However, it is interesting to note that the above mentioned Indo-European languages have both correlative clauses and headed relative clauses, and strikingly, the two structures exploit exactly the same relative morpheme. This is illustrated by the following pairs of examples. (4) is a Latin headed relative featuring the same morpheme *qui* that appears in the dependent clause of (2):

(4)   ex   iis   rebus   *quas*   gerebam intellegebatis
      from those-ABL things-ABL which-ACC did-1SG understood-2SG
      'from those things which I did you understood'   [Cic. *De Sen.* 22]

The same morphological coincidence is also attested by the morpheme *jo* in Hindi (5)–(6) and by the morpheme *se* in Old English (7)–(8):

(5)   *jo*   laṛkii$_i$ khaṛii   hai, vo$_i$ lambii hai
       which girl   standing is, she tall   is

(6)   vo laṛkii *jo*   khaṛii   hai lambii hai
      that girl who standing is tall   is
      'the girl who is standing is tall'   [Srivastav 1991]

(7)   *þone*   stán$_i$ þe ða wyrhtan awurpon, þés$_i$ is
      the-ACC stone-ACC that the workers rejected, that-NOM is
      geworden on þaere hyrnan heafod   [Harbert 1983: 552]
      become   on the   corner head
      'the stone that the workers rejected has become the head-stone'

(8)   ure Drihten araerde anes ealdormannes dohtor   *seo*
      our Lord   raised   an aldorman-GEN daughter-ACC who-NOM
      þe   laeg dead
      that lay dead
      'our Lord resuscitated an aldorman's daughter who lay dead'
      [Allen 1977: 87]

From the perspective of the adjunction analysis, this coincidence is not expected. Compare the schematic representation of the correlative structure in (3) to that of the adjunct relative clause in (9):

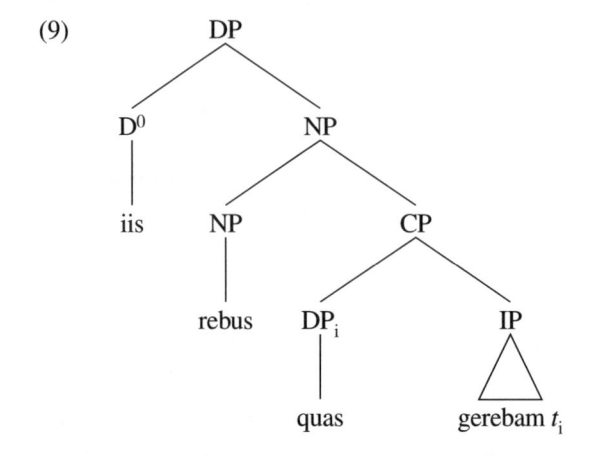

(9)
```
              DP
             /  \
           D⁰    NP
           |    /  \
          iis  NP   CP
               |   /  \
             rebus DPᵢ  IP
                   |    △
                  quas  gerebam tᵢ
```

In (2) the relative morpheme *qui* is a determiner selecting the noun 'head'; in (9), instead, it is an independent pronoun anaphoric to the antecedent NP.

If these two relative structures are completely unrelated, it is unclear why they are both found in various languages, and they exploit the same relative morpheme.

Actually, a diachronic link between the two structures has been proposed by Haudry (1973). Specifically, Haudry argues that the headed relative developed from an earlier correlative structure.[3] The starting point is the structure (10a), which Haudry calls the 'normal correlative dyptic': the correlative clause precedes the main clause and the relative DP is fronted at the beginning of the former. The second step involves the inversion of the NP and the relative determiner, as in (10b). Once this inversion has taken place, the NP preceding the relative determiner can be reanalysed as a constituent of the main clause, that is, as an external 'head' (10c). At this point, the correlative clause becomes a modifier of the NP 'head'; the whole string is no longer a subordinate clause adjoined to the main clause, but a noun phrase embedding a relative clause, and the correlative pronoun in the main clause becomes superfluous.

(10) a. [[qui   vir] ...] [... is ...]
         which man   he
     b. [[vir   qui] ...] [... is ...]
         man   which   he

c. [[vir]   [qui ...]] ... (is) ...   [Haudry 1973: 155]
    man   who   (he)

Haudry's proposal straightforwardly accounts for the cooccurrence of the two structures in the above mentioned languages, since the correlative structure is in fact the surviving ancestor of the headed relative; moreover, the morphological coincidence follows from the fact that the relative morpheme was preserved in this development, though it underwent a reanalysis.

Adopting the adjunction analysis of the headed relative, Haudry's diachronic development in (10) can be rephrased in the X-bar structures (11):

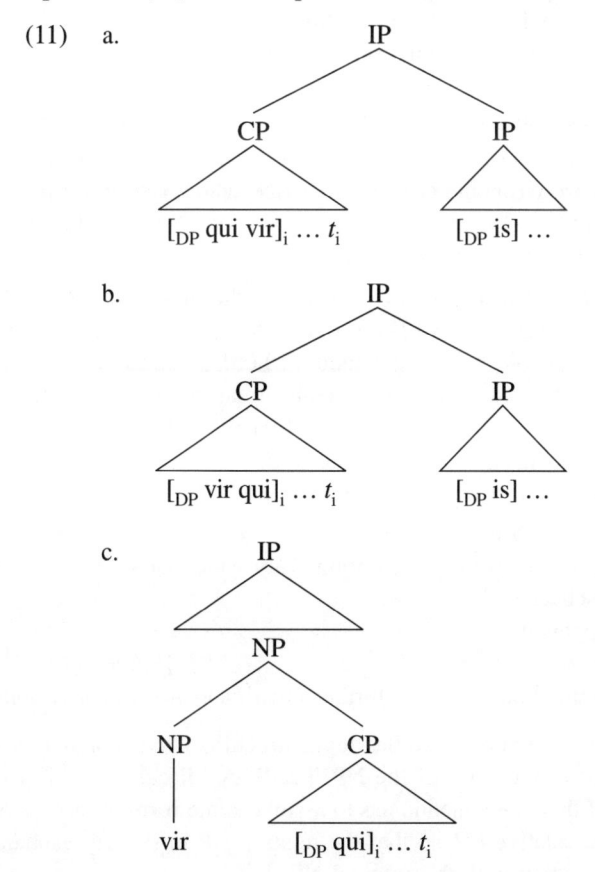

(11) a.

```
                IP
              /    \
            CP      IP
           /  \    /  \
    [DP qui vir]ᵢ ... tᵢ   [DP is] ...
```

b.

```
                IP
              /    \
            CP      IP
           /  \    /  \
    [DP vir qui]ᵢ ... tᵢ   [DP is] ...
```

c.

```
           IP
          /  \
         NP
        /  \
      NP    CP
      |    /  \
     vir  [DP qui]ᵢ ... tᵢ
```

Note however that the evolution from (11b) to the adjunct relative in (11c) requires two radical reanalyses:

I. the NP 'head' must be reanalysed as external to the relative CP;
II. the relative CP originally adjoined to the main clause must be reanalysed as adjoined to the antecedent NP.

2.2 *Case attraction*

Another phenomenon that appears problematic for the adjunction analysis in (1) is Case attraction of the relative pronoun, exemplified in (12) (Latin), (13) (Ancient Greek), (14) (Old English) and (15) (Old High German):

(12) notante   iudice   *quo*   nosti
     judging-ABL judge-ABL   who-ABL   (you) know
     ACC ⇒ ABL
     'judging the judge whom you know'   [Hor., *Sat* 1,6,15]

(13) ἄνδρες ἄξιοι τῆς   ἐλευθερίας   ἧς   κέκτησθε
     men   worthy (of) the-GEN freedom-GEN which-GEN (you) possess
     ACC ⇒ GEN   [Harbert 1982: 245]
     'men worthy of the freedom which you possess'

(14) syþþan hie gefricgeaþ frean   userne ealdorleasne, *þone*   þe
     when   they learn   lord-ACC   our   to be dead,   who-ACC that
     ær   geheold wiþ   hettendum   hord   ond rice
     in the past guarded against the enemies treasure and kingdom
     NOM ⇒ ACC   [Mitchell & Robinson 1982: 77]
     'when they learn that our lord, who in the past guarded the treasure and the kingdom from the enemies, is dead ...'

(15) sie gedâht' ouch maniger leide,   *der*   ir   dâ
     she thought also some   sufferings-GEN which-GEN her   at
     héimé geschach.
     home happened
     NOM ⇒ GEN   [Pittner 1995: 198]
     'She thought about some misfortunes that happened to her at home'

In this phenomenon, a relative pronoun bearing a structural Case (nominative or accusative) is attracted to the Case of the NP 'head'. As discussed by Harbert (1982), any account of this phenomenon has to assume some form of 'accessibility' of the Spec of the relative CP, so that the relative DP in (9) can exchange morphosyntactic information with the external NP 'head'.[4]

This raises a problem for the adjunction analysis. In the latter, the relative CP is a barrier: the dynamic agreement relation between the relative DP and its antecedent NP necessarily crosses this barrier, i.e. it is a non-local relation, contrary to other known instances of Case attraction (e.g. Case agreement of adjectives with the noun within DP).

Actually, the 'agreement chain' proposed by Browning (1987: 53–63) carries out agreement for ϕ-features across the CP barrier (through predication); it is possible to modify this mechanism so as to allow for the dynamic transmission of the Case feature from the antecedent NP to the relative DP. But in this approach it is unclear how to differentiate agreement for phi-features, which is generally attested in headed relatives, from Case attraction, which is a much more marked option.[5]

Note that the phenomenon is even more problematic if we adopt the checking theory of Case (Chomsky 1995: 277–286). In fact, in this approach the relative D^0 is taken from the numeration in an inflected form and checks its Case feature in the course of the derivation. This means that in (13), for instance, the relative D^0 must be inserted in the base direct object position in the genitive form. Even assuming that inherent Cases need not be checked, the genitive DP will presumably be unable to check the structural accusative Case associated to the transitive VP of the relative clause on its way to SpecCP. Note also that the structural relation between the relative DP and the NP 'head' in (9) is not one of checking.[6] Thus, it is unclear whether Case attraction can be reduced to an instance of checking, rather than to a 'surface' dynamic agreement.

In conclusion, it appears that, with or without the checking theory of Case, the phenomenon of Case attraction is problematic for the adjunction analysis of relative clauses and requires the stipulation of an *ad hoc* mechanism.

2.3 *Inverse attraction*

An even worse problem for the adjunction analysis is raised by the phenomenon of 'inverse attraction', exemplified in (16)–(18) (Latin) and (19) (Old High German):

(16) *Urbem* quam statuo vestra est
city-ACC which-ACC I found yours is
NOM ⇒ ACC   [Verg. *Aen.* I, 573)]
'the city which I found is yours'

(17) Ab   arbore abs   terra   *pulli*   qui
      from the tree out of the earth sprouts-NOM which-NOM
      nascentur,   eos   in terram   deprimito
      will germinate them-ACC in the earth (you must) layer
      ACC ⇒ NOM   [Cato, *Agr.* 51]
      'You must layer the sprouts that germinate out of the earth'

(18) *Hunc   chlamydatum* quem   vides,   ei
      this-ACC soldier-ACC whom-ACC (you) see, to-him-DAT
      Mars iratust
      Mars angry is
      DAT ⇒ ACC   [Plautus, *Poen.* 644]
      'This soldier you see here, Mars is angry at him'

(19) *Den   schilt*   den   er vür bôt der   wart
      the-ACC shield-ACC which-ACC he held,   that-NOM was
      schiere zeslagen
      quickly shattered
      NOM ⇒ ACC   [Pittner 1995: 200]
      'The shield he held was quickly shattered'

From the perspective of the adjunction analysis, this structure is mysterious: in fact, if the relative 'head' is generated outside the relative clause, it is unclear how it may come to agree in Case with the structurally lower relative pronoun (cf. Harbert 1983). Furthermore, Case attraction and inverse attraction seem to be perfectly symmetric phenomena, contrasting with the standard non-symmetric conception of agreement.

In conclusion, the adjunction approach to headed relatives in (1) seems unable to provide a satisfactory account for some comparatively uncommon, but well attested and significant relativization phenomena in Latin, Ancient Greek, Hindi, Old English and Old High German. In the following discussion I will show how the raising approach to relative clauses proposed by Kayne (1994) provides a straightforward and unified solution to these and other puzzles.

3. The raising analysis of headed relative clauses

An alternative approach to headed relative clauses has been recently elaborated by Kayne (1994: Chapter 8) in the framework of his Antisymmetry theory. This theory restricts the variety of possible X-bar structures and establishes an invariable mapping from the hierarchical relations between nonterminal nodes in a tree to the linear ordering of the terminal symbols that they dominate. Most relevant to the present discussion are the following consequences of the theory:

I.   adjunct and specifier positions are structurally identified and restricted to one at most per maximal projection;
II. every head has at most one complement;
III. linear precedence is determined by asymmetric c-command, yielding a universal order adjunct-head-complement; consequently, rightward adjunction is excluded.

The restrictiveness of the Antisymmetry theory is incompatible with the adjunction analysis (1) of righthand relative clauses. The relative CP can no longer be right-adjoined to the NP 'head'. Alternatively, Kayne proposes that it is the structural complement of a nominal functional head, the determiner:[7]

(20) [$_{DP}$ the [$_{CP}$ [book]$_i$ that I read t_i]]

The nominal constituent [book] in (20) is not generated as the determiner's complement, but it originates within the relative CP. In this respect, Kayne adopts the raising hypothesis elaborated by M. Brame (in unpublished work), Schachter (1973) and Vergnaud (1974).

Let us consider more closely the derivation of a relative structure like *the book which I read*, featuring an overt relative morpheme. Clearly, in the raising analysis the latter can not be analysed as a DP binding the relative trace, as in (1). Kayne (1994: 89) proposes instead that it is the original determiner of the NP 'head'. The derivation starts from a structure like (21):

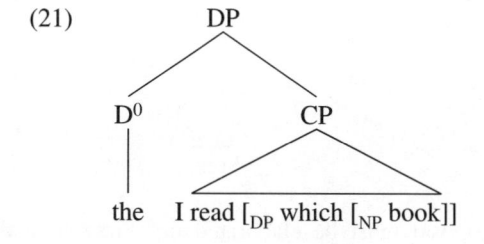

(21)   DP
           / \
         D⁰   CP
         | / \
        the I read [$_{DP}$ which [$_{NP}$ book]]

In this structure the DP headed by the relative D⁰ originates in the argument position within the relative clause. The derivation proceeds by raising the relative DP to SpecCP, as in (22). As a final step, the NP complement of the relative D⁰[8] moves to the Spec of the latter, yielding the desired linear order of the morphemes (23):

(22)

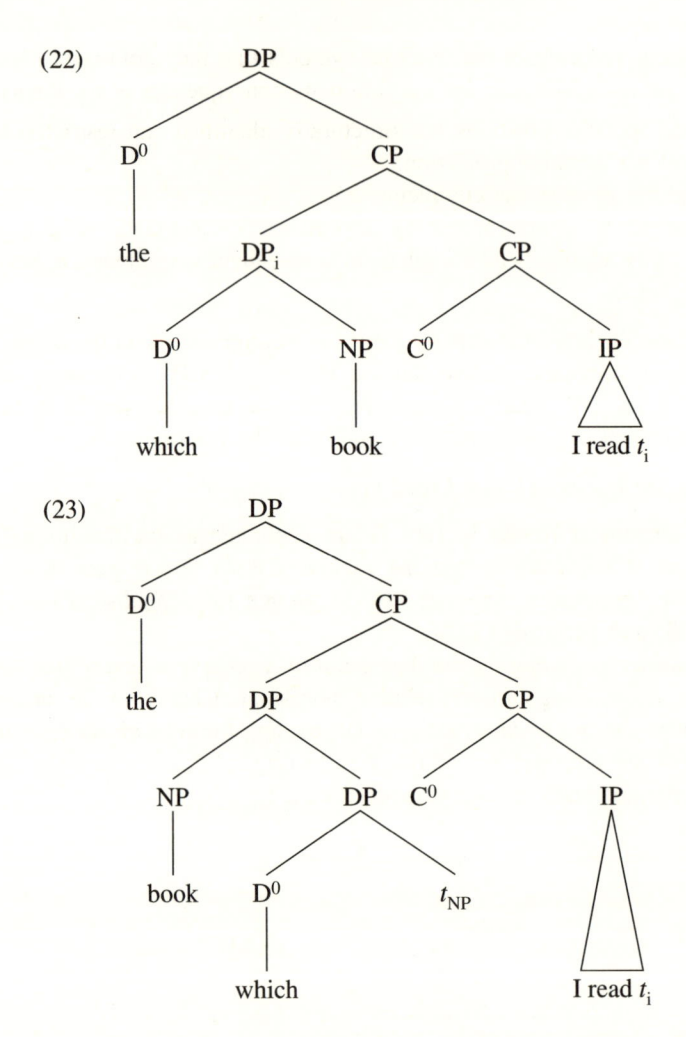

```
         DP
        /  \
       D⁰   CP
       |   /  \
      the DPᵢ   CP
          / \   / \
         D⁰  NP C⁰  IP
         |   |      △
       which book  I read tᵢ
```

(23)

```
         DP
        /  \
       D⁰   CP
       |   /  \
      the DP    CP
          / \   / \
         NP  DP C⁰  IP
         |   / \     △
        book D⁰ t_NP I read tᵢ
             |
           which
```

At least two aspects of this proposal must be elaborated on. First, note that though the 'external' D^0 *the* and the NP 'head' *book* do not form a constituent in (23), they agree for phi-features, and in a language like Latin, they also agree for Case (cf. for instance example (4) above). Furthermore, it is reasonable to assume that the external D^0 also bears a [+N] categorial feature (in the sense of Chomsky 1995: 282), which must be satisfied by the NP 'head'.

Second, it is necessary to explain what triggers the overt raising of the relative 'head', and in particular the step from (22) to (23), which places the NP constituent in front of its original Determiner.[9]

As an answer to the first problem, it is necessary to assume that the syntactic relation between the external D^0 and the NP 'head' in (23) qualifies as a proper agreement (or checking) configuration. Note that this configuration is essentially similar to the pre-minimalist relation of head government: in particular, given the adjoined status of the specifier position in the Antisymmetry theory, the NP 'head' in (23) is only dominated by one segment of the CP barrier.[10] It is then necessary to assume, *pace* Chomsky (1995: 172–73) and in line with Rizzi (1997),[11] that this qualifies as a proper agreement/checking configuration.

In order to implement this idea, let us adopt the definition of minimal domain proposed by Manzini (1994):

(24) The minimal domain of a head X, notated (X), includes all elements that are immediately dominated by, and do not immediately dominate, a projection of X.

This definition has an interesting consequence with respect to the Antisymmetry theory. Recall that in the latter specifiers are adjoined to the maximal projection they are specifiers of and are only covered by one segment of it. Since the relation of domination only holds of categories, and not of segments, it follows that in (23) the NP 'head' in SpecDP does not fall in the minimal domain of the relative D^0 or of C^0, but rather in the minimal domain of the higher head, the external D^0. Let us then assume that being in the minimal domain of this D^0, the NP 'head' can establish an agreement/checking relation with it. This assumption will also cover the more familiar case of (25):

(25) [$_{DP}$ the [$_{NP}$ book]]

Consider then the problem of the trigger for the raising of the NP 'head' to the left of the relative D^0 in (23). I have suggested that the external D^0 bears a categorial feature [+N] which cannot be satisfied by its structural complement CP. Suppose that this categorial feature is strong. Then, we can assume that it is precisely this feature that triggers the overt raising of NP to SpecDP in (23).[12, 13]

Finally, let us turn to the Case problem. It is necessary to explain how the NP 'head', which is originally the complement of the relative D^0, may come to acquire the Case assigned to the complex DP within the matrix clause, possibly disagreeing with the relative D^0, as in (4) above, repeated here:

(26) a. ex   iis   rebus   quas   gerebam
       from those-ABL things-ABL which-ACC did-1SG
       'from those things which I did '
   b. [$_{PP}$ P^0 [$_{DP}$ D$^0_{Abl}$ [$_{CP}$ [$_{DP}$ NP$_{Abl}$ [D$^0_{Acc}$ t_{NP}]] ...]]]

The solution to this problem rests on a particular conception of morphological Case.

Let us assume that the terminal symbol dominated by a functional head is not a morpheme, but a set of morphosyntactic features: this abstract element is turned into a concrete morpheme in the Morpho-Phonological component (cf. Halle & Marantz 1993). The inflected noun can be analysed as a lexical head N^0 combined with a functional head Agr^0, which consists of a bundle of phi-features and is spelled out as a specific inflectional morpheme.

Furthermore, let us assume — following Giusti (1993) — that being Case-marked is a syntactic property of the D^0 position; the noun morphologically agrees for Case with the determiner by which it is governed.[14] More specifically, the Case feature of the governing D^0 is copied into the Agr^0 head which the noun incorporates to; as a result, the noun is spelled out in PF in the form inflected for the corresponding Case.

Interesting support for this approach to Case in terms of 'morphological' agreement under government comes from a phenomenon of Russian and other Slavic languages, discussed by Babby (1987) and Franks (1994). In such languages, the structural Case assigned to an indefinite DP can be realized on the determiner only, while NP realizes the genitive Case assigned by the indefinite determiner itself under government, as in (27) (Russian):

(27)   poslednie pjat'   butylok
       last-NOM five-NOM bottles-GEN   [Babby 1987:92]
       'the last five bottles'

Consider now from this perspective the configuration in (26b). The external D^0 bears the ablative Case assigned to it by the preposition, and the relative D^0 bears the accusative Case assigned to the relative DP within the relative clause. As discussed above, the NP 'head' comes to be governed by (or in the minimal domain of) the external D^0. Therefore, in the Morpho-Phonological component the Case feature of this D^0 is copied into it, and it is spelled out in the ablative form.

To conclude, it is worth to point out some of the aspects of the raising analysis which will be most directly relevant to the following discussion:

I. the relative CP is selected by an external D^0;
II. the relative morpheme is the original determiner of the NP 'head';

III. there exists a morphosyntactic interaction between the external D^0 and the NP 'head' in SpecCP.

Let us now see how this approach can account for the data presented in Section 2.

4. Consequences of the raising analysis

4.1 *Correlative clauses again*

Recall from Section 2.1 that in Latin, Old English and Hindi both correlative clauses and headed relatives are found, and they exploit the same relative morpheme. As discussed above, these coincidences are unexpected from the perspective of the adjunction analysis, according to which the two structures are unrelated (cf. (3) vs. (9)).

From the perspective of the raising analysis, instead, the same element is involved in the two structures. Compare again (3), repeated here as (28), to the raising structure (29):

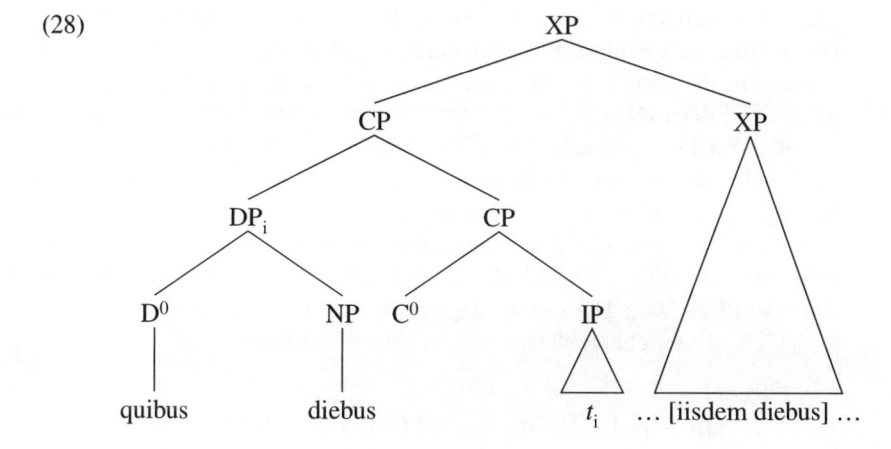

(28)

```
                    XP
                   /  \
                  CP    XP
                 /  \    /\
              DPᵢ    CP
              / \    / \
            D⁰  NP  C⁰  IP
            |   |       /\
         quibus diebus  tᵢ  ... [iisdem diebus] ...
```

(29)

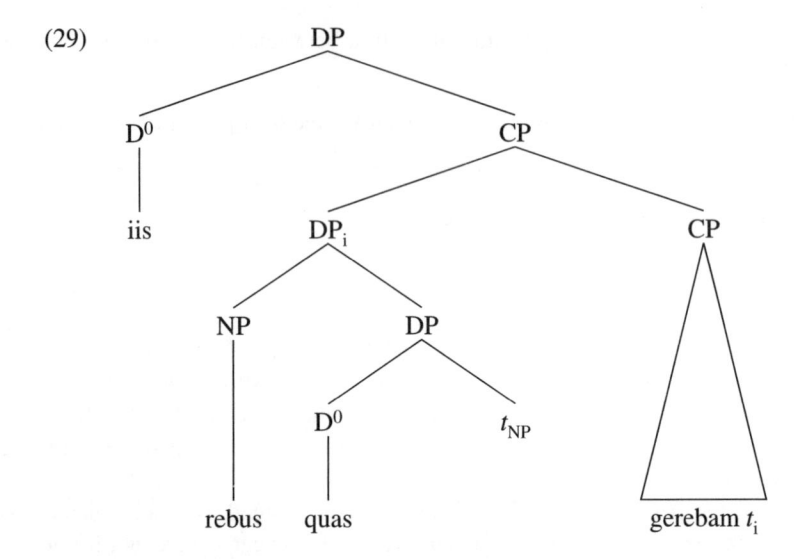

```
              DP
           /      \
         D⁰        CP
         |       /    \
         iis   DP_i    CP
              /   \    /\
            NP    DP  t_NP ...
            |   /  \
          rebus D⁰  t_NP    gerebam t_i
                |
               quas
```

In both structures, the relative morpheme is a determiner selecting the NP 'head'. The crucial difference is that in (29) the 'head' moves to the left of the relative D^0 in order to establish a checking/agreement relation with the external D^0, whereas in the correlative structure (28) it stays in the complement position of the relative determiner.

The raising approach also offers a more straightforward account of the diachronic development from the correlative clause to the headed relative. Haudry's proposal in (10) can be reconstructed in X-bar theoretical terms along the following lines. The first stage (10a) corresponds to the by now familiar correlative structure, in which the relative DP is an internal constituent of the dependent CP (30a). The second stage (10b) is derived by raising the NP 'head' to the left of the relative determiner, as shown in (30b):

(30) a. $[_{CP} [_{DP}$ qui $[_{NP}$ vir$]]_i [_{CP} \ldots t_i]]$
     b. $[_{CP} [_{DP} [_{NP}$ vir$] [_{DP}$ qui $t_{NP}]]_i [_{CP} \ldots t_i]]$

In the resulting structure, the NP 'head' occupies the most prominent position within the CP. It suffices to introduce a nominal functional head above this CP to obtain the headed relative (30c). This external functional head selects the relative CP, turning it into a nominal phrase which can directly occupy an argument position within the main clause (whence the elimination of the correlative pronoun in the latter):

(30) c. $[_{DP} D^0 [_{CP} [_{DP} [_{NP}$ vir$][_{DP}$ qui $t_{NP}]]_i [_{CP} \ldots t_i]]]$

Thus, the crucial step in this diachronic evolution consists in the postulation of a nominal functional head selecting the relative CP. In Latin, this external head is not always realized as a determiner; however, it can be assumed to correspond to the Case declension (K^0).[15]

4.2 Attraction phenomena

The second step of the proposed diachronic evolution (30b) may seem ad *ad hoc* stipulation; but interestingly, it can be taken to correspond to the problematic inverse attraction structure exemplified in (16)–(19) above, where the NP "head" precedes the relative D^0 but agrees with it for Case.[16] In other terms, an example like (17) will have the structure in (31):

(31) [$_{CP}$ ...[$_{DP}$ pulli-NOM [$_{DP}$ qui-NOM t_{NP}]]$_i$ [t_i nascentur]] ...eos-ACC...

The structure is still correlative (as attested by the presence of a correlative pronoun in this and in most other examples): the NP 'head' originates in the complement position of the relative D^0, whose (nominative) Case feature is copied into the noun. The NP 'head' then moves to the left of the relative D^0, but since there is no external D^0/K^0 that can attract it, it is spelled out with the internal (nominative) Case.

The inversion of the determiner and the NP in (30b) is probably an instance of a more general phenomenon also involving numerals and demonstratives.[17] Alternatively, we may assume with Kiparsky (1995: 154–155) that the NP has moved out of the relative DP, stranding the relative D^0 in a lower specifier position (cf. Section 4.3 below).

An intermediate stage between the structures (30b) and (30c) may be represented by examples like (18)–(19). These differ from (16)–(17) in that the NP 'head' is introduced by a demonstrative morpheme which bears the internal Case. It is not quite plausible that the demonstrative be generated within the relative DP and raised together with the NP 'head' to the left of the relative D^0. As a matter of fact, the assimilation of this structure to (30b) would not extend to the following Ancient Greek example, where we observe a definite determiner preceding the NP 'head' and the demonstrative:

(32) τὸν   ἄνδρα   τοῦτον   ὅν   πάλαι ζητεῖς ...,
     the-ACC man-ACC this-ACC whom-ACC you long search for,
     οὗτός   ἐστιν ἐνθάδε
     he-himself-NOM is here   [Sophocles, *Oed. Tyr.* 449]
     'this man who you have long been searching for is here'

More plausibly, the demonstrative morpheme realizes an external functional head selecting the relative CP. This means that examples (18), (19) and (32) are no longer correlative clauses with the structure (30b), but they are headed relative clauses with the structure (30c). The relative CP is no longer adjoined to the matrix clause, but it is selected by an external D^0/K^0; the whole structure is reinterpreted as the left-dislocation of a DP, and the correlative pronoun is reinterpreted as a resumptive pronoun.

But if the demonstrative is generated outside the relative CP, it is necessary to explain how it can share the internal Case of the NP "head" and of the relative D^0. Actually, in almost all the examples that I have encountered so far the shared Case is the accusative. Therefore, I tentatively suggest that the external demonstrative morpheme does not receive the *internal* accusative, but it bears an accusative Case that could be assigned to left-dislocated noun phrases.[18]

If this approach is correct, the left-dislocation structure attested in (18), (19) and (32) may have constituted a crucial intermediate step between the still correlative structure of (16)–(17) and the headed relative occurring directly in argument positions, as in (4).

Let us now turn to the phenomenon of Case attraction of the relative D^0, exemplified in (12) to (15). The structure underlying (12) is (33):

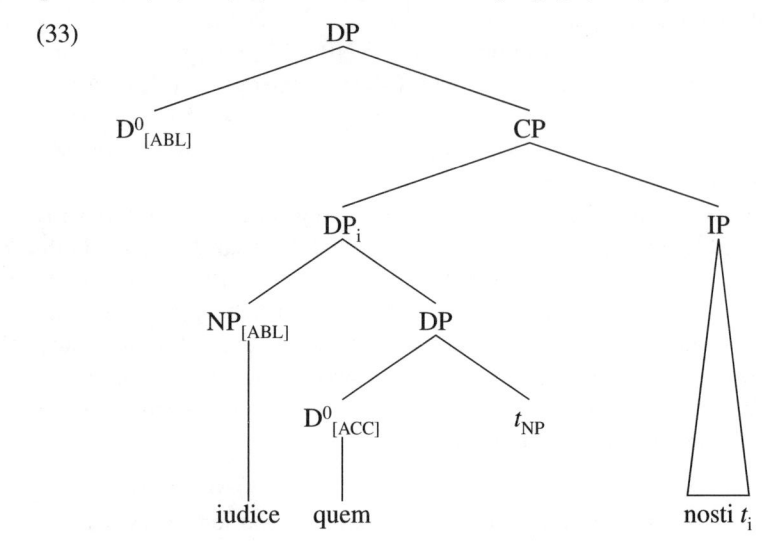

(33)

```
              DP
           /      \
      D⁰[ABL]     CP
                /    \
              DPᵢ     IP
             /  \      |
         NP[ABL] DP    /\
           |    /  \  /  \
           |  D⁰[ACC] t_NP
           |    |
         iudice quem           nosti tᵢ
```

Recall that in the approach proposed in Section 3 the NP 'head' is attracted to the Case of the external D^0 under government. But note that in this configuration the relative D^0 too is governed by the external D^0 and it can be involved in the same process of 'morphological' agreement:[19]

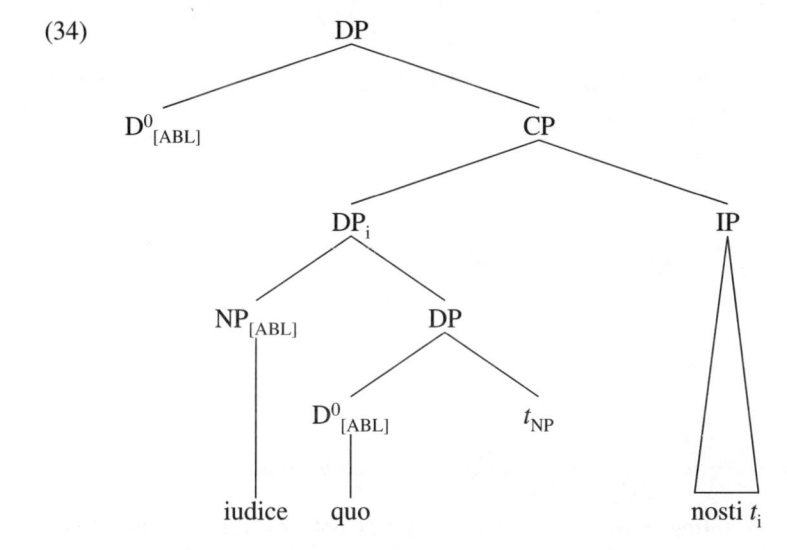

(34)
```
              DP
           /      \
       D⁰[ABL]     CP
                 /     \
               DPᵢ      IP
              /   \      /\
         NP[ABL]  DP    /  \
                 /  \  nosti tᵢ
            D⁰[ABL] t_NP
            
         iudice  quo
```

In order for this to be possible, there must be no conflict with the structural Case that the relative DP receives within CP. There are two possible solutions to this problem. First, the structural Case may be checked off within IP before the relative DP reaches SpecCP; if the checked Case feature is also optionally erased (in the sense of Chomsky 1995: 279–282), then the D^0 can morphologically realize the Case feature that it receives from the external D^0 under government. Alternatively, we may assume that syntactic structural Case can remain morphologically unrealized and is therefore compatible with 'morphological agreement'.[20]

The hypothesis that Case attraction requires government by the external D^0 straightforwardly accounts for Harbert's (1982: 246) observation that a preposition pied piped by the relative DP invariably blocks Case attraction. Following Kayne (1994: 89), I assume that the NP 'head' moves to the Spec of the pied piped PP, stranding the relative determiner in the complement position of P^0:

(35)

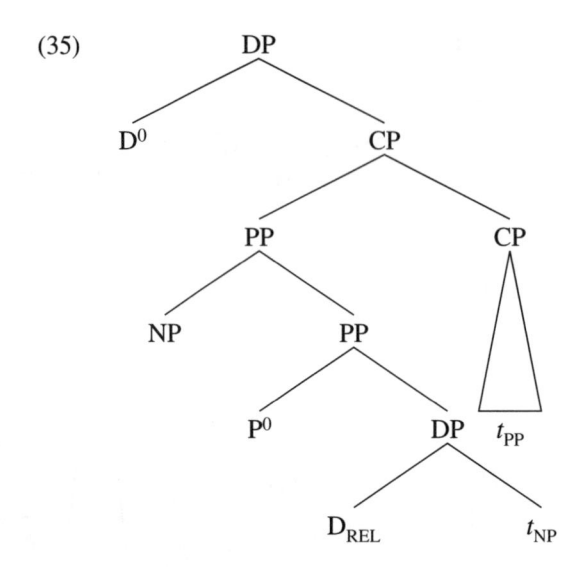

```
                    DP
                   /  \
                 D⁰    CP
                      /  \
                    PP    CP
                   /  \   /\
                 NP    PP
                      /  \
                    P⁰    DP   t_PP
                         /  \
                      D_REL  t_NP
```

In the resulting structure, the relative D^0 is not governed by the external D^0 under relativized minimality (or equivalently, the relative DP falls in the minimal domain of P^0 rather than of the external D^0); hence Case attraction is impossible.

It is not plausible to attribute the structure (34) to examples like (26a) above, where the relative D^0 is not attracted although it bears a structural accusative Case. The logic of the argument leads to the conclusion that in this case the relative D^0 is not in a local syntactic relation with the external D^0, as represented in (26b). Let us instead assume that the relative determiner can be stranded in a specifier position below SpecCP, which is outside the minimal domain of the external D^0.[21]

(36)

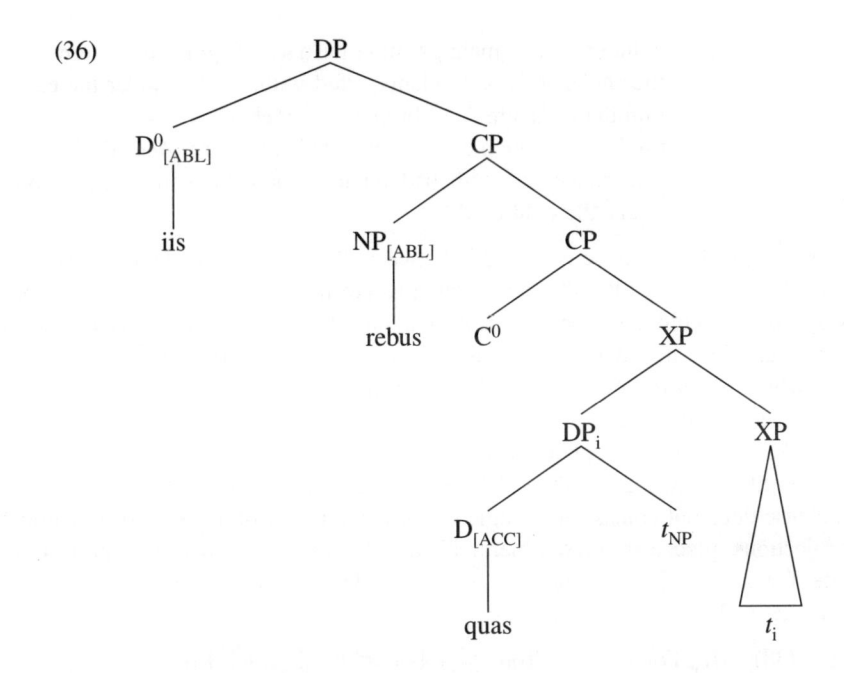

```
              DP
         /         \
    D⁰[ABL]        CP
       |        /      \
      iis   NP[ABL]    CP
              |      /    \
            rebus  C⁰     XP
                       /      \
                     DPᵢ       XP
                   /    \       △
                D[ACC]  t_NP    tᵢ
                  |
                quas
```

4.3 Postposition of the relative pronoun

The proposal in (36) may look at first sight implausible; but interestingly, there is evidence to the effect that (in Latin at least) the NP 'head' and the relative D^0 may occupy two distinct specifier positions. This evidence consists in the phenomenon of postposition of the relative determiner, exemplified in the Latin examples (37):

(37) a. meus vicinus,   meo   viro   qui   liberum
       my   neighbour-NOM (to) my husband-DAT who-NOM free
       praehibet locum
       offers   place
       [Plautus, *Casina* 536]
       'my neighbour, who offers a free place to my husband'
   b. istos captivos duos,   heri   quos   emi...
       those prisoners two-ACC, yesterday who-ACC I bought
       a   quaestoribus
       from the commissioners   [Pl., *Captivi* 110]
       'those two prisoners who I bought from the commissioners yesterday'

c. coluber   mala gramina pastus,   frigida sub   terra
    the snake-NOM bad plants   fed with, cold   under the earth
    tumidum   quem   bruma   tegebat
    tumid-ACC which-ACC the winter kept [Verg. Aen. II, 471–72]
    'the snake fed with bad plants which the winter kept tumid under the cold earth'

Here a topicalized phrase is placed in between the NP 'head' and the relative D^0: this clearly indicates that the two categories are not in a specifier-head relationship. More specifically, the NP 'head' has raised to a position locally related to the external D^0 in order to satisfy the nominal features of the latter; the relative D^0, which is not involved in this checking/agreement relation, has been stranded in a lower position.

An analysis of this phenomenon can be framed in the 'split Comp' hypothesis recently proposed by Rizzi (1997). According to Rizzi, the left periphery of a clause does not consist of a single CP projection, but of an array of functional projections, placed in a fixed hierarchical order, each one providing the landing site for a specific type of A' movement. This 'complementizer system' is schematically represented in (38):

(38) [$_{FP}$ Force^0 [$_{TopP*}$ Top^0 [$_{FocP}$ Focus^0 [$_{TopP*}$ Top^0 IP]]]]

The highest layer, the Force Phrase, is headed by the 'declarative complementizer' and conveys the propositional force of the clause. Below it are recursive Topic projections, which host topicalized or dislocated constituents in their specifiers; in between them, a non-recursive Focus Phrase hosts focussed (and possibly interrogative) phrases.

It is now possible to analyse the postposition of the relative determiner as involving multiple specifiers in the complementizer system. Specifically, I propose that the relative DP moves to a low Topic or Focus position;[22] the NP 'head' is then extracted and moves to the most prominent position, SpecForce Phrase, to the left of the topicalized phrase occuring in the specifier of an intermediate Topic Phrase:

(39) [$_{DP}$ istos [$_{FP}$ [captivos duos]$_i$ Force^0 [$_{TopP}$ [heri] Top^0 [$_{XP}$ [quos t_i] X^0 [$_{IP}$ emi ...]]]]]

4.4 Preposed relative clauses

Another type of evidence in favour of the 'split Comp' structure in (36) comes from the possibility of preposed relative clauses like (40a-b) (Ancient Greek) and (40c-d) (Latin):

(40) a. τούτους   καὶ ἄρκοντας ἐποίει   ἧς
   these ones-ACC and governors (he) made which-GEN
   κατεστρέφετο χώρας
   he conquered country-GEN   [Xenophon, *Anabasis* I,9,14]
   'and he made these ones governors of the country which he conquered'
b. ... ἀποπέμψαι πρὸς ἑαυτὸν ὅ   εἶχε
   to send   to   him   which-ACC (he) had
   στράτευμα
   army-ACC
   'to send to him all the soldiers he had' [Xenophon, *Anabasis* I,2,1]
c. agedum   odorare hanc   quam   ego habeo pallam
   come on, sniff   this-ACC which-ACC I   have mantle-ACC
   'come on, smell this mantle that I have here'
                                        [Plautus, *Maenechni* 166]
d. illa   quae   iniuria depulsa fuerat ancilla totam
   that-NOM who-NOM rudely repulsed had been maid-NOM all
   faciem eius fuligine   longa perfricuit
   face   his (with) signs of soot long   covered
                                        [Petronius, *Satyricon* 22,1]
   'that girl who had been rudely repulsed covered all his face with long signs of soot'

In these examples, the relative clause including the relative determiner has been fronted to a position preceding the NP 'head' (and which in the Latin examples follows the external demonstrative morpheme). This is only possible if the relative D^0 and the NP 'head' occupy two distinct specifier positions of the Comp system, as shown in (41). In this representation, CP_2 indicates a low layer of the Comp system whose Spec hosts the relative DP, CP_1 indicates the highest layer (=Force^0) and F_N indicates a nominal functional head below the external D^0, whose Spec hosts the preposed relative clause:

(41) a. [$_{DP}$ hanc [$_{F/NP}$ F_N^0 [$_{C_1P}$ pallam$_j$ C_1^0 [$_{C_2P}$ [$_{DP}$ quam t_j]$_i$ C_2^0 [$_{IP}$ ego habeo t_i]]]]]
b. [$_{DP}$ hanc [$_{F/NP}$ [$_{C_2P}$ [$_{DP}$ quam t_j]$_i$ C_2^0 [$_{IP}$ ego habeo t_i]] F_N^0 [$_{C1P}$ pallam$_j$ [C_1^0 t_{C_2P}]]]][23]

On the contrary, if the NP 'head' invariably landed in the Spec of the relative D^0, as in (34) above, the derivation of the examples in (41) would have to involve the fronting of a nonconstituent.

5. Concluding remarks

In this paper I have examined some data mainly from Latin, Ancient Greek and Old English that appear problematic for the standard 'adjunction' analysis of headed relative clauses. These data concern the diachronic development of the headed relative from an original correlative structure (Haudry 1973) and Case attraction phenomena (Harbert 1982; 1983). In both respects, the adjunction analysis fails to provide a satisfactory account because it assumes too loose a relation between the NP 'head' and the relative morpheme: the two elements are generated independently of each other and are separated by a barrier.

I have tried to show how the raising analysis proposed by Kayne (1994) can provide a more unified approach to these phenomena, under the specific hypothesis that there exists a 'surface' morphosyntactic interaction between the external D^0 selecting the relative CP and the NP 'head' in the Spec of the latter, in a configuration corresponding to the pre-minimalist notion of head government. This morphosyntactic interaction accounts for Case attraction phenomena; the introduction of an external D^0 selecting CP constitutes the crucial step of the diachronic development leading from the correlative clause to the headed relative.

As a final remark, it is worth pointing out that the analysis proposed for this (limited) empirical domain is fully compatible with the restrictiveness of the Antisymmetry theory.

Appendix

Srivastav (1991) offers a detailed comparison between the correlative clause and the headed relative clause of Hindi, exemplified in (5)–(6) above. She argues that the two relativization strategies do not share a common underlying structure, pointing out various systematic differences:

I. The headed relative allows internal recursion (namely, the relative clause can contain an NP itself modified by another relative clause); the correlative structure does not.
II. Only in the correlative structure can the noun be realised in both members of the correlative pair; in the headed relative, instead, the 'head' only appears to the left of the relative morpheme:

(42) a. *jo   laṛkii* khaṛii   hai *vo   laṛkii* lambii hai
         which girl   standing is, that girl   tall   is
         'the girl who is standing is tall'
     b. **vo   laṛkii jo   laṛkii* khaṛii   hai lambii hai
         that girl   which girl   standing is   tall   is

III. The dependent clause of the correlative structure can contain multiple relative NPs, each one resumed by an appropriate correlative element in the main clause, as in (43) below. The headed relative, on the contrary, cannot have multiple 'heads'.

(43) jis   laṛki-ne$_i$ jis   laṛke-ko$_j$ dekhaa us-ne$_i$ us-ko$_j$ pasand kiyaa
     which girl   which boy   saw,   she   him   liked
     'whichever girl saw whichever boy, she liked him'

Srivastav reduces these contrasts to the different underlying structures, corresponding to (3) and (9) respectively. It is necessary to show that these syntactic differences also follow if one adopts instead the raising analysis for the headed relative.

I. Recursive embedding is impossible in the correlative structure:

(44) *[$_{IP_0}$ [$_{CP_1}$ RelP$_j$ [$_{IP_1}$ [$_{CP_2}$ RelP$_i$ [$_{IP_2}$ ... t_i]] [$_{IP_1}$ ...DP$_i$... t_j ...]]] [$_{IP_0}$ ... DP$_j$ ...]]

In fact, Srivastav proposes that the whole adjoined CP is interpreted as a generalized quantifier binding the correlative element in the matrix clause. In (44) the adjoined CP$_1$ binds the correlative DP$_j$ within the main clause IP$_0$; but CP$_1$ itself contains a correlative DP$_i$ to be bound by a dependent CP$_2$ adjoined to IP$_1$. The configuration is excluded because the quantified clause CP$_2$ adjoined to IP$_1$ prevents the relative phrase raised to SpecCP$_1$ (RelP$_j$) from locally A'-binding its variable t_j.

In the raising structure, instead, recursion is unproblematic, since every NP 'head' is locally bound by the external D^0 selecting the relative CP in which the NP originates:

(45) [$_{DP_1}$ D$_1$ [$_{CP_1}$ NP$_1$ [$_{IP_1}$ ... t_{NP_1} ... [$_{DP_2}$ D$_2$ [$_{CP_2}$ NP$_2$ [... t_{NP_2} ...]]]]]]

II. As for the lexical realization of the noun head in (42a), note that in the correlative structure the relative DP *jo laṛkii* and the correlative DP *vo laṛkii* are generated independent of each other and they do not form a chain. In the headed relative (42b), on the contrary, the NP 'head' moves from a position following the relative determiner *jo* to a position immediately adjacent to the external determiner *vo*:

(46) [$_{DP}$ vo [$_{CP}$ [$_{DP}$ laṛkii [$_{DP}$ *jo* t_{NP}]] [$_{IP}$ t_i khaṛii hai]]] lambii hai
        that   girl   who   standing is   tall   is
'that girl who is standing is tall'

Even assuming that the trace following the relative D^0 is a copy of the NP 'head', it is c-commanded by the first link of the chain, and hence it is obligatorily deleted in the phonetic representation by whatever principle prevents the spellout of traces in a chain.

III. The possibility of multiple heads in the correlative structure (43) follows from the hypothesis that the two relative DPs can be interpreted by an operation of quantifier absorption (Srivastav 1991: 667). Roughly, the relative DPs are intrinsically non-definite, and they can be both bound by an implicit universal unselective quantifier, which yields a 'pair' reading.[24] An unselective binder can bind multiple variables by definition. The raising structure, on the contrary, does not involve unselective binding: the external D^0 binds only one NP 'head', and furthermore, SpecCP can host at most one relative DP. Therefore, multiple 'heads' are excluded.

The most problematic difference between the correlative structure and the headed relative concerns their semantic interpretation. Whereas a headed restrictive relative is an open expression with a variable to be bound by the external determiner,[25] the correlative CP is 'closed' by type shifting (Srivastav 1991) or by an operation of 'maximalization' (Dayal 1995; Grosu & Landman 1996), so that it denotes the unique maximal individual satisfying the properties expressed by the NP 'head' and by IP. If this is the correct semantic characterization for the ancient correlative structures as well,[26] then the diachronic evolution proposed here must also have involved a 'semantic reanalysis'.

If the type shifting or maximalization operation which closes off the correlative CP can be thought of as a sort of default operation applying at the CP level, then it is possible to speculate that this operation failed to take place as soon as an external D^0 was introduced in the structure which could bind the free variable of the NP 'head'.

Notes

1. Cf. Safir's (1986) notion of R-binding or Browning's (1987: 52–63) 'agreement chain'. In the following discussion, the notion of 'head' of the relative clause is always indicated by inverted commas, as opposed to the X-bar theoretic notion of head.

THE SYNTAX OF RELATIVE DETERMINERS 77

2. Actually, the relation is not simply anaphoric but it involves quantification: cf. Srivastav (1991), Dayal (1995), Grosu & Landman (1996). See also the Appendix.
3. It must be pointed out that Haudry's proposal concerns not only relative clauses, but also many types of adverbial clauses and it is also extended to Old English and Sanskrit.
4. Note that no Case conflict arises despite the fact that the relative DP inherits a structural Case from its trace and another Case from the 'head'. On this problem see the discussion around (33) and (34) below.
5. In this respect, it is perhaps possible to exploit Chomsky's (1995: 277–279) distinction between [+interpretable] features (phi-features of nouns and pronouns) and [–interpretable] features (Case); but the formulation of the parameter accounting for the cross-linguistic distribution of Case attraction would remain essentially stipulative.
6. According to Chomsky's (1995: 178) definition of checking domain.
7. The present discussion will only take into account restrictive relatives. On the extension of the raising analysis to appositive relatives, see Kayne (1994: 110–115) and Bianchi (1997: chapters 4 and 5).
8. Actually, the category may be not simply NP, but a larger functional category including adjectives, numerals, etc. I will use the label NP for simplicity.
9. As for the first step from (21) to (22), I assume that the movement of the relative DP to SpecCP is triggered by a 'Relative Criterion' akin to Rizzi's (1996) Wh Criterion.
10. See Bianchi (1999: 54–61) for a more careful assessment of this problem.
11. Cf. also Kayne (1994: 90).
12. This implies that the derivation does not satisfy Chomsky's (1995: 190) extension condition. However, note that in Chomsky (1995: 232–235) the extension condition is no longer postulated, but it is derived from the defining property of strong features: a strong feature must be eliminated by checking as soon as it is introduced in the derivation. This condition is satisfied in the derivation of (23), under the specific assumption that all the members of the minimal domain are visible for checking.
13. An anonymous reviewer points out two alternative solutions to this checking problem which are consistent with Chomsky's minimalist assumptions. A first possibility is that the NP 'head' raises to the Spec of the external D^0 in LF. This implies that the step from (22) to (23) is not triggered by a strong feature of the external D^0, but it is necessary to postulate some independent trigger. The second possibility is that the relative CP in (23) raises to the Spec of the external D^0 in LF: since the relative NP is only covered by one segment of CP and one segment of the relative DP, it will fall in the checking domain of the external D^0 under Chomsky's (1995: 178) definition. This alternative is incompatible with Kayne's (1994: 112) proposal that relative clauses falling outside the c-command domain of the external D^0 in LF receive an appositive interpretation. At present I am unable to fully work out the consequences of these alternatives.
14. Or one of its traces is governed (cf. the discussion around (31)). If other functional projections intervene between D^0 and NP, the Case feature must 'percolate' from every such head to the immediately lower head, again under government.
15. Pittner (1995: 218–221) proposes a different diachronic evolution from the correlative structure to the headed relative clause in Old and Middle High German. The evolution starts from an 'inverse' correlative dyptic, with a cataphoric correlative pronoun in the main clause pointing forward to a following asyndetic relative clause:

(i)   [NP$_i$ correl [pro$_i$ ...

In this stage, the correlative pronoun obviously bears the Case required by the matrix clause. At the next stage the correlative pronoun is reanalysed as a relative pronoun in the Comp of the relative clause, though it still bears the Case required by the matrix:

(ii)   NP$_i$ [(cor)rel$_i$ ...]

Finally, the reanalysed pronoun takes the Case assigned within the relative clause and becomes a well-behaved relative pronoun:

(iii)   NP$_i$ [rel$_i$ ...

The reanalysis of the correlative pronoun as a relative pronoun in SpecCP is motivated by a condition of C-visibility holding in New High German, whereby the Comp projection must be filled by a lexical element endowed with a [+C] feature. In stage (iii), this function is accomplished by the relative pronoun and accordingly, the old invariable relative particles are eliminated. When fulfilling the C-visibility condition, the relative pronoun can not be attracted to the Case required by the matrix clause, because it must be clearly identified as belonging to the relative CP. This accounts for the lack of 'Case attraction' of the relative pronoun in New High German.

Though the correlation between the C-visibility requirement and the elimination of Case attraction is interesting, the proposed development appears problematic. First, note that it requires a radical reanalysis of the structure, symmetric to that in (11) above: here a constituent of the matrix clause (the correlative pronoun) must be reanalysed as belonging to the relative CP. Second, the stage (ii) of the derivation is problematic, as Pittner herself acknowledges: the reanalysed pronoun in SpecCP must still be assigned the matrix Case "by the same rules" which determined Case marking in stage (i). This Case attraction of the relative pronoun is less problematic from the perspective of the raising analysis (cf. Section 4.2).

16. Cf. Kiparsky (1995: 154–155) and Kroll (1912: 13–16).
17. Cf. for instance the following Latin examples:
    (i)   Pater   abhinc   [duos et viginti annos] est mortuus [Cic. *In Verr.* II, 29]
          (My) father from-now twenty two   years is dead
          'my father died twenty-two years ago'
    (ii) Comitia   abhinc   [diebus triginta] habita sunt [Cic. *In Verr.* II, 52]
          the assembly from-now days   thirty held was
          'the assembly was held thirty days ago'
18. These would be instances of the (rare) *Accusativus pendens* mentioned by Ernout & Thomas (1972^5, §§ 31–32). The so called proleptic Accusative is probably irrelevant here, since it was assigned by a matrix transitive verb to a noun phrase left-dislocated from within the complement clause; however, according to Panhuis (1984), in Ancient Greek some instances of prolepsis in front of the matrix clause may actually be 'hanging topics' (e.g. Xenophon, *Mem.* 4,2,33) base generated outside the domain of the matrix verb. Cases of inverse attraction of an external demonstrative to the Nominative (like Plautus, *Poen.* 770) would instead be instances of the *Nominativus Pendens*.

    The sporadic cases of inverse attraction to the Dative in *Truc.* 745, *Aul.* 574, quoted by Stolz-Schmalz (1928: § 193), are potentially problematic if their pronominal 'heads' are not raised from within the relative clause. If the text proposal were to prove untenable, it would be necessary to assume (with Harbert 1983), a marked mechanism that transmits to the external D^0 the internal Case of the relative D^0 in left-dislocation positions.

19. The relative D^0 agrees for phi-features with the NP 'head', which is originally its complement, but it agrees for Case with the external D^0. The two types of agreement are thus correctly differentiated, and the second one constitutes a more marked option.
20. Harbert (1982, 1983) also discusses Case attraction in free relatives. The latter will not be taken into account here, though they also can be reduced to the raising analysis (see Kayne 1994: n. 13 to Chapter 8).
21. An anonymous reviewer suggests that the definite determiner which appears in between the NP 'head' and the relative determiner in Hungarian relative clauses may be the lexicalization of the higher C^0 head in (36). This recalls an observation by Kenesei (1994: 303), according to whom in XVIth century Hungarian the declarative C^0 *hogy* appeared in the same context.
22. An anonymous reviewer points out that in Hungarian relative clauses a focussed phrase may appear to the right of the relative determiner; since the Focus position is unique, this suggests that the relative DP in Hungarian targets a Topic position. The movement of the NP 'head' across SpecTopP in (39) raises questions w.r.t. relativized minimality which I cannot adequately discuss here for reasons of space.
23. Note that in (41b) the relative D^0 is again in the minimal domain of the external D^0, hence subject to Case attraction (cf. (40a), where the relative D^0 is attracted to the external Genitive Case). However, in this context attraction was not obligatory:

    (i)   in ista   quam   dixi   tragoedia [Gellius, *Noctes Atticae* 5, 11, 14]
          in this$_{Abl}$ which$_{Acc}$ (I) have said tragedy$_{Abl}$
          'in this tragedy which I mentioned'

24. Actually, Srivastav (1991: 661–62) proposes a type shifting operation: the dependent CP denotes the unique individual that satisfies the predicates expressed by the NP 'head' and by IP, which contains a trace; type shifting turns the dependent CP into a generalized quantifier, the set of all the sets containing this unique individual.
25. This presupposes that the relative D^0 does not close the variable within the NP head. For justification of this hypothesis see Bianchi (1999: 80–86).
26. From a different perspective, Kroll (1912) and Haudry (1973: 166–168) suggest instead that the relation is simply anaphoric: an indefinite in the first clause is resumed by an anaphoric element in the second clause.

References

Allen, C. L. (1977). *Topics in Diachronic English Syntax*. Doctoral Dissertation, MIT.
Babby, L. (1987). Case, Prequantifiers, and Discontinuous Agreement in Russian. *Natural Language and Linguistic Theory* 5, 91–138.
Bianchi, V. (1999). *Consequences of Antisymmetry: Headed Relative Clauses*. Berlin: Mouton de Gruyter.
Browning, M. (1987). *Null Operator Constructions*. Doctoral Dissertation, MIT.
Chomsky, N. (1995). *The Minimalist Program*. Cambridge, Mass., MIT Press.
Dayal, V. (1995). Quantification in Correlatives. *Quantification in Natural Languages*, edited by E. Bach, E. Jelinek, A. Kratzer & B. Partee, 179–205. Dordrecht: Kluwer.

Downing, B.T. (1978). Some Universals of Relative Clause Structure. *Universals of Human Language. Volume IV: Syntax,* edited by J.H. Greenberg, 375–418. Stanford: Stanford University Press.
Ernout, A. & F. Thomas (1972[5]). *Syntaxe Latine.* Paris: Klincksieck.
Franks, S. (1994). Parametric Properties of Numeral Phrases in Slavic. *Natural Language and Linguistic Theory* 12: 599–676.
Giusti, G. (1993). *La sintassi dei determinanti.* Padova: Unipress.
Gonda, J. (1954). The Original Character of The Indo-European Relative Pronoun **io. Lingua* 4: 1–41.
Grosu, A. & F. Landman (1996). *Strange Relatives of the Third Kind.* Manuscript, Tel Aviv University.
Halle, M. & A. Marantz (1993). Distributed Morphology and the Pieces of Inflection. *The View from Building 20,* edited by K. Hale & S.J. Keyser, 111–176. Cambridge, Mass.: MIT Press.
Harbert, W. (1982). On the Nature of the Matching Parameter. *The Linguistic Review* 2: 237–284.
Harbert, W. (1983). A Note on Old English Free Relatives. *Linguistic Inquiry* 14: 549–553.
Haudry, J. (1973). Parataxe, hypotaxe et corrélation dans la phrase latine. *Bulletin de la Société Linguistique de Paris* 68: 147–186.
Hock, H.H. (1988). Relative Clauses and Rebracketing in Old English. *Germanic Linguistics II: Papers from the Second Symposium on Germanic Linguistics,* edited by E.H. Antonsen & H.H. Hock, 35–55. Indiana University Linguistic Club.
Kayne, R.S. (1994). *The Antisymmetry of Syntax.* Cambridge, Mass.: MIT Press.
Keenan, E. (1985). Relative clauses. *Language Typology and Syntactic Description.*[Vol. II], edited by T. Shopen, 141–170. Cambridge University Press.
Kenesei, I. (1994). Subordinate Clauses. *The Syntactic Structure of Hungarian [Syntax and Semantics 27]* edited by F. Kiefer & K. Kiss, 275–354. New York: Academic Press.
Kiparsky, P. (1995). Indo-European Origins of Germanic Syntax. *Clause Structure and Language Change,* edited by A. Battye & I. Roberts, 140–169. New York: Oxford University Press.
Kroll, W. (1912). Der lateinische Relativsatz. *Glotta* 3: 1–18.
Manzini, M.R. (1994). Syntactic Dependencies and Their Properties: A Note on Strong Islands. *University College of London Working Papers in Linguistics* 6: 205–218.
Mitchell, B. (1985). *Old English Syntax.* Oxford: Clarendon Press.
Mitchell, B. & J. Robinson (1982). *A Guide to Old English.* London: Basil Blackwell.
Panhuis, D.J. (1984). Prolepsis in Greek as a Discourse Strategy. *Glotta* 62: 26–39.
Pittner, K. (1995). The Case of German Relatives. *The Linguistic Review* 12: 197–232.
Rizzi, L. (1996). Residual Verb Second and the *Wh*-Criterion. *Parameters and Functional Heads,* edited by A. Belletti & L. Rizzi, 63–90. New York: Oxford University Press.
Rizzi, L. (1997). The Fine Structure of the Left Periphery. *Elements of Grammar,* edited by L. Haegeman, 281–337. Dordrecht: KLuwer.

Safir, K. (1986). Relative Clauses in a Theory of Binding and Levels. *Linguistic Inquiry* 17: 663–689.
Schachter, P. (1973). Focus and Relativization. *Language* 49: 19–46.
Srivastav, V. (1991). The Syntax and Semantics of Correlatives. *Natural Language and Linguistic Theory* 9: 637–686.
Stolz, F. & J. H. Schmalz (1928[5]). *Lateinische Grammatik.* München: Ch. Becksche.
Vergnaud, J. R. (1974). *French Relative Clauses.* Doctoral Dissertation, MIT.

Type-Resolution in Relative Constructions
Featural marking and dependency encoding[*]

Alexander Grosu
Tel Aviv University

Introduction

This paper constitutes the first part of a two-part study. The first line of the title characterizes the topic of the entire study, the second line characterizes the concerns of this first part. A major impetus for undertaking this research was jointly provided by the proposed theme of the Colloquium on Interface Strategies that was held in Amsterdam between 24–26 September 1997 and by a *prima facie* partial similarity between the 'classical' version of the B(inding) T(heory) (Chomsky 1981) and the typology of relative clause constructions proposed in Grosu and Landman (1998) (henceforth: GL).

The theme of the Colloquium was whether a hierarchy of preferences that had emerged from research on BT (in particular, from Reinhart (1983) and Reuland (1996)) is also applicable in other domains, the hierarchy in question being, essentially, that **pre-encoding** by the Computational System (CSYS) takes precedence over **interpretive interface operations**, and that the latter in turn takes precedence over **inspection of the knowledge base**. The *prima facie* partial similarity with classical BT concerned the fact that the three types of elements named by BT's Conditions A-C are required to be (a) **bound within a particular**

---

[*] I wish to express my gratitude to Julia Horváth and to an anonymous referee, who painstakingly commented on earlier versions of this paper. I am also grateful to audiences at the colloquium on DPs held at the Zentrum für Allgemeine Sprachwissenschaft, Berlin, February 1997, at the 23. Incontro di Grammatica Generativa held at the Scuola Normale Superiore, Pisa, February 1997, and at the colloquium on Interface Strategies organized by the Royal Netherlands Academy of Arts and Sciences, Amsterdam, September 1997. All these persons are in no way responsible for the use I have made of their suggestions, and deserve credit for whatever improvements the final version of this paper contains. All remaining errors are my own.

domain (their governing category), (b) free within that domain, but possibly **bound in a higher domain**, and (c) **free**. The typology proposed by GL exhibits types such that the necessarily present CP-internal variable needs to end up (a′) operator-**bound within a particular domain** (specifically, the relative clause), (b′) operator-**bound within a higher domain**, or (c′) operator-**free**. These two factors, I wish to stress, provided no more than the **initial inspiration** for undertaking the research. As will be seen in what follows, the similarity just noted plays no part in my proposed analysis. As for the above hierarchy of preferences, while it will turn out to have relevance for the theory of relative clause constructions, its significance will be seen to be quite different from the one that was attributed to it in relation to BT. Thus, whereas its relevance to BT was claimed to lie in an ability to shed light on the fact that it consists of three distinct conditions on A-binding, its relevance to relatives is that it can provide an account of the local/non-local character of certain dependencies that are entirely orthogonal to GL's typology.

The division of labour between the two parts of my study on type resolution in the domain of relative clause constructions is as follows: In this paper, I concentrate on **encoding** prior to the syntax-semantics interface, and argue that type-encoding needs to be achieved by means of 'interpretable' formal features (Chomsky 1995), and that dependency-encoding is effected by operations of the CSYS (in particular, by Merge, and possibly by Move). In the second paper, which is currently in preparation for a volume based on contributions to the Colloquium on Interface Strategies, I argue that certain **interpretive operations** and aspects of the **knowledge base** effect type-resolution in a proper subdomain of relatives; this paper refines and revises certain proposals made by GL.

The typology of relatives proposed by GL, like many other proposed typologies of relatives, tacitly assumed the existence of a coherent class of 'relative constructions'. Let us attempt to make this intuition more explicit. But first, let us observe that past literature on relatives has used a variety of criteria to identify and classify them (in particular, morphosyntactic, semantic, and pragmatic), and it is thus far from obvious that the totality of constructions which have been called 'relative' on the basis of **some** criterion or other forms a theoretically interesting class. Furthermore, in contrast to, say, declaratives, interrogatives, and comparatives, for which uniform logical types have been proposed in the literature, in particular, propositions, sets of propositions, and degrees respectively, relatives can evidently not all be assigned a single logical type. Accordingly, if one adopts, for example, the suggestion made in Rizzi (1994) to the effect that the interpretable formal features which express the 'force' of a CP include a feature [REL], one needs to characterize the import of such a feature. I offer the informal definition in (A), which, as will be seen, both characterizes an interesting 'core' of relative constructions and allows natural characterizations of increasingly 'distant' constructions.

(A) In the spirit of Rizzi (1994), [REL] has both 'inside-' and 'outside-oriented' import.
   i. *Inside-oriented:* CP includes (at least) one free variable in the input to semantics.
   ii. *Outside-oriented:* The internal variable(s) of (Ai) is/are **consonant** in syntactic category and logical type with a complex XP that properly contains the relative CP (where 'consonant' is a term with the general import of 'identical', except for categorial differences limited to the 'level' of extended projection, as well as differences in logical type limited to such 'equivalence classes' as the one that consists of individuals and generalized quantifiers).

The core class characterized by (A) is that of continuous 'headed' relative constructions. I note that, under the analysis of relative extraposition proposed in Wilder (1995), extraposed relative constructions belong to the core (because they are continuous at the syntax-semantics interface). — Constructions that are analyzed as 'discontinuous' throughout a derivation, in particular, correlatives left-adjoined to IP, require a slight modification (Aii) in the sense that the variable(s) need(s) to be consonant not with a containing phrase, but with the discontinuous CP-external part of the construction, in particular, the correlate(s). — Existential relative constructions, which are simplex clauses (see below), require a more radical modification of (Aii), in particular, suppression of the reference to syntactic category, with the result that consonance applies to logical type alone. — French clauses like the bracketed one in (1a), which have the approximate distribution and semantics of (certain) small-clause predicates (see Muller 1995 and references therein), may be called '(predicative) relatives', if one wishes (on the grounds that they share internal morphosyntactic properties with French restrictive/appositive relatives), but ought not to bear the feature [REL]. For one thing, (Aii) is inapplicable. As for (Ai), it becomes otiose, since the clause needs to be marked as [PRED], that is, as involving abstraction over a variable in the course of semantics, and this implies (Ai). — Neither should the clause within the inner set of brackets in (1b) bear the feature [REL], since this would be downright misleading. Thus, observe that the constituent within the outer set of brackets is superficially indistinguishable from the one in (1c). But while the latter is an uncontroversial DP that includes a restrictive relative, the former has the semantics of an interrogative clause, and is arguably an extended projection of V (with *ce* a clausal, rather than nominal D; see Zaring 1992 for a comparable *ce* that introduces declarative clauses). I also note that the constructions within the inner sets of brackets in (1b) and (1c) differ in their degree of transparency to extraction in the way in which interrogatives and relatives typically do (see (31) below for illustration). The feature [REL] would thus be completely inappropriate for (1b) (the appropriate feature is, of course, [Q]).

(1) a. Je l'ai   vue [qui partait].
       I her-have seen who was-leaving
       'I saw her leaving' [approximate translation]
    b. Je me demande [ce [qui   lui fait   mal]].
       I me ask   that COMP her makes pain
       'I wonder what is hurting her.'
    c. Je revendrai [ce [qui   m'a   été   vendu]].
       I will-resell that COMP me-has been sold
       'I will resell what was sold to me.'

For the purposes of this paper, I will be concerned with the core constructions in the sense of (A), with the 'near-core' case represented by correlatives, and with the more peripheral existential relatives, noting that, orthogonally to the 'core and periphery' characterization offered above, these constructions may be viewed as part of the continuum in (B). As GL observed, the left to right orientation on this continuum correlates with an increasingly greater contribution made by the relative clause to the semantics of the construction.

(B) Simplex XPs Appositives Restrictives Maximalizers Simplex CPs [Existentials]
         1   2   3   4   5

Following GL, I will refer to the constructions numbered 4 and 5 as 'sortal-internal', and to those numbered 2 and 3, as 'sortal-external', a terminology meant to suggest that the sortal (or 'common noun') is construed within and without the relative clause respectively (I note, however, that this terminology is not fully accurate with respect to restrictives, whose sortal can sometimes be construed clause-internally; for an illustration of this possibility, see example (35) and the paragraph that includes it; for more extensive illustration, see Grosu (1998), which is the second part of this study).

The way in which the clause-internal variables required by [REL] receive a value in sortal-external relatives is well-known and basically uncontroversial. According to most authors, such variables acquire values through co-valuation with an antecedent in appositives, and through syntactic binding by a D(eter-miner) in restrictives. Since the syntax-semantics of sortal-internal relatives is less widely known, I will provide encapsulated characterizations of their major properties in Section 1. The center of gravity of the paper lies in Sections 2 and

3, in which I address the issues of type-resolution and dependency characterization respectively. — The major thrust of Section 2 is that while languages may or may not pre-encode their various types of relatives in configurational terms, a purely configurational treatment cannot succeed in general, and type-resolution needs to be handled in UG in terms of interpretable features, or formal semantic logical types. In Section 2.1, I critically examine a number of past proposals that relied (almost) exclusively on configurational distinctions, and show they are all inadequate in some way or other. In Section 2.2, I argue that such an approach cannot succeed for maximalizers, either. In Section 2.3, I make a concrete proposal for a distinctive featural characterization of the subtypes of relative constructions that fall on the continuum in (B). — In Section 3, I examine the contribution of the Merge and Move operations of the CSYS to the creation of pre-encoded local dependencies of certain kinds in the core constructions defined by [REL]. Special attention is devoted to an exploration of the applicability of a 'Head-raising' analysis to all three semantic subtypes found in the core class of relatives. — Section 4 summarizes the major results of the paper, noting that the proposed analyses pave the way towards a unified treatment of all core relative constructions.

1. Sortal-internal relatives

Sortal-internal relatives contrast with sortal-external ones not only in that sortals, if there are any, are necessarily construed internally, but also in the following respect: Whereas in appositives and restrictives, assignment of a value to internal variables is effected on the basis of **syntactically realized** elements (antecedents or binders), in maximalizers and existentials, internal variables get bound by **'concealed'** operators with uniform force in each case; specifically, with uniqueness force in maximalizers and with existential force in existentials. I provide more details on sortal-internal relatives in the remainder of this section, drawing freely from GL and adding information, where appropriate.

1.1 *Maximalizing relatives*

As GL and the references they cite observe, maximalizing relatives occur in a variety of syntactic and morphosyntactic garbs in the languages of the world, but are nonetheless easily recognizable by the following two properties: the clause-external Ds of the (continuous or discontinuous) constructions to which they belong are restricted to definites and universals, and maximalizing clauses do not 'stack' with intersecting import. The former property is illustrated in (3), where indefinite Ds and *most* are infelicitous (one must resist a possible tendency to construe such Ds as *D of the*).

(2) [{The (three), all the, those, both, every, several, some, three, (a) few, most} student(s) {who, that} attended the party] left early.

(3) [{The (three), all the, every, both, #several, #some, #three, #(a) few #most} student(s) that there were/was at the party] left early.

Observe that there are no comparable restrictions in (2), which exhibits a restrictive construction. The restrictions on external Ds at issue are sometimes associated with certain structural configurations (in correlatives), or with morphological properties of elements in the 'COMP area.' In (3), it is associated with relativization 'out of' the presentational context *there* BE __ (for reasons to which I return below).

GL account for restrictions on external Ds in maximalizing relatives as follows: For arbitrary or motivated reasons, at the interpretive stage where the relative clause has become a lambda-abstract, an operator MAX applies to the set defined by abstraction, picking out of it a unique maximal element, if there is one (if there is no such element, MAX is undefined, with ensuing infelicity). The construction is not exhausted by CP, it exhibits (at least) an additional D, overt or null, and possibly a sortal, numerals, etc. If this external material were unrestricted, the effects of MAX would be undetectable in the construction, and its application pointless. GL suggest that the external material is subject to the restriction that it **preserve** the (individual-sum, cardinality, scale, etc.) values established by MAX within the clause, and point out that only definite and universal operators are suitable for this purpose. Hence, the infelicity of Ds of other kinds.

To avoid misunderstandings, I note that the preservation condition has only a necessary, not a sufficient character, and is thus not contradicted by the deviance of the reduced version of (4b) (noted, but not satisfactorily explained in Carlson 1977). For a suggested explanation for the contrast between the reduced and the full versions of (4b), see GL.

(4) a. The students that there were at the party left early.
     b. The #(only, single, one) student that there was at the party left early.

It should be pointed out that MAX was not invented in *ad hoc* fashion for relatives with restrictions on external Ds, but is independently needed to account for the semantics of other constructions. The most uncontroversial need for

MAX, or at least a concealed uniqueness operator, is in comparatives, where the operator applies to a set of degrees and yields a unique (usually maximal) degree (von Stechow 1984; Rullmann 1995). Note that without MAX, (5a) would incorrectly emerge as true in situations where it is false, and, conversely, (5b) might emerge as false in situations where it is true.

(5)   a.   Mary can run faster than John (can).
        b.   Mary can't run faster than John (can).

MAX has also been appealed to in relation to discourse anaphora (Evans 1980) and questions (Rullmann 1995), but in those cases, it seems to have the character of a default operation, which applies in the absence of certain potentially cancelling pragmatic conditions (Francez and Lappin 1994), rather than an intrinsic ingredient of the semantics of some construction. One notable difference between MAX in comparatives and relatives is that in the latter case, MAX may apply not only to a set of degrees, but also to sets of individuals ordered by the part-whole relation, as well as to n-tuples that include such sets and their cardinalities, and possibly to n-tuples of other kinds (see GL and references therein).

For completeness, I wish to note that the limitation of external Ds to definites and universals in maximalizing constructions may well be true of the overwhelming majority of cases, but does not constitute an absolute universal, there being at least one counterexample in one language (see below).

In the prototypical case, the external material is related to the clause in ways reminiscent of the anaphor-antecedent relation in discourse, *modulo* the obligatory presence of both an 'antecedent' and an 'anaphor' in maximalizing relatives, but not in discourse (in the latter case, some phrase becomes an antecedent just in case there happens to exist an element that is construed as anaphoric to it). Possibly the kind of construction that mimics anaphora most closely are correlatives of the form 'what girls are standing, they/all are tall' (see Srivastav-Dayal 1991 for abundant illustration). At the same time, the relation between 'antecedents' and 'anaphors' may be somewhat 'weaker' than in the example just cited, since consistency with **preservation** of the output of MAX can be satisfied without absolute identity. Illustrations of this state of affairs are provided by most of the data brought up in Carlson (1977). We will make the point clear here in relation to (6), which is one of the versions of (3).

(6)   The three students that there were at the party left early.

GL make the following points about this kind of construction: The clause-internal presentational context requires short-scope existential binding of an individual variable. Since the individual variable is bound existentially, another variable must be found in order to construct a lambda-abstract. This variable is provided by degree (or kind) modifiers of the individual variable, and abstraction over a degree variable in (6) yields essentially 'the set of degrees d such that there were d many students at the party.' Now, in contrast to CP, the construction, due to the nature of the external token of the sortal, designates students, not degrees (more exactly, the set of properties of a unique sum of students having cardinality three); slightly more formally, an ordered pair of a set of degrees and a set of individual sums arises within CP, while a differently ordered pair with comparable members arises outside CP. Due to this 'mismatch', CP cannot intersect with the external sortal. However, the mismatch at issue does not block pointwise maximalization of the internal ordered pair and 'anaphoric' resumption of its members by a differently ordered pair, since the outputs of MAX are preserved. This is then why (6) has only a maximalizing construal (in Grosu, (1998), it will be shown, however, that relativization 'out of' the presentational *there* context blocks a restrictive construal only under certain circumstances, but not in general; in particular, it will be shown that restrictive readings emerge when the internal and external ordered pairs are also ordinally identical).

Let us now turn to a construction of Romanian which falls outside the prototype, in that there are no definite or universal external Ds. The view that this construction is not prototypical converges with the observation that no other language I have examined (in particular, English, French, German, Dutch, Modern Hebrew, and Modern Greek) seems to allow it. Its particular flavour is thus difficult to convey in English, and the best I was able to do in the English translations of (7a-b) was to resort to circumlocutions.

(7) a. [{Opt, *puține} kilograme cât cântărește bagajul
        eight few   kilos   how-much weighs   luggage-the
tău de mână nu reprezintă o problemă
your of hand not represents a problem
'What your hand luggage weighs — and it's at most {eight, *few} kilos — won't be a problem.'
b. [{Trei, *puțini} kilometri cât ai alergat până
    three few   kilometers how-much have-you run   till
acuma] nu reprezintă o distanță suficientă.
now not represent a distance sufficient
'What you have run so far — and it's at most {three, *few} kilometers — does not constitute a sufficient distance.'

Note that both versions of (7a) and (7b) exhibit **indefinite** complex DPs, but only the acceptable version designates a **precise** measure-value. I submit that CP and the external material are related here not as 'antecedent' and 'anaphor', but rather like the two phrases of an equative-specificational construction of the kind illustrated by (8).

(8)   John's weight is {eighty, *few, *some} kilos.

This claim relies on the observation that the restrictions on specificational measure phrases in (8) are entirely parallel to the restrictions on clause-external material in (7), and is moreover consonant with the intuitively perceived meaning of the constructions in (8). Note also that the two equated phrases in (8) are unique and maximal, presumably in virtue of definitional properties of this construction. Thus, (8) implies that (exactly) eighty kilos is John's maximal weight. Significantly, (7a) implies that eight kilos is the maximal weight of your hand-luggage, and (7b), that three kilometers is the maximal distance you have run so far. The claim that the constructions in (7) illustrate the possibility of preserving the outputs of MAX by means of an equative-specificational relation thus appears well supported.

1.2 *Existential relatives*

In contrast to the constructions characterized in the preceding section, infinitival, and, more generally, irrealis free relative constructions are construed just like existential (indefinite) nominals with narrowest scope. Since the latter do not occur in the major Germanic languages, but do occur in Romance, Slavic and Semitic languages, I shall use illustrations from Romance languages in what follows (in particular, from Romanian, except where otherwise indicated). The semantic contrast just alluded to can be appreciated by contrasting the senses of the realis and irrealis free relatives in (9).

(9)   a.   Am   pus [ce   mi-ai   dat]   pe masă
              have-I put   what me have-you given on table
              'I put what you gave me on the table.'
       b.   Avem   deja   [cu   cine negocia]
              we-have already with who negotiate.INF
              'There is already someone with whom we can negotiate.'

(9a) says that I put **that** which you gave me, and not just **something** you gave me, on the table. In contrast, (9b) makes an existential claim, as can be seen by inspecting the English translation. In general, irrealis free relatives are most natural crosslinguistically in presentational constructions, whether these use *have*-type elements, as is the case in the Romanian example (9b), or *be*-type elements, as is the case in corresponding Russian or Hebrew data, and have on the whole a highly restricted distribution (a point to which I return below).

The semantic distinction just proposed is arguably reflected in the following contrast between realis and irrealis free relatives: whereas realis free relatives typically tolerate elements with the import of the English *-ever* morpheme, such elements are uninterpretable in irrealis free relatives. The following data from Romanian illustrate this point.

(10) a. Voi angaja pe [(ori)cine mă respectă].
        I-will hire ACC (ever)who me respects
        'I will hire who(ever) respects me.'
     b. (Nu) am [cu (*ori)cine vorbi].
        Not have-I with (ever)who to-talk
        'There is {someone, no one} with whom I can talk.'

It is well-known that definite Ds are downward entailing with respect to their DP, and that indefinite elements are upward entailing with respect to the maximal extended projection that they head, as illustrated in (11).

(11) a. The students walk ⇒ The smart students walk.
     b. The smart students walk ⇏ The students walk.
     c. Some students walk ⇏ Some smart students walk.
     d. Some smart students walk ⇒ Some students walk.

Kadmon and Landman (1993) argue that elements like 'free choice' *any* or *-ever* are polarity items, and thus licensed in downward entailing contexts (Ladusaw 1979: 1980). Since the relative clause in (10a) undergoes maximalization and thus acquires the force of a definite DP, *ori-* '-ever' is licensed; since the relative clause in (10b) is construed as within the scope of an existential quantifier, polarity items are not licensed. Hence, the contrast between the full versions of (10a) and (10b).

In addition to being semantically distinct from other third-type relative constructions, irrealis free relative constructions are also structurally distinct from them in that they alone consist entirely of a 'bare' clause. That is to say, they contrast with headed relative constructions in occurring in argument positions as CPs, rather than as proper subparts of DP's, and they contrast with correlative constructions in having no 'correlates'. The construction with which irrealis free relatives contrast most minimally in structural terms is that of realis free relatives, and the contrasting property is that the latter, but not the former, are part of a complex DP with a null head. This claim was supported in Grosu (1989, 1994), and also in GL, with a battery of arguments, from which I reproduce two below.

Extraction from realis free relatives results in deviance no less severe than that associated with extraction from overtly-headed definite complex DP's; this is illustrated in (12a) with Romanian and English data. Extraction from an irrealis free relative is, however, quite acceptable, as illustrated in (12b). Moreover, (12b) has the same degree of acceptability as (12d), in which extraction has operated out of an irrealis interrogative, an uncontroversially 'bare' CP (extraction from an embedded interrogative, even a finite one, seems to be easier in Romanian than in English, as noted by Comorovsky 1986; hence, the difference in acceptability ratings between (12d) and its English counterpart). Finally, the relatively degraded status of (12c), where extraction has operated out of an overtly headed relative construction with roughly the existential semantics of the free relative in (12b), indicates that the acceptability of the latter is not (entirely) attributable to its semantics.

(12) a. *Cui   ai   pus [ce   (i-) ai   arătat t] pe masă?
         who.DAT have-you put what (him) have-you shown   on table
         *'To whom did you put what you showed on the table?'
     b. Despre ce   nu ai   [cu cine să   vorbeşti t]?
         about what not you-have with who SUBJ you-talk
         'What do you have [no one] with whom to talk about?'
     c. ?*Despre ce   nu ai   pe nimeni [cu   care să
         about what not you-have ACC no one with who SUBJ
         vorbeşti t]?
         you-talk
         ?*'What do you have no one with whom to talk about?'
     d. Despre ce   nu ştii   [cu cine să   vorbesti t]?
         about what not you-know with who SUBJ you-talk
         ?'What don't you know with whom to talk about?'

In short, the acceptability status of (12b) vis-a-vis the other subcases of (12) is straightforwardly accounted for under a 'bare' CP analysis, but not under a null-headed DP analysis.

Irrealis and realis free relatives further contrast with respect to certain morphosyntactic restrictions that apply to the former, but not to the latter. Thus, in headed relative constructions where either the clause-external material or the corresponding clause-internal nominal, but not both, are null, the ability of the overt element to exhibit Case and/or prepositional properties that are morphologically incompatible with the null element is limited, such limitations varying in severity from language to language; by and large, the overt element must either be fully compatible with the null element, or must exhibit a more 'oblique' morphological Case. These phenomena are well-known from traditional literature, and have also been the focus of a certain amount of interest within generative linguistics; for a summary and partial reinterpretation of the relevant literature, see Grosu (1994: Section 4). Now, such restrictions are abundantly found with respect to the wh-phrases of realis free relatives, as illustrated with a French example in (13a). In contrast, such restrictions are not found in interrogative clauses, as illustrated in (13c), and, crucially, they are absent from irrealis relative clauses, as illustrated in (13b). These facts are straightforwardly accounted for if irrealis free relative constructions are analyzed, just like comparable interrogatives, as bare clauses, and if realis relative constructions are analyzed as null-headed DPs. They remain, however, mysterious, if realis and irrealis relatives are not distinguished in the way just indicated.

(13) a. *Je frapperai [à qui tu parles].
    I will-hit to who you speak
    'I will hit [the person] with whom you are speaking.'
 b. Je n'ai pas [à qui parler].
    I NEG-have not to who to-speak
    'I have [no one] with whom to speak.'
 c. Je ne sais pas [à qui parler].
    I NEG know not to who to-speak
    'I don't know who to speak to.'

The two arguments just provided show that irrealis free relative constructions at least **can** consist of bare clauses. There is, however, another set of facts which suggests — under certain theoretical assumptions — that they can have **no other** analysis. Landman (1998) takes a new look at the presentational *there* construction of English and at the *er* constructions in Dutch (for earlier analyses, see, for example, Milsark 1974; Enç 1991, and the various contributions in Reuland and ter Meulen 1987), and proposes that indefinite (more generally, weak) nominals can have two structural analyses. Under one analysis, they have a null D and are free to occur in argument positions, with short or wide scope. Under the alternative analysis, they lack a D, are of category NP or Num(ber)P, and occur in predicate positions, as well as in certain positions where they can acquire existential force 'from the construction'. The latter possibility is instantiated by *there* and *er* constructions, as well as by *have* constructions like the one in (14b) (note the parallelism between the restrictions on strong DPs in (14a) and (14b);

for details on how the various 'constructions' provide narrow scope existential quantification, see Landman (1998).

(14)   a.   There are {several, three, many, *every, *those, *most} hole(s) in my pocket.
   b.   I have {several, three, many, *every, *those, *most} hole(s) in my pocket.

Now, irrealis free relatives have a distinctly more restricted distribution, in the languages in which they are allowed, than weak nominals with narrow scope. In particular, they cannot occur in subject position, as illustrated by the Romanian minimal pair in (15).

(15)   a.   O persoană cu   care să   ducem   tratativele   la bun
         a person   with who SUBJ carry.1PL negotiations-the to good
         sfârşit va fi greu de găsit.
         en   will be hard of found
         'A person with whom to bring the negotations to a satisfactory conclusion will be hard to find.'
   b.   *Cu cine să   ducem   tratativele   la bun sfârşit
         with who SUBJ carry.1PL negotiations-the to good end
         va fi greu de găsit.
         will be hard of found

Rather, they seem to be strongly preferred and most unhesitatingly accepted in *be* and *have* constructions of the kind illustrated in (14), and to be also possible, with cross-linguistic variations in acceptability, as objects of a small class of verbs which consists of items with the import of *look for, find,* and *give,* and more rarely, *send, buy,* and *sell.* These restrictions strongly suggest that irrealis free relatives cannot occur as objects of a null D, but only as bare CPs having the logical type of NP/NumP (that is, $\langle s, \langle e, t \rangle \rangle$), and that their distribution is 'licensed' only in environments that can provide them with existential quantification. For this proposal to go through, it is necessary to assume that the verbs mentioned a few lines above can provide existential quantification for their NP/NumP objects. I will not attempt to provide independent support for this assumption here, but wish to point out that the obvious ability of the above verbs to take definite objects (e.g., *I found Mary behind that barn*) does not conflict with the suggestion just made, since the verbs *be* and *have* are also found in non-presentational constructions, as illustrated in (16a–b).

(16) a. Most holes are in my left pocket, not in my right pocket.
　　　b. I have most holes in my left pocket, not in my right pocket.

In short, irrealis free relatives are necessarily bare CPs with the logical type of NPs and NumPs, and with narrow-scope existential quantification provided by elements of their local context other than a selecting D. I will conclude this section by exhibiting one more feature they share with bare NPs/NumPs. As Carlson (1977) observed, indefinite nominals with definite degree or kind modifiers are fine in presentational contexts; illustrations are provided in (17). Irrealis free relatives can also have a comparable import, as illustrated in (18).

(17) a. There are exactly that many books on the table.
　　　b. I have just the right (kind of) girl for you.
(18)　Am　　exact　ce　　să　　port　　la nuntă
　　　have-I exactly what SUBJ wear.1SG at wedding
　　　'I have exactly the suitable outfit for the wedding.'
　　　(literally: I have exactly what to wear at the wedding)

2. The characterization of the semantic subtypes of [REL]

As noted in the Introduction, the feature [REL] as characterized in (A) defines a core of 'headed' constructions; with the slight extension needed to encompass correlatives, it defines the classes 2–4 on the continuum in (B). Do we need additional typing features to distinguish these three semantic subtypes? Earlier proposals that have addressed restrictives and appositives have typically answered this question in the negative, explicitly or implicitly. By and large, most writers have sought to derive restrictive vs. appositive readings from **configurational** distinctions.

In Section 2.1, I examine critically a number of past proposals of the kind just indicated, and point to difficulties in all of them. In Section 2.2, I examine the possibility of using configurational properties to characterize maximalizing relatives, and reach a comparably negative conclusion. In Section 2.3, I outline a featural approach to all the subtypes of relatives brought up in the Introduction.

2.1 *Configurational approaches to restrictives/appositives*

In the earlier generative literature, some proposals were confined to post-nominal relatives, and were not assumed to be necessarily extendable to all languages (for example, Emonds 1979). Other more recent proposals attempted to formulate a universally valid configurational basis for the semantic distinctions, essentially by locating them at LF (Kayne 1994). In what follows, I will evaluate their ability to deal with **two** kinds of properties (invidiously neglecting other properties, such as the apparently general requirement that in constructions with co-occurring non-extraposed post-nominal restrictives and appositives, the latter must follow the former).

A first property, which points to a *prima facie* **similarity** between restrictives and appositives, is that the free variable within an appositive, while capable of acquiring a value by co-valuation only, nonetheless contrasts with definite discourse anaphors in that the antecedent needs to be both linguistically present and 'local'. Thus, while the basis for assigning a value to *him* in (19a) can be either of the boldfaced nominals, as well as some individual that was not even linguistically mentioned, the basis for assigning a value to *who* in (19b) can only be the adjacent boldfaced nominal. Let us call this property 'Loc(al)-Ass(ignment)', noting that something quite similar is found in restrictives, where the clause-internal variable gets bound by a maximally local external D (recall we proposed to assume, following Wilder 1995, that extraposed clauses are non-extraposed in the input to the semantics).

(19) a. **John** told **Bill** that Mary loves *him*.
b. John told **Bill**, *who* spoke rudely to Mary, to go to hell.

A second property, which constitutes the fundamental distinction between restrictives and appositives, is that the latter, in contrast to the former, have the essential status of independent discourse sentences, and are thus impervious to syntactic binding by external operators. For the purposes of the ensuing discussion, it will be useful to distinguish two subcases, according as the external operation belongs to the construction or not; the contrasts found in these two subcases are illustrated in (20) and (21) respectively. Let us call these two subcases of the distinguishing property at issue C(onstructional) O(perator) B(inding) A(bility) and N(on-constructional) O(perator) B(inding) A(bility) respectively.

(20) a. **Every** student who *ever* took an exam will get five dollars.
b. ***Every** student, who *ever* took an exam, will get five dollars.
(21) a. **Every** student danced with the girl who likes *him*.
b. ***Every** student danced with Mary, who likes *him*.

Past configurational approaches to restrictives and appositives may be cross-classified with respect to (at least) two criteria: (a) whether the locus of configurational distinctions is overt representation or LF, and (b) whether, at the level where co-valuation applies, appositives do or do not form a constituent with their antecedent; for ease of reference, let us adopt for the nonce the notation [±O(vert)] and [±C(onstituent)].

The approach [+O, +C] is adopted, for example, in Jackendoff (1977), Fabb (1990) and Toribio (1992). Jackendoff assumes a nominal projection with three bar levels, and attaches restrictives and appositives as right sisters to N^2 and N^3 respectively; importantly, (what we would call today) strong Ds are left sisters of N^3. Fabb assumes a nominal projection with two bar-levels, and adjoins restrictives to N^1 and appositives, to N^2; Ds are in SpecN^2. Toribio assumes the DP Hypothesis, and adjoins restrictives to NP, and appositives to DP; Ds are, of course, in head-of-DP position. All these approaches can easily deal with Loc-Ass, since both restrictives and appositives form a constituent with the material that serves as basis for assigning a value to their variables. Fabb's and Toribio's can also deal with COBA, since the appositive is outside the c-command domain of D, but not with NOBA; Jackendoff's can deal with neither COBA nor NOBA.

The approach [+O, −C] is represented by Emonds (1979) and McCawley (1982). While assuming quite different theoretical frameworks, these two studies share the view that appositives are an immediate subconstituent of the main clause. This approach deals straightforwardly with COBA and NOBA, but not with Loc-Ass, as far as appositives are concerned, and thus require an otherwise unmotivated appeal to linear adjacency.

An approach of type [−O, +C] is found in Kayne (1994), who operates within his Antisymmetry syntactic framework, one implication of which is that complements follow heads, and specifiers precede them. Both restrictives and appositives are assumed to originate universally as complements to D (possibly also to some lower functional head within DP; see footnote 67 to Chapter 8), and the (apparently) external NP is raised from some (argument or adjunct position) within IP to SpecCP. More exactly, this type of derivation is found if there are no wh(-like) pronouns; if such pronouns exist, the external NP originates as part of a DP headed by the wh(-like) pronoun, and it is this DP that undergoes movement to SpecDP, after which its NP complement is reordered to SpecDP, stranding the wh pronoun and achieving its seemingly external position. Restrictives and appositives are distinguished at LF in the following way: the former occupy their basic position, possibly due to 'reconstruction', in case they happened to be overtly raised, and the latter are in SpecDP, either through covert raising, or through 'unreconstructed' overt raising. This analysis can deal with Loc-Ass and COBA, but does not deal with NOBA.

The inability of Kayne's analysis to deal with NOBA was noticed by Bianchi (1995), who, while espousing the general framework of Antisymmetry, proposed a [–O, –C] analysis that modifies Kayne's in the following way: appositives need to undergo further covert raising and adjoin to some functional projection of the main clause, thus avoiding the scope of all possible logical operators. This proposal evidently deals with both COBA and NOBA, and since the appositive originates within the complex DP and may be assumed to leave a trace in its base position, it can in principle also deal with Loc-Ass. Bianchi also proposes a number of additional (arguably improving) modifications in Kayne's original analysis, and I return to some of them in Section 3. However, as far as the solution proposed with respect to NOBA is concerned, I believe it is open to at least one serious empirical objection, as well as to certain conceptual reservations. The empirical objection arises in connection with the very assumption of covert raising all the way up to the main clause. Earlier studies within generative grammar assumed that covert movement is exempt from the kind of island constraints that apply to overt movement (Huang 1982). However, a subsequent body of studies has provided substantial evidence that covert movement is not free from locality constraints (see, for example, Reinhart 1991 and references cited therein). Furthermore, a number of recent theoretical approaches — among them, Antisymmetry — have converged on the view that limiting constraints on movement to overt movement is conceptually unprincipled; within Minimalism (Chomsky 1993, 1995), the assumption that constraints do not distinguish between overt and covert movement seems to have a definitional character. Now, observe that the surface distribution of appositives is completely free from island constraints of any sort, they being able to occur, for example, within another appositive, as illustrated in (22a); note the striking contrast between the full acceptability of (22a) and the crashing unacceptability of (22b), where wh-Movement has operated out of an appositive. The assumption of unrestricted LF raising of appositives is thus empirically problematic.

(22)   a.   I sent a letter of protest to John, [who claimed that Mary, whom we all like, is an idiot].
       b.   *Which books did Mary, [who bought e,] visit you yesterday?

In addition to the problem just noted, one may well feel qualms of a more conceptual nature. In general, students of language are suspicious of proposed covert operations that have no overt counterpart in any known language. The 'longest movement' approach to appositives put forward by Bianchi seems to fall in this category. True, some relative clauses do occur overtly left-adjoined to some IP, but to the best of my knowledge, such clauses are always correlative, which means (i) that they are not necessarily adjoined to the highest IP, (ii) that they have not obviously achieved their surface position in virtue of movement, and above all, (iii) that they have maximalizing, not appositive semantics (see Srivastav-Dayal 1991, for discussion of these points). In short, correlatives certainly provide no conceptual support for Bianchi's long-raising analysis. A further observation that further erodes the plausibility of Bianchi's proposal is that, whenever languages distinguish restrictives from appositives in terms of their overt external syntax, they seem to do so by placing the appositives **further to the right** than the restrictives, which is precisely the opposite of what Bianchi proposes. This phenomenon is well-known from English and languages with comparable properties, but is even more pointedly brought home by languages where certain morphemes intervene between the positions of restrictives and appositives. Illustrations of this state of affairs (from Lehmann 1984) are provided in (23)–(26), where the relevant morphological marker is boldfaced; in the Indonesian examples, the marker appears to be the definite D, in the Yucatec examples, the marker has the more general function of signaling the end of some scopal domain.

Indonesian
(23) lelaki [yang sedang tidor] **itu**
man REL PROG sleep the
'The man who is sleeping...' [restrictive]

(24) lelaki **itu**, [yang sedang tidor]
'The man, who is sleeping, ...' [appositive]

Yucatec Mayan
(25) tuʔš yan le tak'in [t-a waʔl-ah he ʔa tas-ik]-**eʔ**?
where be the money [PRT-2 say-TR FUT-2 bring-TR]-D
'Where is the money that you promised to bring?' [restrictive]

(26) le santo k'in-**eʔ**? [k k'ulktabal]-eʔ waʔkum-ah toon teloʔ.
the holy sun-D 1PL worship-PTL preserves us here
'The holy sun, which we worship, keeps us alive.' [appositive]

For completeness, let us also take a look at a somewhat different type of approach to Loc-Ass, COBA, and NOBA. Safir (1986) proposes to assume that operator-binding takes place in the LF component. Appositives — and parentheticals in general — are introduced into syntactic structures in a **later** component called LF'. This approach accounts for COBA and NOBA, and can also deal with Loc-Ass, since appositives may be inserted into the extended nominal projection. However, it is open to both empirical and conceptual objections, some of which are pointed out by Bianchi (see Section 1.3. of her Chapter IV). On the empirical side, it is unclear how introducing parentheticals after LF, and thus covertly, can guarantee their correct positioning in overt representations, since the two branches of a derivation are assumed not to 'communicate' with each other. On the conceptual side, if LF′ lies outside the computational system, Safir's proposal implies that Merge can operate outside the Computational System, a strange position, to say the least (this point was brought to my attention by Julia Horváth).

For perspicuousness, I summarize in Table 1. the gist of the proposals reviewed above, and in Table 2., their degree of success in dealing with Loc-Ass, COBA, and NOBA (asterisks indicate empirical and/or conceptual problems).

Table 1

	Restrictives	Appositives
Both are part of the (extended) N-projection throughout a derivation		
Jackendoff (1977):	Daughter of N^2	Sister of N^2 and of D
Fabb (1990):	Adjunct to N^1	Adjunct to N^2
Toribio (1992):	Adjunct to NP	Adjunct to DP
Only Rs are part of the N-projection throughout a derivation		
Emonds (1979):	Part of N^{max}	Sister of main S
McCawley (1982):	Part of N^{max}	Daughter of main S
Not necessarily configurationally distinguished until LF		
Kayne (1994):	Compl of D	Spec of D
Bianchi (1995)	Compl of D	Spec of main-clause F-head
Configurationally distinguished only until LF		
Safir (1986):	Part of N^{max} throughout	Not part of main S till LF, inserted into N^{max} at LF′

Table 2

	Loc-Ass	COBA	NOBA
Jackendoff	yes	no	no
Fabb, Toribio	yes	yes	no
Emonds, McCawley	no	yes	yes
Kayne	yes?	yes	no
Bianchi	yes?	yes	yes*
Safir	yes	yes	yes*

2.2 A configurational approach to maximalizers?

In contrast the restrictives and appositives, there have been, as far as I know, no attempts to provide a universal characterization of maximalizing relatives in terms of configurational properties. Nonetheless, it is worth considering the likelihood of the success of such an approach.

To be sure, there is one overt configuration which appears to be invariably associated with a maximalizing construal, that of correlatives left-adjoined to IP. Suppose one were to propose that all maximalizing relatives occur in a comparable configuration at LF (in correlatives, through base-generation, and in 'headed' constructions, through covert raising). Would such a proposal be tenable, and if yes, would such a configuration force a maximalizing construal?

In response to the first question, I wish to note certain empirical considerations that argue against such a move. Observe that in (27), the bracketed maximalizing relative includes a pronoun (in italics), and that this pronoun is construable as bound by either of the boldfaced quantifiers.

(27) {**Every, no**} student read the three books [that there were on *his* desk].

Srivastav-Dayal (1996) explicitly notes that in correlative constructions, quantifiers in the matrix clause may not bind a variable in the correlative, which is entirely expected if the correlative maintains its IP-adjoined position throughout a derivation, since the variable it includes is not c-commanded by any matrix quantifier. But on the assumption that scope is decided at LF, the possibility of syntactic binding in (27) is incompatible with a covert correlative-like analysis.

What has just been said renders the second question asked two paragraphs above academic. Nonetheless, let us note that even if the scope facts were different, it would be necessary to show that the configuration at issue **forces** a maximalizing construal. A restrictive construal would certainly be excluded (since D could not bind into the relative), but an appositive one might not be (recall that Kayne and Bianchi proposed to assume comparable configurations precisely for appositives). More generally, it is unclear, in the absence of a theory of maximalization (which, to the best of my knowledge, does not exist at the moment), that a left-adjoined configuration rules out any conceivable construal other than maximalization.

In short, it seems unlikely that a purely configurational account of the semantics of maximalization in relatives can get off the ground.

2.3 A featural approach to relative subtypes

In the two preceding sections, we have seen a number of reasons for being suspicious of the view that both the distinctive semantic properties and the Loc-Ass properties of the three major subtypes of relatives (that is, those numbered 2–4 on the continuum in (B)) can be captured in purely configurational terms. Let us then adopt an approach in terms of interpretable features.

For restrictives, we may adopt the **minimal** characterization [REL, PRED, MOD], noting that it has the same import as the Montagovian type $\langle\langle s, \langle e,t\rangle\rangle, \langle s, \langle e,t\rangle\rangle\rangle$. For maximizing relatives, we may minimally represent them as [REL, MAX], which incorporates the assumption that maximalization is part of their definition. As pointed out in Section 1.2, [MAX] is not used in *ad hoc* fashion in relatives, it must also be assumed to characterize at least comparatives, even if in the latter case, it need not be explicitly stated, having non-distinctive, redundant status (since comparatives are always [MAX], while only some relatives have this property). For a formal semantic characterization of the logical type of maximizing relatives, see GL and references therein. Concerning appositives, they may be minimally characterized as [REL, E], borrowing an idea from Emonds (1979), who proposed that appositives are base-generated under a node 'E(xpression)'. The import of [E] is that the constituent which bears it has an illocutionary force independent of that of the matrix, and thus the essential status of an independent discourse sentence.[1] I leave open the question of the formal semantic counterpart of [E].

Let us now turn to the non-core and non-[REL] constructions mentioned in earlier sections. In line with proposals made in Section 1.2, existential relatives are open sentences that receive existential quantification from some feature of their context. I propose the minimal characterization [REL, PRED]. [PRED] ensures that the variable required by the first part of [REL] (see (Ai)), gets abstracted over, and a 'weakened' version of the second part of [REL] (see (Aii)), that is, a consonance requirement limited to logical type, is satisfied by existential quantification. The Montagovian counterpart to the proposed characterization is $\langle s, \langle e, t\rangle\rangle$. Note that the absence of [MOD] keeps such relatives distinct from restrictives.

Finally, the French constructions in (1a) and (1b) may be minimally characterized as [PRED] and [Q] respectively.

3. On dependency-encoding by the computational system

In the preceding section, I have argued that the semantic properties which distinguish the various types of relative clauses are not retrievable from their configurational properties, and thus cannot be viewed as pre-encoded by the Merge or Move operations of the CSYS; rather, I argued, the relevant distinctions need to be encoded by means of featural (or formal semantic) typing. I nonetheless believe that the CSYS does have something to contribute to the analysis of relative clause constructions, in particular, to the analysis of the dependencies that hold between the clause and the remainder of the construction whenever the latter is not null; that is to say, in cases 2–4 in (B).

In earlier sections, it has been abundantly noted that the nature of dependency between a relative clause and the external part of its construction is semantically different from type to type. Orthogonally to this state of affairs, the dependency formed by the clause and the external material may have a **local** or a **non-local** character. Local dependencies are found in the core cases defined by [REL], that is, in those cases where the clause and the remainder of the construction form a constituent. Non-local dependencies are found in correlatives, more exactly, in those correlatives that are left-adjoined to IP, and whose correlates may occur at an arbitrary linear distance and depth of embedding within IP (the reason for the qualification just expressed is that, as Srivastav-Dayal 1991 points out, correlatives may also occur left-adjoined to a correlate, in which case the correlative-correlate dependency is evidently local). Now, to say that the elements which form a semantic dependency also form a syntactic constituent is to say that the CSYS has pre-encoded a possible dependency one member of which is a relative clause. But we may still wonder why in such a case, the relative clause cannot be involved in a different semantically conceivable dependency. To clarify the issue by means of an example, observe that in *Bob, who — remember — I can't stand, wants to give him a prize, Bob* is the only possible antecedent of *who*, while in the very similar *Bob — and recall I can't stand him — wants to give him a prize*, the leftmost token of *him* may corefer with *Bob*, with the rightmost token of *him*, and possibly even with some third unmentioned individual. An answer to this puzzle may be derived by extending a proposal made in Reuland (1996), and to which I alluded in the Introduction:

(28) If an operator-variable structure at the C[onceptual]-I[ntensional] interface can either be obtained from
  i. a structure in which this dependency has been pre-encoded, or
  ii. a structure without pre-encoding,
  option i. will be taken.

In other words, I am proposing that pre-encoding by the CSYS forces the resulting **possible** dependencies to be **actual** ones in this case.

But how exactly are the dependencies at issue pre-encoded by the CSYS? One possible view, which has often been adopted in past literature, is that the pre-encoding is done entirely by Merge. Another view, which maintains that clause-external sortals undergo raising out of the relative IP, has sometimes been envisaged in earlier literature in relation to specific subtypes of relatives; for example, with respect to restrictives in Schachter (1973), and with respect to 'amount' (maximalizing) relatives in Carlson (1977). Kayne (1994) was, to my knowledge, the first writer who proposed to use such an approach in an attempt to provide a unified account of both restrictives and appositives. Neither Kayne nor Bianchi took maximalizing relatives into account, but had they done so, they would in all likelihood have extended the raising approach to 'headed' maximalizers as well. In what follows, I will explore some of the consequences of adopting the raising approach with respect to all 'headed' relative constructions. For the purposes of this exploration, I will assume the following features of the raising analysis in Bianchi (1995), which is built on Kayne (1994), but also differs from the latter in a number of respects that arguably constitute improvements (some possible improvements will be noted in what follows).

I. What is usually analyzed as the CP-external 'common noun' (in more precise terms, the external NP or NumP) originates as complement to an overt or null D within the relative IP; when this D is overt, it is a wh(-like) relative pronoun.

II. In contrast to earlier analyses, the complex DP that forms the 'headed' relative construction is not, strictly speaking, an extended **nominal** projection. Rather, the relative CP is base-generated as a complement of D, or of some functional head lower than D, such as Num(ber).

III. In relatives introduced by a complementizer (e.g., *that*) and lacking wh(-like) pronouns, a null-headed DP within IP (see (I)) is reordered to SpecCP, and the null D is 'absorbed' into the external D, a step that makes it 'invisible' to the subsequently applicable semantic interpretive mechanisms. The rationale for positing this null D (which Kayne did not posit) is purely syntactic: it ensures that the 'gap' within IP is invariably a DP (see Borsley 1997 on the desirability of this move), and it also yields an account of the impossibility of pied-piping anything other than the 'external' common noun along with the null D.

IV. In relatives with wh(-like) pronouns, the 'common noun' reaches SpecCP in two steps: first, the DP headed by the wh-pronoun is reordered to the Spec of a verbal functional projection lower than CP (which we will refer to simply as FP, since its precise nature is not at issue here); second, the complement of the wh-pronoun is reordered to SpecCP, stranding the wh-pronoun in SpecFP. In Kayne's original analysis, the second movement targeted the Spec of the DP moved in the first step, and this had the undesirable consequence that the string consisting of the wh-pronoun and the relative IP was characterized as a non-constituent (note that in appositives, this string is intonationally separated from the surrounding material); Bianchi's analysis avoids this consequence (which, incidentally, was also pointed out in Borsley's critique of Kayne's monograph).

V. Movement to an A'-position has the major features proposed in Chomsky (1993). Thus, movement leaves 'behind' a **full copy** of the raised element, and the resulting chain can be 'tampered' with at LF in the sense that chain links may be partially or totally deleted, and variables may be inserted; such tampering is restricted by the need to achieve well-formed operator variable configurations, and can be used to account for 'reconstruction' effects. To illustrate these points, consider the question in (29a), which has the essential properties of (29b) in the output of Wh-Movement ((29a) is derived from (29b) by 'tampering' with the chain at PF in a way that does not necessarily parallel LF tampering; PF deletion is of no concern for what follows). (29b) can be turned into well-formed LF outputs in two distinct ways, which give rise to slightly different construals. One option is to delete the material italicized in (29c) and to substitute an individual variable for it; another option is to delete the material italicized in (29d) and to substitute a number variable within the lower chain-link. (29c) asks for a number of books, and is most naturally answered by, for example, 'five books'; (29d) asks for a number, and is most naturally answered by 'five'.

(29) a. [How many books] did you read?
b. [How many books] did you read [how many books]
c. How many books did you read [*how many books*]
d. How many *books* did you read [*how many* books]

VI. Locality is redefined in a manner that makes it in principle possible for the common noun of a 'headed' relative construction to agree with the external D, much like a D and its complement NP may agree with each other in a simplex DP. Instead of the notion 'minimal domain' of Chomsky (1993), Bianchi adopts the notion with the same name in Manzini (1994), where it is proposed that the minimal domain of a head H excludes H's Spec and includes the Spec of its complement; minimal domains are related to each other (they form a 'dependency') if their heads are related by one of the following two kinds of relation: complementation or checking. Now, Bianchi also proposes to assume that the Spec of H's complement belongs to H's checking domain; under this further assumption, agreement between D and the common noun of a 'headed' relative construction can be accounted for.

Let us now examine some further aspects of the analysis of 'headed' relative constructions, keeping in mind (I)–(VI) above.

In (II) above, it was noted that 'headed' relative constructions are not base-generated as extended **nominal** projections. At the same time, it would not be appropriate to view them as extended **verbal** projections, either, since this would make them indistinguishable from constructions with genuine 'clausal determiners', such as the bracketed structures in (30) and (1b) (see Zaring 1992 for discussion).

(30) Je veillerai à [ce que Marie lise ce livre].
I will-take-care of DET COMP Mary read this book
'I will see to it that Mary reads this book.'

(1) b. Je me demande [ce qui lui fait mal].
I me ask DET COMP her makes pain
'I wonder what is hurting her.'

Observe that the bracketed constituents are construed as a proposition and a question respectively, in contrast to the bracketed constituent in (1c), which, although superficially similar to the one in (1b), is construed as a generalized quantifier.

(1) c. Je revendrai [ce qui m' a été vendu].
I will-resell DET COMP me has been sold
'I will resell what was sold to me.'

I suggest that the element *ce* carries the feature [+V] in (30)–(1b) and the feature [+N] in (1c), and that the external Ds of relative constructions in general are [+N]. This featural charaterization makes it possible to account not only for semantic distinctions between relative clause constructions and constructions like those in (30)–(1b), but also for differences in opacity to extraction. Thus, observe that (31a) has the marginal acceptability of extraction out of finite interrogatives, while (31b) has the strong unacceptability of violations of the Complex NP Constraint. While a theory of extractability goes beyond the scope of this paper, it seems to me that the featural contrast just proposed — in particular, the 'switch' from [+V] to [+N] in relatives and the lack of such a switch in data like (30), (1b), and (31a) — provides a promising basis for constructing an account of the contrast in acceptability between (31a) and (31b).

(31) a. ?*A qui* te demandes-tu [ce que Marie a donné *t*]?
to who you ask you DET COMP Mary has given
?'Who do you wonder what Mary gave to?'
b. **A qui* as-tu reçu [ce que Marie a donné *t*]?
to who have-you received DET COMP Mary has given
*'Who did you receive what Mary gave to?'

In (VI) above, it was suggested that a functional head and the Spec of its complement may form a configuration for checking feature-matching, and it was noted that this permits the kind of agreement that operates within simplex DP's to also operate in complex DP's that include a relative clause. But if so, it seems entirely natural to also allow the binding of a common noun by D in the kind of complex DP's at issue with semantic effects comparable to those found in simplex DP's. That is to say, the common noun in SpecCP may be construed just like a nominal complement of D, even though it does not configurationally have complement status. A natural consequence of this state of affairs is that the common noun is semantically 'cut off' from the remainder of CP. In short, complex DP's with a relative clause may receive under the theory just outlined exactly the kind of construals that have been proposed on the basis of more conservative structures (with the relative clause adjoined to some perfect or extended projection of N).

Before examining the derivation of the three subtypes of relatives in more detail, let us briefly confront the issue of the factors that trigger movement within relative CPs. The Manzini-Bianchi theory of locality retains the Spec–Head configuration as a valid one for feature-checking, even though the two elements belong to different minimal domains; without such an assumption, it is hard to see how the strong feature on the C-head of a direct question could be checked. Let us then assume that overt wh-movement in relatives is triggered in essentially the same way as in non-relative wh-constructions; in particular, the trigger may be a strong feature on the head of FP. The next step, raising of the common noun to SpecCP, may be viewed as triggered by a strong N feature on D; the stranding of the wh-pronoun is attributable to the fact that its pied-piping is not required by any principle. In contrast, the non-stranding of a null D is 'forced' by the need to eliminate an 'unidentified' null category (see Bianchi for details).

Let us now consider more closely how the derivation of a sample of relatives of the three semantic types might operate under the assumptions outlined above.

First, consider the wh-construction in (32a), which looks essentially as in (32b) at the stage that immediately follows the two-step raising outlined in (IV) above.

(32) a. **The** boys(,) who Mary dislikes, ...
b. **The** [$_{CP}$ boys [$_{FP}$ *who boys* [$_{IP}$ Mary dislikes *who boys*]]]

(32b) can give rise to either an appositive or a restrictive construal, depending on whether C is marked [REL, E] or [REL, PRED, MOD]. In the former case, the boldfaced D is unable to syntactically bind into the clause, since the feature [E] assigns to it the status of an independent discourse sentence. However, given the theory of locality outlined in (F) and elaborated in the ensuing text, D **can** bind the (variable restricted by the) NP in SpecCP, since this NP escapes the domain of [E]. As a result, the initial sequence *the boys* is construed as a generalized quantifier, much as when this sequence forms a simplex DP, since the theory of locality we are assuming makes the configurational distinction irrelevant.

Assume now that the C in (32) is marked [REL, PRED, MOD]. The variable required by [REL] is created just like in the previously considered case, but the feature [PRED] requires the formation of a lambda-abstract over that variable; in view of the assumed theory of locality, SpecCP escapes the domain of [PRED] and [MOD], just as it escaped the domain of [E] in appositives. The feature [MOD] requires the abstract to intersect with a sortal, if there is one, yielding a more narrowly specified lambda-abstract. This abstract gets turned into a generalized quantifier through application of a D-function.

Let us now consider a construction without wh-pronouns, in particular, (33a), to which Bianchi assigns the essential representation in (33b) in the output of raising to SpecCP.

(33) a. The boys that Mary dislikes ...
b. The [$_{CP}$ Ø boys that [$_{FP}$ [$_{IP}$ Mary dislikes Ø *boys*]]]

In contemporary Standard English, such constructions may be restrictive, but not appositive. Furthermore, as Carlson (1977: 529) observed, there are no principled grounds for excluding a maximalizing construal in such cases, even though a restrictive and a maximalizing construal yield equivalent semantic outputs in the case at hand.

If C is typed [REL, PRED, MOD], the operations are almost the same as for (32b), with the only difference that there is a single copy to delete within CP, and that the null D in SpecCP gets absorbed into the external D. — If C is typed [REL, MAX], things proceed as follows: within the clause, the null D is deleted, but *boys* is retained and used as a restrictor on an individual variable. Abstract formation yields an expression of the form λx [Boy(x) and Mary dislikes(x)], and MAX is applied to this abstract, yielding the unique maximal i(ndividual)-sum within the set defined by the abstract; much as in the previously considered cases, SpecCP falls outside the domain of features that trigger clause-internal operations, in particular, of MAX. Outside MAX's domain, the null D is absorbed into the external D. As for the copy of *boys* in SpecCP, whether it is deleted or not is immaterial, given the constraint that properties fixed within the clause, in particular, by sortal construal and MAX, must be **preserved** in the complex DP. Along the lines proposed by GL, CP together with its Spec is construed just like CP without its Spec, that is to say, as the maximal sum of boys disliked by Mary; application of *the* to CP yields the set of properties of the sum of boys disliked by Mary.

The remark made in the preceding paragraph to the effect that the higher copy of *boys* need not be deleted bears some additional elaboration. As an anonymous referee observed, if two chain links were allowed to be **independently** used in logical form, it would incorrectly be predicted that *himself* in *John wondered which picture of himself Bill saw* could be co-construed as bound by both *John* and *Bill*. What I am suggesting, however, is only that chain links may be used more than once just in case all except one are used redundantly. Srivastav-Dayal (1991) observes that in correlatives, where the same preservation requirements obtain as in 'headed' maximalizing constructions, distinct tokens of the same sortal may overtly occur both within the correlative and within the correlate. The two sortals in the latter case do not belong to a movement chain, but I see no principled grounds for excluding two comparable sortal-tokens that do belong to a movement chain, so long as the preservation requirement is met. At the same time, it should be clear that a second 'higher' sortal-token is certainly not necessary to achieve a generalized quantifier construal for the complex DP. In realis free relatives, which have a null external definite D, but no 'external' sortal, the interpretive operations that lead to the construction of a generalized quantifier may apply to the output of MAX without 'structural support', as noted by GL.

Let us consider one slightly more complex construction which is unambiguously maximalizing (see GL and references therein), in particular, the one in (34a); after raising, the representation is essentially (34b).

(34) a. The three boys that there were at the party ...
b. The [$_{NumP}$ three [$_{CP}$ Ø boys that [$_{FP}$ [$_{IP}$ there were Ø boys at the party]]]]

Observe that CP is here the complement of a Num(ber) head. We must therefore assume that Num, rather than D, carries the strong feature that triggers raising, and presumably also that the null D in the upper chain-link is absorbed into the immediately higher Num, rather than into D (which is 'too' high). Within the clause, we must assume, just as in the preceding case, that the null D is deleted and the sortal is used as a restriction on an individual variable, but since that variable needs to be bound by an existential operator, we must also insert a degree variable, in particular, one which defines the cardinality of the set of individuals, and this, in order to make possible the construction of a lambda-abstract with clausal scope (see Section 1.1). However, no degree variable is needed in the higher chain link, since there is a single CP-external operator in need of a variable to bind, the external D. The preservation condition requires that the cardinality value established by MAX within the clause be preserved in the construal of the complex DP. Note that, in the particular case of (34b), an explicit cardinality specification is provided by the external numeral, and it must, of course, be identical to the value fixed by MAX clause-internally.

For completeness, I wish to note that, if 'reconstruction' is operative in restrictive constructions — and data like (35) suggest that it is (note the **in**definiteness of the complex DP) — then 'sortal-internality' is not a fully adequate characterization of maximalizing and existential relatives.

(35)   [A picture of herself that Mary truly likes] is hard to imagine.

To see this, observe that under any implementation of reconstruction (including the one assumed in Chomsky 1993 and Bianchi 1995), *(a) picture of himself* must be construed as restricting the variable **within the clause**. It would thus appear that what really distinguishes maximalizing relatives from restrictives is that the clause-internal variable characteristic of [REL] must be quantifier-bound clause-internally in the former, rather than the fact that its sortal is construed clause-internally.

Having shown how a raising analysis of the three subtypes of 'headed' relatives might operate within (Bianchi's version of) the Antisymmetry framework, let us attempt to determine what (non-framework specific) advantages, if any, such an approach may have over a more conservative analysis, in particular, one that right-adjoins relatives to some nominal extended projection, which need not be the same for all subtypes (the framework specific advantage being, of course, that the conservative approach is inconsistent with Antisymmetry).

One *prima facie* conceptual advantage emerges from Bianchi's 'unifying' assumption (II) (taken over from Kayne), in particular, from the view that all 'headed' relatives start their syntactic life as complements of some D (recall that under the right-adjunction analysis, adjunction is not necessarily to the same category for all subtypes; see, for example, the first three analyses listed in

Table 1.). However, whether this *prima facie* advantage is a genuine one depends on Antisymmetry's ability to account for surface ordering constraints on the co-occurrence of appositive and non-appositive clauses within the same complex DP. As noted in Section 2.1, co-occurring restrictives and appositives need to occur *in that order* in non-extraposed constructions, sometimes separated from each other by a morphological marker (see (23)–(26)). In the conservative approach, this state of affairs is handled by assuming that appositives are adjoined 'higher' than non-appositives. In the Antisymmetry approach, an account was proposed (Kayne 1994: 113–4) that relied on two doubtful assumptions: (a) that appositives must raise across D at LF (see the critique of this view in Section 2.1), and (b) that in a sequence of 'stacked' relatives, only the rightmost can raise (at LF), on the grounds that raising a non-final relative would violate (some version of) the Left Branch Condition. Assumption (b) rests on the alleged inability of appositives to iterate (Kayne offers (36a) as supporting evidence). But (36b) shows that appositives **can** iterate, subject, apparently, to certain pragmatic felicity conditions that need not concern us here.

(36) a. #The book, which I've read twice, which is on the table...
b. John, who never finished high-school, who can't in fact even read or write, wants to do a doctorate in astrophysics.

Furthermore, assumption (b) assumes that prenominal relatives in languages like Japanese or Turkish do not iterate, and this seems to be incorrect (for illustration, see Wartemberg 1997). In sum, the *prima facie* advantage addressed in this paragraph is not obviously a genuine one.

An empirically-based advantage that was prominently claimed by Kayne and Bianchi with respect to the raising operation *per se* is that restrictives show reconstruction effects for the purposes of the Binding Theory (see (35) above). The strength of this argument is, however, unclear, since reconstruction effects are also detectable in situations where a movement analysis seems implausible; for example, in pseudo-clefts like *the individuals that John and Mary dislike most are each other*.

A somewhat different argument in favour of a raising analysis for certain maximalizing constructions was put forward by Carlson (1977). Carlson observed that comparative constructions contrast with degree relatives in that the former, but not the latter, allow 'subdeletion', as illustrated by the contrast between (37a–b) and (37c). Since the two kinds of construction exhibit many similarities, as Carlson abundantly shows, one might expect whatever mechanism accounts for the 'gap' in comparatives, for example, the A′-movement of a null degree operator, to also be operative in degree relatives; nonetheless, the contrasts in

(37) suggest that this is not so.

(37) a. They drank as much wine as we drank (beer).
b. They ran as many miles as we ran (kilometers).
c. They drank the two liters of wine that we drank (*of beer).

The effect noted by Carlson can also be replicated in languages that use overt wh-forms in the kinds of construction at issue. Thus, wh-like forms (which trigger Pied-Piping) are found in certain 'equative' comparatives of Romanian, as shown in (38a), and also in some degree relatives, as may be seen by inspecting (7a-b). Nonetheless, wh-forms like those in (7) may not 'modify' additional material, as illustrated by (38b). Note that the deviance of the full versions of (37c) and (38b) are unlikely to be semantic, since 'subdeletion' is possible in Hindi correlatives, as shown in (39) (a datum kindly provided to me by Srivastav-Dayal in p.c.).

(38) a. Ion a   alergat exact   atâția   kilometri câte   mile a
       Ion has run   exactly as-many kms.   how-many miles has
       alergat Maria.
       run   Maria
       'Ion ran exactly as many kilometers as Maria ran miles.'
   b. Trei kilometri {cât,   *câte   mile} ți-a   cerut
      three kms.   how-much how-many miles you-has asked
      doctorul   să   alergi zilnic nu reprezintă o distanță prea
      doctor-the SUBJ run   daily not represents a distance too
      mare.
      great
      'The three kilometers that the doctor asked you to run (*miles) daily do not represent too great a distance.'

(39) jiitnii   kilomețer main ek hafte men dauṛtii huun,
     how-many kilometers I   one week in   run
     utnii-hii   miil jaun ek din men dauṛtaa hai
     that-many miles John one day in   runs
     'The kilometers I run in one week, John runs that number of miles in one day.'

Now, observe that data like those in (37) are neatly accounted for if sortal-raising is part of the analysis of 'headed' relatives, but not of comparatives, since under such a view, there would be no source for the full versions of (37c) and (38b). As Carlson observes, such facts are not impossible to account for within an analysis that base-generates the sortal in its surface position and assumes A′-

movement within the clause, but this would require some stipulation, for example, that the constituent that is moved within the clause must match the entire construction in syntactic category. Thus, with respect to the above data, a raising analysis does have a certain edge over its non-raising competitors.

On the whole, the empirical advantages that result from the adoption of the raising analysis are far from overwhelming, and a decision to retain it will largely depend on how strongly one feels committed to the basic tenets of Antisymmetry, and also on how successfully the latter will be able to deal with a variety of objections that have been raised concerning the framework in general (see, for example, Friedemann 1995) and the proposed analysis of relatives in particular (see, for example, Borsley 1997). A thorough evaluation of such objections goes way beyond the scope of this study. I will nonetheless note here two issues that concern a particular aspect of the analysis of relatives outlined in this section, and which need to be addressed in future research.

Thus, a central feature of the Kayne-Bianchi analysis which was taken over in this section is that raising is triggered by properties of an external D, or of some 'lower' functional Head within the complex DP. Now, as Jackendoff (1977) and Borsley (1997) observed, a complete analysis of appositives would need to generalize to such non-nominal constructions as those in (40).

(40) a. Mary is extremely smart, which John, unfortunately, is not.
b. Mary has traveled from Toronto to L.A., which is a pretty long distance.
c. John died yesterday, which is something we had not expected.

Such a generalization depends on the plausibility of positing appropriate functional categories that play a role comparable to that of D in nominal appositive constructions.

A second unresolved issue, which was in fact noted in Bianchi (1995: Chapter II, Section 10), concerns the treatment of 'hydras' (Link 1984), such as the one in (41).

(41) *The* man and *the* woman who disliked each other...

Assuming that the stage following the first raising operation (to SpecFP) is essentially ... [*who [man and woman] disliked each other*] ..., the conjuncts would need to separately raise to distinct targets in order to check features on the two boldfaced items. A solution within the strongest version of Antisymmetry, which insists on linear ordering of all elements, and thus of conjuncts, at all stages of a derivation (see Kayne 1994: Section 5.2) seems unlikely, but it might be possible to handle such facts within a version of Asymmetry that incorporates some of the assumptions in Williams (1978), in particular, the view that conjuncts may be superimposed in a third dimension at the stage where movement operations take place.

Pending solutions to these and other problems, the proposals made in this section must be considered tentative.

4. Summary of results

This paper has argued that the search for a purely configurational characterization of the various semantic subtypes of relatives is likely to prove quixotic even with respect to individual languages, and *a fortiori* with respect to UG. It was proposed instead to use a system of interpretable features which is flexible enough to capture both similarities and differences among subtypes, and which can straightforwardly trigger suitable interpretive procedures.

The paper has also sketched a characterization of a feature [REL], which defines a 'core' class of relative clause constructions in which the dependencies that hold between the clause and certain types of external material are pre-encoded by Merge, with resulting locality effects, and possibly also by Move, if conceivable objections to the raising analysis can be satisfactorily answered. The core status assigned to this class may also be viewed as justified on the grounds that three semantic operations, in particular, those that yield appositives, restrictives, and maximalizers, are in principle available within it, while the non-core correlative and existential constructions apparently allow single semantic interpretations.

The applicability of three semantic operations to the core has been illustrated only in relation to post-nominal constructions, but the same state of affairs is arguably attested in pre-nominal constructions as well. It has often been noted that a restrictive/appositive ambiguity exists in certain pre-nominal adjectival constructions (such as *the industrious Japanese*), as well as in the pre-nominal participial constructions of German, Dutch and Turkish, and in the pre-nominal relatives of Japanese and Korean (even though the distinction is usually not accompanied by morphosyntactic or prosodic reflexes). The restrictive reading can be teased out by using certain Ds or particles that are inconsistent with appositive readings, yielding such unambiguously restrictive constructions as *the only industrious Japanese, every industrious Japanese,* and *no industrious Japanese.* That genuine ambiguity, and not vagueness, is found in such cases is brought out by the impossibility of 'cross-readings' in data like (42).

(42) John admires the industrious Japanese, and so does Bill.

Comparable effects are found in the more elaborate pre-nominal constructions of other languages that were alluded to above (demonstration omitted). If so, we may expect that such constructions will also allow maximalizing construals. I provide confirming evidence based on the German so-called 'extended participial' construction.

Carlson (1977) observed that one clause-internal type of syntactic context that appears to favour maximalizing readings is that of cardinality/measure expressions. This context was already illustrated in (7), where it was noted that German is not among the languages that allow deviations from the diagnostic restriction on the external Ds of maximalizing constructions; that is to say, data like the acceptable versions of (7a-b) cannot be constructed in German. This claim is illustrated in (43a) with respect to post-nominal relatives. That the generalization also holds for pre-nominal participles is shown in (43b).

(43) a. {Die drei, #drei} Meilen, die du noch laufen musst, sind
the three three miles which you still run must are
genau was du brauchst, um deine Aggressionen
just what You need in-order your aggressions
loszuwerden.
to-get-rid-of
'{The three, #three} miles that you must still run are just what you need to get rid of your feelings of aggression,'

b. {Die drei, #drei} von dir noch zu laufenden Meilen sind
the three three by you still to running miles are
genau was du brauchst, um deine Aggressionen
just what you need in-order your aggressions
loszuwerden.
to-get-rid-of
[same meaning as (43a)]

Notes

1. For completeness, I wish to note that Emonds, while base-generating appositives under a separate E-node, proposed that they are subsequently lowered and adjoined to the main clause S′ node (that is, immediately under the main clause E-node), with the implication that the appositive and the main clause form a single illocutionary unit. The justification he offers for this move is that, while parentheticals like the one in (i-a) are asserted, minimally different appositives like the one in (i-b) are — in his view — presupposed.

(i) a. Too much sun made these tomatoes, and we paid a lot for them, rot on the vine.
   b. Too much sun made these tomatoes, which we paid a lot for, rot on the vine.

However, Emonds appears to be wrong concerning the construal of (i-b), as Chierchia and McConnell-Ginet (1990) point out. The property NOBA of appositives is shared by independently asserted discourse sentences, but not by uncontroversially presupposed clauses, as illustrated in (ii), and this points to the conclusion that appositives are asserted, not presupposed.

(ii) a. #**Every boy** stared at Mary. She began to dislike *him*.
   b. #**Every boy** stared at Mary, who began to dislike *him*.
   c. **Every boy** was amazed that Mary disliked *him*.

I conjecture that Emonds may have been misled by the fact that asserted information may nonetheless be known to both speaker and addressee, the pragmatic justification for assertion being, for example, that the speaker wishes to draw the addressee's attention to a point he considers important.

References

Bianchi, V. (1995). *Consequences of Antisymmetry for the syntax of headed relative clauses*. Doctoral Dissertation, Scuola Normale Superiore, Pisa.

Borsley, R. (1997). Relative Clauses and the Theory of Phrase Structure. *Linguistic Inquiry* 28: 629–647.

Carlson, G. (1977). Amount Relatives. *Language* 53: 520–542.

Chierchia, G. & S. McConnell-Ginet (1990). *Meaning and Grammar: An Introduction to Semantics*. Cambridge, Mass.: MIT Press.

Chomsky, N. (1981). *Lectures on Government and Binding*, Dordrecht: Foris.

Chomsky, N. (1993). A Minimalist Program for Linguistic Theory. *The view from Building 20: Essays in linguistics in honor of Sylvain Bromberger*, edited by K. Hale & S. J. Keyser, 1–52. Cambridge, Mass.: MIT Press.

Chomsky, N. (1995). *The Minimalist Program*. Cambridge, Mass.: MIT Press.

Comorovsky, I. (1986). Multiple Wh Movement in Romanian. *Linguistic Inquiry* 17: 171–177.

Emonds, J. (1979). Appositive Relatives have no Properties. *Linguistic Inquiry* 10: 211–243.

Enç, M. (1991). The Semantics of Specificity. *Linguistic Inquiry* 22: 4–25.

Evans, G. (1980). Pronouns. *Linguistic Inquiry* 11: 337–362.

Fabb, N. (1990) The Difference between English Restrictive and Appositive Clauses. *Journal of Linguistics* 26: 57–77.

Francez, N. & S. Lappin (1994). E-Type Pronouns, I-Sums, and Donkey Anaphora. *Linguistics and Philosophy* 17: 391–428.

Friedemann, M.-A. (1995) *Sujets syntaxiques: positions, inversions et* pro. Doctoral Dissertation, Université de Genève.

Grosu, A. (1989). Pied-Piping and the Matching Parameter. *The Linguistic Review* 6: 41–58.

Grosu, A. (1994). *Three Studies in Locality and Case.* London: Routledge.
Grosu, A. (1998) *Type-Resolution in Relative Constructions. Competing Restrictive and Maximalizing Construals.* Manuscript. [To appear in *Interface Strategies,* edited by H. Bennis, M. Everaert & E. Reuland. Holland Academic Graphics.]
Grosu, A. & F. Landman (1998). Strange Relatives of the Third Kind. *Natural Language Semantics* 6: 125–170.
Huang, J. (1982). *Logical Relations in Chinese and the Theory of Grammar.* Doctoral Dissertation, MIT.
Jackendoff, R. (1977). *X-bar Syntax.* Cambridge, Mass.: MIT Press.
Kadmon, N. & F. Landman (1993) 'Any'. *Linguistics and Philosophy* 16: 353–422.
Kayne, R. (1994). *The Antisymmetry of Syntax.* Cambridge, Mass.: MIT Press.
Ladusaw, W. (1979). *Polarity Sensitivity as Inherent Scope Relations,* Doctoral Dissertation, University of Texas at Austin. [Also published by Garland, New York, 1980.]
Ladusaw, W. (1980). Affective *or,* Factive Verbs, and Negative-Polarity Items. *Papers from the Sixteenth Regional Meeting of the Chicago Linguistic Society,* edited by J. Kreiman & A. Ojeda, 170–184, Chicago Linguistic Society, University of Chicago.
Landman, F. (1998) *Parallels between the Nominal and the Verbal Domain: the case of 'definiteness effects.* Manuscript, Tel Aviv University.
Lehmann, C. (1984). *Der Relativsatz.* Tuebingen: Gunther Narr Verlag.
Link, G. (1984). Hydras. On the Logic of Relative Constructions with Multiple Heads. *Varieties of Formal Semantics,* edited by F. Landman & F. Veltman, 245–257. Dordrecht: Foris.
Manzini, M.-R. (1994). Locality, Minimalism, and Parasitic Gaps. *Linguistic Inquiry* 25: 481–508.
Milsark, G. (1974). *Existential Sentences in English.* Doctoral dissertation, MIT.
McCawley, J. (1982). Parentheticals and Discontinuous Constituent Structure. *Linguistic Inquiry* 13: 91–106.
Muller, C. (1995). *Tendances récentes en linguistique française et générale. Volume dédié à David Gaatone,* edited by H. Bat-Zeev Shyldkrot & L. Kupferman, 311–322. Amsterdam: John Benjamins.
Reinhart, T. (1983). *Anaphora and Semantic Interpretation.* London: Croom Helm.
Reinhart, T. (1991). Elliptic Conjunctions — Non-Quantificational LF. *The Chomskyan Turn,* edited by A. Kasher, 360–384. Oxford: Blackwell.
Reuland, E. (1996). Pronouns and Features. *Proceedings of NELS 26,* ed. by K. Kusumoto, 319–333. Amherst, Mass.: GLSA.
Reuland, E. & ter Meulen, A. (eds.) (1987). *The Representation of (In)definiteness.* Cambridge, Mass.: MIT Press.
Rizzi, L. (1994). *The fine structure of the left periphery.* Manuscript, University of Geneva.
Rullmann, H. (1995). *Maximality in the Semantics of WH-Constructions,* Doctoral dissertation, University of Massachusetts at Amherst.
Safir, K. (1986). Relative Clauses in a Theory of Binding and Levels. *Linguistic Inquiry* 17: 663–689.
Schachter, P. (1973). Focus and Relativization. *Language* 49: 19–46.

Srivastav-Dayal, V. (1991). The Syntax and Semantics of Correlatives. *Natural Language and Linguistic Theory* 9: 637–686.

Srivastav-Dayal, V. (1996). *Locality in Wh Quantification*. Dordrecht: Kluwer.

Stechow, A. von (1984). Comparing Semantic Theories of Comparison. *Journal of Semantics* 1: 1–77.

Toribio, A. (1992) Proper Government in Spanish Subject Relativization. *Probus* 4: 291–304.

Wartemberg, I. (1997). *Iteration and Stacking of Japanese Modifiers. A comparison of English, Japanese and Turkish.* Unpublished MA Thesis, Tel Aviv University.

Wilder, C. (1995). Rightward Movement as Leftward Deletion. *Extraction and Extraposition in German*, edited by U. Lutz & J. Pafel, 273–309. Amsterdam: John Benjamins.

Williams, E. (1978) Across-the-Board Rule Application. *Linguistic Inquiry* 9. 31–44.

Zaring, L. (1992). French *ce* as a Clausal Determiner. *Probus* 4: 53–80.

Some Syntactic and Morphological Properties of Relative Clauses in Turkish[*]

Jaklin Kornfilt
Syracuse University

Introduction

The aim of this paper is to describe and explain the distribution of two main types of nominalization[1] morphology found on the modifier clauses in Turkish relative clause constructions (RCs). This is a topic which has been widely discussed in Turkish linguistics. While the debate has centered around questions of facts and the 'correct' generalization(s), there has hardly been an attempt to actually explain those generalizations, i.e. to tie the facts of morphological choice to more general principles of syntax at work in the language at large. It is the latter enterprise which this paper attempts to address. In doing this, I will concentrate on facts of the 'standard' dialect of Modern Turkish (MST).

The account proposed looks at three different areas of relativization in MST: regular simple RCs, complex RCs, and extractions of non-subjects in constructions with expletive subjects (e.g. in impersonal passives and in constructions with non-specific subjects). While the accounts for all three areas are somewhat different, there are points of contact. The main proposal is centered around a generalized version of Binding Theory: choice of nominalization

---

[*] A (partly different) version of this paper was given in an ASG-seminar in Berlin, and more similar, but shorter versions were presented at the Linguistics departments of the University of the Bosphorus in Istanbul and of the CUNY Graduate Center; I thank the audiences for helpful comments, especially Bob Fiengo, Janet Fodor and Richie Kayne at the latter presentation, and Eser Erguvanlı-Taylan and Sumru Özsoy at the former one. I am indebted to Artemis Alexiadou, Manfred Bierwisch and Chris Wilder for making the trip possible that lead to the first presentation in Berlin, and to Artemis Alexiadou and Paul Law for interesting and enriching comments and queries after a close reading of a preliminary draft. Any shortcomings are my sole responsibility.

morphology is explained via (generalized) Binding Condition B as well as the fact that Turkish is a Null Subject Language (NSL). I appeal to the requirement of the basic nominalization form, i.e. -*DIK*,[2] for an agreement morpheme (agreeing with the subject of the clause or with the possessor in a possessive DP),[3] while the 'special' nominalization form, i.e. -(*y*)*An*, lacks overt agreement. Subject (or possessor) agreement is the only type of overt agreement in Turkish. There is no overt agreement with complements or adjuncts. I claim that it is the presence or absence of **overt** subject (and possessor) agreement that determines the choice of the nominalization morphology under certain syntactic conditions, because it is overt agreement which necessitates the application of the Binding Condition just mentioned. This explanation is tied into the observation that Turkish does not permit resumptive pronouns in simple RCs. The reason for taking -*DIK* as the basic form (or 'elsewhere case') is that this morpheme is found on the predicates of factive complement and adjunct clauses, and it also is the nominalization morpheme with the widest distribution in MST.

The paper is organized as follows: In Section 1, facts concerning word order and choice of nominalization morphology in nominalized, right-headed simple RCs in MST are introduced. I show that no overt resumptive pronouns are possible and explain this fact via Binding Condition B, as generalized to A′-binding. I then claim that the special nominalization form lacking overt Agr found on simple RCs with a subject as a target is motivated by the same generalized binding condition. In Section 2, I show how the same principle explains extractions out of larger subjects and non-subjects. Section 3 addresses extractions out of impersonal constructions where the target of relativization is a non-subject and the element in canonical subject position is a non-thematic, i.e. expletive, *pro*. In all of these RC constructions, the generalized binding principle B is implicated as a guiding principle, but in varying degrees of centrality.

This study in the interactions of syntax and morphology also shows that an explanatory account of all the basic facts concerning RCs in Turkish must assume that the nominalized modifier clauses are all indeed clausal (rather than just phrasal as assumed in traditional studies) and consist of operator-variable structures.

While couched in general GB-terms, the account proposed here is not narrowly formulated within the most recent syntactic models, e.g. within the minimalist framework (cf. Chomsky 1995) or within Kayne's (1994) hypothesis of a non-symmetric universal base. However, the analyses proposed are easily translatable into either model.[4]

1. Syntactic and morphological properties of Turkish relative clauses

Turkish is (at least superficially) a head-final language. Relative clauses (RCs) are just one type of construction where this property is clearly observed.[5] Predicates are clause final, and inflectional elements follow the predicate. The modifier clause in RCs is 'nominalized'. How that nominalization morphology is chosen has been a question of long-standing debate. This paper addresses this issue.

There is no overt complementizer in Turkish RCs, nor is there an overt *wh*-element; there is a gap in the position corresponding to the head.[6] The following examples illustrate these characteristics:[7]

(1) a. [[e_i geçen yaz   ada-da   ben-i gör-en]   kişi-ler$_i$]
       last summer island-LOC I-ACC see-*(y)An* person-PL
       'The people who saw me on the island last summer' [Subject as target]
    b. [[*pro* geçen yaz   ada-da e_i gör-düğ-üm] kişi-ler$_i$]
       last summer island-LOC   see-*DIK*-1SG person-PL
       'The people who(m) I saw on the island last summer' [Non-subject as target]

When relativizing a subject,[8] the suffix used is -*(y)An*. There is no agreement morphology when this suffix is used. When relativizing a non-subject,[9] the suffix used is -*DIK*, which is followed by subject agreement morphology.

One basic question that arises here is whether the modifying clause is indeed a clause, and whether there is an empty bound variable in the position of the gap. To put the matter in an 'Anglo-centric' manner, we might ask which type of modification in English corresponds to the Turkish constructions just illustrated:

(2)   a running child

(3)   a child who is running

I claim that the Turkish constructions are rather like (3), despite some superficial similarities with (2).[10] This point of view is not obvious. The view generally found in traditional Turkological studies is that Turkish does not have genuine RCs, and that the nominalized verbal forms found as nominal modifiers are 'just' participles, i.e. deverbal adjectives. No operator-bound variable would be posited in most generative analyses for (2). The Turkish constructions are superficially similar to (2): the verb is nominalized, and it precedes the head; there is no relative pronoun, nor is there an overt complementizer. On the other hand, the nominalized verb in the Turkish constructions can head a clause-like domain;

several arguments as well as adjuncts can be realized:

(4) [her sabah ev-in-den okul-a arkadaş-lar-ı -yla
every morning home-3SG-ABL school-DAT friend-PL-3SG -with
koş-an] bir çocuk
run-*(y)An* a child
'A child who runs early every morning from his home to school with his friends'

Note that the construction in (2) cannot be used here in English:

(4') *an early every morning from his home to school with his friends running child

Similarly, an agent phrase can't be used in pre-nominal English modification as in (5a). In contrast, the corresponding Turkish construction (5b) is perfectly grammatical:[11]

(5) a. *a by his mother loved child
b. [[[*pro*^{i} anne-si^i] tarafindan] sev-il -en] bir çocuk
mother-3SG by love-PASS -*(y)An* a child
'a child loved by his/her mother'

In its ability to host a full array of arguments and adjuncts, the modifying domain in a Turkish RC corresponds much more closely to an English CP (or IP) as in (3), than it does to a participle with one unrealized (external) argument as in (2). Furthermore, (5b) also shows that there can be a resumptive pronoun in the modifying 'domain', as illustrated by the English translation; in the Turkish example, this is a resumptive *pro*, licensed by the possessive agreement. A pronoun which is directly or indirectly bound by the modified head is not a property generally found in modification by participles.

As an additional argument, note the fact that the nominalized modifier clause can host sentential ('speaker-oriented') adverbs, and that the nominalized verb can have modal suffixes:

(6) a. [Oya-nın herhalde e_i sev-e -me -diğ-i] bir insan$_i$
Oya-GEN probably love-ABIL -NEG -*DIK*-3SG a person
'A person whom Oya probably cannot love'
b. [e_i herhalde Oya-yı sev-e -me-yen] bir insan$_i$
probably Oya-ACC love-ABIL -NEG-*(y)An* a person
'A person who probably cannot love Oya'

Such 'higher', sentential adverbs, exemplified by the 'modal adverbs' (cf. Cinque 1999) as the one used in these examples (i.e. such as 'obviously', 'probably') provide additional support to the claim advocated here, namely that the nominalized modifier clause of these RCs has fully spelled-out clausal structure and does not consist of a 'reduced' deverbal adjectival phrase.

I conclude that in Turkish both RC constructions are to be analyzed in a manner akin to the English (3) rather than to (2). This claim includes both 'relativization strategies', i.e. the construction with -$(y)An$ as well as the one with -DIK, as illustrated above. Note that any attempt to render the semantics of such examples by means of pre-nominal, participial modification in English following the pattern in (2) leads to examples like (7) which are grossly ungrammatical:

(7)   a.   *my/I having seen/seeing (on the island) people
        b.   *Mary's probably not being able to love person
        c.   *a probably not being able to love Mary person

If the gap in the modifying domain in Turkish RCs is a phonologically empty bound variable, is it the result of syntactic movement? I claim that it is. The moved element is, in a 'traditional' approach, an empty operator (corresponding to an overt *wh*-element in languages like English), and in a Kaynian approach, the relative head. In most of what follows, I will presuppose a 'traditional' derivation (roughly in the framework of Chomsky 1981) for the sake of exposition; my main concern, i.e. choice of different nominalization morphemes, can be expressed under either derivation.

This claim is based on subjacency effects observed in RCs. Note that RCs in Turkish exhibit island effects, at least where relativization out of RCs is concerned:[12]

(8)   a.   *[Hasan-ın   [[e_i geçen yaz e_j ben-i gör-en]
             Hasan-GEN   last   summer   I-ACC see-$(y)An$
             kişi-ler$_i$]-i   tanı-dığ-ı]   ada$_j$
             person-PL-ACC know-*DIK*-3SG island
             Intended reading: 'The island (such that) Hasan knows the people who saw me (on it) last summer'[13]

I claim that the ungrammaticality of examples like (8a) are instances of Ross's Complex NP Constraint (cf. Ross 1967) and are thus due to violations of subjacency. To see this more clearly, I repeat (8a), 'enriched' with abstract operators, under a 'traditional' derivation:

a'. *[$_{CP}$Op$_j$ [$_{IP}$ Hasan-ın [$_{DP}$[$_{CP}$Op$_i$[$_{IP}$ e$_i$ geçen yaz   e$_j$ ben-i
          Hasan-GEN   last summer   I-ACC
gör-en]] kişi -ler$_i$]-i tanı -dığ -ı]] ada$_j$
see-(y)An person -PL-ACC know -DIK -3SG island
Intended reading: 'The island (such that) Hasan knows the people who saw me (on it) last summer'

The first operator, i.e. Op_i, moves to SpecCP (but see the caveat in footnote 16). Movement of the second operator, i.e. Op_j , violates subjacency, because the specifier position of the lower CP is occupied by Op_i.

In contrast, when the variable whose binding by the head (in a head-raising analysis of RCs) or by an empty operator (in 'traditional' analyses of RCs) violates subjacency is identified by an overt Agr-element (i.e. where such a variable is a non-locally bound resumptive *pro*), no island (i.e. subjacency) effect is observed (a phenomenon often seen with 'repaired' subjacency violations in English):[14]

(8)   b.   [$_{CP}$Op$_j$ [$_{IP}$ pro^l [$_{DP}$[$_{CP}$Op$_i$[$_{IP}$ pro^k_j ben-i e$_i$ davet
                                                                                            I-ACC   invitation
et -tiğ -i^k]] ada] -da$_i$ ev al -dığ -ım^l]] kaptan$_j$
do -DIK -3SG island -LOC house buy -DIK -1SG captain
*'The captain$_j$ who$_j$ I bought a house on the island$_i$ which$_i$ he$_j$ invited me to t_i.'

c. $^{(?)}$[$_{CP}$Op$_j$[$_{IP}$ rektör-ün^l [$_{DP}$[$_{CP}$Op$_i$[$_{IP}$ pro^k_j e$_i$ rüşvet
          rector-GEN   bribery
ver-dik -leri^k]] profesör$_i$]-ü kov -duğ -u^l]] öğrenci-ler$_j$
give-DIK -3PL   professor-ACC fire -DIK -3SG student-PL
*'The students$_j$ such that the rector fired the professor$_i$ whom$_i$ they$_j$ bribed'

Similar contrasts are also seen with overt pronouns in non-subject positions (i.e. in positions where *pro* is not licensed):

(9)   a.   *[$_{CP}$Op$_j$[$_{IP}$ rektör-ün^l [$_{DP}$[$_{CP}$Op$_i$[$_{IP}$ e$_i$ e$_j$ rüşvet ver-en]]
                  rector-GEN   bribery give-(y)An
öğrenci-ler$_i$]-i sınıf-ta   bırak-tığ -ı^l]] profesör$_j$
student-PL-ACC class-LOC leave-DIK -3SG professor
Intended reading: *'The professor$_j$ such that the rector flunked the students$_i$ who$_i$ bribed (him$_j$)'

b. $^{(?)}[_{CP}Op_j[_{IP}$ rektör-ün^l $[_{DP}[_{CP}Op_i[_{IP}\ e_i\ kendisin\ -e_j$ rüşvet
   rector-GEN   him   -DAT bribery
   ver-*en*]]   öğrenci-ler$_i$]-i   sınıf-ta   bırak -tığ   -ı^l]] profesör$_j$
   give-*(y)An* student-PL-ACC class-LOC leave -*DIK* -3SG professor
   *'The professor$_j$ such that the rector flunked the students$_i$ who$_i$ bribed him$_j$'

The ungrammaticality of (9a) is due to a violation of subjacency, itself due to the long-distance dependency between Op_j and e_j. This dependency (and the ungrammaticality it gives rise to) is entirely comparable to the situation we saw in (8a). This example is 'saved' by the resumptive pronoun that replaces the offending phonologically empty variable e_j, as illustrated in (9b).

These facts establish two points. Firstly, it is not the long-distance relationship between operator and variable per se that violates subjacency in the (a)-sentences, since the same relationship is well-formed in the (b)- and (c)-sentences, where the bound variable is overt in (9b) and is a null pronoun (*pro*) in (8b) and (8c). The ungrammaticality of the (a)-sentences is based on a derivational, movement-based definition of subjacency, as has been done traditionally in instances where resumptive pronouns do not exhibit subjacency effects, but corresponding **empty** variables do. (Notice also that the 'offending' variable in ungrammatical examples like (9a) is θ-governed, thus making an ECP-based account implausible as a rival account).[15]

Secondly, the overt pronoun and *pro* pattern together in their ability to 'save' subjacency violations, thus providing additional motivation for treating *pro* as a regular pronominal, representative of the natural class of [+pronominal/-anaphoric] elements, whenever *pro* is licensed. (Additional arguments are provided in Section 1.1.)

I take these facts to argue in favor of an analysis which attributes their island sensitivity to subjacency, in a fashion similar to better-studied European languages like English (see also Kornfilt 1984 and 1991). Thus, the modifying clause in Turkish RCs is once again shown to be more similar to a clause[16] than to a lexical participle as a modifier, in that it involves an operator-variable structure.[17]

The morphology for 'subject relativization' is not used anywhere else in the language (with the exception of a very limited adverbial construction), but the one for 'non-subject relativization' is the most basic morphology found in complementation. There are two basic types in complementation: factive (the basic type) and non-factive (similar to subjunctives in Romance). The factive type uses -*DIK* with obligatory overt Agr, just as in RCs with non-subject targets:

(10) [*pro* sen-i ada-da gör-düğ -üm]-ü
 you-ACC island-LOC see-FNOM 1SG-ACC
 herkes -e anlat-tı-m
 everybody -DAT tell-PAST-1SG
 'I told everyone that I saw you on the island last summer'

Following Kornfilt (1984) and (1991), I propose an analysis which derives Turkish RCs with *-DIK*, i.e. those where the target of relativization is a non-subject (or part of a non-subject) from the regular factive complementation construction. My motivation is based on facts of the sort illustrated above, i.e. identity of the factive nominalization and the non-subject 'relativization' markers and of the obligatoriness of overt Agr in both. Furthermore, it appears reasonable to derive RCs from factive complements on general grounds, as well, and to treat the construction employing *-DIK* as the 'unmarked' or 'elsewhere' case. We now have to explain why the regular 'strategy' is not available for subjects, forcing the use of *-(y)An* instead.

In addressing this question, I claim that what is of interest here is not the morphology of the nominalization per se, but rather whether there is overt agreement morphology present or not[18]. As illustrated in (1b) and the examples in (6), the 'regular' morpheme, i.e. *-DIK*, is followed by (subject) agreement morphology, while the 'subject relativization' morpheme *-(y)An* is 'bare'. The significance of this observation follows from a generalized version of Binding Theory — more specifically, from a principle roughly of the following sort:

(11) The A'-disjointness Requirement: A pronoun must be (A'-) free in the smallest Complete Functional Complex (CFC) which contains it.

This is a special clause of a generalized version of the familiar Condition B of Binding Theory which requires a pronoun to be (A-) free in its Governing Category (or its Complete Functional Complex [CFC]; cf. Chomsky 1986a: 169–172). If the domain of the CFC is CP for A'-binding, and if the requirement that the pronoun be A-free is generalized to a more general requirement that it be A-free as well as A'-free, we get a generalized Condition B, with the requirement in (11) as a subclause.

This subclause and/or this generalized version of Condition B have been advocated in a variety of studies and for a number of languages; see, for example, Aoun & Li (1989), Borer (1984), McCloskey (1990),[19] and Ouhalla (1993). For Turkish RCs, I have advocated this approach in Kornfilt (1984) and (1991).[20] This principle rules out resumptive pronouns in simple RCs, as illustrated by the following examples (in whose representations I have translated the previous IPs as Agr[N]P, and the previous CP as C[N]P, following footnote 16); modifier clauses with -(y)An are represented as Agr[N]Ps with an abstract Agr-head, while modifier clauses with -DIK+Agr are represented as Agr[N]Ps with an overt Agr-head. Only in the latter type is *pro* licensed as a subject:

(12) a. [C[N]P Op_i[Agr[N] P (*o_i/*$kendisi_i$) ada-da ben-i
         he/himself[21] island-LOC I-ACC
         gör-en]] $kişi_i$
         see-*(y)An* person
         'The $person_i$ who_i (*he_i) saw me on the island' [A subject as target]

   b. [C[N]P Op_i[Agr[N] P pro ada-da (*$on-u_i$/ *$kendisin-i_i$)
         island-LOC he-ACC/ himself-ACC
         gör-düğ-üm]] $kişi_i$
         see-*DIK*-1SG person
         'The $person_i$ $who(m)_i$ I saw (*him_i) on the island' [A non-subject as target]

The generalized version of Condition B makes the correct predictions: the modifying clause cannot contain a resumptive pronoun, since that pronoun would be bound by an (in Turkish, abstract) operator (or by the head in a derivation based on Kayne 1994) within the modifying C[N]P, i.e. the smallest CFC for that pronoun.

We must note the importance of locality. Resumptive pronouns, whether overt or *pro*, are ruled out by the condition under discussion in **local** domains, i.e. in their smallest CFC. We saw previously that both *pro* and overt pronouns can be used as resumptive pronouns to 'save' subjacency violations; thus, the A'-binding of both overt and phonologically empty pronouns is allowed, as long as that A'-binding is non-local.

We are now ready to explain the choice of nominalization in RCs: Turkish, as a Null Subject Language (NSL), can have phonologically unrealized subject pronouns in finite clauses as well as in nominalized clauses and in nominal phrases, if the clause or the phrase is headed by *overt* agreement. It is a generally accepted view that the syntactic category of such subject pronouns (i.e. of *pro*) is that of a regular pronominal, with the features [+pronominal/−anaphoric]. If *pro* occupies the position of a relativized subject it violates the A'-disjointness condition as a pronoun which is A'-bound in its smallest CFC.

The target of relativization is a *pro* (rather than a non-pronominal empty variable) whenever *pro* is licensed (as well as identified; cf. Rizzi 1986). In NSLs, this is typically the case when *pro* is a subject which is licensed by a rich agreement element; that this is indeed so for Turkish (in tensed and nominalized clauses as well as in possessive NPs) is argued for in Kornfilt (1984, 1996a and 1996b). I now turn to a brief sketch of the evidence in favor of positing *pro* subjects (and possessors) in the respective specifier positions of syntactic domains headed by overt agreement morphology.

1.1 *Evidence for* pro

Just as in better-studied NSLs like Italian and Spanish, it is possible to omit a subject in Turkish in finite clauses and interpret that subject as a pronoun:

(13) a. *pro* [*pro* sinema-ya git-tiğ -in]-i duy-du-m
       cinema-DAT go-FNOM -2SG-ACC hear-PAST-1SG
       'I heard that you went to the movies'
   b. [*pro* komşu-m] [*pro* çiçek-ler-im]-e bak-acak
       neighbor-1SG flower-PL-1SG-DAT look-FUT
       'My neighbor will look after my flowers'

In these examples, the phonologically empty (subject or possessor) element is referential — obviously, a pronominal property. Since there is no obvious syntactic antecedent for it, this element is unlikely to be a trace. It cannot be PRO, either, since PRO must be ungoverned, while the agreement inflection (whether verbal, as in the root clause of (13a), or whether nominal as in the embedded clause of (13a) and in the possessive phrases of (13b)) would govern the empty element. I now show that the empty element here has indeed the properties of *pro* in other NSLs, and that it has properties which set it apart from other phonologically empty elements in Turkish.

As has been claimed in the literature (e.g. Jaeggli & Safir 1989; Rizzi 1986), *pro* must be licensed; if it is referential, its feature contents must also be identified. This formal requirement holds in Turkish and can't be overridden by pragmatic or discourse recoverability of *pro*'s contents. I claim that the licenser and identifier of a referential *pro* is an overt and strong (i.e. paradigmatic in the sense of belonging to a paradigm with distinct shapes for each of the relevant phi-feature combinations) agreement element, and that it must have a syntactically local relationship to such a *pro*. For third person plural subjects, the number component of the agreement morpheme is optional:

(14) komsu -lar tatil -e çık -tı (-lar)
     neighbor -PL vacation -DAT go out -PAST (-3PL)
     'The neighbors went out on vacation'

This often preferred option to omit number agreement for third person plural subjects becomes unavailable when the subject or possessor associated with the agreement element is null (and, as I claim here, is *pro*):

(15) a. Namzet -ler oda -ya bir-er bir-er gel -sin(-ler)
candidate -PL room -DAT one-by one-by come -OPT(-3PL)
'The candidates should come into the room one by one'
b. Namzet -ler-e$_i$ söyle, [*pro*$_i$ oda -ya bir-er bir-er
candidate -PL-DAT tell(IMP) room -DAT one-by one-by
gel -sin *(-ler)]
come -OPT(-3PL)
'Tell the candidates$_i$ that they$_i$ should come into the room one by one'

Although the omission of the plural part of the third person agreement marker is possible in the first example (and is even stylistically preferred), such omission is not possible in the second example. In the first example, the subject of the clause is overt, while in the second, the subject of the (embedded) clause is not overt. This non-overt subject is fully referential, hence *pro*, thus explaining the contrast between the two examples via the licensing and identification requirement on *pro*: when not all of the relevant phi-features are overtly expressed by the licensing element (i.e. here, overt Agr), *pro* is not properly licensed and identified, hence the prohibition to omit the plural agreement in the second example, but not the first. Note also that in the second example, the *pro* subject has its antecedent, i.e. the dative object of the root clause, nearby; but this is not enough to license *pro*. The required plurality feature must be expressed locally, via overt agreement; it cannot be picked up via syntactic or pragmatic binding.

Similar facts hold even where *pro* is c-commanded by its antecedent:

(16) a. Asker-ler$_i$ [*pro*$_{i/j(3PL)}$ öl-ecek-ler+in]-e inan -ıyor (-lar)
soldier-PL die-FUT-PL+3-DAT believe -PRESPROG
(-3PL)
'The soldiers$_i$ believe that they$_{i/j}$ will die'
b. Asker-ler$_i$ [*pro*$_{*i/*j(3PL)/k(3SG)}$ öl-eceğ-in]-e
soldier-PL die-FUT-3-DAT
inan -ıyor (-lar)
believe -PRESPROG (-3PL)
'The soldiers$_i$ believe that *they$_{i/j}$/(s)he$_k$ will die'

Again, for the *pro* to be licensed and to be interpreted as having plural features, a plural c-commanding binder is insufficient: a local agreement element is required that expresses the relevant feature overtly; otherwise, the *pro* is interpreted as singular.

This contrasts sharply with PRO as the subject of infinitival clauses. The infinitival marker *-mAK* cannot be followed by agreement inflection. Yet, infinitival clauses have phonologically empty subjects. Since partial agreement is insufficient to license *pro* — an element requiring full agreement locally —, the empty subject in a domain without any overt agreement whatsoever can't be *pro*. I posit PRO as the subject of infinitivals and turn to the different syntactic properties of PRO and *pro*.

We observe a series of properties exhibited by these elements which are identical to the properties of such elements in other, better studied, languages; in the case of *pro*, we further observe that it has properties of regular pronominals, i.e. of overt pronominals in a non-NSL like English.

Partee (1975) shows that PRO and pronouns behave differently with respect to binding in certain contexts; the following example with a pronoun is ambiguous:

(17) Only John expected [that he would win]

(18) a. No one except for John expected himself to win.
[Bound variable reading.]
b. No one except for John expected John to win.
[Co-referential reading.]

The corresponding example with an embedded PRO as a subject instead of the pronoun is not ambiguous; only the bound variable reading is possible:

(19) Only John expected [PRO to win]

Turkish is similar, with PRO behaving as its English counterpart, and *pro* as the English overt pronoun:

(20) Sırf Hasan [*pro*^{i} yarışma-yı kazan-acağ -ın^i] -ı
only H. race-ACC win-FUT.NOM -3SG -ACC
um-uyor -du
hope-PROG -PAST
'Only Hasan was hoping that he would win the race'

Just as in English, both the bound variable and the co-referential readings are available in this example, while only the bound variable reading is possible in the corresponding infinitival construction:

(21) Sırf Hasan [PRO yarışma-yı kazan -mağ] -ı   um   -uyor -du
only H.   race-ACC win -INF -ACC hope -PROG -PAST
'Only Hasan was hoping to win the race'

Such systematic and predictable differences between *pro* and PRO are also observed between arbitrary PRO and expletive *pro*. (Example (41a) later in this paper illustrates *pro* as an expletive; for further examples and discussion, showing that PRO$_{arb}$ needs a θ-role, while *pro* doesn't and hence can serve as an expletive as opposed to PRO, see Kornfilt 1996b.)

I conclude that the empty element associated with overt strong agreement is *pro*, since *pro* exhibits properties typical of overt pronouns in non-NSLs, while the empty element associated with obligatory absence of agreement is PRO.

This analysis enables us to explain some additional observations:

(22) Hasan$_i$ [*pro*$_i$ dün   tanış-tığ -ı]   kız-a   telefon   et-ti
H.   yesterday meet-*DIK* -3SG girl-DAT telephone do-PAST
'Hasan$_i$ called up the girl whom he$_i$ met yesterday'

(23) *pro**$_{i/j}$ [Hasan-ın$_i$ dün   tanış-tığ -ı]   kız-a   telefon
H.-GEN   yesterday meet-*DIK* -3SG girl-DAT telephone
et-ti
do-PAST
'He$_{*i/j}$ called up the girl whom Hasan$_i$ met yesterday'

The surface sequences of lexical DPs and agreement are the same in these two examples, and the agreement morphemes themselves are identical, as well. Therefore, the differences in co-reference possibilities can't be due to those elements alone, but rather are due to Condition C: in the second example, the embedded subject is an R-expression which must be (A-)free everywhere. However, under the co-referential reading, it is c-commanded by the co-indexed matrix *pro*. This account is made possible by the assumption that overt agreement locally licenses and identifies a *pro* element it is co-indexed with.

1.2 *Obligatoriness of* pro *whenever licensed*

We have seen that if a relative clause is headed by an overt, paradigmatic agreement element, and if the target of relativization is the subject of that clause, then that subject **could** be *pro*, and that *pro* would violate the condition in (11). But **must** such an element always be *pro*?

An affirmative answer is motivated in a variety of languages as well as in a variety of syntactic phenomena; while space limitations don't permit me to go into such arguments in detail, I refer the reader to Jaeggli (1984) for a detailed discussion of this view:

(24) If an empty category is licensed and identified by AGR, it **must** be *pro*. (Jaeggli 1984, emphasis added: JK)

Neither *-DIK* nor *-(y)An* can be followed by overt Agr morphology:

(25) a. *[_DP_[_C[N]P_ *Op*_i_ [_Agr[N]P_ *pro*_i_ ada-da ben-i gör-düğ -ü]] kişi_i_]
island-LOC I-ACC see-*DIK* -3SG person
Intended reading: 'The person who saw me on the island'
b. *[_DP_[_C[N]P_ *Op*_i_ [_Agr[N]P_ *pro*_i_ ada-da ben-i gör-en -i]]
island-LOC I-ACC see-*(y)An* -3SG
kişi_i_]
person
Intended reading: 'The person who saw me on the island'

In both instances, the reason for the ungrammaticality is the same as that in the examples of (12), namely that there is a resumptive pronoun in a simple RC; the only difference is that in (12), the offending resumptive pronouns are overt, while in (25), they are instances of *pro*. We have here a pronominal which is A'-bound locally; no matter which type of nominalization morpheme we choose, the result will be bad, due to the overt agreement in a relative clause whose target is a subject.

Why can't *-DIK* be used without agreement, instead of *-(y)An*? I suggest that the reason is not a purely syntactic one, but rather that this is a redundancy of the morphology. Alternations between overt agreement morphology and lack thereof are not very salient perceptually, and thus two distinct, phonologically unrelated nominalization markers are used in addition to that alternation. A language is conceivable with essentially the same grammar, with the same nominalization marker for all instances, but without overt Agr for subject and possessor relativization targets, and with overt Agr for all other relativization targets.[22]

Up to now, we have been concerned with the question of why we cannot use the nominalization form with *-DIK* for relativizing subjects. But we also have to ask why the so-called subject participle (cf. Hankamer & Knecht 1976; Underhill 1972), i.e. the morpheme *-(y)An*, cannot be used to relativize non-subjects. We have answered this question earlier, albeit implicitly: the nominalization form with *-DIK* is the 'elsewhere case' in complementation, since it shows up as the general marker of factive complements everywhere in the language. An additional explanation is based on the Case Filter. When a non-subject has been relativized, the subject will show up as a phonologically realized constituent that needs Case, assigned by overt Agr (unless the subject is *pro*, in which case overt Agr is needed for a different reason, namely as a local licenser and identifier of *pro*). If a language does not need overt Agr to assign Case to a subject, i.e. if a mechanism of default Case assignment is available, then RCs may exhibit a nominalization morpheme that does not require overt Agr; the morpheme found with subject targets can then also be used for non-subject targets, and without overt Agr in either instance; Azeri, a Turkic language closely related to MST, appears to be such a language.

In conclusion, I have claimed here that the facts of the choice in simple RCs of a particular nominalization morphology in MST are determined by the agreement on the general nominalization marker *-DIK*. This agreement marker triggers application of the A'-Disjointness Condition, i.e. a subclause in a generalized version of Binding Condition B, for subject 'relativization'. This condition was itself further motivated by observing that Turkish does not allow locally operator-bound pronouns (whereby, as we shall see later on, intermediate traces do not cound as operators[23]), irrespective of whether such pronouns are subjects or non-subjects, and also irrespective of whether they are overt or *pro*. This motivates formulating the condition in a very general fashion and argues for the view that the '-(y)An strategy' for relativizing subjects is nothing but a special instance of applying this very general A'-Disjointness Condition, thus prohibiting the use of the otherwise 'unmarked nominalization strategy' with the *DIK*+Agreement sequence.

There is no problem about the *DIK*+Agreement sequence heading the modifier clause for non-subject relativization targets. Since, as noted earlier, overt agreement in Turkish agrees only with the features of subjects and possessors, but not with the features of non-subjects, the empty variable in these instances will never be licensed as *pro*, and no violation of the principle in (11) will arise. Thus, we make the necessary distinction between relativizing a subject versus a non-subject and account for the correlation between the relativization target and the choice of nominalization morphology.

My analysis for both types of the nominalized modifying clauses has been to posit the same structure for both, namely a structure quite similar to the fully projected one of fully finite clauses. The VP is identical for the nominalized and the fully finite clauses. The differences are at the level of the functional projections that dominate VP: instead of the verbal tense, mood and (subject) agreement projections of fully finite clauses, nominalized clauses have nominal functional projections. This is true, I claim, for nominalized argument clauses as well as adjunct clauses, with the nominal modifying clauses in RC constructions a special instance of the latter.

Returning to the nominal modifier clauses in RC constructions, I have posited structural identity between the two types of clauses with respect to the nominal functional projections above the VP. I have assumed that both types are nominal AgrPs; the 'elsewhere' type with the *-DIK* morphology is headed by overt Agr, while the 'special' type with the *-(y)An* morphology is headed by abstract Agr. However, complete structural identity between the two types of modifier clauses is the least crucial to the main thrust of this paper. My main reasons for adopting such identity are general ones: (a) Unless there are sound empirical reasons for assigning 'reduced' structures to propositional domains, the best *a priori* analysis is to attribute clausal status to such domains; (b) The evidence presented in the introductory section of this paper showed that modifier clauses with *-(y)An* have full clausal properties (e.g. a full array of arguments and adjuncts realized; overt argument-changing morphology like Passive, functional morphology like negation, modality morphology like ability, and sentence-level adverbs).[24]

A slightly different and less abstract analysis is also possible. Suppose that there is no projection of AgrS in instances that lack overt realization of AgrS; *-(y)An* clauses would not be AgrPs, as opposed to *-DIK* clauses which would. However, *-(y)An* clauses would still be higher than VPs, given all the clausal criteria previously listed; i.e. they would be (nominal) TPs or Modal Ps, with the subject variable in specifier position of that phrase. We would need to stipulate, however, that the head of such a phrase is able to assign (or check) Case features on(to) the subject variable, or that default Case is assigned/checked in just that context.

Whether the best analysis will ultimately be one positing identical structures for the two types of modifier clauses or (slightly) different structures is only of tangential interest for us. The main question to be answered here is: **Why** are there two different nominalization forms, one with overt Agr, and the other without? How are these forms related to the 'target of relativization', and why should they be so related? Why is the fully-projected AgrP (with *-DIK* and overt Agr) the 'elsewhere' construction, and why is it not available for subject targets in simple RCs? And why is the (slightly) less fully projected nominal TP (or MoodP) — without an Agr head at all under this analysis — licensed for subject targets, while it remains unavailable for non-subject targets?

The account offered in this paper to explain the choice of morphology is easily transposable into this analysis by ruling out AgrP projections (with *-DIK*) as hosts for (*pro*)-subject variables, while allowing nominal MoodPs (with

-(y)An) as their hosts. The generalized binding condition B would be violated in the former and not in the latter.

2. Extractions out of larger subjects and non-subjects

So far in the discussion, we have limited ourselves to simple RCs. Now, we turn to constructions where the target of relativization is part of a larger subject or non-subject.

It has been noted in the literature (e.g. Hankamer & Knecht 1976; Kornfilt 1984 and 1991; Underhill 1972) that in the standard dialect, extracting a subconstituent out of a larger subject gives rise to a 'Subject Participle' form (i.e. a form in -(y)An) heading the complex RC (even if the target of the relativization is not a subject in its own phrase or clause), while extracting a subconstituent out of a larger non-subject results in an 'Object Participle' form (i.e. a form in -DIK+Agr), even if the target of relativization is a subject in its own phrase or clause; to capture this observation, Hankamer & Knecht (1976) formulate a generalization which they call 'The Mother Node Principle'. This principle states that the grammatical relation of the 'mother node', i.e. of the larger domain that includes the target of relativization, determines the form of the nominalization morpheme to be found on the complex modifier clause in a relative clause construction (cf. Hankamer & Knecht 1976).[25] Such extractions out of larger subjects (e.g. out of possessive phrases and clauses which are themselves subjects)[26] are illustrated below (for the sake of simplicity, I have left out detailed indications of labelled brackets and operators in the following set of examples):

(26) [[müdür-ün e_i kov-acağ -ı] hemen   duy-ul -an]
      director-GEN fire-FUT -3SG immediately hear-PASS -(y)An
      öğretmen$_i$
      teacher
      'The teacher who (it) was heard immediately that the director was going to fire (him)'

(27) *[[müdür-ün e_i kov-acağ-ın] -ın hemen
      director-GEN fire-FUT-3SG -GEN immediately
      duy-ul   -duğ-u] öğretmen$_i$
      hear-PASS -DIK-3SG teacher
      [Same intended reading.]

(28) [[*pro*$_i$ öğretmen-i kov-acağ-ı] hemen duy-ul -an]
       teacher-ACC fire-FUT-3SG immediately hear-PASS -*(y)An*
müdür$_i$
director
'The director who (it) was heard immediately that (he) was going to fire the teacher'

(29) *[[*pro*$_i$ öğretmen-i kov-acağ-ın]-ın hemen
       teacher-ACC fire-FUT-3SG-GEN immediately
duy-ul -duğ-u] müdür$_i$
hear-PASS -*DIK*-3SG director
[Same intended reading.]

Given these facts of MST, we have to ask whether the explanation based on the A′-Disjointness Effect carries over.

Compare the ungrammatical examples above — e.g. (27) and (29) — to the grammatical (28). In (27), the phonologically empty variable is not a subject in its own clause; its contents are not identified by agreement; therefore, it is not *pro*. Hence, the ungrammaticality of this example has certainly nothing to do with the A′-disjointness condition in (11). In (29), the variable is a subject in a domain headed by overt agreement, and is thus *pro*. However, since (according to Kornfilt (1984), where I followed Levin (1983)) intermediate traces don't qualify as operators, it is not operator-bound in its smallest CFC, which is the embedded nominal CP, while the operator is in the specifier position of the higher CP; therefore, condition (11) is not violated by that variable; again, there must be another reason for why this example is ungrammatical. I now repeat a contrasting pair of examples, with more structural information given:

(28′) [$_{CP_2}$ *Op*$_i$ [$_{Agr[N]P_2}$ [$_{CP_1}$ *t*$_i$ [$_{Agr[N]P_1}$ *pro*$_i$ öğretmen-i kov-acağ -ı]]
                                                             teacher-ACC fire-FUT -3SG
hemen duy-ul -an]] müdür$_i$
immediately hear-PASS -*(y)An* director
'The director who (it) was heard immediately that (he) was going to fire the teacher'

(29′) *[$_{CP_2}$ *Op*$_i$ [$_{Agr[N]P_2}$[$_{CP_1}$ *t*$_i$ [$_{Agr[N]P_1}$ *pro*$_i$ öğretmen-i kov-acağ -ın]] -ın
                                                              teacher-ACC fire-FUT -3SG -GEN
hemen duy-ul -duğ-u]] müdür$_i$
immediately hear-PASS -*DIK*-3SG director
[Same intended reading.]

Note that we cannot assume that in (29), the *pro* is operator-bound by the intermediate trace, because if such binding gave rise to ungrammaticality in (29), we should observe the same ungrammaticality in (28), as well.

We draw the (preliminary) conclusion that the generalization expressed as the 'Mother Node Principle' by Hankamer & Knecht (1976) appears to be independent from the A'-Disjointness Effect in (11). How, then, is the choice of the 'relative participle' determined in long extraction?

If condition (11) cannot be appealed to in exactly the same way in which it was invoked for simple RCs, it would nevertheless be desirable if we could still appeal to it in a somewhat different fashion. This is what I will attempt to do in this section.

One possibility is to claim that any such larger subject (whether a sentential subject or a possessive phrase in subject position of a clause) acts as a syntactic island and can therefore not host a target of relativization. In descriptive terms, this would mean that Ross's Sentential Subject Constraint (SSC) does hold for Turkish, in fact it holds for both sentential subjects and possessive phrases as subjects. The fact that the 'elsewhere' morphology with overt agreement is not possible in the standard dialect for relativization targets within such larger subjects is, so I claim, primarily an effect of the SSC (used here as a descriptive label). The motivation for this claim is as follows.

Where the word order of a clause is unmarked, Genitive marking on the subject of a nominalized clause with overt subject agreement is evidence that the subject is in canonical subject position, i.e. in SpecAgrP.[27] Why should a subject in that position be an island? The pre-Barriers account of subjacency did not have a straightforward answer to this (without additional stipulations). In the Barriers framework, the explanation is tied to the notion of L-marking. Since a constituent in canonical subject position is governed by a functional category rather than a lexical one, it is not L-marked. As a consequence, it is a barrier, and extraction of any constituent out of it would violate subjacency.

In order to make such extraction possible, the larger subject could move elsewhere. Chomsky (1986b) suggests a solution along these lines for extractions out of a subject DP (via *wh*-movement of the DP, cf. Chomsky (1986b: 26), and via PP-extraposition of the target of relativization out of the larger subject, cf. Chomsky (1986b: 32)). If so, the movement of that larger subject would leave behind a variable in the canonical subject position; if that variable is a pronominal, it will violate the condition in (11)[28]. In Turkish, this would be the case, given Jaeggli's stipulation in (24) according to which an empty category licensed and identified by overt Agr not only can, but **must** be *pro*.

To see how this would work, let us reconsider example (29), which is ill-formed in the standard dialect due to the 'incorrect' choice of nominalization. I repeat a version of (29) as (30); identification of *pro* by overt Agr is marked via co-superscripting:

(30) *[[[[*pro*$_i$]^l öğretmen-i kov-acağ-ın] -ın^l]$_j$ [*pro*$_j$]^k
teacher-ACC fire-FUT-3SG -GEN
duy-ul -duğ -u^k] müdür$_i$
hear-PASS -*DIK* -3SG director
Intended reading: 'The director who (it) was heard that (he) was going to fire the teacher'

Here, the A'-bound pronominal that would violate the condition in (11) is not the target of relativization, i.e. the *pro* with the index [i], but the *pro* with the index [j]. That *pro* is licensed and identified by the agreement morphology of the 'elsewhere' nominalization morpheme -*DIK*, and it is A'-bound by the 'large subject' that has been moved out of its canonical subject position, i.e. SpecAgrP, to SpecTop(ic)P. (Arguments for this landing site will be presented shortly; one reason for this analysis is that, if the operator has to end up in SpecCP, the 'large subject' must be in a different A'-position.) Since this *pro* is A'-bound in its smallest CFC, the A'-disjointness condition is violated, and thus this type of nominalization is ruled out.

Before continuing the discussion of this solution, I mention an alternative. A rival analysis would posit that the operator in question in fact never leaves its own domain and therefore does not need to land in SpecCP of the relative modifier clause; the operator moves to SpecCP of its own clause (or phrase, in the case of possessive nominal AgrPs), i.e. of the 'large subject', and stays there. The movement of the 'large subject' (presumably to SpecC[N]P, making the assumption of TopP unnecessary) could then be seen as an instance of pied piping, a process that has been posited to take place at LF (cf. Horváth 1996 for Hungarian) and in overt syntax (Ortiz de Urbina 1990 for Basque).[29]

However, the problem of resumptive pronouns appears here again. If the operator remains within its own clause or phrase, it would locally A'-bind a pronominal variable within that clause or phrase. Thus, we would predict that in 'long distance relativization', resumptive pronouns are just as bad as in simple relativization; however, resumptive pronouns are possible (albeit not perfect) in complex RCs, especially if they are focussed (cf. Kornfilt 1995a and 1995b):

(31) ?(?)[[öğretmen-i kendisin-in$_i$^{30} kov-acağ-ı] duy-ul -an] müdür$_i$
teacher-ACC himself-GEN fire-FUT-3SG hear-PASS -*(y)An* director
'The director who (it) was heard that HE was going to fire the teacher'

Similar changes in word order when focussing the overt, pronominal variable does not lead to a similar improvement of an ungrammatical *simple* RC, even where the morphology of the 'relative participle' is otherwise the correct one:

(32) *[müdür-ün   kendisin-i$_i$ kov-duğ -u]   ögretmen$_i$
director-GEN himself-ACC fire-*DIK* -3SG teacher
Still bad under the intended reading: 'The teacher who the director fired HIM'

Note that in a complex RC, too, it does not help to focus the resumptive pronoun, when the 'relative participle' is of the 'wrong' type (at least for the restrictive dialect; compare the following example with (31) to see this point):

(33) *[[öğretmen-i kendisin-in$_i$ kov-acağ -ın] -ın
teacher-ACC himself-GEN fire-FUT -3SG -GEN
duy-ul   -duğ -u]   müdür$_i$
hear-PASS -*DIK* -3SG director
Intended reading: 'The director who (it) was heard that HE was going to fire the teacher'

Furthermore, resumptive pronouns are sometimes even **required** in complex RCs, as we saw earlier when discussing island violations, while they are not possible at all in simple RCs. I conclude that even if there is pied piping in RCs, the operator must leave its host, and we face the problem of having to find a position for the operator, if we assume that a 'large subject' is in the specifier position of the nominal CP.

In order to avoid this problem, let us posit an additional projection in the clausal architecture of a Turkish nominalized clause; suppose that this phrase structural 'layer' is between the nominal AgrP and the 'nominal CP' (or DP) that dominates the AgrP. It is reasonable to characterize such a projection as a Top(ic)P[31]. Suppose, then, that the 'large subject' first moves to the specifier position of the TopP, and that 'relativization' applies afterwards, moving the operator to the specifier position of the 'nominal CP', i.e. of the modifier clause in the RC construction. This idea would capture an early proposal made by Kuno (1973), who suggests that the target of relativization in Japanese is the 'theme', i.e. the topic of a clause.

The representation of example (30) is now as follows:

(30′) *[$_{C[N]P_2}$ [Op_i] [$_{TopP_2}$ [$_{C[N]P_1}$ [t_i] [$_{Agr[N]P_1}$ [pro_i]^l öğretmen-i
                                                                                                 teacher-ACC
kov-acağ -ın^l] -ın]$_j$ [$_{Agr[N]P_2}$ [pro_j]^k hemen   duy-ul
fire-FUT -3SG -GEN   immediately hear-PASS
-duğ -u^k]]] müdür$_i$
-*DIK* -3SG director
Intended reading: 'The director who (it) was heard immediately that (he) was going to fire the teacher'

The offending A′-bound pronominal is the *pro* with the index [j], bound by the 'topicalized' sentential subject; that subject is in the specifier of the TopP, while the empty operator binding the target of relativization is in the specifier position of the 'nominal CP', i.e. the highest 'layer' of the relative modifier clause. (I am assuming that the TopP is not a barrier for the empty operator on its way from the specifier position of the lower CP to the specifier position of the higher nominal CP.)

Now note that, if we did not have the agreement with the superscript [k], no *pro* would be licensed in the specifier position of the nominal modifier clause:

(30″) [$_{C[N]P_2}$ [Op_i] [$_{TopP_2}$ [$_{C[N]P_1}$ [t_i] [$_{Agr[N]P_1}$ [pro_i öğretmen-i kov-acağ-ı]]$_j$
                                                                                       teacher-ACC fire-FUT-3SG
[$_{Agr[N]P_2}$ [e_j] hemen   duy-ul   -an]]] müdür$_i$
              immediately hear-PASS -*(y)An* director
'The director who (it) was heard immediately that (he) was going to fire the teacher'

The result is perfectly grammatical. Where we have no overt agreement heading the nominal modifier clause, we also don't have the 'elsewhere' morphology of -*DIK*; instead, we have the -*(y)An* morphology (which has no overt Agr). No *pro* is licensed and hence not possible. As a result, we have a variable bound by the large subject, but that variable is not a pronominal; consequently, the A′-Disjointness Condition is not violated.

What independent evidence do we have for this topicalization? In our previous discussion of empty object variables with pragmatic or discourse antecedents (cf. footnotes 23 and 31), we had assumed exactly this phenomenon. In the light of more recent theoretical work that has attributed additional structure to the 'COMP-layer' of the clause (as proposed, for example, in Rizzi 1994), this is a reasonable assumption to make. I assume that the topic operator occupies SpecTopP. Since space considerations preclude further discussion of this related, by nevertheless independent point about clause structure, I refer the reader to the evidence discussed in Rizzi (1994) and Bianchi (1994/95) (where an analysis is proposed for RCs that involves movement to SpecTopP, a phrase lower than CP, before further movement to SpecCP).

There might be one particular objection to the application of this analysis to relativization out of a sentential subject, and this is based on the work of Koster (1978), where it is claimed that sentential subjects do not exist in the strict sense. What looks like a sentential subject is actually located in a (left-)dislocated structure, coindexed with a pronoun in subject position. This analysis is designed to explain the fact that 'apparent' sentential subjects are syntactic islands, because dislocated domains are islands in general.[32]

This problem for the account under discussion is only apparent, however. In the account that I have proposed for Turkish relativization out of (apparent) sentential subjects, something similar to Koster's proposal in fact does play a role in the ungrammatical examples, i.e. in those instances where the 'wrong' nominalization choice has been made and where the modifying clause is headed by *-DIK*+Agr. In such instances, the sentential subject is indeed coindexed with a pronoun, and this is clearly bad. This shows that topicalization of a sentential subject in Turkish is not allowed if it is associated with a pronoun. This also means that, just as in German and Dutch, a sentential subject associated with a pronoun is a syntactic island in Turkish, as well.

However, if the domain is not headed by agreement (or is headed by abstract agreement), then topicalization of the sentential subject is possible, since there won't be any association with a pronoun. Sentential (and topicalized) subjects, then, can host a relativization variable only under obligatory absence of overt Agr heading the whole modifier clause (i.e. when the nominalization morpheme *-(y)An* is used rather than the 'elsewhere' nominalizer *-DIK* with its overt agreement).

We have now accounted for the 'Mother Node Principle' for extractions under relativization: extractions out of non-subjects give rise to the 'elsewhere' pattern (involving the *-DIK* suffix with overt agreement), for the same reasons as in simple RCs where non-subjects themselves are extracted. Extractions out of subjects give rise to the special pattern, involving the *-(y)An* suffix without overt agreement. In part, this is due to a Subject Constraint, itself a subjacency effect, now treated within the Barriers-framework. Where the 'large' subject has moved out of the canonical subject position to avoid a subjacency violation, the empty category left behind cannot be *pro*, to avoid a violation of the A'-Disjointness condition. If there is no overt agreement to identify and license *pro*, the result is grammatical in all dialects; if there is such overt agreement, the *pro* which that agreement identifies will lead to such violation and hence to ungrammaticality in the standard dialect.

I now turn to other instances where the 'elsewhere' pattern cannot be used in RCs, even though the target of relativization is not a subject.

3. Relative clauses with impersonal adjuncts

As has been noted in the literature (e.g. Underhill 1972; Hankamer & Knecht 1976), extracting non-subjects out of 'subjectless' clauses requires the 'Subject Participle'. It is more appropriate to analyze the constructions thus characterized by these earlier works as having no thematic subjects. For the time being, I shall be vague about the exact structural analysis of such constructions:

(34)   [e_i otobüs -*e*   bin   -il   -en]   durak$_i$
        bus   -DAT board -PASS -*(y)An* stop
'The stop where one boards the bus (i.e. where the bus is boarded)'

(35)   *[e_i otobüs -e   bin   -il   -diğ -i]   durak$_i$
        bus   -DAT board -PASS -*DIK* -3SG stop
[Intended reading: The same as in the previous example]

Example (34) illustrates relativization into an impersonal passive construction. Impersonal passives are constructions where there is no derived overt subject at S-Structure, because the verb is not genuinely transitive; in other words, the verb is either intransitive or assigns (checks) oblique Case, but no structural Case. Since only direct objects with structural (Accusative) Case can correspond to subjects in passive constructions, the passive structures with verbs like *bin* 'board, mount' which assign only oblique Cases have no overt subject, but rather only expletive subjects. An expletive subject is a *pro* in a NSL like Turkish.

Another type of RC where the target of relativization is a non-subject, yet where the standard dialect requires the 'subject participle' with -*(y)An* (rather than the 'elsewhere case' with -*DIK* with its agreement morpheme attached) is found with non-specific subjects. Such subjects do not occupy the canonical subject position, i.e. SpecAgrSP, but rather must immediately precede the verb. The canonical position of the subject, i.e. SpecAgrSP, is therefore occupied by an expletive *pro*, just as it is in impersonal passive constructions. Hence, the discussion in the text of this paper that centers around relativization out of impersonal passives is also applicable to relativizations out of clauses with non-specific subjects. I won't discuss the latter type of construction separately.

It would be appealing to attribute the choice of nominalization morphology in such constructions to the A'-Disjointness Principle, if one could claim that the target of relativization is in the subject position of the embedded clause, although that target is not a genuine subject. However, such a claim cannot be motivated independently, since non-subjects in such impersonal constructions do not exhibit subjecthood properties otherwise. One of these properties is overt agreement between subject and predicate:

(36)   pro$_{expl}$ otobüs-e bu durak-lar-da bin -il -ir (*-ler)
             bus-DAT this stop-PL-LOC board -PASS -AOR -3PL
             'One boards the bus at these stops'

Agreement facts illustrate only one type of subjecthood behavior; the locative object does not have other subject properties, either (e.g. undergoing ECM, ability of being controlled etc.). The following examples illustrate the difference with respect to such properties between a regular passive and an impersonal passive.

(37)   [Oya-yı öp -ül -dü] san -ıyor -um
         Oya-ACC kiss -PASS -PAST believe -PRESPROG -1SG
         'I believe Oya to have been kissed' [Successful ECM with regular passive.]

(38)   *[Oya-yı yardım ed -il -di] san -ıyor -um
         Oya-ACC help do -PASS -PAST believe -PRESPROG -1SG
         'I believe Oya to have been helped' [Unsuccessful ECM with impersonal passive.]

(39)   Oya$_i$ [PRO$_i$ öp -ül -mek] isti -yor
         Oya   kiss -PASS -INF want -PRESPROG
         'Oya wants to be kissed' [Successful Control with regular passive.]

(40)   *Oya$_i$ [PRO$_i$ yardım ed -il -mek] isti -yor
         Oya   help do -PASS -INF want -PRESPROG
         'Oya wants to be helped' [Unsuccessful Control with impersonal passive.]

The verb *öp* 'kiss' takes accusative objects, while the verb *yardım et* 'help' takes dative objects. While accusative objects correspond to subjects in regular passives, as we see in (37) and (39), dative (and other oblique) objects do not correspond to subjects in intransitive passives. The passive morphology, while obviously having the property of structural Case absorption familiar from better-studied languages, does not absorb oblique Case. Consequently, oblique objects continue receiving (or checking) their Case in the domain of the VP in impersonal passive constructions, and don't have to move to SpecAgrP for Case reasons.

Returning to RCs, we saw that where the relativization target is a locative object, we do not get the expected 'elsewhere' morphology. Not surprisingly, the same also holds for the **non-directional** dative object; in other words, although the dative object does not behave like a subject, its relativization 'triggers' the so-called subject participle morphology, rather than the 'elsewhere' object-participle morphology.

Note that the behavior of oblique objects other than just locatives (i.e. also of non-directional datives, ablatives and instrumentals) as objects rather than subjects in intransitive passive constructions is evidence that none of these oblique objects are subjects. This is important, because locatives have been claimed to exhibit subject properties in certain constructions in a variety of languages; for example, Kuno (1971) claims that in existentials, the locative of existentials is in subject position universally.[33] Supposing that this claim is true, it appears to be irrelevant for our present purposes. Note that the examples at issue presented earlier are not all existential constructions (this is true even for those examples above that do involve locatives), and that all oblique objects (and not just locatives) behave in the same fashion with respect to agreement, ECM, and Control — namely as objects and not subjects. There also is no evidence from adverb placement to show that any of those objects are subjects in impersonal passives. On the contrary, adverb placement remains the same with respect to oblique objects, irrespective of whether they appear in passives or non-passives. If so, the target of relativization in the corresponding RCs is not a subject, either. In turn, if that target, i.e. the variable, is not a subject, it cannot be *pro*, and hence the A'-Disjointness Condition cannot be invoked directly. Yet, when any such object is relativized, the 'subject participle' morphology is found.

That the same generalized binding condition B can be invoked after all is made possible by considering the proposal I made when introducing this section, namely that the non-thematic element occupying the canonical subject position is an expletive empty pronominal, i.e. pro_{expl}, much like in similar constructions in some of the Germanic languages, i.e. an empty counterpart of *es*.[34]

Pro_{expl} is licensed by overt Agr, as well as thematic instances of *pro*.[35] If the principle in (24) is correct for expletive *pro* as well as for referential *pro*, i.e. if an empty subject licensed by Agr **must** be *pro*, then the subject in impersonal passives must also be *pro* and cannot be one of the overt oblique objects. Furthermore, agreement facts point in the same direction. We saw earlier that in root clauses, oblique objects of impersonal passives don't agree with the predicate. In embedded contexts, too, oblique objects in impersonal passives as well as in constructions with non-specific subjects cannot agree with the nominalized verb; the only overt Agr element to be found in such embeddings is the unchanging, 'weak', 3.sg. agreement, which would license an expletive *pro*, but which certainly is not in a Spec/Head relationship with any oblique object, as the following examples illustrate for both types of 'impersonal' constructions:

(41) a. [*pro* bu havuz-lar-da balık ol-ma -sı] ne güzel!
 this pool-PL-DAT fish be-ANOM -3SG what nice
 'How nice it is that there are fish in this pool!'
 b. *[*pro* bu havuz-lar-da balık ol-ma -ları] ne güzel!
 this pool-PL-DAT fish be-ANOM -3PL what nice
 [Intended reading: Same as in the previous example.]

(42) a. [bu durak-lar-da otobüs-e bin -il -diğ -in]- i
 this stop-PL-LOC bus-DAT board -PASS -FNOM -3SG -ACC
 san-ıyor -um
 think-PRESPROG -1SG
 'I think that one boards buses at these stops'
 b. *[bu durak-lar-da otobüs-e bin -il -dik -lerin] -i
 this stop-PL-LOC bus-DAT board -PASS -FNOM -3PL -ACC
 san-ıyor -um
 think-PRESPROG -1SG
 [Intended reading: Same as in the previous example.]

(43) a. [ban-a yardım ed-il -eceğ -in] -e
 I-DAT help do-PASS -FUT -3SG -DAT
 inan -ıyor -um
 believe -PRESPROG -1.SG.
 'I believe that I shall be helped'
 [Literally: 'I believe that to me, help will be done']
 b. *[ban-a yardım ed-il -eceğ-im]-e inan -ıyor -um
 I-DAT help do-PASS -FUT-1SG-DAT believe -PRESPROG -1SG.
 [Intended reading: Same as in the previous example.]

In all of these examples, an oblique object of an embedded impersonal passive or of a clause with a non-specific subject co-occurs with 'weak' third person singular agreement on the nominalized embedded verb; an attempt to match the phi-features of such an oblique object with the nominal agreement on the embedded predicate leads to ungrammaticality in all instances. Furthermore, none of these oblique objects can show up in the Case typical for the subjects of nominalized embeddings, i.e. in the genitive. In addition, as mentioned and illustrated earlier, none of these objects can undergo Control or ECM. Hence, I conclude that the subject in these embedded impersonal passives and embedded clauses with non-specific subjects is an expletive *pro* rather than an oblique object.[36]

Surprisingly, as stated earlier, in constructions with either non-specific subjects or with impersonal passives, relativizing oblique objects necessitates the special morphology with -(y)An, lacking overt agreement. Can the A′-Disjointness Condition be invoked here?

I have been assuming all along that in Turkish RCs, an empty operator (or the head itself, in a Kaynian derivation) moves to SpecC[N]P, leaving behind a co-indexed, A′-bound variable which is an empty category (and is non-pronominal if it is not identified by overt agreement). I shall now also follow Chomsky (1986b) in assuming that the specifier of CP and the head C^0 of CP 'agree', in the sense that they share the index of the operator in the SpecCP position.[37] The additional assumption is made there that the head C^0 properly governs the subject of its IP complement in English RCs in the following configuration, and that such proper government is made possible through such index sharing (cf. Chomsky 1986b: 26–27); the Bavarian facts of complementizers that agree with subjects of their IP and allow for apparently successful ECP violations concerning subject extractions (cf. Bayer 1984) are open to such an analysis, as well:

(44)   NP [$_{CP}$ O [$_C$ that] IP]   [Chomsky 1986b: 27, ex. (51)]

In such a configuration, O is the empty operator of the 'relativization' and transmits its index to the C-head. This idea follows Pesetsky (1981), where this proposal is made to account for the well-known *que*-to-*qui* phenomenon in French; this phenomenon, then, can be viewed as a more concrete instance of the index transmission I am positing here.[38] By virtue of being the proper governor of the subject position, the C-head now transmits that index to the expletive *pro*-subject. Such index transmission to a pronominal subject via proper government is de facto possible, I suggest, only where the pronoun is non-thematic and is thus unable to have any sort of referential index of its own. Where the subject is thematic, it has its own inherent referential index; thus, index transmission is blocked, even for a phonologically empty pronoun, i.e. for a *pro* with a θ-role. Where that pronominal already bears the same index (i.e. where the subject is a pronominal variable), index transmission would be vacuous (and the configuration will be ruled out by the A′-Disjointness Condition as discussed). The proposed blocking of index transmission to a subject with an inherent index rules out a situation where the index of a **non-subject** variable is transmitted to a referential, thematic subject pronominal. Where the subject is a **non-pronominal** variable, such index transmission will be just what we want. If this is so, the **general** Turkish dichotomy between subject and non-subject relativization targets can be viewed as entirely parallel to the French *que*-to-*qui* alternation, and the facts of non-subject targets in impersonal constructions constitute an extention of that phenomenon.

Now, in a relative clause with a non-thematic subject we have a configuration of the following sort (after index transmission from the operator to the C-head, and further index assignment from that C-head to the subject of its complement IP under proper government; I have kept the representation as close as possible to Chomsky's schema for English and French):

(45) *NP$_i$ [$_{CP}$ Op_i [$_C$ e_i] [$_{Agr[N]P}$ [pro]$_i$ [Agr[N]^0] [$_{VP}$ ... t_i ...]]]^{39}

There are a number of ways to interpret this representation, all of which will mark the configuration as ill-formed. Given that the pronominal subject of the IP (i.e. of the nominal AgrP) bears the index of the operator and is thus locally bound by it (or by the contraction of that operator with the governing head C), it has the status of a pronominal bound variable; as such, it violates the A'-Disjointness condition. Further, by virtue of being a pronominal which is co-indexed with a variable (i.e. with the A'-bound target of relativization), the *pro*-subject gives rise to a strong crossover configuration, however analyzed (e.g. the 'leftness condition'; cf. Koopman & Sportiche 1982). Hence, we account for the ungrammaticality of Turkish RCs in which the target is a non-subject and the subject is a non-thematic *pro*.

How are the grammatical versions of such RCs (with the -(*y*)*An* morphology devoid of overt agreement) accounted for? Here is the relevant representation:

(46) NP [$_{CP}$ Op_i [$_C$ e_i] [$_{Agr[N]P}$ [e]$_i$ [$_{VP}$ ... e_i ...]]]

Now, the empty category in the subject position of the nominal AgrP is not *pro*, because *pro* is not licensed: there is no overt agreement element to act as a licenser. Hence, we have a locally A'-bound, nonpronominal variable in subject position which is properly governed and does not violate any known principles. However, if the VP-internal empty category is also a variable, it would be locally A-bound, which would lead to ill-formedness. I would therefore like to suggest that the VP-internal empty category is actually an anaphor in configurations like (46), and thus it is successfully A-bound. In other words, (46) is a representation similar to that of a subject extraction out of a (regular) passive clause. The only aspect of this representation which might appear somewhat out of the ordinary is the fact that the anaphoric empty category is not caseless. However, this should not be too bothersome. What is important about A-chains is that they should have one (and only one) θ-role, and this is what we find here. It is also required of A-chains that they have only one Case position. In the A-chain formed by the embedded subject and the VP-internal empty category, there appear to be two Cases: the oblique Case assigned to the foot of the chain, and the default abstract Case on the subject, i.e. the head of the chain. However, it is plausible to claim that abstract default Case is assigned only when needed, i.e. that this is the meaning of 'default'. When the subject position is contained in a chain that has a position with a Case, the abstract default Case is not assigned. Thus, the A-chain in (46) is well-formed: it has only one θ-role and only one Case. The fact that the unique θ-role is assigned to the foot of the chain is also what we usually find in A-chains. The only unusual aspect of this A-chain is the fact that its unique Case is assigned to the foot and not the head of the chain, and this might well be an option chosen more frequently than was realized heretofore.

In (46), then, we have two chains: an A-chain, as just discussed, consisting of the embedded subject position and the anaphor in embedded VP-internal position, and an A'-chain, consisting of the operator (or the contracted operator and C-head) and the non-pronominal variable in embedded subject position. There is no strong crossover violation, nor a violation of the A'-Disjointness condition.

The account proposed here for RCs with impersonal modifier clauses might appear to be costly (or ad hoc). We have made two assumptions here which (to my knowledge) have not been proposed elsewhere and thus have not been motivated by other phenomena in other languages: transmission of the index of a proper governor to its **pronominal** governee, and an empty anaphor in a Case-marked (or Case-checked) position. I have argued, however, that the second assumption does not really change more general tenets. As for the first assumption, it does not appear to be unnatural, either. If an indexed head governor can transmit its index to an empty variable in the subject position of its clausal complement, as proposed in the literature, it should also be able to transmit that index to a pronominal in that position, if that pronominal lacks any other (assigned or inherent) index.

It might be objected here that, in some sense, I have proposed an account that in effect posits a process which I had claimed earlier does not take place: the chains formed in the configuration of the grammatical examples are the same ones that are formed when relativizing a derived subject in a **regular** passive. In other words, it looks as though the oblique objects have, in fact, become derived subjects. However, in the account proposed here, the configurations I posited owe their existence to the operator and to index-sharing; they do not extend to configurations where there is no operator, and where oblique objects without variable status appear with passive morphology on the verb. In those constructions, we saw ample evidence against analyzing oblique objects as subjects. Thus, the account proposed captures precisely what we observe: oblique objects in impersonal passives behave like subjects **only** when they are relativized; in all other instances, they have properties that set them clearly apart from subjects.

Hence, it is appropriate to attribute their subject-like behavior in RCs to the operator that is part of such constructions.

4. Conclusions

We have now accounted for all the RC constructions in MST: simple RCs with targets in subject and non-subject position, complex RCs with targets within larger subjects (and, as an 'elsewhere' case, those with targets within larger non-subjects), and finally RCs with non-subject targets in clauses with non-thematic subjects. In all of these instances, so I claimed, the basic phenomenon to be explained is not the two different morphological forms heading the modifier clause, but rather the fact that one of these forms is 'linked' to overt (subject) agreement morphology, while the other form has no such overt agreement. In an attempt to explain the appearance of such agreement, this paper has centrally appealed to the A'-Disjointness condition. Thus, overt, rich agreement morphology was argued to be directly implicated syntactically, by a generalized version of Binding Theory. The facts of simple RCs with thematic subjects are exhaustively explained by this condition; when accounting for the facts of RCs with targets within larger subjects and for those with targets in 'impersonal' clauses, we saw that the A'-Disjointness condition continues to play a role, but a less central one, since it has to be complemented by other syntactic principles and phenomena (e.g. subjacency, topicalization, typology of Case, proper government, index transmission, chain formation, the leftness condition). Finally, we saw that the asymmetry in the morphology in Turkish RCs is rather similar to that found in French (*que* versus *qui*) and is best treated similarly, by assuming operator-variable configurations. Future work directed towards extending the account to non-standard varieties of the language is likely to find that it is in the interplay of the A'-Disjointness condition with other principles that dialect variations are likely to be found, and not in those instances where this condition is the only one implicated. A superficial survey of such facts as reported so far appears to bear out this prediction.

Notes

1. By using the term 'nominalization', I wish to remain neutral between the two descriptive terms 'participle' and 'gerund'. For distinguishing criteria see, among others, Trask (1993).
2. In citing morphemes, I follow the established custom in Turkish linguistics and use capital

letters to denote archiphonemes, i.e. phonemes with underdetermined feature values; those values are fully determined by vowel harmony for vowels, and by a variety of (de)voicing rules (in part of assimilatory nature) for consonants. Segments in parentheses are deleted in well-defined phonological contexts; e.g. the palatal glide in *-(y)An* is deleted after a vowel.

Special terms are abbreviated in the glosses as follows: ABL = Ablative, ABIL = Abilitative, FNOM = Factive Nominalization, ANOM = Action Nominalization, AOR = Aorist, OPT = Optative.

3. The only exception to this generalization is overt agreement marker on certain postpositions with the postpositional object. In these instances, it makes sense to analyze the phrase as a postpositional AgrP, and the apparent postpositional object as the specifier of the AgrP, in parallel to regular possessive DPs.
4. While an account of the historical development of these RCs does support Kayne's treatment of right-headed RCs (as involving raising of IP as well as raising of the head), space limitations preclude such a discussion here.
5. Turkish also has a head-initial RC construction, borrowed from Persian. This construction is rarely used in colloquial styles of MST; its use is restricted to written, official styles. I shall not consider this construction in this paper.
6. Resumptive pronouns can show up in simple RCs of the left-headed variety and will not concern us here. The right-headed RCs can also have resumptive pronouns, but only in long distance relativizations, as we shall see later.
7. The bracketing in this example and the following ones implies a derivation in the manner of Vergnaud (1974), with (rightward) raising of the head. As stated earlier, I do not wish to take a stand here on the exact derivation of these constructions; for present purposes, it is irrelevant whether the derivation is as suggested in Vergnaud (1974), or as proposed in Kayne (1994), or whether an empty operator has moved. I am using bracketing and coindexation here merely as a help for the reader in parsing the examples.
8. This generalization is provisional; the situation is more complex, as later discussion will show. I have glossed the occurrences of the nominalization suffixes simply with their corresponding phonologically underlying representations.
9. This generalization, too, is too simple; more discussion is offered later in the paper.
10. The reviewers point out that under the analysis proposed in Kayne (1994), both (2) and (3) have relative clause structure. In this paper, I am neutral between a 'traditional' approach towards RCs and the approach advocated by Kayne. What is important for my purposes here is not how various degrees of reduced RCs can be achieved in English (and other languages), but rather the fact that, despite superficial similarities, the nominalized RC constructions in Turkish are not lexical deverbal adjectives, as often claimed, but rather have syntactic properties that put them on a par with the 'regular' English RC type as in (3).
11. The *pro* in this example is licensed and identified by the agreement on the head of this possessive DP; this is expressed by the superscripts. Overt agreement with the possessor (i.e. with the specifier of this nominal AgrP) in terms of person and number is found in all possessive phrases, and *pro* is possible in all of them as the specifier. For further discussion, see Kornfilt (1984) and (1988).
12. Relativizing into other types of adjunct clauses is bad, as well. An in-depth discussion of this point is impossible here, due to space limitations. Among Ross's constraints, the CNPC is the clearest in Turkish. However, I claim in this paper that the Sentential Subject Constraint does hold in Turkish, despite appearances. The Coordinate Structure Constraint does hold in Turkish,

however that constraint is probably independent of subjacency. The *wh*-island constraint does not appear to hold independently of relativization into CNPs, i.e. it doesn't appear to hold with respect to *wh*-questions. However, note that *wh*-elements in Turkish are in-situ; thus, it is possible that *wh*-movement at LF does not obey subjacency. Note also that certain adjunct island effects with respect to both relativization and *wh*-questions can, in fact, be observed. Thus, Özsoy (1996) discusses some instances where *wh*-questions into certain RCs and into adjunct clauses are ungrammatical. If so, *wh*-movement in Turkish at LF would, in fact, have to obey subjacency, and the grammatical examples could then be analyzed as due to pied piping at LF (in the manner proposed by Nishigauchi 1990). Given that *wh*-movement takes place at LF as shown by the contrast between wide versus narrow-scope *wh*-questions (as in Kornfilt 1984, 1985 and 1993 and contra Kennelly 1997), the fact that the target of the relativization can be within an embedded *wh*-question is not problematic for the view that syntactic movement and subjacency are involved in relative clause formation in Turkish. It is claimed in Kennelly (1997) that a relative clause with a specific head is not an island with respect to further relativization; (8a) in the text shows that this is incorrect.

13. For additional discussion of island constraints in Turkish (in particular, of the Complex Noun Phrase constraint), see Kornfilt (1984) and Kornfilt, Kuno & Sezer (1980).

14. For more examples that illustrate the contrast exemplified in (8a) and (9a) versus (8b, c) and (9b), see Kornfilt (1977).

15. This is not to say that the ECP is irrelevant in Turkish RC constructions. Given that these are operator-variable structures, ECP effects should be expected for phonologically empty variables, and they are indeed found. Thus, where the 'offending', long-distance bound variable is an adjunct as in (8a), the ungrammatical examples such as those discussed in the text deteriorate even further.

16. Is this clause-like modifying domain a CP? The domain obviously has an 'escape hatch', i.e. a specifier position that serves as a landing site for a moving element. If a CP is a functional projection with verbal features, than the projection in question cannot be a CP; given its nominal nature, it would have to be a DP or, as proposed in Kornfilt (1984) and in Borsley & Kornfilt (2000), a nominal AgrP that has CP-like properties. (Note that the analysis based on a nominal AgrP for nominalized clausal domains was translated by Abney (1987) into his system as a DP). Here, I will at times refer to the modifier clause as a nominal(ized) CP.

17. This account of Turkish RCs would lead us to also expect CED-effects (cf. Huang 1982), e.g. adjunct-island effects. Such effects are indeed found; examples are offered in Kornfilt (1997b). It is interesting to note differences between Turkish and Japanese RCs. Tanaka (1998) notes that in Japanese RCs, adjuncts cannot serve as targets even in simple RCs, while complements can. Tanaka concludes that this asymmetry is due to the ECP, and that subjacency is irrelevant in Japanese 'relativization'. In Turkish, however, there is no adjunct/complement asymmetry in **simple** RCs; thus, the ECP plays no role here. The ECP plays a secondary role in explaining relativization **out of** adjuncts, while subjacency is needed in explaining island effects in general.

18. With this statement, I differ from many previous researchers who have described Turkish RCs, and in the generative literature perhaps most extremely from Pustejovsky (1984) . I also differ from Comrie (1997), who analyzes modifiers with *-(y)An* as participles and those with *-DIK* as 'verbal nouns', i.e. presumably as gerunds. I don't want to rule out the possibility that further in-depth analysis might justify positing some structural difference between modifiers headed by *-DIK* and those headed by *-(y)An*. Such an alternative is considered in the text.

19. McCloskey (1990) presents facts about RCs in Modern Irish that are quite similar to their Turkish counterparts, particularly to those concerning simple RCs. However, in Irish as well as

some of the other languages (cf. Suñer 1998) which also appear to have a condition similar to the A′-Disjointness Condition in (11), the situation is more complex than in Turkish, since resumptive pronouns are allowed in non-subject positions in **simple** RCs, and are even obligatory in certain positions. Thus, in Irish, resumptive pronouns in simple RCs are optional (while less preferred than an empty variable) in direct object position (cf. McCloskey 1979 and 1990), and they are obligatory in genitive possessor positions and as prepositional objects.

20. In Ouhalla (1993), it is claimed that in Kornfilt (1984) and (1991), after mentioning an approach to Turkish RC morphology based on a generalized version of Condition B, I reject it. This is not so, however; in those works, I mention that an extension of the account to non-subject targets is not obvious, but without rejecting the account for simple relatives. In the present paper, I make the same claim, and I attempt such an extension.

21. The reflexive here is not a genuine anaphor, but a kind of logophoric pronominal. For discussion, see Kornfilt (1997a).

22. This situation is indeed found in some contemporary languages like Uzbek and Turkmen. A longer version of this paper (Kornfilt 1997b) discusses this point in detail, with reference to data presented in Sjoberg (1962) and Nepesova (1979).

23. Throughout this paper, it has been important to assume that Turkish nominalized RCs are operator-variable constructions, although the operator is not overt (in the traditional approach). Additional evidence for such an operator comes from systematic differences between embedded clauses that are operator-variable structures (e.g. RCs and comparative constructions) and those that are not. Discussion of these would far exceed the limits of this paper. I nevertheless mention two phenomena where an A′-bound variable, bound by an abstract operator, has been posited for similar constructions in other languages; these are parasitic gap constructions and empty objects. Especially the latter phenomenon is of some interest, and the former might possibly be subsumed under the latter in the languages that have both. Turkish is one of the languages (some others are Chinese, Japanese and Portuguese) where constituents can be 'elided' in certain pragmatic or discourse contexts. It has been proposed for similar phenomena in other languages (cf. Huang 1984; Raposo 1986) that these 'elided' constituents are variables that are locally bound by an **empty** operator (and that operator, in turn, is bound by a pragmatic or discourse antecedent). These operator-bound empty variables are not pronouns, in contrast to empty subjects which do have pronominal properties. Evidence for this difference comes from the different binding properties of these elements: while an empty subject variable in these languages exhibits pronominal properties (e.g. obeys Binding Principle B), the empty object variable behaves as an empty R-expression (i.e. obeys Binding Principle C), just like familiar instances of variables. The arguments based on Portuguese and Chinese examples in Raposo (1986) and Huang (1984), respectively, carry over to Turkish straightforwardly. In these works, the topicalization operator is claimed to be located in SpecCP. Later in the text, when discussing relativization out of larger subjects, I shall claim that this operator is instead located in the specifier position of a Topic Phrase which is dominated by CP and itself dominates AgrP.

24. Under the respective frameworks of Alexiadou (1997) and Cinque (1999), different types of adverbs are located in specifier positions of various levels of phrasal projections. The fact that sentential adverbs can be included in modifier clauses with *-(y)An* shows that an analysis positing clausal-level projections (and thus at least a level of TP [Tense Phrase] or MP [Mood Phrase] is indicated.

25. In some more recent work, it has been observed that the situation is more complex. While the facts as characterized in the text do hold for the standard style of MST and are accepted by all speakers, there are some speakers who accept — and produce — RCs with *-DIK*+Agr in some

contexts where the 'standard', restrictive dialect allows only forms with -*(y)An* (cf. Barker, Hankamer & Moore 1990; Zimmer 1987 and 1996; Csató 1985, and, as an early work where similar observations are made, Kornfilt 1974).

26. As mentioned in the introduction, I claim here that the Sentential Subject Constraint holds in Turkish. I shall argue later in the text that apparent successful violations take place only when the sentential subject is not in canonical subject position.

27. An overtly case-marked subject can scramble away from its canonical position, just like any overtly case-marked constituent can — hence the proviso in the text about the unmarked word order.

28. The possibility for a solution along these lines is mentioned by Ouhalla (1993) in passing, but without any discussion as to execution or independent evidence.

29. Another instance of syntactic pied piping of a clausal host for the target of relativization is the construction of pied piped infinitives in German, studied in v. Riemsdijk (1984); I am indebted to one of the referees for pointing this out to me. However, this construction is different in two respects: the host is limited to infinitives in German, but there is no such limitation in Turkish; and under v. Riemsdijk's analysis, the host of the relativization target is situated in the SpecCP position of the modifier clause, while the relativization operator itself remains in the lower SpecCP, i.e. the SpecCP of its host. As we shall see shortly in the text, I claim that the operator binding the relativization variable must leave the domain of the host in the Turkish construction.

30. In this and the following two examples, I have used the logophoric pronoun rather than the regular pronoun, since it is the more felicitous one in long distance binding contexts (cf. Kornfilt 1997a). The contrast which is important here between (relative) acceptability of resumptive pronouns in complex RCs versus unacceptability of such pronouns in simple RCs is found with regular pronouns, as well.

31. In a variety of 'topic-oriented' languages (e.g. Japanese, Korean) it is very reasonable to assume the existence of such a phrase; not only do a number of syntactic phenomena make this assumption plausible, there is also a special morphological topic marker (e.g. *-wa* in Japanese) that marks a topic. It would make sense to posit a similar projection for Turkish, whose syntax exhibits a variety of syntactic similarities to such languages, even though there is no overt topic marker (as opposed to Left Dislocation markers which do exist). Hence, the head of the TopP I just posited as a possibility in the text would have to be empty in Turkish.

32. I am indebted to Richie Kayne for pointing this out to me.

33. There are more recent, detailed studies that make the same point for individual languages and language families. Bresnan & Kanerva (1989) offer a thorough study of Chichewa locative inversion, and Collins (1997) sketches an account of locative inversion in English. In both studies, locative expressions are analyzed as structural subjects. However, the facts described in these studies and those in Turkish impersonal passives are quite different. While an exhaustive description cannot be offered here due to space restrictions, I shall mention just a few. In Chichewa, the finite verb agrees (obligatorily) with the locative phrase in inversion constructions; locative inversion is possible with definite, referential subjects; neither of these properties hold in comparable Turkish constructions. Impersonal passives in Turkish are therefore clearly different from locative inversion. As for Collins's analysis of English locative inversion, it is important for his account that the verbs that allow this phenomenon be unaccusatives. However, there is no such restrictions on impersonal passives in Turkish; one of the verbs that we saw in the text, i.e. *yardım et* 'help' is clearly not an unaccusative verb.

34. If the proposal made in the text is on the right track, Turkish would be more like Yiddish, where the (overt) expletive is in SpecIP, rather than German, where it is in SpecCP. This proposal is further discussed in Kornfilt (1991) and (1996 a, b).
35. For discussion of this point, see Kornfilt (1996 a, b).
36. In addition to what was said earlier about differences between Turkish impersonal passives and Chichewa locative inversion, consider the fact that in contrast to the evidence in Turkish for the existence of expletive *pro* subjects, Chichewa has no evidence in favor of positing such an element (according to Bresnan & Kanerva 1989).
37. Such index sharing between the specifier and the head can be viewed as a special instance of a more generalized version of the *wh*-Criterion proposed in Rizzi (1991). In Kornfilt (1995c: 51), I proposed such an extension, which I call 'Operator Criterion'. That extension is based on quite different facts (in particular, on facts regarding infinitival versus subjunctive versus factive RCs and embedded questions) than those analyzed in the present paper.
38. As a matter of fact, it would be interesting to view the whole area of *-(y)An~-DIK* alternations as akin to the *que*-to-*qui* alternation. I leave the implementation of this idea to further research.
39. Pesetsky proposes that as a result of index transmission from the operator to the C, a process of contraction takes place that merges the operator with the C-head of the CP. Whether such a process applies or not in Turkish RCs is not relevant for our purposes here.

References

Abney, S. (1987). *The English noun phrase in its sentential aspects.* Doctoral dissertation, MIT.
Alexiadou, A. (1997). *Adverb placement: a case study in antisymmetric syntax.* Amsterdam: Benjamins.
Aoun, J. & A. Li. (1989). *Two cases of logical relations: bound pronouns and anaphoric relations.* Manuscript, USC.
Barker, C., J. Hankamer & J. Moore. (1990). *Wa* and *ga* in Turkish. Manuscript, UCSC.
Bayer, J. (1984). COMP in Bavarian syntax. *The Linguistic Review* 3: 209–274.
Bianchi, V. (1994–95). *Consequences of antisymmetry for the syntax of headed relative clauses.* Doctoral dissertation, Scuola Normale Superiore, Pisa.
Borer, H. (1984). Restrictive relatives in modern Hebrew. *Natural Language and Linguistic Theory* 2: 219–260.
Borsley, R. & J. Kornfilt. (2000). Mixed Extended Projections. *The Nature and Function of Syntactic Categories*, edited by R. Borsley, 101–131. New York: Academic Press.
Bresnan, J. & J. M. Kanerva. (1989). Locative inversion in Chichewa: a case study of factorization in grammar. *Linguistic Inquiry* 20: 1–50.
Chomsky, N. (1981). *Lectures on government and binding.* Dordrecht: Foris.
Chomsky, N. (1986a). *Knowledge of language: its nature, origin and use.* New York: Praeger.
Chomsky, N. (1986b). *Barriers.* Cambridge, Mass.: MIT Press.
Chomsky, N. (1995). *The Minimalist program.* Cambridge, Mass.: MIT Press.

Cinque, G. (1999). *Adverbs and functional heads: a cross-linguistic perspective*. Oxford: Oxford University Press.
Collins, C. (1997). *Local economy*. Cambridge, Mass.: MIT Press.
Comrie, B. (1997). Turkic languages and linguistic typology. *Turkic Languages* 1: 14–24.
Csató, E. (1985). A syntactic analysis of participle constructions in modern Turkish. In *Beşinci Milletler Arası Türkoloji Kongresi, Tebliğler: Türk Dili* 1, 39–56. İstanbul: İstanbul Üniversitesi
Hankamer, J. & L. Knecht (1976). The role of the subject/non-subject distinction in determining the choice of relative clause participle in Turkish. *NELS* 4: 123–135.
Horváth, J. (1996). *The status of "*Wh-*expletives" and the partial* Wh-*Movement construction of Hungarian*. Manuscript, Tel-Aviv University.
Huang, J. (1982). *Logical relations in Chinese and the theory of grammar*. Doctoral dissertation, MIT.
Huang, J. (1984). On the distribution and reference of empty pronouns. *Linguistic Inquiry* 15, 531–574.
Jaeggli, O. (1984). Subject extraction and the null subject parameter. *NELS* 14: 132–153.
Jaeggli, O. & K. Safir. (1989). The null subject parameter and parametric theory. *The null subject parameter*, edited by O. Jaeggli & K. Safir, 1–44. Dordrecht: Kluwer.
Kayne, R. (1994). *The antisymmetry of syntax*. Cambridge, Mass.: MIT Press.
Kennelly, S. (1997). The P-focus position in Turkish. *GLOW Newsletter* 38: 34–45.
Koopman, H. & D. Sportiche. (1982). Variables and the bijection principle. *The Linguistic Review* 2: 365–391.
Kornfilt, J. (1974). *Wanderings under some hills and NPs (in some Turkish complex constructions)*. Manuscript, Tel-Aviv University.
Kornfilt, J. (1977). Against the universal relevance of the shadow pronoun hypothesis. *Linguistic Inquiry* 8: 412–418.
Kornfilt , J. (1984). *Case marking, agreement, and empty categories in Turkish*. Doctoral dissertation, Harvard University.
Kornfilt, J. (1985). Infinitival relative clauses and complementation in Turkish. *CLS* 21: 221–235.
Kornfilt, J. (1988). A typology of morphological agreement and its syntactic consequences. *Papers from the parasession on agreement in grammatical theory, CLS* 24: 117–134.
Kornfilt, J. (1991). Some current issues in Turkish syntax. *Turkish linguistics today*, edited by H. Boeschoten & L. Verhoeven, 60–92. Leiden: E. J. Brill.
Kornfilt, J. (1993). Infinitival WH-constructions and complementation in Turkish. *Eurotyp working papers, Group 3: Subordination and Complementation*, vol. 4: edited by K. Börjars and N. Vincent, 66–83. European Science Foundation.
Kornfilt, J. (1995a). *Focusing and de-focusing in Turkish*. Paper presented to the Department of Linguistics, University of Stuttgart.
Kornfilt, J. (1995b). *On problems of so-called free word order in Turkish*. Paper presented to BERLINCO, Technical University, Berlin.

Kornfilt, J. (1995c). Constraints on free relative clauses in Turkish. *FAS Papers in Linguistics* 4, edited by A. Alexiadov, N. Fuhrhop, P. Law, S. Lökken, 36–57. Berlin: Forschungsschwerpunkt für Allgemeine Sprachwissenschaft.

Kornfilt, J. (1996a). NP-movement and 'restructuring'. *Current issues in comparative grammar*, edited by R. Freidin, 121–147. Dordrecht: Kluwer.

Kornfilt, J. (1996b). Turkish and configurationality. *Current issues in Turkish linguistics*, edited by B. Rona, 111–125. Ankara: Hitit Yayınevi.

Kornfilt, J. (1997a). *Long-distance and other reflexives in Turkish*. Manuscript, Syracuse University. Presented at the Workshop on long distance reflexives, LSA Summer Institute, Cornell University.

Kornfilt, J. (1997b). *Synchrony and diachrony of relative clauses and possessive phrases in Turkish*. Manuscript, Syracuse University.

Kornfilt, J., S. Kuno & E. Sezer (1980). A note on crisscrossing double dislocation. *Harvard Studies in Syntax and Semantics*, vol. 3: edited by S. Kuno, 185–242. Cambridge, Mass.: Harvard University.

Koster, J. (1978). Why subject sentences don't exist. *Recent transformational studies in European languages*, edited by S. Keyser, 53–64. Cambridge, Mass: MIT Press.

Kuno, S. (1971). The position of locatives in existential sentences. *Linguistic Inquiry* 11: 333–378.

Kuno, S. (1973). *The structure of the Japanese language*. Cambridge, Mass.: MIT Press.

Levin, J. (1983). Government relations and the structure of INFL. *MIT Working Papers in Linguistics* 5: 121–150.

McCloskey, J. (1979). *Transformational Syntax and Model Theoretic Semantics: A Case Study in Modern Irish*. Dordrecht: Reidel.

McCloskey, J. (1990). Resumptive pronouns, A'-binding, and levels of representation. *Irish. Syntax and Semantics: The Syntax of the Modern Celtic Languages* edited by R. Hendricks, 199–238. New York: Academic Press.

Nepesova, R.G. (1979). *Contrastive morphology of modern English and Turkmen*. Ashkabad.

Nishigauchi, T. (1990). *Quantification in the theory of grammar*. Dordrecht: Kluwer.

Ortiz de Urbina, J. (1990). Operator feature percolation and clausal pied-piping. *Papers on Wh-Movement*, [*MIT Working Papers in Linguistics* 13], edited by L. Cheng & H. Demirdash, 193–208.

Ouhalla, J. (1993). Subject-extraction, negation and the anti-agreement effect. *Natural Language and Linguistic Theory* 11: 477–518.

Özsoy, S. (1996). A'-dependencies in Turkish. *Current issues in Turkish linguistics*, edited by B. Rona, 139–158. Ankara: Hitit Yayınevi.

Partee, B. (1975). Deletion and variable binding. *Formal semantics of natural languages*, edited by E. Keenan, 16–34. Cambridge: Cambridge University Press.

Pesetsky, D. (1981). Complementizer-trace phenomena and the nominative island condition. *The Linguistic Review* 1: 297–343.

Pustejovsky, J. (1984). *Studies in generalized binding*. Doctoral dissertation. University of Massachusetts, Amherst.

Raposo, E. (1986). On the null object in European Portuguese. *Studies in Romance linguistics*, edited by O. Jaeggli & C. Silva-Corvalan, 373–390. Dordrecht: Foris.
van Riemsdijk, H. (1984). On pied-piped infinitives in German relative clauses. *Studies in German grammar*, edited by J. Toman, 165–192. Dordrecht: Foris.
Rizzi, L. (1982). Negation, *Wh*-movement and the null subject parameter. *Issues in Italian Syntax*, 117–184. Dordrecht: Foris.
Rizzi, L. (1986). Null objects in Italian and the theory of *pro*. *Linguistic Inquiry* 17: 501–557.
Rizzi, L. (1991). Residual verb second and the *Wh*-criterion. *Technical Reports in Formal and Computational Linguistics*, Faculté des Lettres, Université de Genève.
Rizzi, L. (1994). *The fine structure of the left periphery*. Manuscript, University of Geneva.
Ross, J. R. (1967). *Constraints on variables in syntax*. Doctoral dissertation, MIT
Sjoberg, A. F. (1962). *Uzbek structural grammar*. Uralic and Altaic Series, vol. 18. Bloomington: Indiana University and The Hague: Mouton.
Suñer, M. (1998). Resumptive restrictive relatives: a crosslinguistic perspective. *Language* 74: 335–364.
Tanaka, H. (1998). *Conditions on logical form: derivations and representations*. Doctoral dissertation, McGill University, Montréal.
Trask, R. L. (1993). *A dictionary of grammatical terms in linguistics*. London: Routledge.
Underhill, R. (1972). Turkish participles. *Linguistic Inquiry* 3: 87–99.
Vergnaud, J.-R. (1974). *French relative clauses*. Doctoral dissertation, MIT.
Zimmer, K. (1987). Turkish relativization revisited. *Studies on modern Turkish*, edited by H. Boeschoten and L. Verhoeven, 57–61. Tilburg: Tilburg University Press.
Zimmer, K. (1996). Overlapping strategies in Turkish relativization. *Current issues in Turkish linguistics*, edited by B. Rona, 159–164. Ankara: Hitit Yayınevi.

On Relative Clauses and the DP/PP Adjunction Asymmetry[*]

Paul Law
ZAS Berlin

1. Introduction

Emonds (1976) pointed out a curious DP/PP asymmetry in non-finite relative clauses (RCs): a *wh*-phrase may occur in the clause-initial position of the RC only if it is preceded by a preposition (cf. also Chomsky and Lasnik 1977). The sharp contrast between DP and PP is illustrated in (1) and (2):

(1) a. *The man who(m) to talk about.
    b. The man about whom to talk.

(2) a. *The man who(m) to discuss linguistics with.
    b. The man with whom to discuss linguistics.

When the RC is finite, however, the DP/PP asymmetry observed in (1) and (2) is completely absent:

(3) a. The man who(m) I should talk about.
    b. The man about whom I should talk.

(4) a. The man who(m) I should discuss linguistics with.
    b. The man with whom I should discuss linguistics.

---

[*] Parts of this paper were presented at the Arbeitsgruppe DP-Modifikation, Deutsche Gesellschaft für Sprachwissenschaft Jahrestagung, Düsseldorf in February 1997, and the School of Oriental and Asian Studies, London in January 1998. I would like to thank Wynn Chao, Norbert Corver, Marcel den Dikken, Ruth Kempson, Annabel Cormack, Anna Pettiward, David Swinburne for stimulating discussions. I am indebted to Chris Wilder for many very helpful comments on earlier versions of this paper. I assume responsibility for any inadequacy.

The examples in (1)–(4) apparently show that the finiteness of the RC has a bearing on the category of the *wh*-phrase that appears in the clause-initial position.

There is another dimension along which the DP/PP asymmetry varies. As shown in (5)–(6), the preposition need not be pied-piped along with its *wh*-DP argument, if the landing site is the clause-initial position of a non-finite embedded question, standardly assumed to be the SpecCP position:

(5) a. I wondered who(m) to talk about.
    b. I wondered about whom to talk.
(6) a. I wondered who(m) to discuss linguistics with.
    b. I wondered with whom to discuss linguistics.

Given the lack of the DP/PP asymmetry in finite RCs as seen in (3) and (4), it comes as no surprise that the *wh*-DP argument of a preposition need not pied-pipe the preposition along when it lands in the clause-initial position of a finite embedded question:

(7) a. I wondered who(m) I should talk about.
    b. I wondered about whom I should talk.
(8) a. I wondered who(m) I should discuss linguistics with.
    b. I wondered with whom I should discuss linguistics.

The examples in (1)–(8) constitute a paradigm case that is all but too familiar in linguistic theory: the surface form often obscures the underlying syntactic properties. For instance, the same surface form *who(m) to talk about* or *who(m) to discuss linguistics with* appears in both (1a)–(2a) and (5a)–(6a), but only the latter are grammatical. The inevitable conclusion is that the same surface form appearing in different syntactic environments may have different syntactic representations and properties.

The limited distribution of *wh*-phrases in RCs and embedded questions can thus be summarized in the table in (9):

(9)
In the left-peripheral position of	finite	non-finite
relative clauses	PP/DP	PP/*DP
embedded questions	PP/DP	PP/DP

The peculiar gap in the distribution of DPs in the table in (9) might seem insignificant from the data point of view in that what has to be accounted for is just a rather small part of a larger paradigm. However, it is precisely this curious small gap in the paradigm that raises many fundamental questions for linguistic theory, and is therefore theoretically interesting. Why should DPs be singled out as having more limited distribution than PPs instead of the other way round? Why should it be that DPs just cannot appear in the clause-initial position of a non-finite RC instead of any one of the other three logical possibilities in (9), or any combination thereof? What syntactic properties of RCs are related to this peculiar ban on DPs? Given the very specific syntactic enviroment in which DP is excluded as indicated in (9), it would be a very remarkable property of English if its grammar contains a special constraint just to rule out DPs in the structures in (1a) and (2a). One thus might wonder whether there are not any other syntactic contexts of which the DP/PP asymmetry holds and which can be related to the paradigm in (9).

From the perspective of language acquisition, the problem is all the more pressing. Competent speakers of English are not likely to be told that examples like (1a) and (2a) are impossible. So the question is how they could, without explicit instructions, come to acquire the knowledge that DPs are not possible in the clause-initial position of a non-finite RC.

In order to solve these syntactic and acquisition problems, linguistic theory should make no appeal to construction-specific constraints. Rather, it must bring independent properties to bear on the limited distribution of DPs. Only in this way can we give an explanatory account for the curious gap in (9) and for why speakers need not be explicitly told of the specific structure in which a DP is excluded, since the peculiarity of the paradigm in (9) necessarily follows from knowledge of independent principles.

I argue that the DP/PP asymmetry in non-finite RCs is not an isolated phenomenon as the table in (9) suggests, but is related to the general asymmetry between DPs and PPs with respect to adjunction. More specifically, it falls under the purview of the constraint on landing sites (cf. Emonds 1976). I show that the analyses by Emonds (1976) as well as by Chomsky and Lasnik (1977) for the DP/PP asymmetry are inadequate in several respects, especially when non-finite contexts other than RCs are taken into consideration (Section 2). I discuss two independent issues regarding infinitivals and RCs. One is the categorial feature of the infinitival marker *to* (Section 3), and the other is the formal properties of questions and RCs (Section 4). I argue that they are related to the general distributional difference between DP and PP in finite clauses, and show that the peculiar gap in the paradigm in (9) falls under the same account without additional assumption (Section 5). To the extent that my claims are correct, they not only shed light on these independent issues bearing on the syntactic difference between DP and PP, but also have far-reaching theoretical consequences for a range of constructions that are thought to involve null operators (cf. Chomsky 1982) (Section 6).

I assume throughout this paper that in English internal arguments of a predicate appearing to its left on the surface are in non-argument positions, but the exact nature of the position, e.g. whether it is a Spec or an adjoined position, must be argued for on independent grounds.

2. Previous accounts for the DP/PP asymmetry

In this section, I discuss two previous accounts for the ban on DP in the clause-initial position of a non-finite clause, which to the best of my knowledge are the only ones that have come to light since the problem was first pointed out more than twenty years ago.[1] I show that these two accounts are inadequate in several respects.

2.1 For-*phrase formation in infinitivals*

Emonds (1976) proposed as a general hypothesis concerning permissible transformations that movement operations are subject to the structure-preserving constraint (SPC) limiting movement of a phrase to positions where it can be base-generated (as they are not directly relevant, root transformations would not be discussed here):

(10)   a.   *Structure-preserving transformation*
          A transformation (or a transformational operation, in the case of a transformation performing several operations) that introduces or substitutes a constituent C into a position in a phrase marker held by a node C is called "structure-preserving".
     b.   *Structure-preserving constraint*
          Major grammatical transformational operations are either root or structure-preserving operations.

The obvious virtue of the SPC is that it puts a constraint on landing sites in requiring that they be independently justified.

Emonds thus argued that the reason why PP may, but DP may not, appear to the immediate left of a RC is due to the interaction between the SPC and a series of transformation operations, which has the consequence that this position can host a PP but not a DP. The analysis runs as follows. A clause is generated in the base by the phrase structure rule in (11), and a rule of *for*-phrase formation in (12) applies to it to create a PP headed by the complementizer *for* with the subject of the infinitive as its argument:

(11)　　S → Comp　　− NP − ..

$$\left(\left\{\begin{array}{l}\text{WH}\\\text{FOR}\end{array}\right\}\right)$$

(12)　　*For*-phrase formation
　　　　$X - [_{\text{COMP}} \text{FOR}] - \text{NP} - Y \Rightarrow 1 - [_{\text{PP}} 2+3] - \emptyset - 4$

Some deletion rules apply to delete *for* and its argument, giving rise to a phonetically empty PP. As a result, a PP, but not a DP, may move to this empty PP position in accord with the SPC. Thus, the derivation of an example like (13a) would be as in (13b) (Δ indicates a phonetically null category):

(13)　a.　I found an usher from whom to buy tickets.
　　　b.　Derivation:
　　　　　Input:　　I found an usher for I to buy tickets from whom.
　　　　　For-phrase formation:
　　　　　　　　$X - [_{\text{COMP}} \text{FOR}] - \text{I} - Y \Rightarrow 1 - [_{\text{PP}} \text{ for me}] - \emptyset - 4$
　　　　　Deletion rules:　　I found an usher [$_{\text{PP}}$ Δ] to buy tickets from whom.
　　　　　Movement of PP:　I found an usher [$_{\text{PP}}$ from whom] to buy tickets.

Thus, from the SPC perspective, the fact that a DP may not move to the immediate left of a RC follows straightforwardly, regardless of whether the *for*-phrase is present or not, there simply being no DP-position for it to move to:

(14)　a.　*I found an usher who(m) (for Mary) to buy tickets from.
　　　b.　*Some tools which (for you) to fix the table will soon arrive.

Emonds (1976: 196–197) argued that the rule of *for*-phrase formation has independent justification, pointing out that the grammatical constrast between (15) and (16) would have exactly the same explanation as that for (17), if the *for* and the subject of the infinitive in (16) is a PP, since adverbials generally cannot intervene between a preposition and its argument:

(15)　a.　Mary asked me if, in St. Louis, John could rent a house cheap.
　　　b.　They built machines that, during lunch hours, businessmen can exercise on.
(16)　a.　*Mary arranged for, in St. Louis, John to rent a house cheap.
　　　b.　*They built machines for, during lunch hours, businessmen to exercise on.

(17) a. *They bought the house for, in St Louis, John.
b. *The built the machines for, in the workshop, the businessmen.

If the infinitival marker *to* appears with verb phrases that are not specially marked by the participle morphemes (*ing* or *en*) and have lost their subjects (for example, as a result of subject raising, equi-NP deletion, or deletion of the subject *one*), then one might take the occurrence of the infinitival marker *to* in a case like (13a) as evidence that the verb phrase in this example has lost its subject, which is precisely the effect of *for*-phrase formation. Moreover, if pronouns have subjective case only if they are dominated by S, i.e. in SpecIP in current frameworks (cf. *it's me/him* and *me and him left* in some dialects), then the fact that the pronominal subjects of infinitivals have objective case implies that they are not dominated by S, consistent with the idea that the subject of the infinitival is reanalyzed by *for*-phrase formation as the argument of the preposition *for*.

The rule of *for*-phrase formation has a number of problems, however. First, it fails to distinguish what may follow *for* when it appears as a complementizer and when it heads a PP. As shown in (18), the subject of an infinitival may be non-argumental, either the expletive *there* or an idiom chunk:

(18) a. Mary arranged for there to be a live band at the party.
b. They allowed for tabs to be kept on Bill.

But neither the expletive *there* nor an idiom chunk can be objects of a preposition:

(19) a. Mary arranged for a party/*there.
b. They allowed for business expenses/*tabs.

Thus, there is no reason to think that *for* forms a PP with the expletive *there* or with an idiom chunk in (18) as a result of the application of the rule of *for*-phrase formation.

Second, it fails to explain the binding properties in the infinitival. As shown in (20), the subject of the infinitival can bind a reflexive in the infinitival, but other phrases outside it may not:

(20) a. Every girl$_i$ found an usher$_k$ [for John$_j$ to buy himself$_{j/*k}$/*herself$_i$ a ticket from]
b. Bill$_i$ looked for a woman$_k$ [for John$_j$ to talk to about himself$_{j/*i}$/*herself$_k$]

According to Emonds' analysis, the PPs *from whom* and *to whom* in (21) would be just like the PP *for John* in (20), the latter being the result of the rule of *for*-phrase formation. Now, given that *John* in (20) may bind the reflexive, *whom* in (21a) should be able to bind it as well, since the two occur in exactly the same position. But it cannot:

(21) a. Every girl$_i$ found an usher$_k$ [from whom$_k$ to buy herself$_i$/*himself$_k$ a ticket]
 b. John$_i$ looked for a woman$_k$ [to whom$_k$ to talk about himself$_i$/*herself$_k$]

Moreover, if the infinitival loses its subject as a consequence of the application of the rule of *for*-phrase formation in both (20) and (21), then there is no obvious reason why the reflexive apparently must be bound by the argument of the preposition *for* within the infinitival in (20) but not in (21).

The problem for binding in (20) and (21) would have a straightforward account if contrary to Emonds' analysis the infinitival in fact does not lose its subject. Suppose the implicit subject of the infinitival in (21) is represented by PRO (cf. Chomsky 1973) coreferential with a matrix constituent as in (22), then it can bind the reflexive in the infinitival, just like the overt subject *John* in (20):

(22) a. Every girl$_i$ found an usher$_k$ [from whom$_k$ PRO$_i$ to buy herself$_i$/*himself$_k$ a ticket]
 b. John$_i$ looked for a woman$_k$ [to whom$_k$ PRO$_i$ to talk about himself$_i$/*herself$_k$]

Third, it goes without saying that the rule of Equi-NP deletion is itself problematic. As is well-known, the example in (23a) cannot be derived from the structure in (23b) by deleting the embedded subject, since the interpretation of the latter is not the same as that of the former:

(23) a. Every girl wanted to leave.
 b. Every girl wanted every girl to leave.

Consequently, there would be no source from which the example in (24a) may be said to have been derived:

(24) a. Every girl found an usher [to buy herself a ticket from]
 b. Every girl found an usher [for every girl to buy herself a ticket from]

More particularly, it cannot be derived by deleting the subject of the infinitival in (24b), the two having different interpretations.

Fourth, the rule of *for*-phrase formation would lead one to expect that *for* and the subject of the infinitival behave as a syntactic unit, but the expection is not borne out. As shown in (25), *for* and the subject of the infinitival do not move as a syntactic unit (the example in (25b) is grammatical with *John* as the benefactive, an interpretation irrelevant to our discussion here):

(25) a. *For there$_i$, Mary arranged t_i to be a live band at the party.
 b. *I found an usher [t_i to buy tickets from for John$_i$]

If the rule of *for*-phrase formation is not warranted, then there must be independent explanations for facts about the adverbial intervention effect observed in (16), the occurrence of the infinitival marker *to* and the objective case of pronominal subjects of infinitivals. Although the examples in (17) show clearly that a preposition does not allow an adverbial to separate it from its argument, it is not obvious whether the intervention effect shows that the complementizer *for* forms a syntactic unit with the subject of the infinitival. An adverb may appear to the left of the subject, as in (26a), but not when it is preceded by an auxiliary, as in (26b):

(26) a. Yesterday, John bought a book.
 b. What did (*yesterday) John buy?
(27) a. With a hammer, the perpetrator can easily break the door.
 b. *Which door can, with a hammer, the perpetrator easily break?

There is surely no reason to suppose that the auxiliary *did* in (26b) or the modal *can* in (27b) forms a syntactic unit with the following the subject. Thus, the adverbial intervention effect observed here, whatever the account for it is,[2] has no bearing on whether the elements on the two sides of the adverb constitute a syntactic constituent. For the same reason, we can conclude that the adverbial intervention effect in (16) is no evidence that the complementizer *for* and the subject of the infinitival form a syntactic constituent.

It is also easy to see that the appearance of the infinitival marker *to* does not bear on the loss of subject as a result of *for*-phrase formation. In other syntactic contexts where the complementizer *for* does not appear and the subject of the infinitival is present, the infinitival marker *to* nevertheless shows up, indicating that its occurrence is not dependent on the absence of the subject:

(28) a. John believed *(there) to be a riot.
 b. John wanted tabs to be kept on Bill.

As in the examples in (18), the expletive *there* and the idiom chunk *taps* in (28) cannot be the object of the matrix verb; they are the subject of the infinitival. Clearly the appearance of the infinitival marker *to* in (28) does not depend on a loss of subject. Therefore, there is no reason to suppose that the rule of *for*-

phrase formation is independently motivated by the loss of the subject of infinitivals.

The objective case of the subject of the infinitival can be alternatively accounted for by assuming that a pronoun is marked subjective case only if it agrees with a (finite) verb. That is, the subject of the infinitival has objective case not because it is not dominated by S, i.e. in SpecIP in current framework, rather, because it does not agree with a finite verb.

In light of its incorrect empirical predictions and the plausible alternative explanations for the independent facts about adverbial intervention effect, the occurrence of the infinitival marker *to*, and the distribution of objective case on pronouns, it is clear that the rule of *for*-phrase formation has no independent justification. Nevertheless, I argue in the Section 3 that with the aforementioned obvious virtue the SPC, with some minor modification, is correct insofar as it provides a unified account for the general different distributions of DP and PP, not only in non-finite RCs but also in finite clauses and constructions with resumptive pronouns as well.

2.2 Surface filters

Chomsky and Lasnik (1977: 464) suggested that syntactic structures in general be constrained by a set of surface filters ruling out specific representations that meet their structural descriptions. The filter relevant to the examples we discuss here is the one in (29):

(29) *[$_\alpha$ NP to VP], unless α is adjacent to and in the domain of [−N] or α=NP.

where the "in the domain of" relation is defined as in (30) in terms of Reinhart's (1976) c-command (Chomsky and Lasnik 1977: 459):

(30) β is in the domain of α if α c-commands β.

The filter thus admits the structures in (31), but excludes those in (32) without *for*:

(31) a. I believe [$_S$ John to be competent]
 b. I thought up a topic [$_S$ for you to work on]
 c. I wonder [$_S$ what to do]
 d. [$_{NP}$ a man to fix the sink] is at the door.
(32) a. His plan [$_S$ *(for) Bill to win]
 b. It is illegal [$_S$ *(for) Bill to take part]
 c. *A topic [$_S$ which to work on]

The impossibility of DPs appearing in the clause-initial position of a non-finite RC as in (32c) thus falls under the general filter in (29), which holds of other non-finite clauses as well.

The filter in (29) fails to account for why the example in (33) is possible, however, even though the DP *what* is not in the domain of the verb:

(33) a. [$_s$ what to do] is unclear.
      b. [$_s$ who to talk to regarding this matter] is an open question.

In theories assuming filters, it is easy to specify exactly the conditions under which a filter applies. Thus, it is possible to state further restrictions in the filter in (29) so that it would apply precisely to cases in (32), but not in (31) and (33). But unless there is independent justification for it, such a solution is simply ad hoc and at best a restatement of facts.

2.3 *The DP/PP asymmetry in other non-finite contexts*

As pointed out in the introduction, it would be a remarkable property of English if the DP/PP asymmetry shows up just in non-finite RCs. It is therefore natural to consider a wider range of constructions other than RCs where the asymmetry holds. We see again the empirical limitation of Emonds' as well as Chomsky and Lasnik's accounts. In a range of other non-finite clauses as well, DP contrasts sharply with PP with respect to occurrence in non-argument positions, as shown in (34)–(35):[3]

– Extraposed infinitivals
(34) a. ??John wanted very much [in the other room to put all the diplomats]
      b. *John wanted very much [all the diplomats to put in the other room]

– Infinitival subjects
(35) a. ??[in the other room [to put all the diplomats]] is unimaginable.
      b. *[all the diplomats [to put in the other room]] is unimaginable.

– ECM-complements
(36) a. ??John considered there [in the other room [to be diplomats]]
      b. *John considered there [diplomats [to be in the other room]]

– Control infinitivals
(37) a. ??John tried [in the other room [to put all the diplomats]]
      b. *John tried [all the diplomats [to put in the other room]]

c. ??John persuaded Bill [in the other room [to put all the diplomats]]
d. *John persuaded Bill [all the diplomats [to put in the other room]]

–Infinitival complements to adjectives
(38) a. ??It is necessary [in the other room [to put all the diplomats]]
b. *It is necessary [all the diplomats [to put in the other room]]

–Infinitival complements to raising predicates
(39) a. ?John seemed [in the other room [to have put all the diplomats]]
b. *John seemed [all the diplomats [to have put in the other room]]
c. ??Mary is alleged [in the other room [to have put all the diplomats]]
d. *Mary is alleged [all the diplomats [to have put in the other room]]

It is not entirely clear how Emonds' analyses accounts for the DP/PP asymmetry in (34)–(39), however. While there are conceivable variants of the examples in (34), (35) and (38) with a *for*-phrase from which these can be derived by moving the PP into the position of the *for*-PP after deletion of *for* and its argument:

(40) John wanted very much [for Bill to put all the diplomats in the other room]

(41) [for John to put all the diplomats in the other room] is unimaginable.

(42) It is necessary [for John to put all the diplomats in the other room]

no such derivations are possible for the examples in (36), (37) and (39) since the structures from which they are derived are ungrammatical:

(43) *John considered for there to be diplomats in the other room.
(44) a. *John tried for him to put all the diplomats in the other room.
b. *John persuaded Bill for Mary to put all the diplomats in the other room.
(45) a. *It seemed for John to have put all the diplomats in the other room.
b. *It is alleged for Mary to have put all the diplomats in the other room.

In other words, there is simply no possible PP created by *for*-phrase formation for the PP in (36a), (37a), (37c), (39a) and (39c) to substitute.

Nor can Chomsky and Lasnik's (1977) account explain the DP/PP asymmetry in these cases, if the "in the domain of" relation is taken to be as in (30). The DP in (34)–(39) is clearly in the domain of the verb according to this definition.

It is worth pointing out that inadequacies of Emonds' as well as Chomsky and Lasnik's accounts for the distribution of DP are due to the specific assumptions they made, namely, the rule of *for*-phrase formation and the filter in (29) respectively, not to the general theoretical frameworks that embed them. These problems that arise in these accounts are thus empirical, insofar as the specific assumptions they make lead to expectations that are not borne out by facts. The account I propose below expressly assumes neither a specific rule of *for*-phrase formation nor the filter in (29); therefore, these empirical problems do not arise. Conceptually, my alternative account also fares better since it employs no grammatical devices like filters. Law (1995a) argued that non-universal filters like that in (29) are problematic for accommodating both cross-linguistic variations and acquisition.

Given the DP/PP asymmetry observed in non-finite contexts other than RCs, it is clear that the gap in the paradigm in (9) is not an accident unique to RCs. To see how finiteness bears on the DP/PP asymmetry, we must consider the categorial feature of infinitivals in addition to the position to the left of the infinitival marker *to*. As it turns out, the asymmetry shows up in some finite clauses as well, yet another problem for Emonds' as well as Chomsky and Lasnik's analyses. The conclusion is therefore inevitable: the explanation for DP/PP asymmetry lies in the account for the general distributional difference between DP and PP independently of RCs and finiteness.

3. The category of the infinitival marker *to*

In order to see why the configuration in (46) involving the infinitival marker *to* is excluded, and to bring it to bear on the independent account of the distributional difference between DP and PP in finite clauses discussed in the last section, we need to identify the categorial feature of the infinitival marker *to* and the nature of the XP position that cannot host a DP:

(46) $[_{ZP}$ XP $[_Y$ *to* ... *XP=DP

There are in principle three possibilities for the XP position. It might be the Spec of a functional projection dominating the projection of the infinitival marker *to* (i.e. ZP≠Y), it might be an adjoined position to the projection of *to* (ZP and Y are segments of a single category, cf. May 1985), or it might be in the Spec position of the projection of *to* (Y=Z′). Given its phonetic identity with the preposition *to*, it is not inconceivable that Y is a PP.

I take it for granted that *to* is neither a noun, nor an adjective, nor an adverb, and assume that there is no functional projection present uniquely in infinitivals; therefore, ZP in (46) can in principle be either Agr or T. However, I argue below that ZP is not a PP, not AgrP or T,[4] but is plausibly a VP.

3.1 *The infinitival marker* to *is not P*

As Pullum (1982) pointed out, the verb is required to carry the *-ing* ending when it follows a preposition:

(47) a. John thought of leaving/*leave the office.
 b. Mary is interested in teaching the class.
(48) a. John looked forward to seeing/*see the chancellor.
 b. John is used to putting/*put up with the noise.

But the base form of the verb must appear when it follows the infinitival marker *to*:

(49) a. John intended to leave/*leaving the office.
 b. John wanted to see/*seeing the chancellor.
 c. John used to put/*putting up with the noise.

In addition, in syntactic contexts like those in (50) the infinitival marker *to* does not require that its complement be overtly realized, but the preposition *to* in (51) does:

(50) a. John wanted to leave, but Mary did not want to (leave).
 b. We hoped that they would hand in the papers on time, and expected them to (hand in the papers on time), too.
(51) a. John went to Chicago, but Mary did not go to *(Chicago/that place).
 b. John talked to Sue, and Bill also talked to *(Sue/her).

Facts in (50) and (51) thus show clearly that the infinitival marker *to* is not of the category preposition.

3.2 *The infinitival marker* to *is not in I*

Since it may cooccur with the complementizer *for* as shown in (52), the infinitival marker *to* is not likely to be of the category C but is contained in a different projection dominated by a CP:

(52) a. [CP [for [IP John [to [leave]]]] would be a pity.
b. It would be a pity [CP for [IP John [to [leave]]]]

If the complementizer *for* is in C, and the subject is in SpecIP (=AgrSP, Chomsky 1993), then it is conceivable that the infinitival marker *to* is in I.

However, evidence from the relative positioning of *to* and negation indicates that *to* is most probably not in I. Negation *not* may follow but can never precede modals:

(53) a. John will not leave.
b. *John not will leave.

As for the relative ordering of *to* and *not*, all speakers accept the order *not to*, although some also permit the order *to not*:[5]

(54) a. Mary wanted John not to be late.
b. ?Mary wanted John to not be late.
(55) a. Bill persuaded Sue not to go to medical school.
b. ?Bill persuaded Sue to not go to medical school.
(56) a. John seemed not to have studied for the exam.
b. ?John seemed to not have studied for the exam.

Now, if modals to the left of negation *not* are in I, then the infinitival marker *to* appearing to the right of *not* cannot be in I.

In this light, it is particularly relevant to consider infinitivals with an overt subject. In the structure in (57a), the infinitival marker *to* to the right of negation *not* is not in I as argued above, and the overt subject is in Spec of the IP dominating the YP projection of *to*:

(57) a. It would be a pity [CP for [IP John [not [YP to [enter the race]]]]]
b. It would be a pity [YP not [to [enter the race]]]

Now, if *to* in (57a) is not in I, i.e. YP≠IP, then there is little reason to suppose that YP in (57b) is IP. Moreover, as YP in (57b) is in a postverbal position, and a (finite) IP is impossible in that position as shown in (58),[6] there is no good motivation for saying that the postverbal YP in (57b) is an IP:

(58) a. *It was a pity [IP John did not enter the race]
b. It was a pity [CP that John did not enter the race]

We can thus reasonably conclude from the facts in (52)–(58) that the category of the YP projection of the infinitival marker *to* is not IP.[7]

3.3 The infinitival marker to is V

At first glance, it is not at all obvious that the infinitival marker *to* might be a (defective) verb, since it takes neither tense nor agreement morphology, and never inverts with the subject in questions. Pullum (1982) gave a number of arguments regarding linear positioning of *to* with respect to other verbs and negation (cf. Section 3.2), subcategorization of non-inflected verbs, stress of stranded *to*, as well as contraction to make a case for the infinitival marker *to* being a verb. For reason of space, I will not repeat them here, but present some particularly clear corroborating evidence from ellipsis, which seems to me to be his most persuasive argument.

In a number of syntactic contexts, among them VP-ellipsis, the position where a VP would otherwise occur must be preceded by a finite verb that also inverts with the subject in matrix questions, as is well-known:

(59) a. They believed that John would go to the movies, and he actually *(will).
b. John has read the book, so Bill *(has) too.

The infinitival marker *to* behaves like these verbs in sanctioning VP-ellipsis. The absence of the infinitival marker *to* leads to ungrammaticality:

(60) a. John read the paper, although noone expected him *(to).
b. Mary seems to be happy, but Sue does not seem *(to).

In addition, the infinitival marker *to* patterns like auxiliary verbs in that it must follow the negation *never* in contexts of VP-ellipsis, even though they may precede it in some other syntactic contexts:

(61) a. John resigned, although he had promised that he never would.
b. *John resigned, although he had promised that he would never.

(62) a. John never has cried.
b. John has never cried.

(63) a. John resigned, although he had promised never to.
b. *John resigned, although he had promised to never.

(64) a. John pretends never to have known Bill.
b. John pretends to never have known Bill.

If the infinitival marker *to* is of a different category from the auxiliary verbs, then one must resort to a disjunction of the conditions sanctioning VP-ellipsis:

(65) a. Be, can, could, dare, do, have, may, might, must, need, ought, shall, should, will, would.
b. To.

Pullum (1982: 199) thus argued that the disjunction in (65) can be collapsed, if the infinitival marker *to* is considered to be of the category auxiliary verb.

Consider now the examples in (66) with a string of verbs occurring in between the subject and the object:

(66) a. Bill has been writing the letter since this morning.
b. John should have read the book.
c. Mary may have been painting the house.

The infinitival marker *to* thus resembles a verb in being able to interevene between a finite verb and a non-finite one:

(67) a. Bill has to write the letter.
b. John ought to read the book.
c. Mary may need to paint the house.

One might argue that the fact that *to* may appear in between two verbs does not show that it is a verb, as adverbs may also do so:

(68) a. Bill has (probably) been (carefully) writing the letter since this morning.
b. John should (really) have (seriously) read the book.
c. Mary may (happily) have (happily) been (slowly) paint it.

There are two indications showing that *to* is not an adverb, however. A rather general property of adverbs is that they may occur in different positions (possible exceptions are those like *merely* and *hard*, cf. Jackendoff 1972), but *to* must precede a non-finite verb. Furthermore, there are restrictions on the verbs flanking *to*. The preceding verb can be the auxiliary *have* or *be*, but not modals like *can* or *would*, and the following verb must be in the base form. This suggests strongly that *to* selects the following verb and is selected by the preceding one (cf. Pullum 1982: 199). No adverbs have this selectional property. Thus, whatever explanation one gives for the examples in (66) where a particular form of a verb is required when it occurs between two verbs, e.g. selection, perfective *have* selecting participial form of the verb, progressive *be* selecting V with the suffix *-ing*, etc, then one can maintain the same selectional account for the examples in (67) if the infinitival marker *to* is considered to be of the category verb, selected by the modals *have*, *ought* and *need*.

Zagona (1988) proposed that syntactically the string of verbs in examples like those in (66) have a VP-structure as in (69) in which each verb heads a VP-projection taking the following VP as complement, with finite auxiliary verbs including modals moving to I (cf. Pollock 1989, variants of the same ideas were proposed in Emonds 1970; Jackendoff 1972; Akmajian and Wasow 1975; Pullum and Wilson 1977):

(69) a. ... has$_i$ [$_{VP}$ [t_i [$_{VP}$ [been [$_{VP}$ [writing ...
b. ... should$_i$ [$_{VP}$ [t_i [$_{VP}$ [have [$_{VP}$ [read ...
c. ... might$_i$ [$_{VP}$ [t_i [$_{VP}$ [have [$_{VP}$ [been [$_{VP}$ [painting ...

Along these lines, then, the strings of verbs including *to* in the examples in (67) would likewise have the same VP-structure as in (70), if the infinitival marker *to* is considered to be a verb:

(70) a. ... has$_i$ [$_{VP}$ [t_i [$_{VP}$ [to [$_{VP}$ [write ...
b. ... ought$_i$ [$_{VP}$ [t_i[$_{VP}$ [to [$_{VP}$ [read ...
c. ... may$_i$ [$_{VP}$ [t_i[$_{VP}$ [have [$_{VP}$ [to [$_{VP}$ [paint ...

Clearly, clusters of verbs with the infinitival marker *to* and those without it may have a unified analysis only if *to* is taken to be of the category verb.[8]

4. On formal features of questions and relative clauses

As mentioned in the introduction, the grammatical contrast between the examples in (1a) and (2a) on the one hand and those in (5a) and (6a) on the other, repeated here as (71) and (72) respectively, is a clear illustration of the obscure relationship between the surface form and the underlying property:

(71) a. *The man [who(m) to talk about]
b. *The man [who(m) to discuss linguistics with]

(72) a. I wondered [who(m) to talk about]
b. I wondered [who(m) to discuss linguistics with]

The bracketed constituents in (71) and (72) are superficially the same, but their underlying grammatical properties are radically different as reflected in their sharp grammatical contrasts.

I argue that despite their identical surface forms the bracketed constituents in (72) differ from those in (71) not only in the formal features that characterize them semantically as (embedded) questions, but also in their categorial feature. Specifically, while embedded questions have the formal feature [+Q] in the head position projecting a CP as standardly assumed, non-finite RCs lack a comparable formal feature (eg, [+PRED], cf. Rizzi 1990: 67), and are simply VP-projections of the infinitival marker *to*. Thus, in contrast to the *wh*-phrases in (72), which occur in SpecCP, those in (71) are adjoined to VPs headed by *to*. The examples in (71) can now be excluded for the same reason why in finite clauses a DP may not be adjoined to a position where it cannot be base-generated (cf. Section 3).

4.1 *A selected formal feature for embedded questions*

On the view that lexical items are bundles of abstract (formal) features (cf. Chomsky 1957), a formal feature can be justified insofar as it interacts with other principles of grammar. In this light, consider the principle of selectional restriction according to which lexical items may, in accordance with their inherent lexical properties, impose specific requirements on the complements they select. If the structural constraint on a selectional restriction is that the head-head relation, then a selected property, e.g. a formal feature, must be located in the head position of the selected category.

Along these lines, there is good reason to assume a formal feature [+Q] for questions, for it would otherwise be very difficult to state in a simple way how the requirement of a verb selecting an interrogative complement can be satisfied. On the one hand, with a formal feature [+Q], one can state the selectional property of a verb like *wonder* as requiring that the formal feature [+Q] be in the head of its complement, a property that the complementizer *if* has but the complementizer *that* does not, and that of a verb like *think* as demanding that the head of its complement not contain the formal feature [+Q], accounting for the grammatical contrasts in (73) and (74):

(73)   a.   John wondered [$_{CP}$ [if [$_{IP}$ he should leave]]]
        b.   *John wondered [$_{CP}$ [that [$_{IP}$ he should leave]]]
(74)   a.   *John thought [$_{CP}$ [if [$_{IP}$ he should leave]]]
        b.   John thought [$_{CP}$ [that [$_{IP}$ he should leave]]]

On the other hand, a problem arises as to how selectional restrictions are satisfied in embedded questions where the *wh*-phrase is not in the head position of CP. In matrix questions, the finite verb occurs in C^0 so the argument *wh*-phrases cannot occur in that position but in SpecCP, as standardly analyzed:

(75)   a.   [$_{CP}$ what$_i$ [did [$_{IP}$ John see t_i]]]?
        b.   [$_{CP}$ who$_i$ [did [$_{IP}$ John give a book to t_i]]]?

If in embedded questions argument *wh*-phrases also occur in SpecCP, then one has to explain how selectional restriction of the matrix verb is satisfied. A simple solution to this problem would be to assume, quite standardly, that the head position of the embedded question, though phonetically empty, actually contains the (abstract) formal feature [+Q]:

(76) a. I wondered [$_{CP}$ what$_i$ [[$_{IP}$ John saw t_i]]]
     b. I wondered [$_{CP}$ who$_i$ [[$_{IP}$ John gave a book to t_i]]]

The same argument holds for embedded non-finite questions as well. That is, the head position of the embedded CP questions, though phonetically empty, actually contains the (abstract) formal feature [+Q], satisfying the selectional restriction of the matrix verb:

(77) a. I wondered [$_{CP}$ what$_i$ [[$_{IP}$ to see t_i]]]
     b. I wondered [$_{CP}$ who$_i$ [[$_{IP}$ to give a book to t_i]]]

The motivation for an abstract [+Q] feature is even stronger in Chinese. As is well-known, Chinese *wh*-phrases in questions must remain in-situ in argument positions (cf. Huang 1981). Thus, the example in (78a) can only be a matrix question since the matrix verb *renwei* 'think' does not select an interrogative complement, while that in (78b) can only be an embedded question, since the verb *xian-zhidao* 'want-know, wonder' requires an interrogative complement, even though the *wh*-phrase *sheme* 'what' occurs in argument position in both cases:

(78) a. Ni renwei [Zhangsan mei-le sheme]
        you think Z.   buy-ASP what
        'What do you think Zhangsan bought?'
    b. Wo xian-zhidao [Zhangsan mei-le sheme]
        I wonder   Z.   buy-ASP what
        'I wonder what Zhangsan bought.'

With an abstract [+Q] feature, the way selectional restriction is satisfied in Chinese would be exactly like that in English, namely, the [+Q] feature is contained in the head position of the complement of the matrix verb.

4.2 *No selected formal feature in relative clauses*

In contrast to questions, there seems to be no comparable motivation for a formal feature characterizing RCs. No category specifically selects a RC,[9] which may but need not cooccur with a nominal projection:

(79) a. The student (who passed the exam) is a genius.
  b. I bought a car (which nobody liked).
  c. Every politician (who I talked to) is corrupt.
  d. Most cities (where there are subways) are chaotic.
  e. The reason (why they fired Bill) was dubious.

One might conceivably argue that the absence of selectional restriction in RCs only shows that a formal feature for selection of RCs is lacking, not that such a formal feature cannot be justified on other grounds. For instance, it might still be motivated as the trigger for syntactic movement (Chomsky 1991).

Along these lines, one might invoke the movement asymmetry in Chinese questions and RCs to justify a formal feature as trigger of movement in RCs. As pointed out above, *wh*-phrases in Chinese questions must remain in-situ:

(80) a. Zhangsan mai-le   sheme?
       Z.   buy-PERF what
       'What did Zhangsan buy?'
   b. *Sheme$_i$ Zhangsan mai-le t_i?
(81) a. Ni renwei shei zui congming?
       you think who most intelligent
       'Who do you think is the most intelligent.'
   b. *Shei$_i$ ni renwei t_i zui congming?

The absence of island effects in the example in (82) further shows that *wh*-phrases in Chinese questions do not move in overt syntax the way those in English do (Huang 1981):

(82) Ni xiang-zhidao shei mai-le sheme?
     you wonder   who bought what
     'What do you wonder who bought?'
     or 'Who do you wonder what bought?'

In (82), as indicated in the English translations, the example is ambiguous in that either one of the two embedded *wh*-phrases is interpreted as having matrix scope, and the other as having embedded scope. If wide scope interpretion is represented as in (83a) at some (abstract) level of representation, on a par with extraction in overt syntax (the order of the traces irrelevant):

(83) Abstract representation for wide scope *wh*-phrases
     wh-phrase$_i$ ... [$_{CP}$ *wh*-phrase$_j$ [... t_i ... t_j ...]]

then in both cases of (82) Ross's (1967) *Wh*-island Constraint or Chomsky's (1973) subjacency condition, more generally represented as in (84), is violated:

(84) Subjacency condition on movement
 *... X ... [$_\alpha$ ... [$_\beta$ ... Y ...] ...] ... X ..., where α and β are bounding nodes.

The wide scope *wh*-phrase is extracted out of an embedded question, a *wh*-island, since the embedded SpecCP escape hatch is occupied by the narrow scope *wh*-phrase. Huang (1981, 1982) thus argued that the grammaticality of the Chinese examples in (82), in contrast with their English counterparts, would be accounted for if Chinese *wh*-phrases differ from English *wh*-phrases in that they move abstractly at LF, where, he suggested, the subjacency condition on movement is irrelevant. Abstract movement of *wh*-phrases apparently gives another desirable result, namely, LF representations in both Chinese and English would be the same.

Now, given that *wh*-phrases remain in-situ in Chinese, it is rather surprising that movement is obligatory in RCs as evidenced by the island effects. In sharp contrast with the example in (82), those in (85) are impossible (the examples in (85a) and (85b) are from Huang (1982:459), ASP for aspect, DE is the relative marker):

(85) a. *Wo bu xiangxin [[[$_{IP}$ Lisi kanjian t_i] zheju hua]   de ren$_i$]
        I   not believe   L.   see   this saying DE man
        'The man who I don't believe the statement that Lisi saw.'
    b. *Wo mai-le   [[[$_{IP}$ Lisi mei kan t_i] zhen qiguai] de neiben shu$_i$]
        I   buy-ASP   L.   not read   real strange DE that book
        'I bought the book that Lisi didn't read is really strange.'
    c. *Wo kan-le   [[$_{IP}$[$_{IP}$ Zhangsan zuo-le t_i zihou]
        I   read-ASP   Z.   make-ASP   after
        [$_{IP}$ tamen qiu   kaihui]]] de neifen baogao$_i$]
             they immediately meet   DE that report
        'I read the report that they immediately met after Zhangsan made.'

The gap to which the head of the RC is related is inside an extraction island in these examples: it is a complement to a noun in (85a), a sentential subject in (85b) and a clausal adjunct in (85c). One can thus take the ungrammaticality of these examples as evidence that (some sort of) overt movement (obligatorily) takes place in RCs.

From the point of view that overt syntactic movement is driven by the need to check formal features, one might take the ungrammaticality of the examples in (85) as motivation for a (strong) formal feature in RCs, which must be checked in overt syntax. The conclusion does not seem to be warranted, however. First, apart from driving overt movement, there seems to be no independent justification for a (strong) formal feature specifically for RCs. Second, when we consider in-situ *wh*-phrases in questions, which do not have a movement-driving formal feature according to this view, the motivation for a formal feature in RCs is especially dubious. In questions *wh*-phrases, with all their overt morphologies and semantic features, must remain in-situ. In RCs, by contrast, it is not even clear what categogy in the RC moves; consequently, it is not obvious what category in the RC carries the feature.[10] Third, insofar as no other facts can be brought to bear on why RCs contain a strong movement-driving formal feature, but questions do not, positing of the feature is but a restatement of the difference between the two constructions with respect to movement, not an explanation for it.

If there is indeed no formal feature present specifically in RCs, then the movement in this construction cannot be to a Spec position (of CP) as commonly thought, but must be adjunction (to IP if it is finite, or to VP headed by *to* if it is non-finite), in contrast with *wh*-phrases in questions, which land in SpecCP as standardly assumed. I claim that the different landing sites for *wh*-phrases in RCs and in questions, schematically represented in (86), are what explains the presence of the DP/PP asymmetry in RCs and the absence of it in questions:[11]

(86)   a.   Relative clauses: ... [$_{IP}$ *wh*-phrase$_i$ [$_{IP}$ ... t_i ...]] ...
        b.   Questions: ... [$_{CP}$ *wh*-phrase$_i$ [[$_{IP}$ ... t_i ...]]] ...

We will see presently how this result for RCs bears on the more general different distributions of DP and PP.

5. The distributional difference between DP and PP

Most of the examples in the preceding section involve non-finite clauses. To see the different syntactic distributions of DP and PP more generally, it is necessary to consider them in finite clauses. We will see that in these cases as well, DP has a more limited distribution than PP.

5.1 *Movement of DP and PP to non-argument positions in finite clauses*

As shown in (87)–(88), DP differs sharply from PP in finite clauses in not occurring in any position between the auxiliary and the thematic verb (the example in (87a) is due to Emonds 1979: 213, footnote 1):

(87) a. We had, in the other room, put all the diplomats.
     b. *We had, all the diplomats, put in the next room.
(88) a. John will, to his friends, be sending chapters of his book.
     b. John will be, to his friends, sending chapters of his book.
     c. *John will, chapters of his book, be sending to his friends.
     d. *John will be, chapters of his book, sending to his friends.

Apart from the intonation break indicated by the commas (cf. Section 3.2), the fact that the DP arguments of the PPs *in the other room* in (87) and *to his friends* in (88) may not be extracted shows clearly that the PPs occur in an adjoined position, given Huang's (1982) Condition on Extraction Domain (CED):

(89) a. Which room$_i$ had we put all the diplomats in t_i?
     b. *Which room$_i$ had we, in t_i, put all the diplomats?
(90) a. Who will John be sending chapters of his book to t_i?
     b. *Who will John, to t_i, be sending chapters of his book?
     c. *Who will John be, to t_i, sending chapters of his book?

Furthermore, since the verbs *put* and *send* take a PP complement, the PPs *in the other room* in (87) and *to his friends* in (88) must have moved from a postverbal position (cf. the positions of the PPs in (89a) and (90a)).

The grammatical contrast in the examples in (87) is most problematic for Emonds' as well as for Chomsky and Lasnik's analyses. For the former, although the ungrammaticality of the examples in (87b), (88c) and (88d) may follow from the assumption that the position between the auxiliary and the thematic verb is not a base-position for DP, it is not clear how the examples in (87a) and (88a) are to be derived, under this view, with *for*-phrase formation. There is no reason to suppose that the rule of *for*-phrase formation applies in these cases to create an empty PP, which is subsequently substituted by the PP *in the other room* or *to his friends*. For the latter, the filter (29) is simply inapplicable since the examples in (87) and (88) do not have the infinitival marker *to*, and hence do not meet its structural description. Hence, there should be no DP/PP contrast in these examples, contrary to fact.

I suggest to relate the grammatical contrasts in (87) and (88) as well as the curious DP/PP asymmetry in the paradigm in (9) to the base-positions of DP and PP.

5.2 *The base-positions of DP and PP*

All the examples that we have been considering so far have in common the property that the DP in a non-argument position is related to a gap. The examples in (91) are different in that the DP to the left of the subject is related to a phonetically overt pronoun or an epithet in a Case position as indicated by co-indexation, a construction that is known as left-dislocation (Ross 1967; Chomsky 1977):[12]

(91)   a.   John$_i$, I like him$_i$.
            b.   Such noble causes$_i$, it is worth fighting for them$_i$.
            c.   Bill$_i$, nobody thinks that the fool$_i$ would win the race.
            d.   That book$_i$, I told Bill that Mary had written a review of it$_i$.

Left-dislocation differs minimally from the construction known as topicalization (Ross 1967; Chomsky 1977) shown in (92) where a gap occurs instead of a resumptive pronoun (cf. also Section 6):

(92)   a.   John$_i$, I like t_i.
            b.   Those noble causes$_i$, it is worth fighting for t_i.
            c.   Bill$_i$, nobody thinks t_i would win the race.
            d.   That book$_i$, I told Bill that Mary had written a review of t_i.

Apart from the intonation break indicated by the commas, the two differ in yet two other respects: topicalization does, but left-dislocation does not, obey the subjacency condition on movement (cf. Chomsky 1973, 1977 and Cinque 1977), and what follows the left-peripheral DP in the left-dislocation construction is a grammatical sentence by itself, i.e. an IP.[13] Moreover, since an overt pronoun or an epithet fills the argument positions in (91), the left-peripheral DPs in these examples cannot possibly be said to have moved from argument positions, but must be base-generated in their surface positions.

The examples in (93) show that the pre-verbal non-argument position for DP in (91) and (92) must be to the immediate left of the subject, regardless of whether a resumptive also appears:

(93)   a.   *I, John$_i$, like him$_i$.
            b.   It (*those noble causes$_i$,) is (*, those noble causes$_i$,) worth (*, those noble causes$_i$,) fighting (*, those noble causes$_i$,) for them$_i$.
            c.   I (*, that book$_i$,) told (*, that book$_i$,) Bill (*, that book$_i$,) that (, that book$_i$,) Mary (*, that book$_i$,) had (*, that book$_i$,) written a review of it$_i$.
            d.   Nobody (*, Bill$_i$,) thinks (*, Bill$_i$,) that (??, Bill$_i$,) the fool$_i$ would win the race.

In sum, examples of topicalization, left-dislocation and the grammatical contrasts in (93) constitute evidence that the IP-adjoined position may be a base-position for DP.

As for PP, it can only appear in the topicalization construction, but not in the left-dislocation construction with a resumptive pronoun (cf. Cinque 1990):

(94) a. With students, I never talked about politics.
b. *With students, I never talked about politics with them.

Therefore, we must consider other constructions in the search for evidence for the base-position of PP. Examples as those in (95)–(97) are pertinent in this regard; they contain PP-adjuncts in different positions fulfilling different semantic roles:

(95) a. In the next meeting, we will be discussing the homework.
b. We will, in the next meeting, be discussing the homework.
c. We will be, in the next meeting, discussing the homework.
d. We will be discussing the homework in the next meeting.

(96) a. Because of the strike, the boys are likely to be staying at home.
b. The boys, because of the strike, are likely to be staying at home.
c. The boys are, because of the strike, likely to be staying at home.
d. The boys are likely, because of the strike, to be staying at home.
e. The boys are likely to be, because of the strike, staying at home.
f. The boys are likely to be staying at home because of the strike.

(97) a. The president will, on Sunday, deliver the message.
b. They have, in a hasty manner, destroyed the evidence.
c. Mary did, without exception, hand in her homeworks on time.
d. Fred should, in the big room, receive the guests.
e. Sue will, in any event, lead the group to the convention.

Given the locality and the lack of island effects, it is anything but obvious that movement is involved in (95)–(97). In fact, there seems to be no particular reason to think that in these examples one of the positions where the PP-adjunct occurs is the base-position and the others are derived. Insofar as there is no natural way to exclude base-generation of PP-adjuncts, the PP in these examples might very well be base-generated there in the first place. The examples in (95)–(97) therefore show that PP has a wider range of base-positions than DP.

5.3 *Case theory and the distribution of DP and PP*

The issue that immediately arises is why PP should have more base-generated positions than DP. A natural answer to this question is to exploit the obvious difference between DP and PP, namely, Case. In contrast with PP, DP almost always need Case (cf. Rouveret and Vergnaud's (1980) Case Filter for DP, but not for PP), the only exception being when it occurs in the left-dislocation construction. Now, if the distribution of DP is tied to Case, then it is understandable that it has a more restricted distribution than PP, since there are only a few Case positions.

Indeed, PP quite generally can be base-generated in adjunct positions to various categories, including VPs as we have seen and NPs as shown in (98):

(98) a. The [$_{NP}$ [$_{NP}$ picture] [$_{PP}$ on the wall]]] (was painted by Picasso).
b. The [$_{NP}$ [$_{NP}$ meeting] [$_{PP}$ on Sunday]]] (was called off).

Thus, DP complements of Ns must be preceded by the preposition *of* (Chomsky 1970), sometimes *to* as in *our help to/*of the victims*, showing their difference from PPs with respect to Case:

(99) a. The Romans' destruction *(of) the city.
b. The city's destruction (*of) by the Romans.

Evidence for PP being adjunct to AP is not easy to come by, but examples of the sort in (100a) seem to me to be reasonable illustration of PP appearing as AP-adjunct. The PP is optional, may move along with the AP, but its argument may not be extracted:

(100) a. John was crazy about Mary (to a considerable degree).
b. It was [$_{AP}$ [$_{AP}$ crazy about Mary] [$_{PP}$ to a considerable degree]] that John was.
c. *What degree$_i$ was John [$_{AP}$ [$_{AP}$ crazy about Mary] [$_{PP}$ to t_i]]?
d. *The degree$_i$ (that) John was [$_{AP}$ [$_{AP}$ crazy about Mary] [$_{PP}$ to t_i]]
(cf. the degree to which John was crazy about Mary)

Appositive DPs may be said to be DP-adjuncts to DPs, as shown in (101), and the example in (102) is a good case of PP being adjunct to PP (Chris Wilder, p.c.), although others are rather difficult to find:

(101) [$_{DP}$ Bill Clinton], [$_{DP}$ the president of the United States], is also the commander-in-chief.
(102) The lamp is [$_{PP}$ [$_{PP}$ in the dining room] [$_{PP}$ next to the door]]

Thus, if adjunction is not related to Case and the distribution of PP is not constrained by Case theory, then it follows directly that PP may be base-generated as adjuncts to various categories, corresponding exactly to facts.

Now it is appropriate to ask what kind of position the position to the immediate left of an independent sentence, i.e. an IP, is which hosts a DP or a PP. Is it a Spec or an adjoined position? For DP, it is often assumed that it is the Spec position of a Topic projection (cf. Chomsky 1977), and the DP appearing there is the Topic of the sentence. In recent literature, the topic DP is even said to check a Topic feature (cf. Rizzi 1997). On the one hand, although the assumption might not seem implausible for DP at first glance, it is much less clear whether it can be justified for a range of different categories like PP, AP, VP, adverbs and clauses occurring in the same position:

(103) a. Without any preparation, they immediately discussed the details of the plan.
　　　b. Ashamed of his error, Sam lied to his boss.
　　　c. (they hoped that John would resign, and) resign he did.
　　　d. Slowly the ammunition expert removed the batteries from the bomb.
　　　e. Frankly, the conference was a failure.
　　　f. Because the noise at home was intolerable, Bill spent the night in the office.

For DP in the left-dislocation construction, one might say that it denotes an individual and is the Topic on which the following sentence comments, but such an explanation is not readily available for the examples in (103) where it is not at all clear if there is a Topic. Particularly problematic are the examples in (103a), (103c) and (103e), where it makes no sense to say that the Topics of the sentences are respectively the non-preparation, the resigning of John or the frank attitude of the speaker. Semantically, the left-peripheral phrases in (103) are properties of individuals (PP, VP, AP) or of properties (manner adverbs), or are simply an embedded clause. It would therefore require some extra machinery to formally relate the left-peripheral non-DP phrases in (103) to DP in order to give a uniform treatment of topics.

When one looks at the categories of the left-peripheral phrases in (103), one can hardly see what these various otherwise different categories have in common that justifies a specific functional projection in whose Spec position they can occur. In the view where Spec is a position for checking of a formal feature (Chomsky 1995), it is even harder to see what formal feature the different categories have in common and how one can reasonably motivate a head position with a particular formal feature for these cateogies to check in the Spec position. On the other hand, if adjunction itself has no categorial constraint so that any category may adjoin to any other category,[14] then the relatively free adjunction of different categories to IP is just as expected.

In sum, then, facts presented in this section warrant the conclusion that DP, being constrained by Case theory, has fewer base-positions than PP, and more relevantly, that for DP the surface non-argument position to the left of the verb is the IP-adjoined position (modulo footnote 13).

5.4 *Structure-preservation and the syntactic distributions of DP and PP*

Recall that the structure-preserving transformation in (10a), repeated in (104), limits movement of a phrase to a position occupied by a phrase where it can be base-generated:

(104) *Structure-preserving transformation*
A transformation (or a transformational operation, in the case of a transformation performing several operations) that introduces or substitutes a constituent C into a position in a phrase marker held by a node C is called "structure-preserving."

Koster (1986: 103) pointed out that the concept of structure-preservation is at odds with the notion of derivation in that there is no longer motivation for structures derived by movement if the structures so formed can be independently generated in the base in the first place. This odd property of structure preservation would evaporate if one relaxes it slightly in not requiring that the position to which a phrase moves is already held by (another instance of) the same phrase. In other words, what is required of the landing site is that it be able to host a phrase by base-generation independently.[15]

With this slight modification, the SPC accounts straightforward for why DP may not move to certain non-argument positions in finite clauses (Section 5.1). Recall our conclusion that the left non-argument position for a DP is an IP-adjoined position (Section 5.2). The examples in (87b), (88c) and (88d) are now excluded by the SPC, since the DPs in these cases adjoin to a VP, a position where a DP cannot be independently base-generated. Exactly the same account can be given for DP in non-argument positions in non-finite clauses as well. The examples in (1a) and (2a), i.e. the gap in paradigm in (9), that in (14a) as well as the ungrammatical examples in (34)–(39) are all ruled out by the SPC, since the DP to the immediate left of the infinitival marker *to* in these cases does not occur in an IP-adjoined position.[16] The SPC also correctly admits structures with

PP-adjuncts in various positions (modulo footnote 14), since they are not constrained by Case theory.

6. Conclusion

In the account for the different distributions of DP and PP that I propose here, answers to the questions raised in the introduction are straightforward. In contrast to PP, DP is constrained by Case theory. It must be assigned Case in accord with its morphological property, and therefore has a more restricted distribution in the base than PP. As the categorial projection of the infinitival marker *to* is not IP and the left-adjoined base-position for DP can only be to an IP, two independently established assumptions, the SPC, a constraint on landing sites, bans DP-adjunction to the projection of *to*. Thus, there is no construction-specific constraint applying specifically to non-finite RCs barring DP-adjunction to the clause-initial position. The pecular gap in the paradigm in (9) is expected, since it is part and parcel of the general distribution of DP. The acquisition problem is also resolved without further assumptions. Since Case theory and the SPC are parts of their language competence, i.e. Universal Grammar (Chomsky 1957), speakers need not be explicitly instructed where DP may not be adjoined to.

RCs with no overt relative pronouns have so far not been mentioned. They are often assumed to have a null operator (Chomsky 1982), the counterpart to the overt relative pronoun:

(105) a. The man [O_i [to talk about t_i]]
 b. The man [O_i [to discuss linguistics with t_i]]
(106) a. The man [O_i [I should talk about t_i]]
 b. The man [O_i [I should discuss linguistics with t_i]]

One major reason for assuming null operators is to derive the island effects by movement of the operators, the same effects observed in cases of movement of overt relative pronouns (cf. Chomsky 1977). The question that immediately arises then is why the examples in (105) and (106) are impossible with overt relative pronouns, if null operators, except for their empty phonetic matrix, are just like overt relative pronouns. In the analysis of RCs I suggest here, relative pronouns are adjoined to the RC. Therefore, if null operators and relative pronouns are categorially the same, i.e. DP, then it should also be impossible for null operators to adjoin to the non-finite RC, just like it is for overt relative pronouns.

One can certainly assume some (abstract) feature distinguishing null operators from overt relative pronouns, and impose a constraint on landing sites to the effect that null operators may, but overt relative pronouns may not adjoin to a RC. There are two problems with this idea, however. First, it seems difficult to justify null operators on grounds other than the island effects. The problem is especially acute given their empty phonetic matrix, independent evidence for which is hard to come by. Second, like the first problem, there does not seem to be independent motivation for a formal feature distinguishing overt relative pronouns and null operators that bears just on the landing site.

A solution to this problem is to do away with null operators. From the Occam's Razor point of view, this is a desirable result. If island effects are a property of movement and there are no null operators, then it must be that something else moves in RCs without an overt pronoun, given the observed island effects in these cases. On the view that movement may involve not only the whole category, but also (abstract) formal features as suggested by Chomsky (1995: 261 ff.), it is conceivable that in cases like those in (105)–(106) some formal feature, instead of a null operator, moves. Possibly the θ-feature of the verb or preposition whose argument not syntactically present in argument position must move to the head noun (in overt syntax, given the island effects); otherwise, the feature on the verb would not be assigned or checked. There is no need to assume an additional grammatical entity like the null operator. The reason why the movement cannot be detected morphologically is because the abstract formal feature, e.g. the θ-feature, has no morphological manifestation.

Exactly the same issues arise in a range of constructions commonly thought to involve null operators (cf. Chomsky 1982; Browning 1987), which conceivably can have the same feature movement analysis:

(107) a. John$_i$ is easy [O_i [to please t_i]]　　　　　　[*tough* construction]
　　　 b. Which article$_i$ did you file [O_i　　　[parasitic gap construction]
　　　　　 [without reading t_i]]?
　　　 c. Bill bought the book$_i$ yesterday [O_i　　　　　[purposive clause]
　　　　　 [to read t_i to the children]]
　　　 d. This book$_i$, [O_i [I really like t_i]]　　　　　　[topicalization]
　　　 e. It is War and Peace$_i$ [O_i [that I like t_i]]　　　　　　[cleft]

The advantage of the feature-movement analysis for the constructions in (105)–(107) is that both null operators and a formal feature specifically for can be dispensed with. However, the two problems as to which feature moves and why it moves remain. Sastisfactory solutions to these two problems unfortunately must await another occasion.

Notes

1. Sag (1997:461) surely missed a unified account for the DP/PP asymmetry in non-finite RCs and non-RCs (Section 2.3) as well as the distributional difference between DP and PP in finite clauses (Section 5) in the remark that it appears to be simply an idiosyncracy of English infinitival *wh*-relatives that the filler daughter [i.e. the category in the clause-initial position of an infinitival RC, PL] must be a PP.
2. The grammatical contrasts in (26) and (27) (cf. also Keyser 1968) recall theories of Case-assignment according to which (non-nominative) Case is assigned under adjacency at S-structure in English (Chomsky & Lasnik 1977; and Stowell 1981). Even if adjacency is relevant to Case assignment (cf. Law 1995b for arguments that it is not), the point still holds that there is no reason to suppose that the finite auxiliary or modal, carrying Case-assigning tense morphology, forms a syntactic constituent with the subject receiving Case. The same remarks apply to the contrasts in (16) and (17).
3. Some speakers of (British) English rejected the example (37a) as ungrammatical. I have no account for this fact.
4. Stowell (1982: 561) claimed that the grammatical difference between (i) and (ii) shows that just like finite clauses infinitivals have COMP (=SpecCP) where the Tense operator is located, in contrast with gerunds:

   (i)   a.   I don't remember who we should visit.
             b.   I don't remember who to visit.
   (ii)   *I don't remember who visiting.

   While there is good reason to suppose that embedded infinitival questions are CPs (Section 4.1.), the gap in non-finite RCs in the paradigm in (9) implies that at least some infinitivals, especially those without an overt complementizer and an overt subject, do not have COMP. Now, if COMP hosts the Tense operator, then the lack of COMP implies the lack of a Tense operator. There would then be no motivation for a projection of T in these cases.

   The contrast between (i) and (ii) would follow directly from the analysis I propose below, without appeal to a projection of T, if it can be independently shown that the projections of gerunds are not IPs (cf. Section 5.4.), a task which I am not prepared to take up here for reason of space.
5. The order *to not* sounds best when it is read contrastively, e.g. when the sentence is continued with a verb phrase (e.g. *Bill persuaded Sue to not ignore but reply to the letter*). According to McCawley (1988: 591), this order is subject to dialectal variation and personal preference.
6. Stowell (1981) suggested that extraposed clauses without an overt complementizer are ruled out by the Empty Category Principle (Chomsky 1981) if they are assumed to be CPs with an empty head, which would not be governed in extraposed (i.e. adjoined) positions. Along these lines, the YP in (57b) must be headed by *to*, and is therefore not an IP. I should like to point out, though, that this account does not explain why extraposed clauses cannot be IPs, as in (58a), whose head is lexically filled with a modal.
7. According to the predicate-internal subject hypothesis (Kitagawa 1985; Koopman & Sportiche 1985; Kuroda 1988), the (logical) subject is base-generated in the Spec position of the projection of the predicate. On this view, then, the syntactic representations for the examples in (57) would be as in (i), where the subject most probably originates from the Spec of the VP headed by *enter*:

(i) a. It would be a pity [$_{CP}$ for [$_{IP}$ John$_i$ [not [$_{YP}$ t_i [to [enter the race]]]]]]
b. It would be a pity [not [$_{YP}$ PRO [to [enter the race]]]]

While an overt subject moves to SpecIP, presumably for Case reasons, the phonetically null subject PRO either remains in the Spec of the YP projection of *to* or raises to the Spec of *to* to avoid government by *to*, if PRO may not occur in governed positions (cf. Chomsky 1981).

The categorial projection of the infinitival need not always be smaller than a CP, however. If embedded questions are CPs (cf. Section 4.1), then the categorial projection of the infinitival marker *to* is possibly dominated by CP, but it is hard to tell if there is an IP between CP and YP, the projection of *to*:

(ii) I wonder [$_{CP}$ what [[$_{YP}$ PRO to do]]

If the distribution of PRO is couched in terms of Case in that it cannot be assigned a non-null Case (cf. Chomsky & Lasnik 1993: 561), then PRO in (i) and (ii) might very well be staying in the Spec of the verb *enter* and *do* respectively. In any event, there seems to be no reason to suppose that the projection of the infinitival marker *to* is an IP.

A related issue that arises is the grammatical contrast in (iii), which Kayne (1990) attributed to *if* illicitly governing of PRO from the C^0 position, in contrast with *whether* in SpecCP:

(iii) a. *John wondered [$_{CP}$ [if [PRO to leave]]]
b. John wondered [$_{CP}$ whether [[PRO to leave]]]

This would be a problem for the null case account for PRO since it is assigned null case in both cases. Other facts about the complementizer *if* and *wh*-phrases in non-finite embedded questions appear to suggest that the contrast in in (iii) is likely to be unrelated to government. As shown in (iv), a (finite) embedded question headed by *if* may not appear in subject position, and the *wh*-phrase *why* may not occur in a non-finite embedded question:

(iv) a. [whether/*if we should leave now] is the question.
b. John wondered [when/where/how/*why to talk to Bill]

The ungrammatical versions of the examples in (iv) are certainly not attributable to government of PRO, since there is no PRO in (iva), and *why* in (ivb), like *whether* (iiib), is standardly assumed to be in SpecCP, where it does not govern PRO. Thus, the restricted distribution of *if* (and that of *why*) may be due to some other reasons than government.

8. As it will become clear in Section 5.4, my analysis remains unchanged should *to* turn out to be of a category other than V. What is crucial is that it is not in I, i.e. its projection is not IP.

9. One can take the grammatical contrast in (i) as evidence that the determiner takes the RC as an argument, since its presence is obligatory:

(i) a. *The John left.
b. The John [$_{CP}$ that I know] left.

The impression is further reinforced by the difference in (ii). One might suppose that the RC must be selected by the determiner:

(ii) a. John left.
b. *John [$_{CP}$ that I know] left.

In fact, the contrasts in (i) and (ii) are sometimes used to argue for the head-raising analysis of RCs (Schachter 1973; Vergnaud 1974 and Kayne 1994) according to which the proper name in (ib) originates in argument position in the embedded clause, since it cannot be base-generated in its surface position as shown in (ia).

However, the grammatical difference in (i) and (ii) does not necessarily show that the relationship between the determiner and the RC is selection. First, if the determiner selects the RC as argument, then it is not clear why the RC need not appear in cases like (79). If the reason for the ungrammaticality of the example in (ia) is because the RC argument of the determiner is missing, then why is its presence not obligatory in (79)? Second, a selectable formal feature does not require that its distribution be limited to selection, i.e. a selectable formal feature need not be selected. Consider the examples in (iii):

(iii) a. [whether John will come tomorrow] is an open question.
  b. [what to wear outdoors] depends on the weather.

Recall from Section 4.1 that the abstract [+Q] is a selectable formal feature, but in (iii) the feature is located in the head C position of a CP in the non-selected subject position. If there is a selectable formal feature in RCs, then clearly one has to explain why it differs from the [+Q] feature in that it must be selected (by the determiner).

The grammaticality contrasts in (i) and (ii) are arguably related to the syntax of proper names. In English, a proper name may cooccur with a determiner not only when a RC cooccurs, but also when a PP follows it, or when an AP precedes it:

(iv) a. Every Fred I know is a genius.
  b. The Paris of my youth was delightful.
  c. The short Smith is the master, and the tall Smith is the apprentice.

Apparently, proper names in English may be used as a common noun (only) in these cases, just like other run-of-the-mill common nouns like *table* and *chair*.

Semantically, the proper names in (iv) do not denote individuals, but properties. *Fred* or *Smith* in (iv) denote not the individual named Fred or Smith, but the property of being called Fred or Smith. The subjects in (iv) are then interpreted as generalized quantifier (Barwise & Cooper 1981) with the determiner taking a conjunction of two (extensional) properties (Stockwell, Schachter and Partee 1973), just like cases like *the round table* and *the small chair*. The obligatoriness of the RC when it co-occurs with a proper name as shown in the contrast in (ii) then follows. Here, the proper name cannot be interpreted as individual, since the adnominal predicate would fail to predicate of it, the two structurally not being in the subject-predicate relation (ie the subject in SpecIP, and the predicate in the VP). It may be interpreted as a property, but then its conjunction with the RC would yield a property, and the example would fail to have an individual-type subject for the predicate *left* to predicate of. The example is then excluded for the same reason as *man left or **man that I know left*.

Proper names in English may also be used as common nouns without an adnominal RC, PP or AP modifier, especially when they take the plural ending -*s*, (the grammaticality of the example in (ia) with the plural ending -*s* on the proper name also improves considerably, if not perfectly grammatical):

(v) a. Exactly three Johns came into the room.
  b. There are more than five Bills in my class.
  c. No two Joneses are alike.
  d. I don't know any Charlotte.
  e. The Xerox has been claimed to be a better photocopier than the Canon.

In (v), the numerals do not denote properties but are, semantically, most likely to be part of the preceding determiners, i.e. *exactly three*, *more than five*, and *no two* are complex determiners (Keenan 1987).

The impossibility of the example in (ia) requires a different explanation, although I have no specific proposal to make. There is apparently no reason why the proper name cannot be interpreted as a predicate on a par with *man* as it is in (iv) and (v). Languages seem to vary in this regard; Greek and German allow it, to name but two well-known cases. As a RC does not necessarily co-occur with the determiner, there is no ground to suppose that the relation between the two is selection.

10. Notice that the morpheme *de* appearing in Chinese RCs also shows up between the possessor and the head noun in non-RCs, as shown in (i):

(i)   a.   Zhangsan de shu.
           Z.   DE book
           'Zhangsan's book'
     b.   Neige-ren de fangzi.
           that-person DE room
           'That person's room.'

Even if the *de* in RCs and that in (i) can somehow be related, it does not seem to be a good reason to assume that *de* in RCs is the morphological manifestation of a formal feature in RCs.

Given the island effects, one might ask what moves in Chinese RCs and why the movement is obligatory, two issues that also arise in English RCs when no overt *wh*-phrase is present, eg. *the man I saw*. It may be that in a range of cases involving what is commonly thought of as null operators (Chomsky 1982) some formal feature on the verb, at least the θ-feature, moves to the head noun in the manner suggested by Chomsky (1995), and the movement is obligatory since the feature on the verb would otherwise not be assigned or checked (cf. Section 6).

11. If head-movement is also taken to be triggered by the need to check a formal feature, then one must allow in addition to the Spec–Head relation either the head position or the adjunction structure in the head position as configurations for feature-checking, depending on whether head-movement is a subsitution or adjunction operation) (Chris Wilder, p.c.). This complication does not bear directly on cases discussed here since they clearly involve XP-movement.

In Kayne's (1994) theory of phrase structure, there is no true distinction between subjects and adjuncts. Hence, the conclusion that relative pronouns adjoin to IP is largely compatible with Kayne's analysis of RCs according to which the head noun is in the Spec of the relative pronoun, the projection of which is in the Spec of the RC (cf. Borsley 1997 for some problems with this view). However, it is not clear how the DP/PP asymmetry discussed in the text is to be explained on this view, as one must distinguish adjunction to CP (or movement to SpecCP), which is possible for both DP and PP, from that to IP, which shows the DP/PP asymmetry. Kayne (1994: 88–90) gives an account for the general lack of an overt relative pronoun for subject and object arguments in Romance languages (cf. Bianchi 1995), which recalls the DP/PP asymmetry discussed in the text, but has no explanation for why English may have an overt relative pronoun for subject and object arguments in finite clauses.

12. There may be two additional base-positions for DP, both are post-verbal. One is in the right-dislocation construction, and the other figures in Heavy NP Shift (Ross 1967):

(i)   a.   I gave him a quarter, that guy over there.
     b.   They never consider it very seriously, the proposal that I made.
(ii)   a.   John sent to the publisher an article that has received little attention in the mainstream media.
     b.   Mary will bring for the children various small toys that she collected as donations last summer.

I put these two base-positions for DP aside here, since the non-argument positions discussed in this paper are pre-verbal.

13. Based largely on facts about word-order in English and Romance, Rizzi (1997: 296) suggested a more elaborate structure for clauses, as in (i) (Top=Topic, Foc=Focus):

    (i)   ... C⁰ (Top*) Foc (Top*)

    On this view, the relative pronouns and topicalized phrases (topicalized PP and DP as well as left-dislocated DP) land in different positions, the former in the Spec of TopP, and the latter in SpecFocP, accounting for the word-order contrast in the Italian examples in (i):

    (ii) a.   Un uomo a cui,   il premio Nobel, lo daranno   senz'altro.
                A man to whom the prize   Nobel it give-FUT-3-PL undoubtedly
                'A man, to whom, the prize Nobel, they will give it undoubtedly.'
          b.   *Un uomo, il premio Nobel, a cui,   lo daranno   senz'altro.
                A man the prize   Nobel to whom it give-FUT-3-PL undoubtedly
                'A man, the prize Nobel, to whom, they will give it undoubtedly.'

    Obviously, the analysis I propose here is incompatible with this view, since both relative pronouns and topicalized and left-dislocated DP are adjoined to IP, whence comes the unified account for the different distributions of DP and PP for both RCs and non-RCs. For the cases considered in this paper, DP behaves uniformly with respect to occurrence in non-argument positions, regardless of whether it is a *wh*-phrase or not. If relative pronouns and other DPs do not land in the same positions in the structure in (i), then it seems to be an accident that the different landing sites have the same restriction with respect to the DP/PP difference.

    The grammatical contrast in (ii) also holds in English, but to a much lesser degree. The English counterpart of the example (iia) is quite marginal, although it seems better than the counterpart of the example in (iib). The difference can be excluded on independent grounds, however. As is well-known, relative pronouns c-command the RC (and consequently all the arguments appearing in it), a fact that also holds in Italian:

    (iii) a.   A man (who) I know got the Nobel prize.
          b.   *A man I know who got the Nobel prize.
    (iv) a.   A man (to whom) I know they gave the Nobel prize.
          b.   *A man I know to whom they gave the Nobel prize.
    (v)   a.   Un uomo a cui   so   daranno   senz'altro   il premio Nobel.
                A man   to whom I-know give-FUT-3-PL undoubtedly the prize Nobel
                'A man to whom I know, they will give the prize Nobel undoubtedly.'
          b.   *Un uomo so   a cui   daranno   senz'altro   il premio Nobel.
                A man I-know to whom give-FUT-3-PL undoubtedly the prize Nobel
                'A man I know to whom they will give the prize Nobel undoubtedly.'

    Thus, the ungrammaticality of the example in (iib) may be reduced to that in (vb). A close examination of the facts and the arguments for the structure in (i) deserves more space than I can afford here.

14. This statement might seem too strong at first glance. There are certainly cases where a PP may not be adjoined to a category that in some other syntactic contexts allows PP-adjunction:

    (i)   a.   *John came to the office early [on the shelf [to put all the books]]
          b.   *These books are easy [to the children [to read]]
          c.   *Mary believed [these stories [to the New York Times [to have been leaked]]]

Notice that DP is also banned from the same adjoined positions, indicating that adjunction in these cases might be excluded independently, for reasons that are unclear:

(ii)   a.   *John came to the office early [all the books [to put on the shelf]]
       b.   *These books are easy [the children [to read to]]
       c.   *Mary believed [these books [the New York Times [to have been leaked to]]]

Apart from the left-dislocation construction (cf. Section 5.2), there seem to be no other non-argument positions where a DP is allowed but PP is not, in accord with the observation that PP has a wider distribution than DP.

These cases recall facts about adverbials. There seems to be no categorial restriction on the adjunction sites for adverbials, but that does not mean that adverbials may freely adjoin to any category. Thus, speaker-oriented adverbials do not occur naturally before a thematic verb (cf. Jackendoff 1972):

(iii)   a.   George (probably) will (probably) have (probably) been (*probably) reading the book when you arrive.
       b.   (as far as I can tell,) John (, as far as I can tell,) has (, as far as I can tell,) been (*, as far as I can tell,) lying.

The facts in (i)–(ii) on the one hand, and those in (iii) on the other may not have the same explanation, but it seems clear that there is no categorial restriction on the adjunction site.

15. The account in the text still holds even if it turns out that the SPC has no independent status, but is reducible from theories of Morphology and feature-checking (Chomsky 1995: 318–319).

As discussed in Section 5.2, one can demonstrate whether a position can host a (base-generated) DP or PP by exhibiting a DP or PP in that position. For SpecCP, however, the demonstration is rather tricky since the only piece of evidence for a phrase being base-generated in that position is the occurrence of *whether* (Emonds 1976: 190):

(i)   a.   I wonder whether he will show up.
      b.   I wonder whether to show up.

Given its limited distribution of *whether*, it is almost impossible to determine its category, but the fact is that SpecCP can host either a DP or PP. Therefore, the SPC should be taken to mean that a phrase XP with some property R may move to a position P only if XP with Q may independently appear in P, where the value of R ranges over categorial features ([±N] and [±V]) and formal features like ([±Q]) (cf. Section 4.1).

16. The examples in (i) show that at least categorially, DP and PP may be generated as adjuncts to CP:

(i)   a.   This book, who do you think would read it?
      b.   When you have a problem, who do you talk to?

From the perspective of SPC, it should be possible to adjoin DP to an embedded CP, but the examples in (14) where a DP occurs to the left of *for* show that it is not the case. These cases are arguably related to the general ban on adjunction to embedded clauses (cf. Chomsky 1986), regardless of the category appearing in the adjoined position:

(ii)   a.   *They believed [this book [that no one would read it]]
        (cf. They believed that no one would read this book)
       b.   *I wonder [when you have a problem [who you talk to]]
        (cf. I wonder who you talk to when you have a problem)
       c.   *John asked Bill [in case of emergency [what number to call for help]]
        (cf. John asked Bill what number to call for help in case of emergency)

d. *They will soon announce [yesterday [that the minister decided to resign]]
    (cf. They will soon announce that yesterday the minister decided to resign)

The SPC does not predict, however, that a PP may not intervene between a preposition and its NP argument (cf. also the examples in (17)):

(iii) a. To [$_{DP}$ the man in the room]
      b. *To [$_{DP}$ in the room the man]

Two facts indicate that the contrast in (iii) is not due to adjacency on Case assignment (cf. footnote 2), but to the position where adnominal PP may occur. First, the same contrast holds of subjects, which need not be assigned Case adjacently:

(iv) a. [$_{DP}$ the man in the room] obviously was the boss.
     b. *[$_{DP}$ in the room the man] obviously was the boss.

Second, it also holds in German postpostional phrases even though the DP argument is adjacent to the postposition from which it receives Case:

(v) a. [$_{DP}$ dem Bild   mit goldenem Rahmen] gegenüber.
             the picture with golden   frame   opposite
         'Opposite the picture with a golden frame.'
    b. *[$_{DP}$ mit goldenem Rahmen dem Bild] gegenüber.

If adnominal modifiers syntactically must form a right-constituent with the projection of N (at least in English and German), however this is to be derived (cf. Jackendoff 1977; Abney 1987), possibly due to the independent fact that a predicate follows the subject of which it is predicated, then the examples in (iiib), (ivb) and (vb) would be excluded. Hence, the restricted distribution of adnominal PP is not a problem specifically to the SPC.

References

Abney, S. (1987). *The English noun phrase and its sentential aspects*. Doctoral dissertation, MIT.
Akmajian, A. & T. Wasow. (1975). The constituent structure of VP and AUX and the position of the verb BE. *Linguistic analysis* 1: 205–245.
Barwise, J. & R. Cooper. (1981). Generalized quantifiers and natural language. *Linguistics and Philosophy* 4: 159–219.
Bianchi, V. (1995). *Consequences of antisymmetry for the syntax of headed relative clauses*. Doctoral dissertation, Scuola Normale Superiore, Pisa.
Borsley, R. (1997). Relative clauses and the theory of phrase structure. *Linguistic inquiry* 28: 629–647.
Browning, M. A. (1987). *Null operator constructions*. Doctoral dissertation, MIT.
Chomsky, N. (1957). *Syntactic structures*. Mouton: The Hague.
Chomsky, N. (1965). *Aspects of theory of syntax*. Cambridge, Mass.: MIT Press.
Chomsky, N. (1970). Remarks on nominalization. *Readings in English transformational grammar*, edited by R. Jacobs & P. Rosenbaum, 184–221.Waltham, Mass.: Ginn.

Chomsky, N. (1973). Conditions on transformations. *A festschrift for Morris Halle*, edited by S.R. Anderson and P. Kiparsky, 232–286. New York: Holt, Rinehart and Winston.
Chomsky, N. (1977). On *Wh*-movement. *Formal syntax*, edited by P. Culicover, T. Wasow & A. Akmajian, 71–132. New York: Academic Press,
Chomsky, N. (1981). *Lectures on government and binding*. Dordrecht: Foris.
Chomsky, N. (1982). *Some concepts and consequences of theory of government and binding*. Cambridge, Mass.: MIT Press.
Chomsky, N. (1986). *Barriers*. Cambridge, Mass.: MIT Press.
Chomsky, N. (1991). Some notes on economy of derivation and representation. *Principles and parameters in comparative grammar*, edited by R. Freidin, 417–454. Cambridge, Mass.: MIT Press.
Chomsky, N. (1993). A minimalist program for linguistic theory. *A view from building 20: Essays in honor of Sylvain Bromberger*, edited by K. Hale & S.J. Keyser, 1–52. Cambridge, Mass.: MIT Press.
Chomsky, N. (1995). *The minimalist program*. Cambridge, Mass.: MIT Press.
Chomsky, N. & H. Lasnik. (1977). Filters and control. *Linguistic Inquiry* 8: 425–504).
Chomsky, N. & H. Lasnik. (1993). The theory of principles and parameters. *Syntax: An International Handbook for Comtemporary Research*, edited by J. Jacobs, A. von Stechow, W. Sternefeld, & T. Vennemann, 506–569. Berlin: de Gruyter.
Cinque, G. (1977). The movement nature of left-dislocation. *Linguistic Inquiry* 8: 397–411.
Cinque, G. (1990). *Types of A'-dependencies*. Cambridge, Mass.: MIT Press.
Emonds, J. (1970). *Root and structure-preserving transformations*. Doctoral dissertation, MIT.
Emonds, J. (1976). *A transformational approach to English syntax*. New York: Academic Press.
Emonds, J. (1979). Appositive relatives have no properties. *Linguistic Inquiry* 10: 211–243.
Huang, J. C-T. (1981). Move-WH in a language without Wh-movement. *Linguistic Review* 1: 369–418.
Huang, J. C-T. (1982). *Logical relations in Chinese and the theory of grammar*. Doctoral dissertation, MIT.
Jackendoff, R. (1972). *Semantics interpretation in generative grammar*. Cambridge, Mass.: MIT Press.
Jackendoff, R. (1977). *X'-Syntax*. Cambridge, Mass.: MIT Press.
Kayne, R. (1990). Romance clitics and PRO. *NELS* 20: 255–302.
Kayne, R. (1994). *Antisymmetry in syntax*. Cambridge, Mass.: MIT Press.
Keenan, E. (1987). A semantic definition of (in)definiteness. *The Representation of (In)definiteness*, edited by E. Reuland & A.G.B. ter Meulen, 286–317. Cambridge, Mass.: MIT Press.
Keyser, S.J. (1968). Review of Sven Jackobson, adverbial positions in English. *Language* 44: 357–374.

Kitagawa, Y. (1985). *Subjects in Japanese and English*. Doctoral dissertation, University of Massachusetts, Amherst.
Koopman, H. & D. Sportiche. (1985). θ-theory and extraction. *Abstract in GLOW Newsletter*, number 14: Department of Language and Literature, Tilburg University.
Koster, J. (1986). *Domains and dynasties*. Dordrecht: Foris.
Kuroda, S-Y. (1988). Whether we agree or not: A comparative syntax of English and Japanese. *Lingvisticae Investigationes* 12: 1–47.
Law, P. (1995a). On learning and grammatical theory. *ZAS Papers in Linguistics* 4: 58–82.
Law, P. (1995b). On the adjacency constraint on case assignment. *ZAS Papers in Linguistics* 5: 53–84.
May, R. (1985). *Logical Form*. Cambridge, Mass.: MIT Press.
McCawley, J.D. (1988). *The syntactic phenomena of English*, Vol. 2: Chicago: The University of Chicago Press.
Pollock, J.-Y. (1989). Verb movement, Universal Grammar, and the structure of IP. *Linguistic Inquiry* 20: 365–424.
Pullum, G. & D. Wilson. (1977). Autonomous syntax and the analysis of auxiliaries. *Language* 53: 741–788.
Pullum, G. (1982). Syncategorematicity and English infinitival *to*. *Glossa* 16: 181–215.
Reinhart, T. (1976). *Syntactic domain of anaphora*. Doctoral dissertation, MIT.
Rizzi, L. (1990). *Relativized minimality*. Cambridge, MA: MIT Press.
Rizzi, L. (1997). The fine structure of the left periphery. *Elements of Grammar: A handbook in generative syntax*, edited by L. Haegeman, 281–337. Dordrecht: Kluwer.
Ross, J.R. (1967). *Constraints on variables in syntax*. Doctoral dissertation, MIT.
Rouveret, A. and J-R. Vergnaud. (1980). Specifying reference to the subject. *Linguistic Inquiry* 11: 97–202.
Sag, I. (1997). English relative clause constructions. *Journal of Linguistics* 33: 431–483.
Schachter, P. (1973). Focus and relativization. *Language* 49: 19–46.
Stockwell, R., P. Schachter & B. Partee. (1973). *The major syntactic structures of English*. New York: Holt, Rinehart and Winston.
Stowell, T. (1981). *Origins of phrase structure*. Doctoral dissertation, MIT.
Stowell, T. (1982). The tense of infinitives. *Linguistic Inquiry* 13: 561–570.
Vergnaud, J.-R. (1974). *French relative clauses*. Doctoral dissertation, MIT.
Zagona, K. (1988). *Verb phrase syntax*. Dordrecht: Kluwer.

Relative Asymmetries and Hindi Correlatives[*]

Anoop Mahajan
UCLA

1. Introduction

Hindi has a variety of relative clause constructions with a number of interesting properties that are hard to account for in terms of standard treatments of other familiar relative clause constructions in Indo-European languages. The relativized noun, its demonstrative head and the modifying relative clause appear in a number of possible permutations and combinations. Within the finite clause relative clause types (the correlative constructions), the relative clauses can either appear immediately to the right of the modified noun, or in a preposed position, or in a postposed position. Given various options available in the finite relatives in Hindi, this area of Hindi syntax provides an interesting challenge to the standard theories of relative clauses and relative clause positioning.

The investigations into Hindi correlative constructions within the generative tradition go back to the research initiated on this topic in the early seventies. These investigations, exemplified by Donaldson (1971), Subbarao (1974) and Kachru (1978), provide a variety of analyses for the Hindi correlative constructions. This paper develops a somewhat new perspective on Hindi relative clauses in light of some recent theoretical developments in the general study of relative clauses. The essential purpose of the paper is to suggest that most of the properties of various Hindi correlative constructions can be accounted for within a head movement approach to relative clauses as presented in Kayne (1994)

---

[*] I wish to thank the participants of the Relative Clause Workshop held at ZAS, Berlin, on November 22–24, 1996, for their comments on the version of this paper that was presented at that workshop. Special thanks to Chris Wilder for his detailed comments on an earlier draft of this paper.

supplemented by the Copy theory of movement proposed in the minimalist framework (cf. Chomsky 1995).

The main aims of this paper are:

I.   to describe Hindi correlatives in terms of a head movement analysis.
II. to present and provide a unified account of different types of correlatives.
III. to account for certain well known asymmetries found between different types of correlative constructions within a unified approach that adopts movement as a basic strategy yielding various positions of the relative clauses in Hindi relative constructions.
IV. to suggest that various properties of preposed correlatives follow from a leftward scrambling analysis of this construction type.

On the basis of the treatment of various correlative constructions in Hindi developed here, I also aim to construct a limited argument against a base generation analysis for the Hindi preposed relatives. Furthermore, I would like to suggest that a unified movement approach would be conceptually superior to an approach that takes movement and base generation as coexisting strategies for describing various positions of the relative clauses. While a unified (movement based) approach will face a greater empirical and explanatory burden, if we find independent motivation for the existence of the movement operations utilized by the descriptive mechanisms adopted, a unified approach will be more appealing.

2. Types of relative clause in Hindi

There is a basic distinction between two type of relativization strategies in Hindi. The first strategy covers various types of prenominal nonfinite relatives. These relatives usually employ a non-finite participial form of the verb in a relative clause preceding the modified NP. These relative clauses do not use a relative pronoun.[1]

(1) meri: paṭʰi: hui   kita:b ...
     my   read-PERF-FEM be-PART-FEM book (FEM)
     'The book that I read'

A variation of this type of prenominal relative clause employs an agentive marking following an infinitival form of the verb preceding the modified NP.

(2) mehnat   karne va:la: a:dmi:
     hard work do-INF (agentive marking)   person
     'a person who works hard'

I will not investigate these kind of non-finite prenominal relative constructions in this paper. The main focus of our current investigation are various kinds of finite correlative constructions that fall into three major categories:

I. Normal: Dem N [*jo* ......]
II. Postposed: Relative clause appears extraposed
III. Preposed: Relative clause appears to the left of the Dem N

These types of relative clauses are exemplified below:

- Normal:
(3) mujhe vo aːdmiː [jo siːtaː-ko accʰaː lagtaː hɛ] pasand
     I-DAT DEM man REL Sita-DAT nice seem-IMP be-PRES like
     nahĩː hɛ
     not be-PRES
     'I do not like the man who Sita likes.'

- Postposed:
(4) mujhe vo admiː pasand nahĩː hɛ [jo siːta-ko accʰaː
     I-DAT DEM man like not be-PRES REL Sita-DAT nice
     lagtaː hɛ]
     seem-IMP be-PRES
     'I do not like the man who Sita likes.'

- Preposed:
(5) [jo siːtaː-ko accʰaː lagtaː hɛ] mujhe vo aːdmiː
     REL Sita-DAT nice seem-IMP be-PRES I-DAT DEM man
     pasand nahĩː hɛ
     like not be-PRES
     'I do not like the man who Sita likes.'

These basic types of finite relative constructions allow for a number of additional variations. For instance, in all of the finite relative clauses exemplified above, the relative pronoun is positioned at the beginning of the relative clause (a standard position for the relative pronoun in most of the well-known finite relative constructions in English type languages). However, Hindi allows the relative pronoun to stay in its base position (in the position in which the relative pronoun would be expected to be base generated).

That is, the relative pronoun *jo* does not have to be fronted. It can appear in its base position. Given this option, the finite clauses exemplified above will have the following possible optional variants:

(6) mujhe vo a:dmi: [si:ta:-ko jo acc^{h}a: lagta: hɛ]
    I-DAT DEM man Sita-DAT REL nice seem-IMP be-PRES
    pasand nahĩ: hɛ
    like   not   be-PRES
    'I do not like the man who Sita likes.'

(7) mujhe vo a:dmi: pasand nahĩ: hɛ   [si:ta:-ko jo acc^{h}a:
    I-DAT DEM man like   not be-PRES Sita-DAT REL nice
    lagta: hɛ]
    seem-IMP be-PRES
    'I do not like the man who Sita likes.'

(8) [si:ta:-ko jo acc^{h}a: lagta: hɛ]   mujhe vo a:dmi: pasand
    Sita-DAT REL nice seem-IMP be-PRES I-DAT DEM man like
    nahĩ: hɛ
    not   be-PRES
    'I do not like the man who Sita likes.'

Given the fact that Hindi is generally a *wh*-in-situ language, the variation exemplified in (6)–(8) is not surprising. Normal *wh*-pronouns in Hindi do not undergo obligatory movement to a sentence initial position in simple sentences though they can (optionally) scramble to this position (cf. Mahajan 1990). Relative pronouns seem to behave in a similar manner yielding (6)–(8) variants of (3)–(5). Thus, a simple independent fact about *wh*-in-situ and the scrambling possibilities in Hindi accounts for one type of variation found in the relative constructions in Hindi. While I will not entirely adopt the approach that I have illustrated above to account for the variation exemplified above, I will argue for the general validity of this type of approach. The essential point being made above is that given two independent properties about Hindi syntax, *wh*-in-situ and leftward scrambling, we can give a unified descriptive account of two similar relative constructions in Hindi. I will follow this strategy in suggesting that given these two properties of Hindi syntax, and given the mechanisms of Copy theory of movement, we can account for a large amount of variation found in correlative constructions in Hindi. Central to what I will be arguing for is the idea that Hindi has rather productive mechanisms of leftward movement (scrambling) and these mechanisms can themselves account for various positions and properties of relative clauses in Hindi. In taking this view, I am indirectly arguing against the approaches that posit base generation as one of the mechanisms for accounting for certain types of correlative constructions while they employ movement as a separate mechanism to account for the other types of correlative constructions. The relevant issues will become clearer once we examine various approaches that have been developed to account for different types of relative clauses. We will turn to those directly in the next section.

3. Various approaches to Hindi finite relatives

Let us take the three types of correlative clauses illustrated above (normal, preposed and postposed relatives) as the basic divisions in the typology of finite relative constructions in Hindi. Within this empirical domain, we can distinguish three essential approaches to the study of the finite relative clauses in Hindi and certain other closely related languages.

3.1 *Unified base approach I*

This is represented by Subbarao (1974, 1984), Kachru (1978) (for Hindi) and Wali (1982) (for Marathi). The general idea behind all of these studies is that all three types of relative constructions (exemplified above) are derived from the same underlying structure by movement/deletion rules.

3.2 *Unified base approach II*

This is represented by McCawley (1992) and Donaldson (1971). In this approach, all the three types of relative clauses discussed above have a different underlying structure. Displaced (preposed as well as postposed) relative clause are base generated in their surface positions, thus eliminating the role of movement rules.

3.3 *Mixed base approach*

Represented by the works of Dasgupta (1980) and Srivastav (1991), these approaches posit different underlying structures for postposed and preposed relative clauses. The general idea that this approach follows is that while the postposed relative clauses are placed in their surface position by an extraposition operation, the preposed relative clauses are base generated in their surface (sentence initial) position.

3.4 *Justification for the three approaches*

The three logically possible explanations that are summarized above have their respective advantages and disadvantages. The mixed base approach seeks empirical justification from the differences between the syntactic/semantic properties of the preposed relative clauses as compared to the properties of postposed relatives. This view, developed first by Dasgupta (1980) for Bangla, has recently been argued for extensively by Srivastav (1991). She discusses a number of differences between preposed and postposed relatives and on the basis of these asymmetries proposes that both movement as well as base generation strategies must be available in order to account for the asymmetries between preposed and postposed relatives. I discuss the asymmetries in some detail in the next section before presenting my own proposal.

The two unified approaches take a totally opposite view from each other. While the first approach uses movement as a basic mechanism to account for the position of all the displaced relative clauses, the second approach takes base generation as the mechanism for placing the displaced relative clauses in their surface positions. One of the arguments that McCawley (1992) uses to justify the generality of base generation for preposed as well the postposed relative clauses is that the postposed relative clauses in Hindi do not obey the right roof constraint (as noted by Subbarao 1984). However, as discussed in Mahajan (1995), there are reasons to doubt the invalidity of the right roof constraint for Hindi extraposition. Apart from this point (see McCawley 1992 for the details of this discussion), this approach essentially has the basic advantage over the mixed base approaches in that it uses one single mechanism for accounting for the various positions of the relative clauses. As would be obvious, this approach, therefore, bears the empirical burden of explaining the asymmetries between the preposed and postposed relatives. For some of the relevant discussion on this, the reader is referred to McCawley (1992).

The most traditional approach in the domain of our discussion of displaced relatives is the approach which uses movement as a general mechanism for deriving the surface positions of the various types of relative clauses. The obvious advantage of this approach is that most theories of syntax do employ movement operations to change the base generated order of constituents and therefore using an operation that is an integral part of the theory comes "for free". This theory, however, has a problem that it shares with the other unified approach in that it has to face the empirical burden of accounting for the asymmetries in the behavior of the different kind of relative clauses in Hindi. In addition, while it is a well known fact that extraposition to the right is relatively frequently encountered, extraposition to the left is not a commonly attested movement operation (cf. Baltin 1985). Therefore, it would be difficult to motivate a leftward extraposition rule to account for the position of the preposed relatives.

Given the recent developments in the syntactic theory, especially the antisymmetry approach of Kayne (1994), the movement based approach also faces a somewhat different kind of problem. Kayne's framework essentially disallows rightward movement rules making the classical rightward extraposition operation unavailable to derive the position of the postposed relatives. The unified movement based approach will therefore have to come up with an alternative to account for the positioning of the extraposed relatives.

3.5 Movement based unified base approach revived

As indicated in the introduction of this paper, I am essentially going to argue for the unified movement approach despite the apparent difficulties that it faces. The essential reason for taking this stand is that (as mentioned above) the movement operations are essentially an integral part of the theory and in that sense, come for free. As I will demonstrate, it is possible to account for most of the positions of the displaced relative clauses using independently motivated movement operations (XP and X^0 movement). In addition, it is also possible to account for the asymmetries between the preposed relatives and postposed relatives in this approach. This can be achieved within a sufficiently constrained Copy theory of movement. Given the unavailability of the rightward extraposition operation (in the theory of movement that I am adopting), I will suggest an alternative treatment of extraposition as remnant leftward movement which appears to yield the desirable results. To derive the leftward positioning of preposed relatives, I employ a leftward DP/DemP scrambling operation (that is independently available in Hindi). This eliminates the need for leftward extraposition which may be a dubious movement operation to employ.

In this paper, I will not directly argue against the non-movement approaches (either for the preposed relatives alone or for all types of relatives). However, the essential purpose of this paper is to sketch out a movement based approach to all kinds of relative clauses that accounts for the various properties of the correlative clauses. Most of the mechanisms used in the arguments that I develop are independently motivated movement options available in Hindi. I also employ certain mechanisms made available by the Copy theory of movement.

4. Relative asymmetries

As indicated above, the major argument for the mixed base approach is the existence of certain known asymmetries (cf. Subbarao 1974; Srivastav 1991) between preposed relatives and the postposed relatives. These asymmetries are described in the following sub-sections (for more details, see Srivastav 1991).

4.1 *Head restrictions*

The head of the relative clause in preposed relative clause constructions can appear in the relative clause as well as in the main clause. Normal and postposed relatives vary from preposed relatives in this respect. According to Srivastav (1991), the head must not appear in the relative clause in the normal and the postposed relatives. My judgments differ somewhat from that of Srivastav though the central point about the asymmetries between the different types of relatives does remain.[2] The relevant distinctions are illustrated in the examples below (the head of the relative clause is italicized in these examples):

I. Preposed relatives:
Preposed relative constructions allow for the head noun to be present in the main clause as well as in the relative clause. The head can also be absent from either of these two positions.[3]

– Head in the preposed relative clause:
(9) [jo a:dmi: si:ta:-ko pasand hɛ] mujhe vo acc^{h}a: nahĩ:
     REL man Sita-DAT like be-PRES I-DAT DEM nice not
     lagta:
     seem-IMP
     'I do not like the man who Sita likes.'

– Head in the relative clause as well as in the main clause:
(10) [jo a:dmi: si:ta:-ko pasand hɛ] mujhe vo a:dmi: acc^{h}a: nahĩ:
     REL man Sita-DAT like be-PRES I-DAT DEM man nice not
     lagta:
     seem-IMP
     'I do not like the man who Sita likes.'

– Head in the main clause:
(11) [jo si:ta:-ko pasand hɛ] mujhe vo a:dmi: acc^{h}a: nahĩ:
     REL Sita-DAT like be-PRES I-DAT DEM man nice not
     lagta:
     seem-IMP
     'I do not like the man who Sita likes.'

II. Normal relatives:

- Head in the main clause:
  (12) mujhe vo a:dmi: [jo si:ta:-ko pasand hɛ] accʰa: nahĩ:
       I-DAT DEM man REL Sita-DAT like be-PRES nice not
       lagta:
       seem-IMP
       'I do not like the man who Sita likes.'

- Head in the relative clause as well as in the main clause:
  (13) *mujhe vo a:dmi: [jo a:dmi: si:ta:-ko pasand hɛ] accʰa: nahĩ:
       I-DAT DEM man REL man Sita-DAT like be-PRES nice not
       lagta:
       seem-IMP
       'I do not like the man who Sita likes.'

- Head in the relative clause (but not in the main clause):
  (14) %mujhe vo [jo a:dmi: si:ta:-ko pasand hɛ] accʰa: nahĩ:
       I-DAT DEM REL man Sita-DAT like be-PRES nice not
       lagta:
       seem-IMP
       'I do not like the man who Sita likes.'

Srivastav (1991) marks sentences like (14) as ungrammatical while (14) is acceptable for me. However, independent of this judgement, there is an obvious asymmetry between the preposed and normal relatives in that preposed relatives allow for the head to be present both in the main clause as well as in the relative clause. Normal relatives do not allow for this dual head option.

III. Postposed relatives:

- Head in the main clause:
  (15) mujhe vo a:dmi: accʰa: nahĩ: lagta: [jo si:ta:-ko pasand
       I-DAT DEM man nice not seem-IMP REL Sita-DAT like
       hɛ]
       be-PRES
       'I do not like the man who Sita likes.'

– Head in the main clause as well as in the relative clause:
(16) %mujhe vo aːdmiː accʰaː nahĩː lagtaː   jo aːdmiː
     I-DAT DEM man nice   not seem-IMP REL man
     siːtaː-ko pasand hɛ
     Sita-DAT like   be-PRES
     'I do not like the man who Sita likes.'

– Head in the relative clause but not in the main clause:
(17) *mujhe vo accʰaː nahĩː lagtaː   [jo aːdmiː siːtaː-ko pasand
     I-DAT DEM nice not seem-IMP REL man   Sita-DAT like
     hɛ]
     be-PRES
     'I do not like the man who Sita likes.'

Here again my judgments differ from the ones reported in Srivastav (1991) in that she finds sentences like (16) ungrammatical while I find them acceptable.[4] However, once again the central point about the differences between the postposed and preposed relatives is established by the ungrammaticality of (17) in that postposed relatives do not allow the head to be absent in the main clause while this is allowed in preposed relatives.

Thus, the normal and the postposed relatives form a natural class as opposed to the preposed relatives in Srivastav's data. For me, the three types of relative clauses all behave somewhat differently with respect to the restrictions on the presence of the head.

4.2 *Demonstrative restrictions*

Subbarao (1984) notes that there is a indefiniteness requirement associated with the position of the relative clauses in Hindi. If the head noun is an indefinite then the relative clause must be to the right of it (either in a normal position or postposed but not preposed). This restriction is illustrated by the examples below:

(18) mujhe kuch kitaːbẽ [jo siːtaː-ne khariːdiː thĩ]   paṭʰniː hẽ
      I-DAT some books REL Sita-ERG buy-PERF be-PST read-INF be-PRES
      'I have to read some books that Sita bought.'

(19) mujhe kuch kitabẽ paṭʰniː hẽ   [jo siːtaː-ne khariːdiː thĩː]
      I-DAT some books read-INF be-PRES REL Sita-ERG buy-PERF be-PST
      'I have to read some books that Sita bought.'

(20) *[jo siːtaː-ne khariːdiː thiː] mujhe kuch kitaːbẽ paṛʰniː
    REL Sita-ERG buy-PERF be-PST I-DAT some books read-INF
    hẽ
    be-PRES
    'I have to read some books that Sita bought.'

Srivastav (1991: 648–649) notes that an overt partitive or an overt demonstrative before the head noun improves these constructions:

(21) [jo siːtaː-ne khariːdiː thiː] mujhe un mẽ se kuch
    REL Sita-ERG buy-PERF be-PST I-DAT those from some
    kitaːbẽ paṛʰniː hẽ
    books read-INF be-PRES
    'I have to read some books that Ram bought.'

(22) [jo accʰiː hẽ] mujhe vo kuch kitaːbẽ paṛʰniː hẽ
    REL good be-PRES I-DAT DEM some book read-INF be-PRES
    'I have to read those few books that are good.'

Furthermore, bare NPs do not allow preposed relatives (Srivastav 1991: 649).

(23) *[jo accʰiː hɛ] mujhe kitaːb paṛʰniː hɛ
    REL good be-PRES I-DAT book read-INF be-PRES
    = 'I have to read book which is good.'

(24) *[jo kitaːb accʰiː hɛ] mujhe kitaːb paṛʰniː hɛ
    REL book good be-PRES I-DAT book read-INF be-PRES
    = 'I have to read book which is good.'

4.3 *Multiple relatives*

Srivastav (1991) points out that preposed relatives allow multiple relativization while the normal and postposed relatives do not.

(25) jis aːdmiː-ne jo kitaːb dekhiː, us-ne vo khariːd
    REL man-ERG REL book see-PERF DEM-ERG DEM buy-PERF
    liː
    take-PERF
    = 'Whichever man saw whichever book, he bought it.'

(26) jis aːdmiː-ne jo kitaːb dekhiː, us aːdmiː-ne vo kitaːb
    REL man-ERG REL book see-PERF DEM man-ERG DEM book
    khariːd liː
    buy-PERF take-PERF
    'Whichever man saw whichever book, he bought it.'

(27)*/%us a:dmi:-ne vo kita:b khari:d li:, jis-ne jo dekhi:
DEM man-ERG DEM book buy-PERF takePERF REL-ERG REL see-PERF
= 'Whichever man saw whichever book, he bought it.'

While (27) is not acceptable for Srivastav, the sentence is acceptable to me and many other speakers of Delhi Hindi.[5] However, I have no proposal to make about the multiple relative constructions, so I will not pursue this issue here.

4.4 *Summary of this section*

It is clear from the evidence presented in this section that there are a number of asymmetries between the three types of relative clauses in Hindi. This evidence (though not exactly in this form) is taken by the mixed base approach taken by Srivastav (1991) to indicate that the source for the preposed relatives is different from that of the normal and the postposed relatives. Her basic proposal is that the preposed relatives are CPs base generated as adjuncts to the left of the main clause. Postposed relatives are derived from normal relatives by rightward extraposition. An obvious advantage of this approach is that it does not require a mechanism of leftward extraposition. Srivastav suggests that the various asymmetries noted above can be accounted by treating the base generated left adjoined relative clause as a quantifier that binds a variable (Dem or Dem+Head Noun) in the main clause.

In what follows, I will suggest a different account of the derivation of various types of relative constructions in Hindi and then suggest how we can account for some of the asymmetries noted above within this framework.

5. A head movement analysis of normal Hindi relatives

The analysis that I develop here is based essentially on Kayne's (1994) proposal about the derivation of relative clauses (Kayne's proposal is based on an analysis suggested by Vergnaud a number of years ago). The essential idea behind this approach is that the relative head that appears outside the relative clause is actually base generated inside the relative clause (next to the relative pronoun) and is moved to the left (to its surface position) by a movement operation.

5.1 *Normal relatives in a head movement analysis*

In a head movement analysis, to derive a normal relative like (28) below, we start with an underlying structure like (29) (I give only the relative clause in this illustration since it is next to its head and not further displaced).[6]

(28) mujhe vo aːdmiː [jo siːtaː-ko acc^{h}aː lagtaː hɛ] pasand
I-DAT DEM man REL Sita-DAT nice seem-IMP be-PRES like
nahĩː hɛ
not be-PRES
'I do not like the man who Sita likes.'

(29) [$_{DemP}$ vo [$_{CP}$ [$_{IP}$ siːtaː-ko jo aːdmiː acc^{h}aː lagtaː hɛ]]]
DEM Sita-DAT REL man nice seem-IMP be-PRES

(29) actually corresponds to a well formed output and can be used in a sentence like (30):

(30) mujhe vo siːtaː-ko jo aːdmiː acc^{h}aː lagtaː hɛ pasand
I-DAT DEM Sita-DAT REL man nice seem-IMP be-PRES like
nahĩː hɛ
not be-PRES
'I do not like the man who Sita likes.'

Given that Hindi is an *wh*-in-situ language with optional leftward movement of *wh*-phrases in questions, this is not entirely unexpected. Hindi's *wh*-in-situ property seems to generalize (as expected) to the relative clauses. This overt appearance of the underlying structure could be taken to support Kayne's proposal about generating the head inside the relative clause. The remaining steps required to derive the desired output from (29) are outlined below.

– Step 1: Leftward movement of REL+NP *jo aadmii*. This would be leftward scrambling of the *jo*-phrase to a IP initial position (possibly an A-position, as discussed in Mahajan 1990).[7]

(31) [$_{DemP}$ vo [$_{CP}$ [$_{IP}$ jo aːdmiː [siːtaː-ko t_i acc^{h}aː lagtaː hɛ]]]]
DEM REL man Sita-DAT nice seem-IMP be-PRES

This also corresponds to a well formed output and can be used in sentences like (32).

(32) mujhe vo jo aːdmiː siːtaː-ko acc^{h}aː lagtaː hɛ pasand
I-DAT DEM REL man Sita-DAT nice seem-IMP be-PRES like
nahĩː hɛ
not be-PRES
'I do not like the man who Sita likes.'

214   ANOOP MAHAJAN

- Step 2: Head noun *aadmii* moves to SpecCP.[8]

(33)   [$_{DemP}$ vo [$_{CP}$ aːdmiː$_j$ [$_{IP}$ [jo t_j]$_i$ [$_{IP}$ siːtaː-ko t_i acc^{h}aː lagtaː
              DEM   man   REL   Sita-DAT   nice   seem-IMP
       hɛ]]]]
       be-PRES

This essentially completes the derivation of normal relative clauses in Hindi. To derive the relevant structure, we have used a leftward scrambling operation (independently available in Hindi) followed by movement of the phrase containing the head into SpecCP. None of these moves is problematic from the point of view of the standard movement theory.

5.2 *Preposed relatives*

As opposed to the base generation approaches to the preposed relatives, I propose to derive the position of the preposed relatives using movement operations. The essential idea that I wish to follow is that the preposed relatives involve leftward scrambling of the whole DemP followed by CP deletion in the copy.

We start with an input like (33) which we have already derived for the normal relatives. The complete input is shown in (34).

(34)   mujhe [$_{DemP}$ vo [$_{CP}$ aːdmiː$_j$ [$_{IP}$ [jo t_j]$_i$ siːtaː-ko t_i acc^{h}aː
       I-DAT   DEM   man   REL   Sita-DAT   nice
       lagtaː   hɛ]]]   pasand nahĩː hɛ
       seem-IMP be-PRES like   not   be-PRES
       'I do not like the man who Sita likes.'

- Step 1: Copying of DemP to the left of the matrix subject:

(35)   [$_{DemP}$ vo [$_{CP}$ aːdmiː$_j$ [$_{IP}$ [jo t_j]$_i$ siːtaː-ko t_i acc^{h}aː lagtaː
              DEM   man   REL   Sita-DAT   nice   seem-IMP
       hɛ]]]   [mujhe [$_{DemP}$ vo [$_{CP}$ aːdmiː$_j$ [$_{IP}$ [jo t$_j$]$_i$ siːtaː-ko t_i acc^{h}aː
       be-PRES I-DAT   DEM   man   REL   Sita-DAT   nice
       lagtaː   hɛ]]]   pasand nahĩː hɛ]
       seem-IMP be-PRES like   not   be-PRES

- Step 2: CP deletion in the copy:[9]

(36) [$_{\text{DemP}}$ vo [$_{\text{CP}}$ a:dmi:$_j$ [$_{\text{IP}}$ [jo t_j]$_i$ si:ta:-ko t_i acc^{h}a: lagta:
         DEM   man   REL   Sita-DAT   nice   seem-IMP
hɛ]]]   [mujhe [$_{\text{DemP}}$ vo [$_{\text{CP}}$ a:dmi:$_j$ [$_{\text{IP}}$ [jo t_j]$_i$ si:ta:-ko t_i acc^{h}a:
be-PRES I-DAT   DEM   REL   Sita-DAT   nice
lagta: hɛ]]]   pasand nahĩ: hɛ]
seem-IMP be-PRES like   not   be-PRES

This derives the one version of the surface output of the preposed relatives. In this version, the head is not present in the main clause since it is deleted with CP deletion leaving the Dem head of the DemP intact.

If the head noun had not moved into SpecCP (recall that this movement is optional as was illustrated earlier), then instead of (36), we will get (37):

(37) [$_{\text{DemP}}$ vo [$_{\text{CP}}$ [$_{\text{IP}}$ [jo a:dmi:]$_i$ si:ta:-ko t_i acc^{h}a: lagta:
         DEM   REL man   Sita-DAT   nice   seem-IMP
hɛ]]]   [mujhe [$_{\text{DemP}}$ vo [$_{\text{CP}}$ [$_{\text{IP}}$ [jo a:dmi:]$_i$ si:ta:-ko t_i acc^{h}a:
be-PRES I-DAT   DEM   REL man   Sita-DAT   nice
lagta: hɛ]]]   pasand nahĩ: hɛ]
seem-IMP be-PRES like   not   be-PRES

(37) is also a well formed output.

To derive *jo*-initial preposed relatives, we have to allow for the possibility of deletion of the Dem in the fronted DemP (I discuss the issue of possible conditions on deletion later):

(38) [$_{\text{DemP}}$ vo [$_{\text{CP}}$ [$_{\text{IP}}$ [jo a:dmi:]$_i$ si:ta:-ko t_i acc^{h}a: lagta:
         DEM   REL man   Sita-DAT   nice   seem-IMP
hɛ]]]   [mujhe [$_{\text{DemP}}$ vo [$_{\text{CP}}$ [$_{\text{IP}}$ [jo a:dmi:]$_i$ si:ta:-ko t_i acc^{h}a:
be-PRES I-DAT   DEM   REL man   Sita-DAT   nice
lagta: hɛ]]]   pasand nahĩ: hɛ]
seem-IMP be-PRES like   not   be-PRES

If the head noun has moved to SpecCP prior to deletion, the possibility of left deletion of Dem and SpecCP will yield another well-formed output.

(39) [$_{\text{DemP}}$ vo [$_{\text{CP}}$ a:dmi:$_j$ [$_{\text{IP}}$ [jo t_j]$_i$ si:ta:-ko t_i acc^{h}a: lagta:
         DEM   man   REL   Sita-DAT   nice   seem-IMP
hɛ]]]   [mujhe [$_{\text{DemP}}$ vo [$_{\text{CP}}$ a:dmi:$_j$ [$_{\text{IP}}$ [jo t_j]$_i$ si:ta:-ko t_i acc^{h}a:
be-PRES I-DAT   DEM   REL   Sita-DAT   nice
lagta: hɛ]]]   pasand nahĩ: hɛ]
seem-IMP be-PRES like   not   be-PRES

This essentially outlines the derivation of preposed relatives. The mechanisms used are leftward DemP movement (scrambling, which is independently available in the language), copying and deletion, mechanisms that are readily available in the theory.[10]

We do need to make precise the conditions on deletions in copies. The basic assumption that I am making here is that copies can be either totally or partially deleted. Under the copying theory of movement, complete deletion of a copy left behind after movement is not problematic. That is what allows for standard movement. I make a reasonable assumption that deletion takes place under identity. This is possibly forced by conditions on recoverability. It is also likely that the precise definition of identity will involve a phonological specification (cf. Truckenbrodt 1994), which by itself is not surprising given the fact that these deletions take place on the PF side of the derivation. I will continue assuming that partial deletions are also possible only under identity with a non deleted copy elsewhere in the sentence (that is, at the minimum, the original material of the input has to be present in the output). I am also assuming that deletions can be forward (in the original copy) as well as backwards (in the moved copy). I assume that one of the relevant conditions on deletion involves c-command as proposed by Kayne (1994). The condition is given in (40) below:[11]

(40) "A given chain link c_k can license PF deletion of another link c_i of the same chain only if c_i does not c-command c_k." (Kayne 1994: 96).

It would be obvious by the derivations that I have proposed above that deletions can affect non-constituents as long as the condition on phonological identity is met. I assume further that prosodic conditions may further regulate the outputs.[12] For instance, when a Dem + head N are deleted, they do not form a syntactic constituent in our analysis but they do seem to form a prosodic constituent in Hindi. I will, however, not be able to discuss the exact nature of the phonological condition on deletions in Hindi in this paper.[13]

5.3 *Postposed relatives*

If we assume that rightward movement is not allowed (cf. Kayne 1994; see Mahajan 1997, for arguments against a rightward movement analysis of extraposition in Hindi), then an extraposition analysis is not an available option for deriving the postposed relatives.

The essential issue concerns the derivation of sentences like (41):

(41) us-ne vo aːdmiː dekhaː jo siːtaː-ko accʰaː lagtaː hɛ
he-ERG DEM man see-PERF REL Sita-DAT nice seem-IMP be-PRES
'He saw the man who Sita likes.'

One of the problems in the derivation of sentences like (41) is that in our analysis of relative clauses, *vo aadmii* does not form a constituent so it cannot move leftwards as a unit. I suggest then that the apparent leftward movement of *vo aadmii* is derived by remnant movement as follows.

We start with the input given in (42).[14] This input differs from the our original input for other types of relative clauses in that it has the object DemP in the postverbal position where it should be generated under the Kaynian view about the initial representation of head final structures (and as noted earlier, the other inputs that we used earlier were simply intermediate steps of the derivations).

(42) us-ne dekhaː [$_{DemP}$ vo [siːtaː-ko jo aːdmiː accʰaː lagtaː
he-ERG see-PERF DEM Sita-DAT REL man nice seem-IMP
hɛ]]
be-PRES
'He saw the man who Sita likes.'

- Step 1: Leftward scrambling of the *jo*-phrase (yields an acceptable output again):[15]

(43) us-ne dekhaː [$_{DemP}$ vo [$_{IP}$ [jo aːdmiː]$_i$ [siːtaː-ko t_i accʰaː
he-ERG see-PERF DEM REL man Sita-DAT nice
lagtaː hɛ]]]
seem-IMP be-PRES
'He saw the man who Sita likes.'

- Step 2: *aadmii* movement to SpecCP (yields an acceptable output that corresponds to a DemP in a postverbal position with a normal relative):

(44) us-ne dekhaː [$_{DemP}$ vo [aːdmiː$_j$ [$_{IP}$ [jo t_j]$_i$ [siːtaː-ko t_i accʰaː
he-ERG see-PERF DEM man REL Sita-DAT nice
lagtaː hɛ]]]]
seem-IMP be-PRES
'He saw the man who Sita likes.'

- Step 3: IP movement to a pre-DemP position (this could be a Spec position above DemP (possibly DetP)):

(45) us-ne dekha: [IP [jo tj]i [si:ta:-ko ti accha: lagta: hɛ]] [DemP
 he-ERG see-PERF REL Sita-DAT nice seem-IMP be-pres
 vo [a:dmi:j [IP tIP]]]
 DEM man
 'He saw the man who Sita likes.'

- Step 4: Leftward remnant DemP movement (scrambling):

(46) us-ne [DemP vo [a:dmi:j [IP tIP]] dekha: [IP [jo tj]i [si:ta:-ko ti
 he-ERG DEM man see-PERF REL Sita-DAT
 accha: lagta: hɛ]] [DemP tDemP]]
 nice seem-IMP be-PRES
 'He saw the man who Sita likes.'

This yields the desired output. This analysis of extraposition is somewhat different from what was proposed in Mahajan (1997) for relative clause extraposition in Hindi and adopts the ideas used to handle Germanic remnant movement.

There is a 'partial deletion' variant of the derivation that I have outlined above for relative clause extraposition. Following the treatment suggested in Wilder (1995), this variant essentially handles the remnant movement effects using partial deletions (within the Copy theory of movement). In this variant, we begin with an input such as (44), followed by leftward DemP copying as in (47). This is then followed by the deletion of the IP in the fronted copy along with the deletion of Dem-*aadmii* in the original copy as shown in (48):

(47) us-ne [DemP vo [a:dmi:j [IP [jo tj]i [si:ta:-ko ti accha: lagta:
 he-ERG DEM man REL Sita-DAT nice seem-IMP
 hɛ]]]]
 be-PRES
 dekha: [DemP vo [a:dmi:j [IP [jo tj]i [si:ta:-ko ti accha: lagta:
 see-PERF DEM man REL Sita-DAT nice seem-IMP
 hɛ]]]]
 be-PRES

(48) us-ne [DemP vo [a:dmi:j [IP [jo tj]i [si:ta:-ko ti accha: lagta:
 he-ERG DEM man REL Sita-DAT nice seem-IMP
 hɛ]]]]
 be-PRES
 dekha: [DemP vo [a:dmi:j [IP [jo tj]i [si:ta:-ko ti accha: lagta:
 see-PERF DEM man REL Sita-DAT nice seem-IMP
 hɛ]]]]
 be-PRES

Wilder (1995) argues that the partial deletion approach of the sort that I have outlined above is superior to the standard remnant movement approach since it avoids a problematic aspect of the remnant movement analysis. The problem concerns IP movement (to the pre-DemP) of the remnant movement analysis. In terms of the treatment that I have outlined for (41), this would imply that the copy theory alternative would avoid the Step 3 of the remnant movement analysis. Wilder (1995) suggests that this is desirable since this step of movement is otherwise unmotivated for languages like English and German. It is, however, difficult to choose between the two alternatives that we have considered on the basis of the Hindi data since (45) itself appears to correspond to a well-formed output in Hindi. I will not discuss the relative merits of these alternatives for the treatment of relative clause extraposition in this paper (for the details of the relevant discussion for English and German, see Wilder 1995).

This completes our illustration of how some of the word orders associated with various kinds of relative clauses can be derived within the head movement theory of relative clauses that uses the copying and deletion approach to movement. As noted earlier, the devices used to derive various word orders are devices that have to be available in the theories of movement.

6. Deriving the asymmetries

Within the approach that I have outlined above, it now becomes possible to reexamine the asymmetries that we noted earlier in the three types of relative clause. In the subsections that follow, I suggest a treatment for three of these asymmetries (leaving out the issue of multiple relatives) within the framework that I am developing.

6.1 *Head restrictions*

The essential observation made in Section 4.1 was that the distribution of the head of the nominal head varies in three type of the relative clauses. This variation is summarized in Table 1:

Table 1

	Head only in the relative clause	Head only in the main clause	Head in both clauses
Preposed	+	+	+
Normal	+	+	−
Postposed	−	+	+

For the preposed relatives, the possibilities of the relative internal as well as the main clause internal heads was derived in the discussion of the preposed relatives in the previous section. These possibilities were illustrated in (38) and (39), which are repeated below.

(38) [$_{DemP}$ vo [$_{CP}$ [$_{IP}$ [jo   aːdmiː]$_i$ siːtaː-ko t_i acc^{h}aː lagtaː
        DEM   REL man   Sita-DAT   nice seem-IMP
   hɛ]]]   [mujhe [$_{DemP}$ vo [$_{CP}$ [$_{IP}$ [jo   aːdmiː]$_i$ siːtaː-ko t_i acc^{h}aː
   be-PRES I-DAT   DEM   REL man Sita-DAT   nice
   lagtaː   hɛ]]]   pasand nahĩː hɛ]
   seem-IMP be-PRES like   not   be-PRES

(39) [$_{DemP}$ vo [$_{CP}$ aːdmiː$_j$ [$_{IP}$ [jo t_j]$_i$ siːtaː-ko t_i acc^{h}aː lagtaː
        DEM   man   REL   Sita-DAT   nice seem-IMP
   hɛ]]]   [mujhe [$_{DemP}$ vo [$_{CP}$ aːdmiː$_j$ [$_{IP}$ [jo t_j]$_i$ siːtaː-ko t_i acc^{h}aː
   be-PRES I-DAT   DEM   man   REL   Sita-DAT   nice
   lagtaː   hɛ]]]   pasand nahĩː hɛ]
   seem-IMP be-PRES like   not   be-PRES

To derive the presence of the head in both the clauses in preposed relatives, we simply have to spell out what is represented as a trace of the head in the fronted *jo* phrase in (39) as is illustrated in (49) below:

(49) [$_{DemP}$ vo [$_{CP}$ aːdmiː$_j$ [$_{IP}$ [jo   aːdmiː]$_i$ siːtaː-ko t_i acc^{h}aː lagtaː
        DEM   man   REL man   Sita-DAT   nice seem-IMP
   hɛ]]]   [mujhe [$_{DemP}$ vo [$_{CP}$ aːdmiː$_j$ [$_{IP}$ [jo   aːdmiː]$_i$ siːtaː-ko t_i
   be-PRES I-DAT   DEM   man   REL man Sita-DAT
   acc^{h}aː lagtaː   hɛ]]]   pasand nahĩː hɛ]
   nice   seem-IMP be-PRES like   not   be-PRES

The essential idea is that the head *aadmii* is moved to SpecCP as for the derivation in (39) and then Dem + *aadmii* are deleted in the fronted DemP while the remaining IP is deleted in the original copy. This yields an output where the head is present both in the main clauses as well as in the relative clause.[16]

For the normal relatives (as in (32), repeated below), the options of main clause internal head and the relative clause internal head were derived in the representation (33) (also repeated below):

(32) mujhe vo jo aːdmiː siːtaː-ko accʰaː lagtaː hɛ pasand
I-DAT DEM REL man Sita-DAT nice seem-IMP be-PRES like
nahĩː hɛ
not be-PRES
'I do not like the man who Sita likes.'

(33) [$_{DemP}$ vo [$_{CP}$ aːdmiː$_j$ [$_{IP}$ [jo t_j]$_i$ [$_{IP}$ siːtaː-ko t_i accʰaː lagtaː
DEM man REL Sita-DAT nice seem-IMP
hɛ]]]]
be-PRES

It now remains for us to account for the ungrammaticality of sentences like (13) (repeated below) where both the head is realized in the relative clause as well as the main clause.

(13) *mujhe vo aːdmiː [jo aːdmiː siːtaː-ko pasand hɛ] accʰaː nahĩː
I-DAT DEM man REL man Sita-DAT like be-PRES nice not
lagtaː
seem-IMP
'I do not like the man who Sita likes.'

(13) is essentially a variant of (33) in which the trace of the moved head (in (33)) is spelled out. Putting it differently, if the original copy of the head moved into SpecCP in (33) was not deleted, we would derive (13). That is, in order to rule out (13), we need a condition that ensures that t_j of (33) cannot be spelled out since it is c-commanded by $aːdmiː_j$. This would essentially be a condition that prevents out multiple spell-outs in cases of normal movement to a c-commanding position. One possible formulation of such a condition could be along the following lines (suggested by Chris Wilder, p.c.): two copies x_i and y_i can be spelled-out simultaneously in a representation only if neither c-commands the other. Given that movement is always to a c-commanding position, this condition would rule out multiple spell-outs in most normal cases while allowing for partial deletions where this condition is not a factor.

Postposed relatives allow for a main clause head or the head being present in both the main clause as well as the relative clause. The derivation of the standard postposed relative with the head in the main clause was achieved using a remnant movement operation or its copying theory variant in the previous section. This is shown in (48), repeated below from the previous section:

(48) us-ne [~DemP~ vo [a:dmi:~j~ [~IP~ [jo *t*~j~]~i~ [si:ta:-ko *t*~i~ acc^h^a: lagta:
       he-ERG   DEM man   REL   Sita-DAT   nice   seem-IMP
       hɛ]]]]
       be-PRES
       dekha: [~DemP~ vo [a:dmi:~j~ [~IP~ [jo *t*~j~]~i~ [si:ta:-ko *t*~i~ acc^h^a: lagta:
       see-PERF   DEM man   REL   Sita-DAT   nice   seem-IMP
       hɛ]]]]
       be-PRES

Since postposed relatives are similar to the preposed relatives in allowing for the dual presence of the head (in the relative clause as well as in the main clause), it seems justified to extend the analysis we utilized for the preposed relatives to the postposed relatives. What we need in this particular case is to spell out the trace of the moved head *aadmii* in the original copy. The rest of the mechanics remain the same, Dem+*aadmii* are deleted in the original copy while the IP is deleted in the fronted copy. The final output corresponds to (50) below:

(50) us-ne [~DemP~ vo [a:dmi:~j~ [~IP~ [jo *t*~j~]~i~ [si:ta:-ko *t*~i~ acc^h^a: lagta:
       he-ERG   DEM man   REL   Sita-DAT   nice   seem-IMP
       hɛ]]]]
       be-PRES
       dekha: [~DemP~ vo [a:dmi:~j~ [~IP~ [jo a:dmi:~j~]~i~ [si:ta:-ko *t*~i~ acc^h^a:
       see-PERF   DEM man   REL man   Sita-DAT   nice
       lagta: hɛ]]]]
       seem-IMP be-PRES

It now remains for us to derive the fact that postposed relatives do not allow a relative clause internal head along with the presence of the head in the main clause. This is illustrated by the unacceptability of (51) below ((51) is similar to (17) used earlier to illustrate this effect):

(51) *us-ne vo dekha: [jo a:dmi: si:ta:-ko acc^h^a: lagta: hɛ]
       he-ERG DEM see-PERF REL man   Sita-DAT   nice   seem-IMP be-PRES
       'He saw the man who Sita likes.'

If (48) is taken to be the input for postposed relatives (our revision of remnant movement analysis of extraposition), then to derive an output such as (51) we will have to perform the following deletions in the input.

(52) *us-ne [$_{DemP}$ vo [a:dmi:$_j$ [$_{IP}$ [jo ~~a:dmi:$_j$~~]$_i$ [si:ta:-ko t_i acc^{h}a:
he-ERG   DEM man   REL man   Sita-DAT nice
~~lagta: hɛ~~]]]]
seem-IMP be-PRES
dekha: [$_{DemP}$ ~~vo~~ [a:dmi:$_j$ [$_{IP}$ [jo a:dmi:$_j$]$_i$ [si:ta:-ko t_i acc^{h}a:
see-PERF   DEM man   REL man   Sita-DAT nice
lagta: hɛ]]]]
seem-IMP be-PRES
'He saw the man who Sita likes.'

(52) violates the condition on identity of the deleted material, the essential problem being that instead of deleting *vo aadmii* in the left copy, we are attempting to delete just *aadmii*. This rules out the output (51) from an input such as (52).[17]

This account of the asymmetries between the different head realization possibilities in different types of relative clauses then uses conditions on the deletions of copies in the copy theory of movement to derive the required results.

6.2 *Demonstrative restriction*

This restriction covers two cases. The first one is Subbarao's observation about the problem that indefinite nominals are incompatible with preposed relatives. This is illustrated in (20) repeated below from Section 4.2.

(20) *[jo si:ta:-ne khari:di: thi:] mujhe kuch kita:bẽ paṛ^{h}ni:
     REL Sita-ERG buy-PERF be-PST I-DAT some books read-INF
     hẽ
     be-PRES
     'I have to read some books that Sita bought.'

Recall that we have analyzed the preposed relatives using leftward scrambling of the DemP containing the relative clause and then deleting the relative clause in the copy left behind and deleting Dem+N in the fronted copy. One well-known property of Hindi leftward scrambling is that indefinite nominals resist leftward scrambling (cf. Mahajan 1990: 92). This is a somewhat general property of leftward scrambling and has been discussed extensively in literature on scrambling. In Hindi, nominals like *kuch kitaabe* 'some books' are resistant to leftward movement as exemplified by (53):

(53)   */??Kuch kita:bẽ ra:m khari:dega:
       some books Ram buy-fut
       'Some books, Ram will buy.'

The derivation of a sentence like (19) in our analysis will have to involve leftward movement of an indefinite nominal. I suggest that this is not possible independent of the issue of the preposed relatives (as illustrated by (53)). Srivastav (1991: 648–649) notes that the presence of an overt partitive or an overt demonstrative on the head allows for the possibility of preposed relatives with such nominals. This is shown in (21) and (22) (repeated below):

(21)   [jo si:ta:-ne khari:di: thĩ:]   mujhe un mẽ se kuch
       REL Sita-ERG buy-PERF be-PST I-DAT those from some
       kita:bẽ paṭʰni: hẽ
       books read-INF be-PRES
       'I have to read some books that Ram bought.'
(22)   [jo accʰi: hẽ]   mujhe vo kuch kita:bẽ paṭʰni: hẽ
       REL good be-PRES I-DAT DEM some book read-INF be-PRES
       'I have to read those few books that are good.'

Once again, when we look at the behavior of such nominals in scrambling constructions, we find that overt partitive/demonstrative bearing nominals undergo leftward scrambling quite easily.

(54)   un mẽ se kuch kita:bẽ mujhe paṭʰni: hẽ
       those from some books I-DAT read-INF be-PRES
       'I have to read some of those books.'
(55)   vo kuch kita:bẽ mujhe paṭʰni: hẽ
       DEM some books I-DAT read-INF be-PRES
       'I have to read those few books.'

Given the possibility of leftward scrambling of such NPs, it is not surprising that they allow for preposed relative clauses too since they also require leftward scrambling of the nominal phrases headed by partitive or Dem elements to derive sentences like (21) and (22).

A very similar argument applies to the observation that bare singular NPs do not allow preposed relatives as demonstrated by the ungrammaticality of (23) repeated below:

(23)   *[jo accʰi: hɛ]   mujhe kita:b paṭʰni: hɛ
       REL good be-PRES I-DAT book read be-PRES
       = 'I have to read book which is good.'

Once again the ungrammaticality of (23), under our analysis, reduces to the problem with leftward scrambling of bare singular NPs in Hindi as shown by (56):

(56) */???kita:b mujhe paṭʰni: hɛ
 book I-DAT read be-PRES
 = 'I have to read book.'

Thus the fact that preposed relatives are not possible with bare singular nominals or with indefinite DET nominals gets a straightforward treatment in our account in which preposed relatives are derived using leftward scrambling. Given independent constraints on leftward scrambling of such NPs, this restriction follows automatically in our analysis.

This essentially completes our illustration of the derivation of some of the asymmetries between various kind of correlatives in Hindi within a movement based approach that I developed in this paper. I have no proposal to make about multiple relatives here. However, I think that the plausibility of a movement based approach is obvious from the derivations that I have proposed.

7. Conclusion

I have provided here an analysis of various types of correlative constructions in Hindi with an approach that incorporates the head movement analysis of Kayne (1994) and the Copy theory of movement proposed in the minimalist framework (Chomsky 1995). I have discussed some aspects of the known asymmetries between the different types of correlatives in Hindi and have shown that these asymmetries can be accounted for within our framework either by known restrictions on leftward scrambling or by certain conditions on copy deletions. Given this approach, we can adopt a movement based analysis of all kinds of correlative constructions. While I have not directly argued against the approaches that either posit different types of sources for different types of correlative structures or base generate all relatives in their surface position, it is clear that a movement based approach to all kind of relative clauses can account for most of the properties of Hindi correlatives. Given the general availability of movement in most theories of displaced constituents, I suggest that a unified movement based approach is to be preferred in principle over the other approaches. There has been some recent work on providing movement based accounts for various other construction types that were earlier taken to justify base generation of discontinuous dependencies. A recent example of this is Kayne's (1994) treatment of right dislocation (also extendable to constructions like clitic doubling and clitic left dislocation, cf. Kayne 1994; also Mahajan 1991). This paper essentially extends the domain of movement theory to those construction types that were earlier taken to justify the existence of base generation (of dislocated phrases) as a mechanism allowed by UG. As I indicated earlier, on purely conceptual grounds, we would prefer theories that adopt one single mechanism to account for discontinuous dependencies rather than allowing for base generation and movement as two coexistent mechanisms for this purpose. Empirical arguments of the sort proposed by Kayne, and also in this paper, then strengthen the conceptual argument for a unified approach to discontinuous dependencies.

Notes

1. The abbreviations used in this paper: ERG=ergative, DAT=dative, PART=participial, IMP=imperfect, INF=infinitive, FEM=feminine, MASC=masculine, PRES=present, PST=past, DEM=demonstrative, REL=relative pronoun.
2. These judgments have been further verified by some of the speakers of Delhi Hindi. One of the relevant judgments is also reported as a possibility in a footnote by Srivastav (1991).
3. It is also possible for the head noun to be missing from both the main clause as well as the relative clause. I do not discuss this possibility here.
4. Srivastav (1991: 647 fn.9) notes that a reviewer for her paper finds sentences like (16) acceptable. My judgment thus matches the judgment of that reviewer.
5. Srivastav (1991: 651 fn.15) does note that sentences like (27) are acceptable for some speakers. She also notes that in such cases there appears to be an intonational break between the two clauses which may indicate that in sentences like (27), the main clause has been fronted. I myself do not perceive any intonational difference between sentences like (25)/(26) and sentences like (27). Furthermore if fronting was a possible available strategy, then it should be possible to derive (i) below from (26) by fronting the main clause. Yet there is a significant difference between (i) and (26) and between (i) and (27).

    (i) *us aːdmiː-ne vo kitaːb khariːd liː,   jis aːdmiː-ne jo kitaːb dekhiː
        DEM man-ERG DEM book buy-PERF take-PERF REL man-ERG REL book see-PERF
        = 'Whoever saw whichever book, he bought it.'

6. I am ignoring at this point the fact that even the structure like (29) must be derived from a head medial structure under Kayne's assumptions. (29) can therefore be taken as an intermediate step in the derivation of the relative clause.
7. The fronted relative phrase can bind a pronoun to its left of its trace in pretty much the same way as the normal *wh*-question phrases in Hindi can (cf. Mahajan 1990):

    (i) jo ciːz$_i$ raːm-ne uske$_i$ maːlik-ko loṭaːiː ...
         REL thing Ram-ERG its   owner   returned

8. Strictly speaking what moves into SpecCP is a phrasal category inside the relative phrase containing the head noun.
9. I am assuming that the deletion indicated in (36) applies at PF. I should note that some

speakers of Hindi find (36) somewhat odd. The sentence improves for these speakers if the Dem *vo* is also deleted in the original copy. A possible explanation for this may be that what is being deleted (not spelled-out) in (36) is not a prosodic unit (see also footnote 16).

10. Chris Wilder (p.c.) points out that if the preposed relatives are indeed derived by leftward movement (as I have suggested), we should be able to detect movement using the standard movement diagnostics such as the island effects. (i) below shows that a relative clause can appear to the left of its head separated by a couple of CP boundaries as long as there are no intervening movement barriers:

(i) [jo siːtaː-ko accha lagtaː hɛ] mɛ soctaː hu [_CP ki mohan-ne kahaː
     REL Sita-DAT nice seem be-PRES I think be-PRES that Mohan-ERG said
     thaː [_CP ki vo aːdmiː paːgal hɛ]]
     be-PST that DEM man crazy be-PRES
     'I think that Mohan said that the man who Sita likes is crazy.'

However, in the presence of an intervening factive island, such preposed relatives are ill-formed:

(ii) *[jo siːtaː-ko achaː lagtaː hɛ] mɛ̃ [_DP yah baːt [_CP ki vo aːdmiː
     REL Sita-DAT nice seem be-PRES I this fact that DEM man
     paːgal hɛ]] jaːntaː hū̃
     crazy be-PRES know be-PRES
     'I know the fact that the man who Sita likes is crazy.'

The contrast between (i) and (ii) favors a movement analysis of the sort that I have sketched above over the non-movement analyses of the sort proposed by Srivastav (1991) and McCawley (1992).

11. There is a potential issue regarding the status of this condition and the derivations given in (38) and (39) where the Spec of the fronted constituent is deleted. For the purposes of this paper, I will have to assume that in (38) *vo* 'Dem' does not c-command out of the fronted clause which is itself adjoined to the matrix clause. That is, Spec of an adjunct which is itself adjoined to a constituent cannot c-command out of out that adjunct into that constituent. (39) will also be taken care of by this assumption.

12. For some interesting ideas regarding conditions on deletions within copy theory, see Wilder (1995) who also allows for non-constituent deletions in his theory.

13. For some general discussion of a promising framework in this respect, see Truckenbrodt (1994).

14. As is becoming a regular pattern for most of our inputs and intermediate steps of derivation, (42) corresponds to a well formed output also.

15. I sometimes represent a trace in the position of a deleted copy. This is done just to keep the derivations simple for illustrative purposes.

16. Chris Wilder (p.c.) points out a potential problem with the derivation in (49). In the preposed DemP in (49), the deleted copy of the head N *aadmii* c-commands the spelled-out copy of *aadmii*. This would violate Kayne's condition on PF deletions (Condition (40)). We are therefore forced to assume that PF deletion of Dem+N in the preposed DemP in (49) is 'licensed' by the Dem+N of the non-preposed DemP. That is, *aadmii* following the REL in the preposed DemP is not a relevant 'licenser' for the relevant deletion. It is obvious that this idea needs further elaboration. That elaboration is, however, beyond the scope of this paper. I therefore simply note the problem here along with a possible direction (mentioned above) for solving the problem.

I should note that there is an alternative to the derivation outlined in (49). This alternative derivation takes (38) as an input and moves the head N in the original copy of the DemP to SpecCP (this operation does not take place in the fronted copy). IP deletion in the original DemP then yields the desired PF output:

(i) [$_{DemP}$ ~~vo~~ [$_{CP}$ [$_{IP}$ [jo aːdmiː]$_i$ siːtaː-ko t_i acc^{h}aː lagtaː hɛ]]] [mujhe
　　　　DEM　　　　　　REL man　Sita-DAT　nice　seem-IMP be-PRES I-DAT
[$_{DemP}$ vo [$_{CP}$ aːdmiː$_j$ [$_{IP}$ [~~jo~~ t_j]$_i$ ~~siːtaː-ko~~ t_i ~~acc^{h}aː lagtaː~~ ~~hɛ~~]]] pasand
DEM　　　　man　　　　REL　　Sita-DAT　nice　seem-IMP be-PRES like
nahĩː hɛ]
not be-PRES

The problem with this alternative is that it is not consistent with cyclicity (it requires a movement operation within the original copy).

17. This analysis does predict that if the Dem is not deleted in the second copy, then the resulting output will be good since now the deleted part is identical to the non deleted part. This seems to be true given the relative acceptability of an output such as (i) below.

(i) ?us-ne [$_{DemP}$ vo [~~aːdmiː~~$_j$ [$_{IP}$ [~~jo~~ aːdmiː$_j$]$_i$ [~~siːtaː-ko~~ t_i ~~acc^{h}aː lagtaː~~ ~~hɛ~~]]]]
he-ERG　　　　DEM man　　　　REL man　Sita-DAT　nice　seem-IMP be-PRES
dekha: [$_{DemP}$ vo [~~aːdmiː~~$_j$ [$_{IP}$ [jo aːdmiː$_j$]$_i$ [siːtaː-ko t_i acc^{h}aː lagtaː hɛ]]]]
see-PERF　DEM man　　　　REL man　Sita-DAT　nice　seem-IMP be-PRES

However, (i) does not have the same status as, for instance, (50). One could speculate that the reason for this is prosodic. *vo aadmii* is a prosodic unit (even though it is not a syntactic constituent) and deletions of the sort that we have been dealing with may be subject to prosodic constraints. I will, however, not explore this aspect of conditions on deletions in this paper.

References

Baltin, M. (1985). *Towards a theory of movement rules*. New York: Garland.
Chomsky, N. (1995). *The Minimalist Program*. Cambridge, Mass.: MIT Press.
Dasgupta, P. (1980). *Questions and Relative and Complement Clauses in a Bangle Grammar*. Doctoral dissertation, New York University.
Donaldson, S. (1971). Movement in restrictive relative clauses in Hindi. *Studies in the Linguistic Sciences* 1: 1–74.
Kachru,Y. (1978). On relative clause formation in Hindi-Urdu. *Linguistics* 207: 5–27.
Kayne, R. (1994). *The antisymmetry of syntax*. Cambridge, Mass.: MIT Press.
Mahajan, A. (1990). *The A/A-bar distinction and theory of movement*. Doctoral dissertation, MIT.
Mahajan, A. (1991). Clitic Doubling, Object Agreement and Specificity. *NELS* 21, 263–277. University of Massachusetts. Amherst.
Mahajan, A. (1995). *Upward Bounding and Hindi Extraposition*. Manuscript, UCLA.
Mahajan, A. (1997) Against a rightward movement analysis of extraposition and rightward scrambling in Hindi. *Scrambling*. edited by S. Tonoike, 93–124. Tokyo: Kurosio Publishers.

McCawley, J. (1992). *Remarks on adsentential, adnominal, and extraposed clauses in Hindi*. Manuscript, University of Chicago.
Srivastav, V. (1991). The syntax and semantics of correlatives. *Natural Language & Linguistic Theory* 9: 637–686.
Subbarao, K. V. (1974). *Complementation in Hindi Syntax*. Doctoral dissertation, University of Illinois, Urbana-Champaign.
Subbarao, K. V. (1984). *Complementation in Hindi Syntax*. Delhi: Academic Publications. [Revision of Subbarao 1974].
Truckenbrodt, H. (1994). *Towards a prosodic theory of extraposition*. Paper presented at the Tilburg Conference on Rightward Movement, October.
Wali, K. (1982). Marathi Correlatives: A Conspectus. *South Asian Review* 6: 78–88.
Wilder, C. (1995). Rightward movement as leftward deletion. *Extraction and Extraposition in German*, edited by U. Lutz & J. Pafel, 273–309. Amsterdam: John Benjamins.

An Antisymmetry Analysis of Japanese Relative Clauses[*]

Keiko S. Murasugi
Nanzan University

1. Introduction

The purpose of this paper is two-fold. The first is to discuss the basic properties of Japanese relative clauses, both head-external and head-internal. The second is to consider how those properties may be analyzed within Kayne's (1994) antisymmetry theory.

In Section 2, I will first go over the basic properties of head-external relatives in Japanese. The most important among them is that those relatives are never derived by movement. Then, I will briefly discuss the hypothesis I proposed in Murasugi (1991) that Japanese relative clauses are IPs, as opposed to CPs. It will be shown that this hypothesis provides a straightforward explanation for the non-movement property and also for some curious acquisition data.

The IP hypothesis mentioned above shares some similarities with Kayne's antisymmetry analysis of N-final relatives. According to his analysis, prenominal relative clauses are IPs. Yet, Kayne's theory, overall, is much more radical. In the remainder of this paper, I will present a detailed analysis of Japanese relatives within his theory. In Section 3, I will consider how the non-movement property of Japanese relatives may be derived within his theory. There, I will suggest the possibility that this property is related to another peculiar property of Japanese relative clauses: According to Keenan (1985), Japanese relatives are unique among N-final relatives in that their main verbs appear in the regular finite form.

---

[*] This is a slightly revised version of the paper presented at the Berlin Workshop on Relative Clauses held in November, 1996. I would like to thank the audience there and Mamoru Saito for helpful comments and suggestions on the earlier version.

In Section 4, I will turn to Kayne's analysis of head-internal relatives. I will first show that his analysis, together with the non-movement property of Japanese relatives, predicts that Japanese does not have head-internal relatives. This is apparently a wrong prediction as it is widely assumed since Kuroda (1976) that there are head-internal relatives in Japanese. But I will argue, following Murasugi (1994) and Mihara (1994), that what have been called Japanese head-internal relatives are not relative clauses, but adverbial adjuncts, and hence, that the prediction is borne out.

Finally, in Section 5, I will reexamine the antisymmetry analysis of Japanese head-external relatives presented in Section 3, and suggest that Japanese, after all, does not have relative clauses. This suggestion is based on the observation that the antisymmetry analysis makes Japanese relatives virtually indistinguishable from sentential modifiers in pure complex NPs. Further, I will show that if Japanese relatives are not relatives but pure sentential modifiers, the acquisition data considered in Section 2 receive a natural account.

2. The basic properties of Japanese relative clauses

In this section, I will discuss the basic properties of Japanese relative clauses. I will first consider the generalization proposed in Kuno (1973) and Perlmutter (1972) that Japanese relative clauses need not involve movement. I will then discuss the stronger generalization found in Hoji (1985) that Japanese relative clauses cannot involve movement. Finally, I will briefly present a slightly revised version of the analysis proposed in Murasugi (1991), which is based on the hypothesis that Japanese relative clauses are IPs, and not CPs.

2.1 *The absence of movement in Japanese relative clauses*

Kuno (1973) notes that Japanese relative clauses need not contain a gap as shown in (1), and also do not exhibit Subjacency effects as illustrated in (2).

(1)　[$_{NP}$[$_{IP}$ syuusyoku-ga　muzukasii] [$_{NP}$ buturigaku]]
　　　　　getting job-NOM is-hard　　　physics
　　'physics, which is hard to get a job in'

(2)　[$_{NP}$[$_{IP}$[$_{NP}$[$_{IP}$ e_i e_j kiteiru]　yoohuku$_j$]-ga yogoreteiru]
　　　　　　　　is-wearing suit　　　-NOM is-dirty
　　[$_{NP}$sinsi$_i$]]
　　gentleman
　　'the gentleman who [the suit that he is wearing] is dirty'

He argues, based on the former fact, that there need not be a relative operator movement in Japanese relatives, and that what is required between the relative head and the relative clause is only the "aboutness relation". Perlmutter (1972) demonstrates convincingly that nothing prevents the gap in a Japanese relative clause from being *pro*, and hence, the gap need not be produced by movement. This accounts for the absence of Subjacency effects noted above.

Hoji (1985) proposes a stronger generalization based on the absence of the connectivity or reconstruction effect. (3) is an example illustrating the connectivity effect in an English relative clause.

(3)   the picture of himself that John likes best

This kind of effect is observed with movement, but not with a based-generated NP-pronoun structure, as shown in (4).

(4)   a.   That picture of himself, John liked
        b.   *That picture of himself, John liked it

Hoji (1985) observes that the Japanese counterpart of (3) is out. A relevant example is shown in (5).

(5)   *[$_{NP}$ [John$_i$-ga e_j taipu-sita] [zibun$_i$-no ronbun]$_j$]
              J.-NOM   typed   self-GEN paper
        'self$_i$'s paper that John$_i$ typed' (lit.)

As Hoji notes, this absence of the connectivity effect indicates that Japanese relative clauses **cannot** involve movement.

Further evidence for Hoji's generalization can be found when we examine the relativization of adjuncts. First, (6) apparently shows that the relativization of reason/manner adjuncts, in distinction with that of arguments, is constrained by Subjacency.

(6)   a.   *[$_{NP}$[$_{IP}$[$_{NP}$[$_{IP}$ e_i e_j kubi-ni natta] hito$_j$]-ga   minna okotteiru]
                                        was fired   person-NOM all   angry
               riyuu$_i$]
               reason
               'the reason that [all of the students who were fired (for it)] are angry'

b. *[$_{NP}$[$_{IP}$[$_{NP}$[$_{IP}$ e_i e_j mondai-o   toita] hito$_j$]-ga   minna
         problem-ACC solved person-NOM all
   siken ni otiru] hoohoo$_i$]
   exam in fail   method
   'the method that [all of the people who solve problems (by it)] fail the exam'

The grammatical status of these examples parallels that of the English (7a)–(7b).

(7) a. *[the reason$_i$ [for which [all of the students who were fired t_i] are angry]]
    b. *[the method$_i$ [by which [all of the people who solve problems t_i] fail the examination]]

This parallelism can be accounted for straightforwardly if *pro* can occur only in argument positions in Japanese. Then, (6a-b), as opposed to (2), must be derived by movement.

But the restriction on the relativization of reason/manner phrases is much tighter. As noted in Saito (1985), they are clause-bound. Some relevant examples are provided in (8)–(9).

(8) a. [[Mary-ga e_i kaetta] riyuu$_i$]
       M.-NOM   left   reason
       'the reason$_i$ Mary left e_i'
    b. *[[Mary-ga [John-ga e_i kaetta to] omotteiru] riyuu$_i$]
       M.-NOM J.-NOM   left C think   reason
       'the reason$_i$ Mary thinks [that John left e_i]'

(9) a. [[Mary-ga e_i mondai-o   toita] hoohoo$_i$]
       M.-NOM   problem-ACC solved method
       'the method$_i$ Mary solved the problem e_i'
    b. *[[Mary-ga [John-ga e_i mondai-o   toita   to] omotteiru]
       M.-NOM J.-NOM problem-ACC solved C think
       hoohoo$_i$]
       method
       'the method$_i$ Mary thinks [that John solved the problem e_i]'

If (8b) and (9b) can be derived by movement, we expect them to be grammatical exactly like their English counterparts in (10a-b).

(10) a. [the reason [(for which) John thinks [that Mary was fired t_i]]]
     b. [the method [(by which) John thinks [that Mary solved the problem t_i]]]

Based on the examples in (8)–(9) and others, I argued in Murasugi (1991) that the relativization of manner/reason adjuncts is simply impossible in Japanese. According to this analysis, (8a) and (9a) do not contain any gap and they are pure complex NPs, exactly like (11a-b).

(11) a. [[sakana-ga yakeru] nioi]
     fish-NOM burn   smell
     'the smell that a fish burns' (Lit.)
   b. [[doa-ga   simaru] oto]
     door-NOM shut   sound
     'the sound that a door shuts' (Lit.)

Then, the interpretation of (8a), for example, parallels the English (12).

(12) the reason for John's leaving

This analysis, if correct, provides support for Hoji's generalization. The examples in (8) and (9) cannot be base-generated with *pro*, since *pro* can appear only in argument positions. And they cannot be derived by movement either, if Japanese relative clauses can never involve movement as Hoji proposed. Hence, it follows that they cannot contain a gap.

2.2 *The IP hypothesis*

Given Hoji's generalization, a question arises why Japanese relative clauses cannot involve movement. One straightforward hypothesis is that Japanese relative clauses are IPs, and not CPs. If they do not have a SpecCP position for the relative operator to move to, they cannot be derived by movement.

In Murasugi (1991), I argued in fact that Japanese relative clauses are IPs, on the basis of the adjunct relativization data discussed above and also some acquisition data.[1] Some Japanese speaking children, around the age 2 to 4, produce ungrammatical relative clauses like those in (13).

(13) a. buta san-ga tataiteru no taiko.
        piggy-NOM is-hitting *no* drum   [M: 2;11]
        'the drum that the piggy is playing'
   b. ohana motteru   no wanwa
      flower is-holding *no* doggie   [T: 2;6]
      'the doggie that is holding a flower'

Here, the problem is the particle *no* following the relative clause, which is not allowed in adult grammar. I first argued that this particle is of the category C.

No as a C appears in cleft sentences as shown in (14).

(14) a. [[Yamada-ga atta] no]-wa Russell da
　　　　　Y.-NOM　　met　C　-TOP　R.　　　is
　　　　'It was Russell that Yamada met.'
　　b. [[Yamada-ga atta] no]-wa Russell ni　da
　　　　　Y.-NOM　　met　C　-TOP　R.　　with　is
　　　　'It was with Russell that Yamada met'

Then, I argued that Japanese speaking children initially hypothesize that a Japanese relative clause is a CP, and hence, produce *no* in its head position.

This analysis of (13) implies that CP is the unmarked category for relative clauses. It also implies that Japanese-speaking children eventually discover that Japanese relative clauses are IPs, and thus, cease to produce *no*. And there is positive evidence that they can use to make this shift. As shown in (15), an overt complementizer is not allowed in Japanese pure complex NPs.

(15) a. [[sakana-ga yakeru (*no)] nioi]
　　　　　fish-NOM　burn　　　C　　smell
　　　　'the smell that a fish burns' (Lit.)
　　b. [[doa-ga　　simaru (*no)] oto]
　　　　　door-NOM shut　　　C　　sound
　　　　'the sound that a door shuts' (Lit.)

This is in clear contrast with English pure complex NPs. As shown in (16), an overt complementizer is required in English.

(16) [the claim [$_{CP}$ *(that) [Bill had left the party]]]

That is, in examples such as (16), *that* must be present in the head position of the CP. Stowell (1981), extending the hypothesis of Kayne (1981), analyzes this fact as follows. If the complementizer *that* is missing, there must be an empty category in the C position. But this empty category would then violate the ECP. Thus, the complementizer *that* must be present in examples like (16).

If we extend this analysis to the Japanese (15), it follows that the sentential modifier cannot be of the category CP. If it is, its head C position would be occupied by an empty category, and the empty category would be in violation of the ECP. Hence, given the ECP, the sentential modifier in (15) must be of the category IP. This means that Japanese speaking children can infer, on the basis of positive evidence like (15), that the sentential modifier in a pure complex NP is of the category IP. Suppose, as seems plausible, that the children generalize this conclusion to all prenominal sentential modifiers. Then, (15) serves as positive evidence that Japanese relative clauses are of the category IP.

If this analysis of the acquisition data in (13) is correct, it provides further support for the IP hypothesis for Japanese relative clauses. According to this analysis, the category for relative clauses is parametrized between CP and IP, CP being the unmarked case. And Japanese speaking children eventually choose IP.

In the remainder of this paper, I will examine how Kayne's (1994) analysis of N-final relatives fares with the data discussed so far. First, in Section 3, I will show that his analysis makes it possible to present a different, yet, quite attractive account for why Japanese relative clauses can never involve movement.

3. An antisymmetry analysis

3.1 *Kayne's proposal and the non-movement property*

Kayne (1994), based on his antisymmetry theory, proposes that N-final relative clauses have the structure in (17).[2]

(17) $[_{DP} [_{IP} \ldots t_i \ldots]_j [_{D'} D [_{CP} NP_i [_{C'} C t_j]]]]$

This structure is derived as in (18).

(18) a. $[_{DP} [_{D'} D [_{CP} [_{C'} C [_{IP} \ldots NP \ldots]]]]]$
 b. $[_{DP} [_{D'} D [_{CP} NP_i [_{C'} C [_{IP} \ldots t_i \ldots]]]]]$

From (18a), first, the relative head moves to the SpecCP position as in (18b). Then, the IP moves to the SpecDP position to yield (17).

This analysis appears, at first sight, to be totally inconsistent with the non-movement property of Japanese relative clauses discussed above: It includes the movement of the relative head to the SpecCP position. But if we can find in this analysis a principled reason that prevents this movement particularly in the case of Japanese, then, the non-movement property of Japanese relatives will turn out to be supporting evidence for Kayne's analysis. In what follows, I will argue that there is in fact such a principled reason.

As Kayne notes himself, the structure in (17) contains an unbound trace, namely t_j. It thus apparently violates the Proper Binding Condition, shown in (19).

(19) Traces must be bound. (Fiengo 1977)

However, Kayne also notes that this is not necessarily a problem, since there are cases where unbound traces are allowed. The case he cites is remnant topicalization in German.

At this point, let us examine more closely the contexts where unbound traces are allowed. Saito (1986) argues that there is a clear asymmetry between A and A′ traces with respect to the application of Proper Binding.[3] For examples, (20a) is fine, but (20b) is totally out.

(20) a. [How likely [t_i to win]]$_j$ is John$_i$ t_j
 b. *[Which picture of t_i]$_j$ does John wonder who$_i$ Mary likes t_j

In (20a), *John* raises to the matrix subject position, and then, the *Wh*-phrase *how likely t_i to win*, which contains the trace of *John*, moves to the SpecCP position. The trace of raising t_i is not bound, and yet the example is grammatical. In (20b), on the other hand, the Wh-phrase *who* first moves to the embedded SpecCP, and then, the larger Wh-phrase *which picture of t_i*, which contains the trace of *who*, moves to the matrix SpecCP. The example is simply uninterpretable. It seems then that traces of A-movement such as t_i in (20a) can be licensed through reconstruction or connectivity, but those of A′-movement, like t_i in (20b), have to be bound in the strict sense.

Let us apply this generalization to the structure in (17). If movement to SpecCP is in general A′-movement, the trace t_i should be an A′-trace. Since A′-traces must be bound, the structure should be excluded. As long as t_i is a trace of movement, there does not seem to be any way to save the structure. It follows then that the structure in (17) cannot be derived by movement. Thus, the non-movement propery of Japanese relative clauses is derived. The only way to generate the structure in (17) would be to base-generate NP_i in the SpecCP position, and to base-generate *pro* in the place of t_i, as in (21).

(21) [$_{DP}$ [$_{IP}$ ... pro_i ...]$_j$ [$_{D'}$ D [$_{CP}$ NP$_i$ [$_{C'}$ C t_j]]]]

This is a variant of Perlmutter's (1972) analysis discussed above.[4]

3.2 *The peculiarity of Japanese relatives among N-final relatives*

We saw above that the non-movement property of Japanese relative clauses follows from Kayne's analysis in a principled way. At this point, we may ask if this explanation implies that all N-final relatives cannot involve movement to SpecCP. The answer, I think, is not necessarily positive. My guess is that it very much depends on the property of the SpecCP position and the nature of the relative clause itself.

Keenan (1985), who discusses the typology of relatives, singles out Japanese relatives as being unique among the N-final relatives. His discussion is quoted directly in (22).

(22) A more regular difference between prenominal and postnominal RCs concerns the form of the main verb of S_{Rel}, which we shall denote by V_{Rel}. In prenominal RCs, V_{Rel} is almost always in some sort of non-finite form, that is a form different from the one it would have as the main verb of a simple declarative sentence. Typically V_{Rel} exhibits a reduction in tense-aspect marking and in verb agreement morphology compared with main clause declarative verbs. ... We may note that the prenominal RCs in Japanese do not put V_{Rel} in a non-finite or specifically relative form, but the Japanese case appears to be the exception among prenominal RCs here. (Keenan 1985: 160–161)

Simply put, Japanese relatives are unique among N-final relatives in that their main verbs are in the regular finite form.

Mahajan (1990) observes that the non-finite/finite distinction relates to the A/A' distinction in Hindi scrambling in an interesting way. As it is shown in Nemoto (1993) that his generalization holds in Japanese as well, I will use Japanese examples to illustrate his observation here. Let us first consider the examples in (23) and (24).[5]

(23) ?Karera-o$_i$ [[otagai$_i$-no sensei]-ga t_i hihansita]
they-ACC each other-GEN teacher-NOM criticized
'Them$_i$, each other's$_i$ teachers criticized t_i.'

(24) a. Karera-o$_i$ [John-ga [Mary-ga t_i hihansita to] itta]
they-ACC J.-NOM M.-NOM criticized C said
'Them$_i$, John said that Mary criticized t_i.'

b. *Karera-o$_i$ [[otagai$_i$-no sensei]-ga [Mary-ga t_i hihansita
they-ACC each other-GEN teacher-NOM M.-NOM criticized
to] itta]
C said
'Them$_i$, each other's$_i$ teachers said that Mary criticized t_i.'

(23) shows that a phrase preposed by clause-internal scrambling can serve as the antecedent for a lexical anaphor. This implies that clause-internal scrambling can be A-movement. (24a) shows that long scrambling out of a finite clause is possible in Japanese. On the other hand, (24b) shows that a phrase preposed by this kind of scrambling cannot be the antecedent of a lexical anaphor. This means that long scrambling out of a finite clause is necessarily A'-movement.

Here, interestingly, long scrambling out of a non-finite clause patterns with clause-internal scrambling, and not with long scrambling out of a finite clause.

The Japanese example in (25) is adopted from Nemoto (1993).

(25) ?Karera-o$_i$ [Mary-ga [otagai$_i$-no sensei]$_j$-ni [PRO$_j$ t_i homeru
 they-ACC M.-NOM each other-GEN teacher-to praise
 yooni] tanonda]
 to asked
 'Them$_i$, Mary asked each other's$_i$ teachers to praise t_i.'

This shows that long scrambling out of a non-finite clause can be A-movement. Mahajan (1990) thus arrives at the generalization in (26).

(26) a. Long scrambling out of a finite clause must be A′-movement.
 b. Long scrambling out of a non-finite clause can be A-movement.

Since it is shown convincingly in Webelhuth (1989) and Saito (1989) that scrambling is not to the SpecIP position and yet it is non-operator movement, it is reasonable to suppose that the generalization in (26) holds for this kind of movement in general.[6]

Let us now return to the discussion of relative clauses, and consider again the structure in (17).

(17) [$_{DP}$ [$_{IP}$ ... t_i ...]$_j$ [$_{D'}$ D [$_{CP}$ NP$_i$ [$_{C'}$ C t_j]]]]

Suppose that the SpecCP position in a relative clause, at least in some languages, can be a non-operator position. This is not implausible, since relativization does not establish an operator-variable relation in the way that *Wh*-question movement does. Then, the generalization in (26) implies that relativization, that is, the movement of *NP*$_i$ to SpecCP in (17), can be an A-movement as long as the relative clause is non-finite. In this case, t_i is an A-trace, and there is nothing wrong with the structure in (17). As shown in (20) above, an A-trace need not be bound in the strict sense, and can be licensed through reconstruction or connectivity.

The discussion here is quite speculative. But I believe it shows that Kayne's analysis need not imply that an N-final relative can never be derived by movement. There seems to be a way to allow movement in those languages where relative clauses have non-finite main verbs. Note that even if this speculation is correct, Japanese relative clauses still cannot be derived by movement to SpecCP. Since Japanese relatives have finite main verbs, the movement to SpecCP will involve extraction out of a finite clause. Hence, the movement is necessarily A′-movement, and t_i in (17) is an A′-trace. The structure is ruled out in this language exactly like (20b). Therefore, the non-movement property of Japanese relative clauses still follows.

4. Head-internal relatives in Japanese

It was shown above that one of the main properties of Japanese relative clauses, i.e., the non-movement property, can be derived from Kayne's analysis in a principled way. I would now like to turn to the so called head-internal relative clauses in Japanese. It has been assumed since Kuroda (1976) that Japanese has head-internal relative clauses. An example is shown in (27).

(27) Keikan-wa   [doroboo-ga ginkoo-kara detekita no]-o
    policeman-TOP robber-NOM bank-from   came out *no*-ACC
    tukamaeta
    arrested
    'The policeman arrested the robber who came out from the bank.'

It is assumed that this example has the same basic meaning as (28), which contains a regular head-external relative.

(28) Keikan-wa   [[*pro* ginkoo-kara detekita] doroboo]-o tukamaeta
    policeman-TOP   bank-from   came out robber-ACC arrested
    'The policeman arrested the robber who came out from the bank.'

I will argue that Kayne's analysis makes another correct prediction here, that is, contrary to appearance, Japanese does not have head-internal relative clauses.

I will first briefly discuss Cole's (1987) analysis of head-internal relatives, which forms the basis of Kayne's proposal. Then, I will go over Kayne's analysis and the prediction it makes for Japanese. Finally, I will present the arguments in Murasugi (1994) and Mihara (1994) that Japanese does not have head-internal relatives.

4.1 *Cole's generalization and analysis*

Cole (1987) observes that head-internal relatives are found only in languages with *pro* and N-final relatives. Given this fact, he first proposes that the head position of a head-internal relative clause is occupied by *pro*, as shown in (29).

(29)
```
        NP
       /  \
     CP/IP   NP
      /\     |
    ...NPᵢ... proᵢ
```

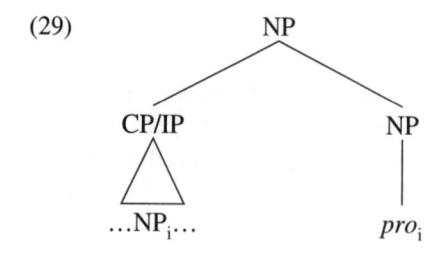

Here, the *pro* is coindexed at S-structure with the lexical NP to be interpreted as the head of the relative clause. This explains why only *pro*-drop languages have such relative clauses.

Then, he turns to the question regarding why only languages with N-final relatives have head-internal relatives. Given that the head position is occupied by *pro*, the structure of an N-initial head-internal relative would be as in (30).

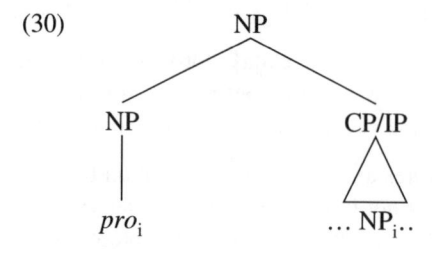

(30)
```
        NP
       /  \
      NP   CP/IP
      |     /\
    proᵢ  ...NPᵢ...
```

He points out that the structure in (30), with the proposed coindexation, is ruled out by Condition C of Binding theory. This is rather straightforward, since the head pronoun binds the coindexed R-expression in the relative clause. And this explains why head-initial languages, or languages with N-initial relatives, do not have head-internal relatives.

However, one problem remains. It must be explained why the structure in (29), as opposed to that in (30), is allowed with the proposed coindexation. As Cole notes, this structure is also ruled out by Condition C, if the condition is formulated only in terms of command along the lines of Reinhart (1976). Thus, he proposes that, at least in those languages with the head-internal relatives, Condition C is formulated as in (31), in terms of precedence and command.

(31)   An anaphor cannot both precede and command its antecedent.

This condition rules out (30) with the proposed coindexation, since the *pro* both precedes and commands the coindexed R-expression in the relative clause. And importantly, it allows (29) since in this structure the *pro* does not precede the coindexed R-expression.

Cole's (1987) hypothesis is very attractive. However, there is reason that it cannot be maintained for Japanese. As Cole (1987) notes himself, it has been controversial whether precedence plays any role in the Binding theory, and in particular, in the formulation of Condition C. Discussing this problem, Saito (1985: 45) presents the examples in (32) as evidence against 'precedence'.

(32) a. [[kare$_i$-no hahaoya-ga genkidatta koro]-no John$_i$]
    he-GEN mother-NOM was-fine time-GEN J.
    'John$_i$ of the time when his$_i$ mother was well
    = John$_i$ as he$_i$ was when his$_i$ mother was well'
 b. *[[John$_i$-no hahaoya-ga genkidatta koro]-no kare$_i$]
    J.-GEN mother-NOM was-fine time-GEN he
    'He$_i$ of the time when John's$_i$ mother was well
    = John$_i$ as he$_i$ was when his$_i$ mother was well'

These examples are directly relevant for the assessment of the configuration in (29). If Condition C is formulated as in (31), then (32b) is incorrectly allowed since the pronoun *kare* does not precede *John*. On the other hand, if the condition is stated only in terms of a command relation, the example is correctly ruled out. Independently of the controversy on the role of precedence in the Binding theory, (32b) clearly indicates that a pronoun in the nominal head position cannot be coindexed with an R-expression in a modifying phrase.[7]

The discussion above indicates that the structure in (29) is illicit in Japanese. And if coreference is constrained in the same way across languages, as seems plausible, then it casts doubts on Cole's analysis in general.[8]

4.2 *Kayne's suggestion*

Interestingly, given Kayne's analysis of N-final relatives, it is not clear that Cole's *pro*-head analysis of head-internal relatives is incompatible with Condition C. Let us consider again the structure in (17):

(17) [$_{DP}$ [$_{IP}$ ... t_i ...]$_j$ [$_{D'}$ D [$_{CP}$ NP$_i$ [$_{C'}$ C t_j]]]]

As noted above, NP_i does not bind t_i in this structure. Thus, even if we substitute *pro* for NP_i and a full NP for t_i, the resulting structure will not violate Condition C. This is illustrated in (33).

(33) [$_{DP}$ [$_{IP}$ ... NP$_i$ ...]$_j$ [$_{D'}$ D [$_{CP}$ *pro*$_i$ [$_{C'}$ C t_j]]]]

However, if we interpret the fact in (32) more generally, and assume, as seems reasonable, that a pronoun in the head position cannot take an NP in a modifying phrase as its antecedent, the problem remains. And Kayne in fact suggests an alternative which does not have this problem.

Kayne's alternative is based on the copy + deletion analysis of movement. According to this analysis, the movement to SpecCP is copying as shown in (34).

(34)   [$_{DP}$ [$_{IP}$ ... NP$_i$ ...]$_j$ [$_{D'}$ D [$_{CP}$ NP$_i$ [$_{C'}$ C IP$_j$]]]]

The standard copy + deletion analysis assumes that the PF representation is derived by the deletion of the NP_i and the IP_j in the tail positions of their respective chains. But it is possible to modify this slightly without any effect on the analysis of the core cases: Kayne suggests that in a chain (A$_1$, A$_2$), one of A$_1$ and A$_2$ must delete, and further, that A$_2$ must delete when A$_1$ c-commands A$_2$. This suggestion is illustrated in (35).

(35)   Given a chain (A$_1$, A$_2$),
       a.   A$_2$ → Ø when A$_1$ c-commands A$_2$.
       b.   A$_1$ or A$_2$ → Ø when there is no c-command relation between A$_1$ and A$_2$.

Then, by (35a), the second IP_j must be deleted in (34). But when it comes to NP_i, by (35b), either one can be deleted. If we delete the NP_i within the preposed IP, we obtain a regular head-external relative clause. On the other hand, if we delete the NP_i in SpecCP, we obtain a head-internal relative clause. This predicts, as in Cole's account, that head-internal relative clauses are possible only in languages with N-final relatives. There is no IP movement to SpecDP in N-initial relatives. Thus, the NP_i in SpecCP c-commands the NP_i within the IP. Hence, by (35a), only the latter can be deleted. Consequently, N-initial relatives are necessarily head-external.

This analysis is clearly an improvement over Cole's, which was based on the dubious assumption that a pronoun can appear as the relative head, coindexed with a full NP within the relative clause. And it also makes different predictions from Cole's analysis. It relies on the copy + deletion analysis of movement, and more specifically, on this analysis as it is applied to the movement to SpecCP. As the movement to SpecCP results in the configuration in (34), either NP_i can be deleted. In paricular, the NP_i in SpecCP can be deleted, and this is how a head-internal relative is derived. This implies that head-internal relatives are possible only when there is movement of the relative head to SpecCP. In other words, if there is no movement to SpecCP, there is no way to derive a head-internal relative.

Let us take the case of Japanese as a concrete example. I argued above that Japanese relatives do not involve movement to SpecCP, and have the structure in (21), repeated in (36).

(36) [$_{DP}$ [$_{IP}$ ... pro_i ...]$_j$ [$_{D'}$ D [$_{CP}$ NP$_i$ [$_{C'}$ C t_j]]]]

Here, *pro* is base-generated within the relative clause IP, and the relative head *NP$_i$* is based-generated in the SpecCP position. As no copying takes place, no deletion applies either. In particular, no operation is available to delete the *NP$_i$* in the SpecCP position. It follows that Japanese does not have head-internal relative clauses.

This prediction goes against the prevailing view that Japanese has head-internal relatives, (27) being a typical example. (27) is repeated as (37).

(37) Keikan-wa [doroboo-ga ginkoo-kara detekita no]-o
 policeman-TOP robber-NOM bank-from came out *no*-ACC
 tukamaeta
 arrested
 'The policeman arrested the robber who came out from the bank.'

In what follows, I will argue, presenting the discussion in Murasugi (1994) and Mihara (1994), that examples like (37) are not head-internal relative clauses, and hence, that Kayne's prediction is indeed correct.

4.3 *Head-internal relatives as sentential adjuncts*

4.3.1 *The status of* no
The first thing that has to be investigated in the analysis of (37) is the status of the particle *no*, which appears at the end of the embedded clause. *No* in Japanese is categorially three-ways ambiguous, as illustrated in (38).

(38) a. John-no berurin e-no ryokoo [Genitive]
 J.-GEN Berlin to-GEN trip
 'John's trip to Berlin)'
 b. [[Yamada-ga atta] no]-wa Russell ni da [Complementizer]
 Y.-NOM met C-TOP R. with is
 'It was with Russell that Yamada met.'
 c. John-ga [akai no]-o tabeta [Pronoun]
 J.-NOM red one-ACC ate
 'John ate the red one.'

In (38a), *no* is the genitive Case marker, corresponding to *'s* in English. (38b) shows that *no* appears as a complementizer in a cleft sentence. And in (38c), *no* is a pronoun, corresponding roughly in meaning to *one* in English.

It is often assumed that there is another *no* of the cateogory N, in addition to the pronoun *no*. This is the so called nominalizer *no*, shown in (39).

(39) a. [Tabesugiru no] -wa yokunai
eat too much -*no* -TOP is-not-good
'It is not good to eat too much.'
b. John-wa [Mary-ga ringo-o hirou no]-o mita
J.-TOP M.-NOM apple-ACC pick up *no*-ACC saw
'John saw Mary pick up an apple.'

Here, the function of *no* is simply to turn a sentence into a nominal category. This *no* is somewhat difficult to distinguish from the *no* as a complementizer.

Then, which one is the *no* in (37)? It does not seem plausible that it is the genitive Case marker. Can it be the pronoun *no*? If it is, (37) goes very well with Cole's analysis. The example would have a pronoun in the relative head position, coindexed with a full NP within the relative clause. But we have seen already that this analysis is untenable. Further, Kuroda (1976), who first analyzed (37) as a head-internal relative clause, presents a convincing argument that the *no* is not a pronoun.

The pronoun *no* has a derogatory connotation, and is not compatible with the honorific marking on the main verb as shown in (40).

(40) a. Wakai sensei-ga oozei orareru
young teachers-NOM many there-are (Hon.)
'There are many young teachers.'
b. #Wakai no-ga oozei orareru
young ones-NOM many there-are (Hon.)
'There are many young teachers.'

The 'strangeness' of (40b) is due to the incompatibility of the derogatory connotation imposed on the subject by the pronoun *no* and the verb in the 'subject honorification' form. On the other hand, the nominalizer *no* does not have any such connotation, since it simply has no reference. (41) is a perfectly natural sentence, since the *no* in this example does not refer to *otosi-no sensei* 'old teachers'.

(41) [otosi-no sensei-ga otabeninarisugiru no]-wa yokunai
old-GEN teacher-NOM eating-too-much (Hon.) *no* -TOP not-good
'It is not good for old teachers to eat too much.'

Here, Kuroda (1976) and Ito (1986) point out that the *no* in what they call head-internal relatives do not have any derogatory connotation. A relevant example is shown in (42).

(42)   John-wa [sensei-ga   kuukoo-ni otukininatta   no]-o
       J.-TOP   teacher-NOM airport-at arrived (Hon.) *no* -ACC
       omukaesita
       greeted (Hon.)
       'John greeted the teacher, who arrived at the airport.'

If the *no* in (42) is a pronoun coindexed with the full NP *sensei*, it should be incompatible with the 'object honorification' form of the matrix verb. But the example does not at all have the 'strangeness' of (40b). Hence, the *no* in head-internal relatives cannot be the pronoun *no*.

The discussion above suggests that the *no* in question is either a complementizer or the 'semantically empty' nominalizer.[9] Then, the structure of the so called head-internal relative clause in Japanese is as in (43a) or (43b).

(43)   a.   [$_{CP}$ [$_{IP}$ ...] [$_C$ no]]
       b.   [$_{NP}$ [$_{IP}$ ...] [$_N$ no]], where *no* is a semantically empty nominalizer.

This indicates that syntactically, what has been called a head-internal relative clause in Japanese is a simple embedded clause.

4.3.2 There are no head-internal relatives in Japanese

Kuroda's hypothesis is that the simple embedded clause in (43) is interpreted as a referential argument NP. Let us consider again the example in (37).

(37)   Keikan-wa   [doroboo-ga ginkoo-kara detekita   no]-o
       policeman-TOP robber-NOM bank-from   came out *no*-ACC
       tukamaeta
       arrested
       'The policeman arrested the robber who came out from the bank.'

According to Kuroda, the embedded clause refers to 'the robber who came out from the bank', and is interpreted as the object of the matrix verb *tukamaeta* 'arrested'. However, there is another possibility. That is, the embedded clause in question is an abverbial, and the object position of the matrix sentence is occupied by *pro*. This possibility is illustrated in (44).

(44)   Keikan-wa   [doroboo$_i$-ga ginkoo-kara detekita no]-o   pro$_i$
       policeman-TOP robber-NOM bank-from   came out *no* -acc
       tukamaeta
       arrested
       'The policeman arrested the robber as he came out from the bank.'

And arguments for this latter analysis are in fact presented in Murasugi (1994) and Mihara (1994). I will here briefly go over those arguments.

In Japanese, interestingly enough, there is another construction which is very similar to what has been called the head-internal relative. In this construction, a pure complex NP headed by *tokoro* appears as an adverbial, as shown in (45a).

(45) a. Keikan-wa [[doroboo-ga ginkoo-kara detekita] tokoro]
policeman-TOP robber-NOM bank-from came out place
-o tukamaeta
-ACC arrested
'The policeman arrested the robber as he came out from the bank.'

b. Keikan-wa [[doroboo$_i$-ga ginkoo-kara detekita] tokoro]
policeman-TOP robber-NOM bank-from came out place
-o *pro$_i$* tukamaeta
-ACC arrested

Tokoro literally means 'place', and the *tokoro*-phrase in this example is a circumstantial adverbial indicating the scene of the matrix event. It is marked by the accusative Case marker *o*, as adverbials can be marked by *o* in Japanese, as shown in (46).

(46) John-ga sono miti-o aruku
J.-NOM that road-ACC walk
'John walks on that road.'

And the semantic object of the matrix verb in (45a) is *doroboo* 'the robber', which is contained within the *tokoro*-phrase. It is the robber coming out from the bank that the policeman arrested.

For examples like (45a), Harada (1973) proposes that *doroboo* does appear as the matrix object at D-structure, but is deleted under identity with the subject of the adverbial *tokoro*-phrase. He calls the relevant rule "counter equi NP deletion." If we express his main idea in more modern terms, we would say that there is an empty pronoun, *pro*, in the matrix object position, coindexed with *doroboo* within the *tokoro*-phrase, as in (45b). This analysis with *pro* is proposed in Hale & Kitagawa (1976).

Given this analysis, a possibility arises that head-internal relatives are adverbials exactly like *tokoro*-phrases, and the matrix object position of examples like (37) is occupied by *pro*, as in (44). And in fact, Harada's arguments for the adverbial status of the *tokoro*-phrase are directly applicable to what have been called head-internal relative clauses.

One of Harada's arguments is based on examples such as (47).

(47) ??Keikan-wa [[doroboo$_i$-ga ginkoo-kara detekita] tokoro]-o
 policeman-TOP robber-NOM bank-from came out place-ACC
 soitu$_i$-o tukamaeta
 the guy-ACC arrested
 'The policeman arrested the robber as he came out from the bank.'

This example shows that when the matrix object is overt in examples like (45), the sentence is degraded. Harada first attributes this marginality to the constraint described in (48):

(48) *The double-'o' constraint* (Harada 1973)
 A derivation is marked as ill-formed if it terminates in a surface structure which contains two occurrences of NPs marked with *o* both of which are immediately dominated by the same VP nodes.

Then, he goes on to show that this constraint has a weak effect when one of the accusative NPs is an adverbial, but has a much stronger effect when the two accusative NPs are both arguments. The contrast between (49b) and (50b) illustrates the difference.

(49) a. John-ga sono miti-o aruku
 J.-NOM that road-ACC walk
 'John walks on that road.'
 b. ??Mary-ga John-o sono miti-o arukaseta
 M.-NOM J.-ACC that road-ACC walk-made
 'Mary made John walk on that road.'

(50) a. John-ga sono hon-o yomu
 J.-NOM that book-ACC read
 'John reads that book.'
 b. *Mary-ga John-o sono hon-o yomaseta.
 M.-NOM J.-ACC that book-ACC read-made
 'Mary made John read that book.'

The accusative NP in (49a) is an adverbial. Thus, the sentence becomes marginal when it is embedded in a causative structure as in (49b), where the causee argument is marked with accusative Case. On the other hand, since the accusative NP in (50a) is an argument, the sentence becomes totally ungrammatical when it is embedded in a causative structure as in (50b). Since (47) is only marginal, and *soitu* is clearly an argument, the *tokoro*-phrase in this example must be an adverbial.

This argument for the adjuncthood of the *tokoro*-phrase is directly applicable to what have been called head-internal relatives. Let us consider the example (51).

(51) Mary-wa [[syasin-ga teeburu-ni oiteatta] no]-o
M.-TOP picture-NOM table-on was put *no* -ACC
sutetesimatta
have thrown away
'Mary has thrown away the picture when it was on the table.'

Our hypothesis is that this example has the structure in (52).

(52) Mary-wa [[syasin$_i$-ga teeburu-ni oiteatta] no]-o *pro*$_i$
M.-TOP picture-NOM table-on was put *no* -ACC
sutetesimatta
have thrown away

Here, the sentence becomes marginal, but only marginal, when the matrix object is expressed overtly, as shown in (53).

(53) ??Mary-wa [[syasin$_i$-ga teeburu-ni oiteatta] no]-o sore$_i$-o
M.-TOP picture-NOM table-on was put *no* -ACC it-ACC
sutetesimatta
have thrown away
'Mary has thrown away the picture when it was on the table.'

This is exactly what we expect if the embedded clause in (53) is an adverbial. The same argument can be constructed on the basis of (37). This example also becomes only marginal, as shown in (54), when the matrix object is overtly expressed.

(54) ??Keikan-wa [[doroboo$_i$-ga ginkoo-kara detekita] no]-o
policeman-TOP robber-NOM bank-from came out *no*-ACC
soitu$_i$-o tukamaeta
the guy-ACC arrested
'The policeman arrested the robber as he came out from the bank.'

Note that if the embedded clauses in (53) and (54) are indeed head-internal relatives and hence matrix objects, as is widely assumed, then these examples should be completely out. They should show a strong violation of the double-*o* constraint like (50b). In addition, they should have two object NPs receiving the same thematic role. Hence, they should be as bad as the completely ungrammatical examples in (55).

(55) a. *Mary-wa [[teeburu-ni oiteatta] syasin]$_i$-o sore$_i$-o
M.-TOP table-on was put picture-ACC it-ACC
sutetesimatta
have thrown away
'Mary has thrown away the picture that was on the table.'
b. *Keikan-wa [[ginkoo-kara detekita] doroboo]$_i$-o
policeman-TOP bank-from came out robber-ACC
soitu$_i$-o tukamaeta
the guy-ACC arrested
'The policeman arrested the robber that came out from the bank.'

In (55), we have head-external relatives, which are clearly interpreted as the matrix objects. The marginality of (53) and (54), thus, provides strong evidence for the adverbial status of what have been called head-internal relatives.

Another piece of evidence Harada presents for the adverbial status of the *tokoro*-phrase is that it cannot be passivized. Thus, the passive counterpart of (45a), shown in (56), is totally ungrammatical.

(56) *[[Doroboo-ga ginkoo-kara detekita] tokoro]-ga (keikan-ni yotte)
robber-NOM bank-from came place-NOM policeman-by
tukamaerareta
was-arrested
'The robber was arrested by the policeman as he came out from the bank.'

Since *o*-marked adverbials, as opposed to *o*-marked objects, resist passivization, as shown in (57), this fact shows that the *tokoro*-phrase is an adverbial.

(57) *Sono miti-ga (John-ni yotte) arukareta (cf. (46))
that road-NOM J.-by was-walked
'John walked on that road.'

The same argument establishes the adverbial status of 'head-internal relatives' as well. The examples in (58) illustrate a straightforward case of passive with a head-external relative, and those in (59) show that what have been called head-internal relatives cannot be passivized.

(58) a. Keikan-wa [[ginkoo-kara detekita] doroboo]-o tukamaeta
policeman-TOP bank-from came out robber-ACC arrested
'The policeman arrested the robber that came out from the bank.' [=(28)]

b. [[Ginkoo-kara detekita] doroboo]-ga (keikan-ni yotte)
   bank-from came out robber-NOM policeman-by
   tukamaerareta
   was-arrested
   'The robber that came out from the bank was arrested by the policeman.'

(59) a. Keikan-wa [[doroboo-ga ginkoo-kara detekita] no]-o
        policeman-TOP robber-NOM bank-from came out *no* -ACC
        tukamaeta
        arrested
        'The policeman arrested the robber as he came out from the bank.' [=(27, 37)]
     b. ?*[[Doroboo-ga ginkoo-kara detekita] no]-ga
        robber-NOM bank-from came out *no*-NOM
        (keikan-ni yotte) tukamaerareta
        policeman-by was-arrested
        'The robber was arrested by the policeman as he came out from the bank.'

It was shown above that Harada's arguments for the adverbial status of *tokoro*-phrases apply directly to what have been called head-internal relatives. The parallelism between the two goes further. For example, the *tokoro*-phrases resist relativization for some reason, as shown in (60).

(60) a. Keikan-wa [[doroboo-ga ginkoo-kara detekita] tokoro]-o
        policeman-TOP robber-NOM bank-from came out place-ACC
        tukamaeta
        arrested
        'The policeman arrested the robber as he came out from the bank.' [=(45a)]
     b. *[[keikan-ga tukamaeta] [doroboo-ga ginkoo-kara
         policeman-NOM arrested robber-NOM bank-from
         detekita tokoro]]
         came out place
         'the scene of the robber coming out from the bank which the policeman arrested'

It seems then that this type of adjuncts, say, circumstantial adjuncts, cannot be relativized.

As shown in (61), the so called head-internal relatives behave exactly as the *tokoro*-phrases in this respect.

(61) a. Keikan-wa [[doroboo-ga ginkoo-kara detekita] no]-o
policeman-TOP robber-NOM bank-from came out *no*-ACC
tukamaeta
arrested
'The policeman arrested the robber that came out from the bank.' [=(59a)]

b. *[[keikan-ga tukamaeta] [[doroboo-ga ginkoo-kara
policeman-NOM arrested robber-NOM bank-from
detekita] no]]
came out *no*
'the scene of the robber coming out from the bank which the policeman arrested'

In contrast, the regular externally headed relatives relativize without any problem, as shown in (62).

(62) [[keikan-ga tukamaeta] [[ginkoo-kara detekita] doroboo]]
policeman-NOM arrested bank-from came out robber
'the robber that came out from the bank who the policeman arrested'

(62) is the relativized version of (58a).

The discussion so far indicates that the so-called head-internal relatives in Japanese are adverbial clauses, exactly like the *tokoro*-phrases. This implies that they are not relative clauses at all. There is one piece of direct evidence for the latter conclusion, i.e., that they are not relative clauses. It is noted in Kuroda (1976), Ishii (1988), and also Hoshi (1994) that what they assume to be a head-internal relative cannot appear as the complement of P. The examples in (63) illustrate this generalization.

(63) a. *Keisatu-wa [[doroboo-ga mise-kara detekita] no]-kara
police-TOP robber-NOM shop-from coming out *no*-from
[nusunda hooseki]-o toriageta
robbed jewelry-ACC took
'The police took the robbed jewelry away from the robber that came out from the shop.'

b. *Keisatu-wa [[doroboo-ga mise-kara detekita] no]-ni
police-TOP   robber-NOM shop-from coming out *no*-to
taihozyoo-o   miseta
arrest warrant-ACC showed
'The police showed the arrest warrant to the robber that came out from the shop.'

If what they call head-internal relative clauses are in fact interpreted as regular relative clauses, it is not at all clear why the examples in (63) are out. These examples are fine with regular externally headed relatives, as shown in (64).

(64) a. Keisatu-wa [[mise-kara detekita]   doroboo]-kara [nusunda
police-TOP   shop-from coming out robber-from   robbed
hooseki]-o   toriageta
jewelry-ACC took
'The police took the robbed jewelry from the robber that came out from the shop.'

b. Keisatu-wa [[mise-kara detekita]   doroboo]-ni
police-TOP   shop-from coming out robber-to
taihozyoo-o   miseta
arrest warrant-ACC showed
'The police showed the arrest warrant to the robber that came out from the shop.'

On the other hand, if what they call head-internal relatives are not relative clauses, but circumstantial adverbials, the ungrammaticality of the examples in (63) is straightforwardly predicted. It is simply impossible to take away stolen jewelries from, or show an arrest warrant to, the scene of an event.[10]

I have presented several pieces of evidence that what has been called the head-internal relative in Japanese is not a relative at all, but a circumstantial adverbial phrase. This implies that Japanese does not have head-internal relatives. As noted above, Kayne's analysis of head-internal relatives, together with the generalization that Japanese relatives cannot involve movement, predicts that Japanese does not have head-internal relatives. What was shown above is that this prediction is indeed borne out.

5. Does Japanese have relative clauses?

To summarize the discussion so far, I first discussed the basic properties of Japanese relative clauses. The most prominent one is that they do not involve movement. I then discussed the hypothesis in Murasugi (1991) that Japanese relative clauses are IPs, and not CPs. This was motivated by the non-movement property and also the acquisition data I briefly discussed. In the third section, I started to examine how Kayne's antisymmetry analysis of N-final relatives fares with Japanese relatives. In this section, I suggested a possible way to derive the non-movement property in his theory. And in Section 4, I considered Kayne's suggestion on the derivation of head-internal relatives. I pointed out that this suggestion, together with the non-movement property, predicts that Japanese does not have head-internal relatives. I argued that this prediction is indeed borne out.

The final problem that remains is the acquisition data in (13), repeated in (65).

(65) a. buta san-ga tataiteru no taiko
piggy-NOM is-hitting *no* drum [M: 2;11]
'the drum that the piggy is playing'
b. ohana motteru no wanwa
flower is-holding *no* doggie [T: 2;6]
'a doggie that is holding a flower'

As noted above, children around the age 2 to 4 produce ungrammatical relatives, with *no* between the relative clause and the relative head. I proposed in Murasugi (1991) that this *no* is a complementizer, and showed how children can retreat from this overgeneration of *no* on the basis of positive evidence.

Within Kayne's antisymmetry analysis, it seems difficult to maintain that the overgenerated *no* is of the category C. This is so, since if it were a C, it should follow the relative head. It is possible to pursue the hypothesis that it is a D, but it is not clear to me at this point that this approach is promising. It has been proposed in the literature (for example, in Zushi (1996)) that the Japanese genitive Case marker *no* is generated under D. But if the *no* in (65) is the genitive Case marker, it is not clear why it appears only in child Japanese, and is not allowed in adult Japanese. That is, it is not clear how children can retreat from the overgeneration of *no*.

In this section, instead of pursuing a radical alternative analysis for the acquisition data, I would like to speculate on how the analysis of Murasugi (1991) can be accommodated under the antisymmetry theory.

Let us consider again the antisymmetry analysis of Japanese relatives we entertained in Section 3. As in (21), repeated in (66), the relative head NP_i is base-generated in SpecCP, and the gap is base-generated as *pro*.

(66) $[_{DP} [_{IP} \ldots pro_i \ldots]_j [_{D'} D [_{CP} NP_i [_{C'} C t_j]]]]$

This analysis follows Kayne's basic assumption that relative clauses universally have the D-CP structure. But let us put aside this assumption for a moment, and consider the structure in (66) on its own right. The structure, it seems, has much redundancy.

In (66), the IP originates as the complement of C and is preposed to the SpecDP position. This is necessary if the relative head moves out of the IP to SpecCP. If the IP is base-generated in SpecDP, then the relative head NP_i cannot move to the SpecCP position. But in (66), the relative head is base-generated in SpecCP. Hence, nothing seems to go wrong even if the IP is base-generated in SpecDP, as in (67).

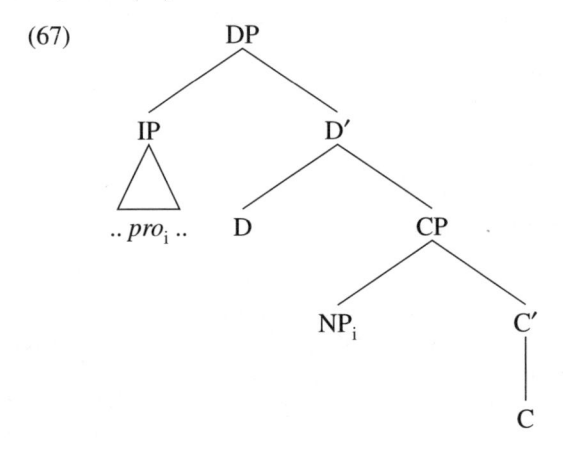

(67)
```
           DP
          /  \
         IP   D'
        /\   /  \
    ..pro_i.. D   CP
                 /  \
               NP_i  C'
                     |
                     C
```

In (67), the C projection plays no role and is completely redundant. If we eliminate this, we obtain (68).

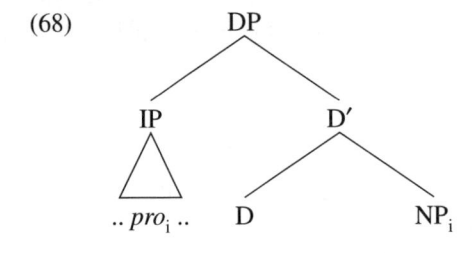

(68)
```
           DP
          /  \
         IP   D'
        /\   /  \
    ..pro_i.. D   NP_i
```

(68) is very close to (69), the structure of Japanese relative clauses argued for in Murasugi (1991).

(69)
```
      NP
     /  \
    IP   NP
```

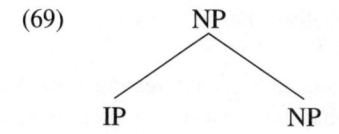

And more interestingly, it is similar to the structure of a pure complex NP. Suppose, as seems reasonable, that the structure of N-final pure complex NPs is as in (70a).

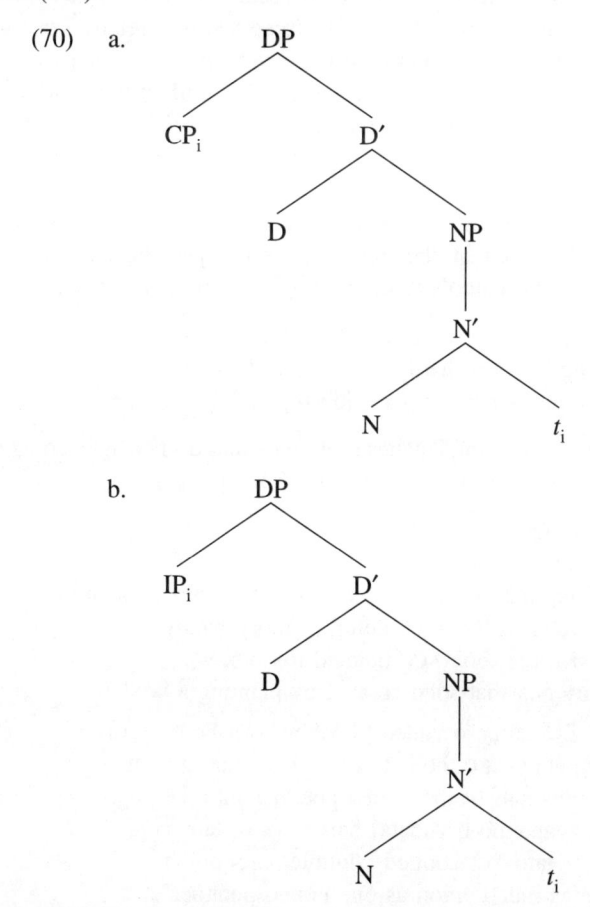

(70) a.
```
         DP
        /  \
      CP_i  D'
           /  \
          D    NP
               |
               N'
              /  \
             N    t_i
```

b.
```
         DP
        /  \
      IP_i  D'
           /  \
          D    NP
               |
               N'
              /  \
             N    t_i
```

If we adopt the conclusion in Murasugi (1991) that prenominal sentential modifiers in Japanese are of the category IP, we have (70b) instead of (70a). The only difference between (68) and (70b) is whether the IP is base-generated in SpecDP, or is moved there from within the NP.

This similarity between (68) and (70b) suggests an interesting possibility. Since there is no clear reason not to suppose that the IP in (68) is preposed from within the NP, it seems possible that Japanese relative clauses have the structure of pure complex NPs, or more straightforwardly, are pure complex NPs. This implies that Japanese does not have relative clauses.

Within the context of the discussion in the preceding sections, this conclusion can be interpreted as follows. As Kayne hypothesizes, relative clauses universally have the D-CP structure, and involve movement of the relative head to SpecCP. But as suggested in Section 3, this results in an illicit unbound trace in Japanese. Therefore, Japanese cannot have relative clauses. The only way in which the language can express the meaning of a relative clause is by employing a pure complex NP.

The idea that Japanese relatives are pure complex NPs seems plausible on independent grounds. As noted at the outset of this paper, Japanese allows relative clauses without gaps. Kuno's example in (1) is repeated in (71).

(71)   [$_{NP}$[$_{IP}$ syuusyoku-ga   muzukasii] [$_{NP}$ buturigaku]]
       getting job-NOM hard   physics
       'physics, which is hard to get a job in.'

And there are many other kinds of Japanese relatives that do not have counterparts in English. Let us consider the examples in (72) and (73).

(72)   a.   [$_{NP}$[$_{IP}$ zyagaimo-o yudeta] mono]
               potato-ACC boiled   thing
               'the thing that resulted from boiling potatoes = boiled potatoes'
   b.   [$_{NP}$[$_{IP}$ John-ga hako-o   nutta] omotyabako]
               J.-NOM box-ACC painted toy box
               'the toy box that John created by painting a box'

(73)   a.   [$_{NP}$[$_{IP}$ Zyagaimo-o yudeta] hanbun]-o nabe-ni ireru
               potato-ACC boiled half-ACC   pan-in   put
               'One puts half of the boiled potatoes into the pan.'
   b.   [$_{NP}$[$_{IP}$ zyagaimo-o yudeta] bai]   -no   tamanegi
               potato-ACC boiled   double -GEN onion
               'twice as much onion as one boiled potatoes'

Examples like (72a) and (72b) are discussed in Kuroda (1976). In these examples, the head noun refers to a result of the action or event denoted by the relative clause. In (73a), the head noun is 'half', and the whole complex NP means "half of the thing obtained by boiling potatoes." As noted by Ishii (1991), this kind of comlex NPs can refer to an amount instead of a thing. Thus, the complex NP headed by *bai* in (73b) means "the amount twice as much as that of the thing that resulted from boiling potatoes." In general, the modification relation between the relative clause and the relative head is very loose in Japanese.

A similar observation can be made with pure complex NPs in Japanese. Thus, examples like (11), repeated in (74), are possible.

(74) a. [$_{NP}$[$_{IP}$ sakana-ga yakeru] nioi]
          fish-NOM burn   smell
          'the smell that a fish burns' (Lit.)
      b. [$_{NP}$[$_{IP}$ doa-ga   simaru] oto]
          door-NOM shut   sound
          'the sound that a door shuts' (Lit.)

These examples are similar to (72) and (73) in their interpretation. The nominal head refers to a result of the action or event denoted by the sentential modifier.

It has been assumed in the literature that (74a) and (74b) are pure complex NPs, in part because (74a), for example, can be paraphrased as 'the smell of a fish burning'. As the examples (71), (72), and (73) cannot be paraphrased in a similar way, they have been assumed to be relatives. But when we consider the similarity in interpretation, it is natural to treat (72) and (73) exactly like (74). And given that the modification relation is in general quite free in Japanese pure complex NPs, it seems quite possible that examples like (71), or even those like (75), are pure complex NPs.

(75) [$_{NP}$[$_{IP}$ John-ga *pro*$_i$ yonda] hon$_i$]
            J.-NOM   read   book
      'the book that John read'

If Japanese relatives are pure complex NPs, the analysis of the acquisition data in (65) proposed in Murasugi (1991) can be maintained as such. The unmarked structure for pure complex NPs is N-CP, and Japanese speaking children initially assume the structure in (70a). Thus, they generate *no* in the Comp position. But they receive as positive evidence examples of pure complex NPs without an overt complementizer. As an empty complementizer is excluded by the ECP, they conclude that the sentential modifiers do not contain a C projection, and are of the category IP. Thus, they obtain the adult grammar and cease to overgenerate *no*.

6. Conclusion

In this paper, I discussed a possible analysis of Japanese relatives within the antisymmetry theory, and suggested as a consequence that Japanese relative clauses are pure complex NPs. It is not clear that all aspects of Japanese nominal structure can be accommodated in a principled way under this theory, and I am not yet committed to such an analysis. But in this discussion, two major conclusions emerged. First, as far as Japanese relative clauses are concerned, the antisymmetry theory makes it possible to explain their major properties in a plausible way. And secondly, the antisymmetry analysis of Japanese relative clauses may not be as radically different from the traditional analysis as one might think. If Japanese relative clauses are pure complex NPs, as I sugested above, then their structures are arguably as in (70b). It is a radical departure from the traditional analysis that the sentential modifier IP originates in an N-initial structure and is preposed to the prenominal position. But aside from this, the structure is very similar to (69), for example. It appears that most of the proposals based on the traditional analysis can be maintained quite straightforwardly even with an antisymmetry analysis.

Notes

1. The account for the absence of adjunct relativization in Murasugi (1991) is actually more complicated than the analysis suggested above. I assumed at that time that Japanese relativization can involve IP-adjunction, and proposed an ECP analysis for why IP-adjunction is impossible in the case of adjunct relativization. In retrospect, the assumption was not well-founded, and the complicated ECP analysis was unnecessary.
2. According to Kayne, Spec is an adjoined position. But since this particular proposal is not relevant to the discussion here, I will ignore it in this paper.
3. See also Saito (1989: fn. 14) for relevant discussion. Saito (1989) and Lasnik & Saito (1992) adopt a different generalization.
4. Honda, et al. (1996), on independent grounds, propose a structure virtually identical to (21) for Japanese relative clauses. Their proposal is based on a detailed examination of the parallelism between relativization and topicalization in Japanese, which was initially noted and discussed in Kuno (1973).
5. These Japanese examples are discussed in detail in Tada (1990) and Saito (1992). The "translations" of scrambling examples are mere illustrations of their structures, and not meant to be the the real translations.
6. (26) clearly does not hold with movement to SpecIP or operator movement. Movement to SpecIP out of a finite clause is simply impossible. And operator movement is necessarily an A'-movement.
7. See also Tsubomoto (1991) and Hoshi (1994) for relevant discussion on this point.

8. It should be noted here that (32) does not constitute a direct counter-example for Cole's analysis. As I will be arguing below that Japanese does not have head-internal relatives, it is technically possible to say that those languages with head-internal relatives have (31), whereas Condition C is formulated only in terms of command in Japanese. But this would be unattractive on conceptual grounds, since, as noted in the text, it is only natural to suppose that coreference is constrained in the same way across languages.
9. See Kuroda (1976), Ito (1986), and Murasugi (1993) for more detailed discussion on the syntactic properties of this *no*.
10. There are limited cases where a 'head-internal relative' is accompanied by the dative marker *no*. The following example is adopted from Ito (1986):

(i)   Watasi-wa [[sensei-ga   tyoodo deteirasita]   no]-ni oaisuru   koto-ga
    I-TOP   teacher-NOM just   came out (Hon.) *no*-DAT meet (Hon.)   -NOM
    dekita
    could
    'I could meet the teacher as he just came out.'

Examples like this seem problematic since the dative *ni* apparently marks the complement of the verb *oaisuru* 'meet (Hon.)', and intuitively, the semantic object of this verb is *sensei* 'teacher'. In addition, the sentence becomes totally ungrammatical when this semantic object is overtly expressed.

(ii)   *Watasi-wa [[sensei$_i$-ga   tyoodo deteirasita]   no]-ni kare$_i$-ni oaisuru   koto-ga
    I-TOP   teacher-NOM just   came out (Hon.) *no*-DAT he-DAT meet (Hon.)   -NOM
    dekita
    could

This fact indicates more clearly that the embedded clause in (i) is not a circumstantial adverbial, but the dative object.

Although I do not have an account for examples like (i), it is not clear that they are indeed problematic for the hypothesis argued for in the text that the typical cases of what have been called head-internal relatives are circumstantial adjuncts. As was discussed in detail in the text, a *tokoro*-phrase refers to the scene of an event. And interestingly, it also can appear in examples like (i), as shown in (iii).

(iii)   Watasi-wa [[sensei-ga   tyoodo deteirasita]   tokoro] -ni   oaisuru
    I-TOP   teacher-NOM just   came out (Hon.) place   -DAT meet (Hon.)
    koto-ga   dekita
    -NOM could
    'I could meet the teacher as he just came out.'

Further, (iii), like (i), becomes ungrammatical when the semantic object of *oaisuru* is made overt.

(iv)   *Watasi-wa [[sensei$_i$-ga   tyoodo deteirasita]   tokoro]-ni kare$_i$-ni oaisuru
    I-TOP   teacher-NOM just   came out (Hon.) place-DAT he-DAT meet (Hon.)
    koto -ga   dekita
    -NOM could

It thus appears that *oaisuru* allows scenes, as opposed to persons, as its dative object.

References

Cole, P. (1987). The structure of internally headed relative clauses. *Natural Language & Linguistic Theory* 5: 277–302.
Fiengo, R. (1977). On trace theory. *Linguistic Inquiry* 8: 35–61.
Hale, K. & C. Kitagawa. (1976). Counter to counter equi. *Papers in Japanese Linguistics* 5: 41–61.
Harada, S. I. (1973). Counter equi NP deletion. *Annual Bulletin of the Research Institute of Logopedics and Phoniatrics* 7: 113–47. University of Tokyo.
Hoji, H. (1985). *Logical form constraints and configurational structures in Japanese*. Doctoral Dissertation. University of Washington.
Honda, K, K. Ichikawa, T. Inoue, K. Yurugi & S. Sunami. (1996). The structure of Japanese relative clauses. Manuscript. Dokkyo University.
Hoshi, K. (1994). The syntax of the head-internal relative clause construction in Japanese. Manuscript. University of Rochester.
Ishii, Y. (1988). Head-internal relative clauses in Japanese and related issues. Manuscript. University of Connecticut.
Ishii, Y. (1991). *Operators and empty categories in Japanese*. Doctoral dissertation. University of Connecticut.
Ito, J. (1986). Head movement at LF and PF. *University of Massachusetts Occasional Papers in Linguistics* 11: 109–38.
Kayne, R. (1981). ECP extensions. *Linguistic Inquiry* 12, 93–133.
Kayne, R. (1994). *Antisymmetry of syntax*. Cambridge, Mass.: MIT Press.
Keenan, E. (1985). Relative clauses. *Language typology and syntactic description II: complex constructions*. Edited by Timothy Shopen, 141–170. Cambridge: Cambridge University Press.
Kuno, S. (1973). *The structure of the Japanese language*. Cambridge, Mass.: MIT Press.
Kuroda, S.-Y. (1976). Pivot-independent relativization in Japanese. Reprinted in Kuroda, S.-Y. (1992), *Japanese syntax and semantics*. Dordrecht: Kluwer, 91–111.
Lasnik, H. & M. Saito. (1992). *Move alpha*. Cambridge, Mass.: MIT Press.
Mahajan, A. (1990). *The A/A' distinction and movement theory*. Doctoral dissertation. MIT.
Mihara, K.-I. (1994). Iwayuru syuyoobu-naizaigata-kankeisetu ni tuite (On the so-called head-internal relative clauses [translated by the present author]). *Nihongogaku* 13: 80–92.
Murasugi, K. (1991). *Noun phrases in Japanese and English: a study in syntax, learnablity and acquisition*. Doctoral dissertation. University of Connecticut.
Murasugi, K. (1993). Two notes on head-internal relative clauses. *Treaties and Studies by the Faculty of Kinjo Gakuin University* 34: 233–242. Kinjo Gakuin University.
Murasugi, K. (1994). Head-internal relative clauses as adjunct pure complex NPs. *Synchronic and diachronic approches to language*, edited by Shuji Chiba, 425–437. Tokyo: Kaitakusha.

Nemoto, N. (1993). *Chains and case positions: a study from scrambling in Japanese*. Doctoral dissertation. University of Connecticut.

Perlmutter, D. (1972). Evidence for shadow pronouns in French relativization. *The Chicago which hunt*, edited by P.M. Peranteau, et al, 73–105. Chicago Linguistic Society.

Reinhart, T. (1976). *On the syntactic domain of anaphora*. Doctoral dissertation, MIT.

Saito, M. (1985). *Some asymmetries in Japanease and their theoretical implications*. Doctoral dissertation. MIT.

Saito, M. (1986). LF effects of scrambling. Paper presented at the Princeton workshop on comparative grammar.

Saito, M. (1989). Scrambling as semantically vacuous A'-movement. *Alternative conceptions of phrase structure*, edited by M. Baltin & A. Kroch, 182–200. Chicago: University of Chicago Press.

Saito, M. (1992). Long distance scrambling in Japanese. *Journal of East Asian Linguistics* 1: 69–118.

Stowell, T. (1981). *Origins of phrase structure*. Doctoral dissertation. MIT.

Tada, H. (1990). *Scrambling(s)*. Manuscript. MIT.

Tsubomoto, A. (1991). Syuyoobu-naizaigata-kankeisetu. (Head-internal relative clauses [translated by the present author]). *Gendai-eigogaku-no ayumi*, edited by Toshio Gunji, et al, 253–262. Tokyo: Kaitakusha.

Webelhuth, G. (1989). *Syntactic saturation phenomena and the modern Germanic languages*. Doctoral dissertation, University of Massachusetts, Amherst.

Zushi, M. (1996) An antisymmetric analysis of Japanese *no*. *The Journal of the Faculty of Foreign Studies* 28: 31–60, Aichi Prefectural University.

A Complement-of-N⁰ Account of Restrictive and Non-Restrictive Relatives
The case of Swedish[*]

Christer Platzack
University of Lund

1. Introduction

The theory of phrase structure proposed in Kayne (1994), where asymmetric c-command has a central role to play, successfully derives several properties of X-bar syntax, previously stipulated. As a consequence, however, many widely assumed analyses are rejected. With respect to relative clauses, Kayne (1994: 91) reaches the conclusion that a raising/promotion analysis is by far the most natural. Developing earlier ideas by Smith (1969) and Vergnaud (1974), Kayne suggests that relative clauses have the base structure in (1a), and that the relative head is created by movement of a NP to SpecCP of the relative clause, as illustrated in (1b):

(1)   a.   [$_{DP}$ D⁰ CP]
        b.   [$_{DP}$ the [$_{CP}$ picture$_i$ [$_{C_0}$ that] [John bought t_i]]]

Kayne's analysis has several virtues, in addition to being compatible with the antisymmetric approach. It offers for instance a costless account of reconstruction cases, i.e. cases where an anaphor contained in the head seems to be bound

---

[*] This article is a revised version of a paper with a slightly different title, published in Working Papers in Scandinavian Syntax 59, June 1997. It has been presented at the Lund University Grammar Seminar in the fall of 1996, and at a workshop on relative clauses hosted by Zentrum für Allgemeine Sprachwissenschaft Berlin, 22–24 November 1996. Thanks to both audiences for corrections and suggestions. I have also greatly benefitted from the insightful remarks of an anonymous reviewer, as well as from valuable comments by Lars-Olof Delsing, Elisabet Engdahl, Gunlög Josefsson, Henrik Rosenkvist and Øystein Vangsnes. The usual disclaimers apply, naturally.

by the subject of the relative clause, as in the English example *the picture of himself that John bought*. However, the raising approach also faces certain problems; see Wilder (1995) and Borsley (1997) for critical reviews. Some of these problems will be discussed below. In this paper I will explore an analysis of relative clauses, according to which the relative clause is a complement of N^0, as outlined in (2):

(2)   [$_{DP}$ D^0 ... [$_{NP}$ ... N^0 CP]]

According to Kayne (1994: 155, fn. 17), this is the only alternative configuration of relative clauses permitted by his phrase structure theory.[1]

I will discuss relative clauses from the point of view of Swedish. Taking into consideration the rich surface structure of the Scandinavian DP (see Delsing (1993) for an overview), it is not inconceivable that a study of relatives based on Scandinavian data will help us to a better understanding of certain aspects of this construction.[2]

The main difference between Kayne's account and mine concerns the status of the relative head: it is raised from a position within the relative clause to SpecCP in Kayne's analysis, but base generated outside the relative clause in my account; see (1) and (2). I will argue that my account preserves the virtues of Kayne's approach without having its drawbacks. For such a claim to be sustained, it is important to show how reconstruction cases (see above) are handled; this is the subject of the last part of this introduction.

My paper is organized in the following way. In Section 2 I present the general outline of my account. Section 3 contains a discussion of two properties that hold irrespectively of the restrictive — non-restrictive distinction, whereas Section 4 highlights a number of differences between these two types of relatives. Section 5 is about extraposed relatives, Section 6 about stacked relatives, and Section 7 focuses on the similarities and differences between non-restrictive relatives and contrastive left dislocation. Section 8 is the conclusion.

1.1 *Reconstruction cases*

One of the strongest arguments for a raising analysis of relatives is that it seems to account for cases like (3a), where an anaphor in the head of the relative appears to be bound by the subject of the relative clause; see Kayne (1994: 87). Given the raising analysis, the relative construction is described analogously to similar cases with topicalization and left dislocation, where the possibility of having an anaphor in the fronted phrase is accounted for in terms of reconstruction.

(3)   a.   John$_i$ bought the picture of himself$_{i/j}$ that Bill$_j$ [Relative]
saw.
        b.   The picture of himself$_i$ John$_i$ found on the   [Topicalization]
table.
        c.   The picture of himself$_i$, John$_i$ found it on   [Left Dislocation]
the table.

However, a closer study reveals a less clear-cut picture. A reconstruction analysis would predict that the following Swedish examples should be equally good, but they are not:

(4)   a.   *Var   la   du   brevet   från   sin   lärare   som   Sara
where put you letter-the from her.REFL teacher that S.
fick igår? [Relative]
got yesterday
'Where did you put the letter from her teacher that Sara got yesterday?'
        b.   Brevet   från   sin   lärare   la   Sara   på
letter-the from her.REFL teacher put S.   on
bordet. [Topicalization]
table-the
'The letter from her teacher Sara put on the table.'
        c.   Eva$_i$ besökte det av sina$_{i/*j}$ slott   som kungen$_j$
E.   visited that of her/*his.REFL castles that king-the
bor i. [Relative]
lives in
'Eva visited the castle of hers (/*his) which the king lives in'
        d.   Det av sina$_i$ slott   som kungen$_i$ bor i är från
that of his.REFL castles that king-the lives in is from
1500-talet. [Relative]
16thcentury-the
'The castle of his which the king lives in is from the 16th century'

Given reconstruction and a raising analysis of relatives, it is a mystery why (4a) should be out and why (4c) is not ambiguous. Whatever the reason for the variation in (4) might be, it is obvious that cases where a reflexive in the relative head appears to be bound by the subject of the relative clause cannot be taken as argument for a raising analysis. On the contrary the facts given in (4) indicate a problem for such an analysis.[3]

2. The relative clause as complement of N⁰

2.1 *Introduction*

The main function of a relative clause is to modify the noun to which it is attached, usually called the antecedent or the relative head; I will use both terms in my article. Based on the nature of this modification, relative clauses are traditionally considered to be of two kinds, restrictive and non-restrictive. The restrictive relative clause is a necessary modification, delimiting the set of elements referred to by the relative head and thereby determining its referent. The non-restrictive relative, on the other hand, gives additional information concerning the relative head, the reference of which is independently established.[4]

Swedish non-restrictive relatives contrast with restrictive relatives in several respects, although some differences are not syntactic in nature but a result of the different types of modification. Such a property is the possibility to expand a non-restrictive relative with speaker-oriented adverbs like *för övrigt* 'by the way', 'incidentally', which cannot be used in a restrictive relative clause. Another non-syntactic property is that non-restrictive relatives do not take proper names as heads under normal circumstances.

In this section I will present the basics of my account of relative clauses, arguing that all relative clauses are generated as the complement of N. My claim is that a relative construction is a DP with the structure outlined in (5), where the dots indicate functional projections not specified here:

(5)

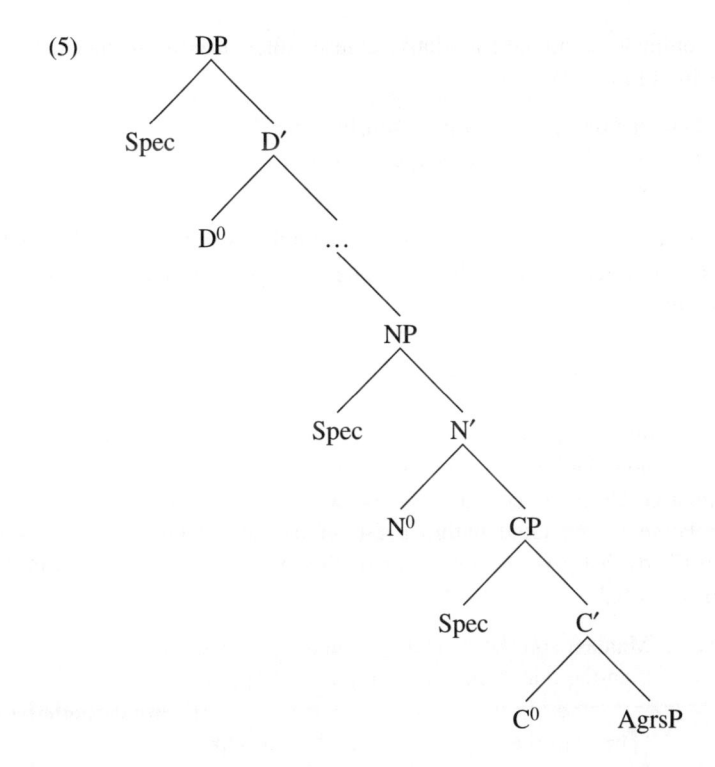

```
              DP
             /  \
          Spec   D'
                /  \
              D⁰    ...
                      \
                       NP
                      /  \
                  Spec    N'
                         /  \
                       N⁰    CP
                            /  \
                         Spec   C'
                               /  \
                             C⁰    AgrsP
```

In the prototypical case, the relative complementizer (*som* in Swedish) is generated in C⁰.[5] With Chomsky & Lasnik (1993) I take SpecCP of the relative clause to contain an operator phrase, either an empty operator *Op* or a *wh*-phrase, which is raised to SpecCP from a position within the clause.[6] This operator is linked to the relative head via C⁰: the relative complementizer in C⁰ shares Φ-features with the operator, since the two are in a spec-head relation.

In addition I will assume that relative *som* contains a feature δ. This feature, which is attracted by D, is also present both in the definite and the indefinite article. When the corresponding feature in D is strong, the closest element carrying δ moves to D in overt syntax; in the absence of a δ in front of the relative complementizer, *som* must move to D, as further discussed below.[7] It follows that a relative clause must be embedded under a DP, hence the analysis predicts that nominal phrases lacking a DP in their extended projection cannot host a relative clause. This prediction seems to be correct. As Delsing (1993: 31) observes, classifying predicatives in Swedish do not take any article, definite or indefinite, which indicates that there is no DP in their extended projection. Such predicative nominals cannot take a relative clause either. The following example is from Delsing (1993: 32):

(6) Han är *(en) karl som man kan lita på.[8]
 he is a man that one can trust on
 'He is a man to trust.'

The ɸ-features associated with *som* (ultimately with the operator in SpecCP) will follow δ as free riders, thereby being brought in spec-head relation to the ɸ-features of the relative head.[9]

2.2 The Restrictive — Non-restrictive Distinction

To capture the difference between restrictive and non-restrictive relatives, I propose that the nominal head of a restrictive relative is generated in N^0 in (5), taking the relative CP as its complement, whereas the nominal head of a non-restrictive relative is generated within a DP in the specifier of N^0.[10] This is illustrated in (7c,d) that give the structures of the restrictive and non-restrictive interpretations of (7a,b):[11]

(7) a. Mannen som kom igår har försvunnit.
 man-the that came yesterday has disappeared
 [Restrictive relative]
 'The man that came yesterday has disappeared.'
 b. Mannen, som (f.ö.) kom igår, har försvunnit.
 man-the that by the way came yesterday has disappeared
 [Non-restrictive relative]
 'The man, who by the way came yesterday, has disappeared.'

c. *Restrictive interpretation*

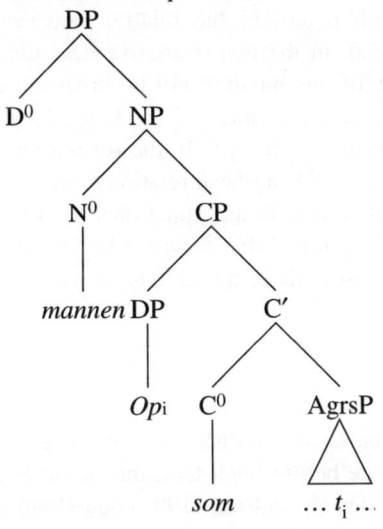

```
            DP
           /  \
          D⁰   NP
              /  \
             N⁰   CP
             |   /  \
         mannen DP   C'
                |   /  \
               Opᵢ C⁰   AgrsP
                   |    /\
                  som  … tᵢ …
```

d. *Non-restrictive interpretation*

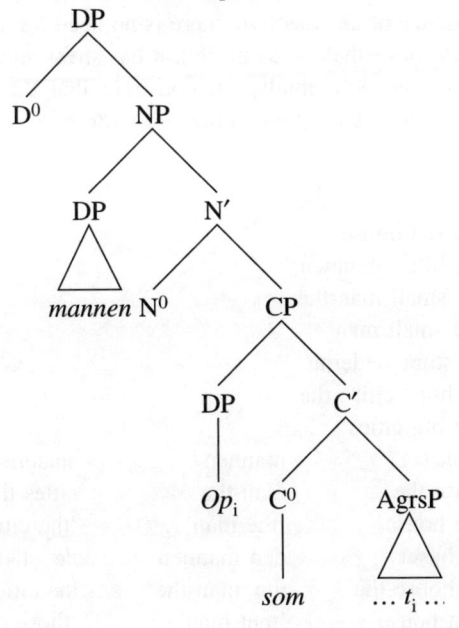

```
            DP
           /  \
          D⁰   NP
              /  \
             DP   N'
             /\  /  \
        mannen N⁰   CP
                   /  \
                  DP   C'
                  |   /  \
                 Opᵢ C⁰   AgrsP
                     |    /\
                    som  … tᵢ …
```

The proposed analysis immediately predicts a difference between restrictive and non-restrictive relatives with regard to the relation between the operator in SpecCP and the relative head: in the non-restrictive case the ɸ-feature bundle hosted by *som* (or the trace of this bundle) will be in spec-head relation to the entire relative head after having been attracted to D, and for this reason it must agree with the relative head in its totality.[12] In the restrictive case, on the other hand, the feature bundle will be in head-head relation to the N taking the relative clause as its complement, as well as to any functional head within the extended projection of this head, making it possible for the relative clause to modify only parts of the relative head. Cases where this difference is of importance will be discussed in Section 4.3.[13]

2.3 *The strong D-feature*

It is commonly assumed that D in Swedish hosts a strong feature which must attract a corresponding feature before Spell-Out; this is the δ-feature introduced above. Arguments are provided by Delsing (1993) and Holmberg & Sandström (1995). Among the arguments, I will cite the following one, based on the (nearly obligatory) presence of a free determiner in front of adjectives taking definite NPs (8a).[14] In the absence of an adjective, there is no need for a free determiner, see (8b). If there is one nevertheless, as in (8c), it has stress and a demonstrative reading. The examples in (8d), finally, demonstrate that the free determiner cannot occur with a noun lacking the definiteness ending.[15]

(8) a. det röda huset;
the red house-the
'the red house'
den lille mannen;
the small man-the
'the small man'
de stora städerna
the big cities-the
'the big cities'
b. huset   mannen   städerna
house-the   man-the   cities-the
'the house'   'the man'   'the cities'
c. det huset   den mannen   de städerna
the house-the   the man-the   the cities-the
'that house'   'that man'   'those cities'

d. *Det röda hus brann.
   the red house was-burning
e. *Den lille man skrattade.[16]
   the little man laughed

Note that Swedish like English lacks a plural indefinite marker, and that definiteness is expressed inflectionally, hence contrasts like *ett hus* 'a house' / *huset* 'the house', *en man* 'a man' / *mannen* 'the man', *städer* 'cities' / *städerna* 'the cities' (the different forms -*en*, -*et* are due to a gender difference between *man* 'man' and *hus* 'house').[17]

A strong D forces the raising of *huset* 'house-the' etc. to D in (8b), since the definite ending carrying the feature δ is part of this word. The examples in (8a) illustrate the case where this raising is blocked, presumably by the phonological features of the intervening adjective (see Delsing (1993: 77–86) for arguments indicating that A^0 is in the head line from D^0 to N^0 in Scandinavian DPs). In cases like (8a) the free determiner seems to function as an expletive, lexicalizing the strong feature in D — following Groat (1995) I take expletives to lexicalize strong features, thereby making them weak (i.e. postponing the checking to invisible syntax). In covert syntax, then, δ is raised to D^0; since no phonological features accompany δ in this case, the raising is not blocked by the intervening adjective. Examples (8c) show the use of the free determiner in the absence of an adjective; recall that the free determiner cannot occur solely with a noun lacking the definite ending (8d), which indicates that the free determiner does not carry the feature δ.[18]

In a restrictive relative like (7a/c) the topmost D overtly attracts the feature d, which is present in the definite noun *mannen* 'man-the'. In a non-restrictive relative like (7b/d) there are two Ds attracting δ, one in the topmost DP and one in the DP inside SpecNP. The second one must find a δ within its DP, since it does not c-command the relative clause and hence cannot get access to the δ in the relative complementizer. The δ in C is attracted by the higher D, an attraction that must result in movement prior to Spell-Out, since the feature in D is strong. Hence the complementizer must move overtly to D in non-restrictive relatives.[19, 20] Since the relative head precedes *som* also in non-restrictive relatives, where *som* is assumed to have been raised overtly to D, there must be a further raising of the relative head DP to SpecDP before Spell-Out. A similar raising to SpecDP is postulated by Holmberg & Sandström (1995), in their account of prenominal possessors in Scandinavian.[21] As a matter of fact, there is a striking similarity in the surface structure they propose for a DP with a prenominal possessor (9a), and the topmost DP of a non-restrictive relative under my account (9b):

(9) a.

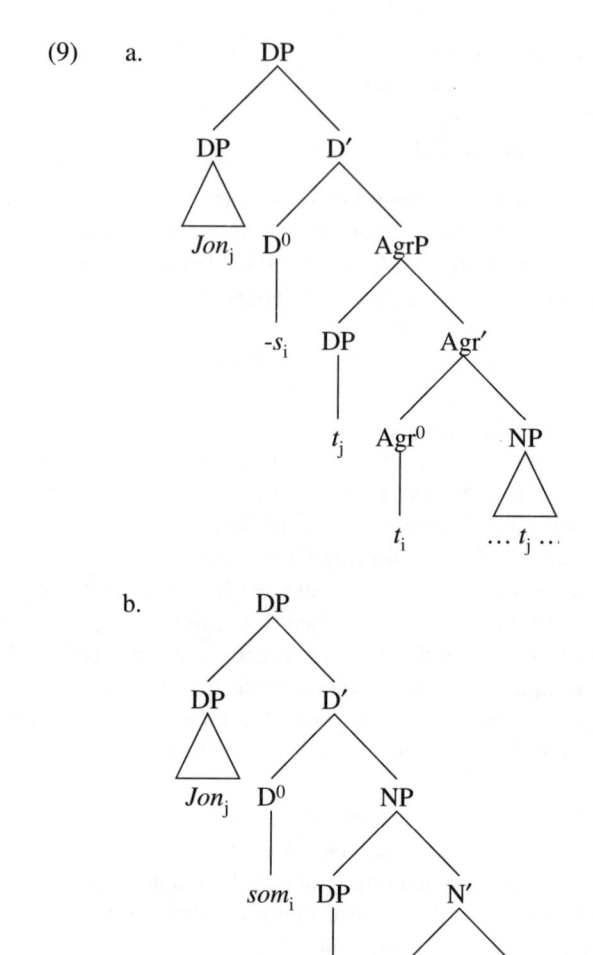

```
           DP
          /  \
        DP    D'
       /|\   / \
      Jonⱼ  D⁰   AgrP
            |   /   \
           -sᵢ DP    Agr'
               |    /   \
               tⱼ  Agr⁰   NP
                   |     /|\
                   tᵢ   ...tⱼ...
```

b.

```
           DP
          /  \
        DP    D'
       /|\   / \
      Jonⱼ  D⁰   NP
            |   /  \
           somᵢ DP   N'
                |   / \
                tⱼ N⁰  CP
                   |  /|\
                   tᵢ ...tᵢ...
```

In Chinese the similarity between a non-restrictive relative construction and a possessive one is even more striking. Consider the examples in (10), taken from Xu (1997), showing that D is filled by the same morpheme *de* in both cases. According to Xu, *de* raises to D⁰ in (10a) from the embedded C, in (10b) from an Agr-position; compare the structures in (9). To derive (10a), Xu assumes that the IP of the embedded clause is overtly raised to SpecDP, as illustrated in (10c).

(10) a. Zhangsan you de shu
   Z. has *DE* book
   'the book that Zhangsan has'
 b. Zhangsan de shu
   Z. *DE* book
   'Zhangsan's book'
 c. [$_{DP}$ [$_{IP}$ Zhangsan you *pro*]$_j$ [$_{D_0}$ de$_j$] [$_{NP}$ [$_{DP}$ shu [$_{CP}$ [$_{C_0}$ t_j] [$_{IP}$ t_j]]]]]

2.4 *Extractions out of relative clauses*

The possibility to extract out of relative clauses in the Scandinavian languages Danish, Norwegian and Swedish, known at least since Erteschik-Shir (1973), Andersson (1974) and Allwood (1976), offers an immediate support for the structural difference between restrictive and non-restrictive relative clauses outlined in (7c,d). As pointed out by Engdahl (1997), extraction is only possible out of restrictive relative clauses:

(11) a. Den här teorin$_i$ känner jag mannen som uppfann t_i.
   this here theory know I man-the that invented
   'I know the man who invented this theory.'
 b. *Den här teorin känner jag Kalle som uppfann t_i.
   this here theory know I Kalle that invented
   'I know Kalle, who invented this theory.'

This difference is predicted by the structural proposals in (7c,d). Extraction out of DP presupposes the availability of an extraction hatch; analoguous with extraction out of CP, I assume SpecDP to perform this role.[22] This position is not available in non-restrictive relative clauses, where it is occupied by the relative head, as illustrated in (9b).[23]

In the following sections I will focus on various parts of the proposed analysis in order to show how it works. I will begin with a discussion of two properties that hold independently of the interpretation of the relative clause as restrictive or non-restrictive, proceeding to a discussion of factors of importance for describing grammatical differences between the two types of relatives.

3. Some general properties of relative clauses

In this section I will discuss two properties of relative clauses predicted by the structures in (7), that hold irrespectively of the restrictive – non-restrictive distinction. As we will see, these facts are problematic (although probably not devastating) for Kayne's approach.

3.1 Case disagreement

The analysis proposed in (7) avoids a Case problem associated with Kayne's account: assuming NP to be raised to SpecCP, Kayne's account predicts that the head of the relative clause should have the case of the embedded clause, whereas in fact it bears the Case of the external determiner. This is illustrated by the examples in (12), where (12a) is Standard German and (12b) Bavarian (the Bavarian example is from Bayer (1984: 213)):

(12) a. der Junge, den wir kennen
the boy.NOM pron.ACC we know
'The boy who we know'
b. die Frau dera wo da Xaver a Bussl g'gem hod
the woman.NOM pron.DAT that the X. a kiss given has
'The woman who Xaver kissed'

Kayne (1994: 86 ff.) accounts for the case situation in (12) by LF-raising the head of the NP raised to SpecCP to the highest D for Case-checking reasons. It is not clear how this is possible when the raised NP has a morphological case different from the morphological Case of the head, as in (12), since the raising will lead to a situation with two distinct cases associated with one position.

There is a further problem in Kayne's analysis related to the raising hypothesis: the raised element in standard cases like *the house I built* is not a DP but an NP. Being an NP, it is not expected to be an argument, see e.g. Stowell (1991), Delsing (1993) or Longobardi (1994). Hence Kayne has to extend his analysis with some auxiliary assumptions to bypass this problem.[24]

It should be clear that the facts of (12) do not constitute problems for my account, where there are two D-heads available, one carrying the Case needed in the matrix clause (*der Junge, die Frau* in (12)), and the other carrying the case needed in the embedded clause (*den, dera* in (12)). Neither does my account have a problem with the status of the relativized element: this is a nominal operator, and hence a DP.

3.2 Pied Piping

A second problem with Kayne's analysis derives from his account of pied piping. Consider an example like *the boy with whom I spoke*, which according to Kayne involves raising of the complex (*with whom boy*) to SpecCP, and the subsequent raising of *boy* to SpecPP, presumably via SpecWh. Applied to the base structure of the sequence *the boy that I spoke with*, it is hard to see how to prevent the mechanism introduced to derive the ill-formed **the boy with that I spoke*. I do not see how Kayne's approach can prevent the PP *with boy*[25] from raising to SpecCP, followed by the raising of *boy* to the specifier of PP, which will result in the ill-formed sequence.

In my analysis of relatives, the incorrect fronting of the preposition would involve raising of *with Op*. However, we are never allowed to front P together with a non-overt nominal, hence this structure is out for independent reasons. Consider e.g. the fact that although *pro* (or a nominal operator, depending on the analysis[26]) may be contextually interpreted in SpecCP, as in ordinary cases of Topic Drop (see the Swedish example in (13a)), the gap may never be preceded by a preposition, as illustrated in (13b):

(13) a. Den mannen?! – *pro* Mötte vi på bussen igår.
       that man   met we on bus-the yesterday
       'That man?! We met him on the bus yesterday.'
    b. På torget?!   – *På *pro* var jag i morse   och köpte
       at market-place-the   at   was I this morning and bought
       några tulpaner.
       some tulips.
       [Intended: 'At the market-place?! I was there this morning and bought some tulips.']

4. Differences between Restrictive and Non-restrictive relatives

In this section I will discuss a number of differences between restrictive and non-restrictive relatives emerging as a result of the different status of the relative head. To recapitulate, under my analysis a restrictive relative clause is the complement of the nominal head of its antecedent, whereas a non-restrictive relative clause is the complement of an empty N^0, the specifier of which is the antecedent of the relative clause. See the structures outlined in (7c, d).

4.1 Free determiner without a definite noun

One particularly clear difference between restrictive and non-restrictive relatives in Swedish is the fact that only restrictive relatives can be headed by a free determiner and a noun without a definite ending, as in (14a,b,c); the impossibility to insert the adverbial *för övrigt* 'by the way' in the relative clauses (see the examples in (14d–f)) unambiguously indicates that only restrictive relatives are possible in these cases:

(14) a. Den man som kom igår har försvunnit.
 the man that came yesterday has disappeared
 'The man that came yesterday has disappeared.'
 b. Det hus som han köpte var rött.
 the house that he bought was red
 'The house that he bought was red.'
 c. De hästar som betar därborta tillhör min far.
 the horses that are-grazing over-there belong-to my father
 'The horses that aregrazing over there belong to my father'
 d. *Den man, som för övrigt kom igår, har försvunnit.
 the man that by the way came yesterday has disappeared
 e. *Det hus, som han för övrigt köpte, var rött.
 the house that he by the way bought was red
 f. *De hästar, som för övrigt betar därborta, tillhör
 the horses that by the way are-grazing over-there belong-to
 min far.
 my father

When not followed by a restrictive relative clause, a noun preceded by a free determiner must take the definite ending, as already shown in (8d) and further illustrated in (15). Note that both restrictive and non-restrictive relatives can take an antecedent consisting of a free determiner and a noun with the definite suffix (15c,d):

(15) a. Den man*(-nen) har försvunnit.
 that man-the has disappeared
 'That man has disappeared.'
 b. Det hus*(-et) var rött.
 that house-the was red
 'That house was red.'

c. Det huset som han talade om ligger där borta.
the house-the that he talked about is over there
'The house that he was talking about is over there.'

d. Det huset, som han för övrigt ville riva, är
the house-the that he by the way wanted to-demolish, is
nu till salu.
now for sale
'The house, which, by the way, he wanted to demolish, is now for sale.'

Consider now the analysis of examples like (14a–c), where a free determiner occurs with a restrictive relative clause and a noun lacking definite ending, and the corresponding ungrammatical cases in (14d–f). My account assigns the structure in (16b) to the restrictive relative in (16a), whereas the ungrammatical case with a non-restrictive relative in (16c) is assigned the structure in (16d):

(16) a. Den bil som jag mötte var röd.
the car that I met was red
'The car that I encountered was red.'
b. [$_{DP}$ [$_{D_0}$ den] ... [$_{NP}$ [$_{N_0}$bil] [$_{CP}$ Op_i [$_{C_0}$ som] [jag mötte t_i]]]]...
c. *Den bil, som jag för övrigt mötte, var röd.
d. [$_{DP}$ [$_D$ e] ..[$_{NP}$ [$_{DP}$ [$_{D_0}$ den] [$_{NP}$ [$_{N_0}$ bil]]] N^0] [$_{CP}$ Op_i [$_{C_0}$ som] [jag mötte t_i]]]]...

Although the presence of the free determiner postpones the checking of the strong feature in δ to covert syntax, there must be an instance of the feature δ around to be attracted by D. Since the noun *bil* 'car' lacks a definite ending, it is not supposed to host this feature, as is evident from (15a,b). The only available δ is provided by the relative complementizer; convergence will occur when the δ-feature of this complementizer is attracted to D. This is unproblematic in the restrictive case, where the only instance of δ c-commands C. In the non-restrictive case, however, there are two instances of D, each needing a δ to attract, as mentioned in Section 2.3. The top-most δ will attract the δ-feature of C just as in the restrictive case. However, the second δ is in SpecNP, where no δ is available in (16c), and since the δ of this DP does not c-command the relative clause it cannot attract δ of the relative complementizer.

Related to the difference demonstrated in (14)–(16) is the following one. A proper name can only be the antecedent of a non-restrictive relative clause; English and Swedish are alike in this respect. However, when the name is preceded by a free determiner, the relative clause is interpreted as restrictive;

consider the examples in (17), and note the fact that neither language accepts an NP consisting solely of a determiner and a proper name (*the Paris, *det Paris, cf. Vergnaud 1974: 265, Kayne 1994: 103):

(17) a. det Paris som jag kände
         the P. that I knew
         'The Paris that I knew'
     b. the Paris that I knew

Summarizing, a free determiner can occur together with a non-restrictive relative clause in Swedish just in case it precedes a definite noun (15d). The sequence free determiner plus definite noun can also precede a restrictive relative clause (14c). The restrictive interpretation is the only possible one in all other cases of a free determiner and a relative clause, as illustrated in (14d–f), (15), and (16a,b). As this subsection has demonstrated, the distribution of cases with a free determiner and a relative clause follows directly from my account.

4.2 *Scopal facts and Kayne's analysis of Non-restrictive relatives*

The account in (7) captures the well known fact (see e.g. Ross 1967; Jackendoff 1977; and Emonds 1979) that only restrictive relatives are in the scope of the definite article at PF; note that the definite article in the head of a non-restrictive relative does not c-command the relative clause, as mentioned above, since it is embedded within a DP in SpecNP. Consider the English examples in (18a,b). To describe this difference, Kayne (1994: 112) assumes that non-restrictive relatives involve the covert raising of the IP of the relative clause to SpecDP, as indicated in the LF-structure (18c); NP in SpecCP is the relative head raised out of IP prior to IP fronting.

(18) a. The young man, who I saw yesterday, is a linguist.
                                              [Non-restrictive]
     b. The young man who I saw yesterday is a linguist.
                                              [Restrictive]
     c. $[_{DP}\ IP_i\ [D^0\ [_{CP}\ NP\ [C^0\ t_i]]]]$

In Kayne's analysis, the LF position of IP is outside the scope of the definite article. Hence, Kayne accounts for the observation in (18). Note, however, that the difference is only present at LF in Kayne's approach, since it is the raising of IP in covert syntax which brings about the scope relation. According to my analysis in (7), the difference is present already at PF.

To compare the two accounts, we will consider a case where PF-scope is operative, namely the licensing of polarity items. The PF-sensitivity of such items is indicated by the contrast in (19), where the polarity item *någonsin* 'ever' is licensed in (19a) but not in (19b); only in the first case is it within the PF-scope of the negation. An ordinary time adverbial may be fronted without problem, as indicated by (19c):

(19) a. Han reste inte någonsin till Paris.
he went not ever to Paris
'He never went to Paris'
b. *Någonsin reste han inte till Paris.
ever went he not to Paris
c. Förra söndagen reste han inte till Paris.
last Sunday went he not to Paris
'He didn't go to Paris last Sunday'

It is well-known that a polarity item in a relative clause is licensed by an appropriate element in the antecedent; thus, e.g., *någonsin* 'ever' is allowed when the antecedent hosts a negation, a question word or a superlative. My approach correctly predicts that polarity items are licensed from the antecedent only in restrictive relatives, since the licensing element does not c-command into the relative clause in the non-restrictive case; see (20):

(20) a. Den vackraste flicka han någonsin hade sett
the most-beautiful girl he ever had seen
stod framför honom.
was-standing in-front-of him
'The most beautiful girl that he had ever seen was standing in front of him.'
b. *Den vackraste flickan, som han f. ö. någonsin
the most-beautiful girl that he by-the-way ever
träffat, var läkare.
(had)met, was a-doctor

Kayne's account does not predict the difference in (20), since the two types of relatives have identical PF structures in his account. With respect to polarity items in relative clauses, then, my approach is superior to Kayne's.

4.3 *Uncountable heads and Hydras*

Although an extended projection usually has the same feature specification as its lexical head, this is not always the case, e.g. with DPs that are ambiguous between a countable and an uncountable interpretation. A predicate adjective in Swedish agrees with the nominal head of such a DP in its countable reading, but not in the uncountable reading. This is illustrated in (21):[27]

(21) Blommor   är   vackra   / vackert.
      flowers.UTER.PL. are beautiful.UTER.PL. / NEUTER.SG.
      'Flowers are beautiful.'

The account proposed in (7) now predicts that only non-restrictive relatives are allowed with an uncountable interpreted relative head, since only in this case is it possible to avoid agreement with the nominal head. This prediction is correct, as shown by the contrast between (22) and (23):

(22) Han serverade fisk   som var god/   *gott.   [Restrictive]
      he   served   fish.UTER   that was good.UTER/ NEUTER.SG
      'He served fish that was good.'

(23) Han serverade fisk,   som för övrigt var god/
      he   served   fish.UTER   that by the way was good.UTER/
      gott.   [Non-restrictive]
      good.NEUTER
      'He served fish, which by the way was good.'

A similar case where (7) predicts a difference between restrictive and non-restrictive relatives is illustrated in (24) and (25):

(24) En av poliserna,   som f. ö.   blev sjuk / *sjuka,
      one of policemen-the   that by the way got ill.SG / ill.PL
      heter   Blom.   [Non-restrictive]
      is-named B.
      'One of the policemen, who by the way became ill, is called Blom.'

(25) En av poliserna   som blev sjuk / sjuka heter   Blom.
      one of policemen-the   that got ill.SG / ill.PL is-named B.
                                                               [Restrictive]
      'One of the policemen who became ill is called Blom.'

My analysis in (7) correctly predicts that agreement with the object of the preposition is not available in the non-restrictive case, since the relative clause must be attached to the entire DP constituting the antecedent. In the restrictive case, on the other hand, there are two possible ways to attach the relative clause to the antecedent, as outlined in (26) and (27):

(26) [_DP_En ...[av [poliserna som blev sjuka]] heter Blom
(27) [_DP_En ...[av poliserna] som blev sjuk] heter Blom

In the restrictive case, the relative clause is either attached to the object of the preposition, yielding the plural form of the adjective (the adjective *sjuka* 'sick.PL' agrees with *poliserna* 'the policemen'), or it is attached to the numeral head of the antecedent, yielding singular form of the adjective (the adjective *sjuk* 'sick.SG' agrees with *en* 'one').

A third case of the same type is constituted by multiple-headed relative clauses ("hydras" in the terminology of Link (1984)) as illustrated in (28):

(28) a. mannen och kvinnan som blev arresterade
man-the and woman-the that were arrested.PL
'the man and the woman who were arrested'
b. varje man och kvinna som blev arresterad
every man and women that was arrested.SG
'every man and woman who was arrested'

In (28a), which may be interpreted as a non-restrictive relative clause, two singular nouns are coordinated, and the past participle must be in plural form. This follows straightforwardly from my analysis, since the head of the non-restrictive relative is a conjoined DP in this case. On the other hand, the participle has singular form in (28b), and the relative clause is interpreted as restrictive. Once again this follows from my analysis: in this case there is no DP antecedent, but just a combination of two singular nouns in the scope of the quantifier *varje* 'every'.

4.4 *An aspectual difference*

Schmitt (1996: 198 ff.) has observed that restrictive and non-restrictive relatives have different influences on the aspectual interpretation of their matrix clauses. Consider first the aspectual effect of the definite article, illustrated in (29) and (30): a definite object of a transitive non-stative verb triggers a bounded interpretation of the event referred to, whereas a naked object triggers an unbounded interpretation; in the examples below, the use of the durational adverbial *i x tid* 'for x time' signals an unbounded event, whereas the use of the durational adverbial *på x tid* 'in x time' signals a bounded event. Swedish and English are alike in this respect:

(29) Han målade porträtten på tre veckor.
      he   painted portraits-the in three weeks
                              [definite object, bounded event]
      'He painted the portraits in three weeks.'
(30) Han målade porträtt i flera år.
      he   painted portraits for several years
                              [naked object, unbounded event]
      'He painted portraits for several years.'

Inserting a non-restrictive relative in the object of (29) does not change the aspectual interpretation, as shown in (31):[28]

(31) Han målade på tre   veckor porträtten, som f.ö.
      he   painted in three weeks portraits-the that by-the-way
      alla   ville   köpa.
      everybody wanted to-buy
      'He painted in three weeks the portraits, which by the way everybody wanted to buy.'

However, if we insert a restrictive relative clause with the same meaning, both a bounded and an unbounded reading is available:[29]

(32) Han målade i flera år   / på tre   veckor porträtten
      he   painted for several years / in three weeks portraits-the
      alla   ville   köpa.
      everybody wanted to-buy
      'He painted in three weeks / for several years the portraits everybody wanted to buy.'

In Schmitt's account, the bounded/unbounded distinction is partly determined by the semantic feature [±S(pecified) Q(uantity)], where [+SQ] is associated with the bounded reading, and [−SQ] with the unbounded reading. To account for the unbounded reading of definites with restrictive relatives, Schmitt (1996: 200) proposes an analysis where the complementizer in C^0 with the feature [−SQ] is raised to D^0, by-passing the definite noun with the feature [+SQ], which in this case will have no influence on the aspectual interpretation.

Schmitt's analysis can easily be implemented in my framework. Consider first the non-restrictive case. The δ-feature of the relative complementizer is attracted by D^0 to check the strong feature of this position. As a consequence a spec-head relation between δ and the relative head is established. Given the optionality of features (see Chomsky 1995: 236), there are now two possibilites:

either the nominal head of the antecedent has the feature [+SQ], or it lacks SQ; a definite noun cannot be [-SQ]. In the first case the DP will be marked [+SQ], in the second case it will lack this feature. The complementizer is either marked [+SQ] or [-SQ], depending on the value of the operator. Since the complementizer must agree with the relative head, only the [+SQ]-value will lead to a convergent derivation. Consequently, the non-restrictive relative cannot have any influence on the aspectual reading.

Consider next the restrictive case. As in the non-restrictive case, the δ-feature of the relative clause is raised to D^0, carrying along its SQ-feature. Let us assume that this feature has the value [-SQ], and that no SQ-value is selected for the definite noun (the optionality of features, see above). In this case the [-SQ]-feature of the relative is raised to D together with δ, giving a [-SQ]-interpretation to the definite DP, producing the unbounded reading of (33). Naturally, if the definite noun is marked [+SQ], only this value is possible for the complementizer as well, leading to the bounded reading of (33). Thus, my analysis accounts for the aspectual ambiguity in DPs with restrictive relatives, without implying a similar ambiguity in DPs with a non-restrictive relative, or in DPs without a relative.[30]

5. The relative complementizer and extraposed relatives

Both restrictive and non-restrictive relative clauses may be extraposed; when extraposed the relative clause must always be introduced by an overt relative complementizer.

(33) a. Nu är flickan här *(som) du frågade efter.
now is girl-the here that you asked for
'Now the girl is here that you were asking for.'
b. Jag träffade flera elever förra veckan *(som) hon hade
I met several students last week that she had
talat med.
talked to
'I met several students last week that she had spoken with.'
c. Kan du säga mig var den där flickan finns *(som) Anna
can you tell me where that girl is that A.
nämnde?
mentioned
'Can you tell me where that girl is that Anna mentioned?'

(34) Jag gav boken   till den flicka igår,   *(som) Anna hade
      I   gave book-the to the girl yesterday   that A.   had
      nämnt.
      mentioned
      'I gave the book to the girl yesterday that Anna had mentioned.'

The existence of extraposed relatives has been problematic for the antisymmetrical hypothesis, which does not allow for rightward movement. Kayne (1994: 118) claims that examples like (33) and (34) involve relative clause *stranding* and not extraposition: according to Kayne, the relative head is raised out of the relative clause into its surface position. Hence in (33a), *flickan* 'the girl' has been raised from SpecCP of the relative clause to the subject position of the main clause. Discussing the structural position of the relative clause, Kayne (1994: 121) suggests the presence of a position below the normal position for direct objects.

Kayne's analysis has several unclear aspects. One of them regards the structure of the raised head. As Wilder (1995) has remarked, D+SpecCP is not a constituent in Kayne's account (see (1b) above), hence it should not be allowed to move.

A case like (34) might also be problematic for Kayne — here the relative head is in the complement of a preposition, i.e. a position from which it cannot c-command its trace.[31]

The structural difference between restrictive and non-restrictive relative clauses proposed in (7) above indicates different analyses for extraposed restictive and extraposed non-restrictive relative clauses.

Consider first example (35a) with an extraposed non-restrictive relative clause; the analysis proposed is indicated in (35b):

(35) a. Jag träffade Anna förra veckan, som f.ö.   också
          I   met   A.   last week   that by the way also
          gillar Brahms.
          likes B.
          'Last week, I met Anna, who by the way also likes Brahms.'
      b. ....Anna$_k$ ....[$_{DP}$ t_k [$_{D_0}$som$_i$] ...[$_{NP}$ t_k [$_{N_0}$ t_i] [$_{CP}$ Op$_j$ t_i [$_{AgrSP}$ t_j också gillar Brahms]]]]

Since the antecedent in this case is a full DP, it may move from SpecNP through SpecDP into its position in the matrix clause. As in ordinary non-restrictive relative clauses, *som* has raised overtly to D^0.[32]

Whereas the antecedent of a non-restrictive relative might be available for raising, as just illustrated, my theory predicts that no raising is possible with restrictive relatives, since the antecedent is not a phrase. Nevertheless, restrictive relatives may be extraposed, as explicitly shown by the form of the relative heads in (36):

(36) a. Nu är den flicka här som du frågade efter.
now is the girl here that you asked for
'Now the girl is here that you were asking for.'
b. Den man vill jag se som kann lösa den här uppgiften.
the man want I see that can solve this here task
'I would like to see the man who can solve this task.'
c. Den vill jag prata med som har stulit min cykel.
the want I talk to that has stolen my bike
'I would like to talk to the one who has stolen my bike.'

Contrary to both Kayne and the traditional view, I will argue for a representational analysis of such cases. The fact that extraposed restrictive relatives, like non-restrictive ones, are obligatorily introduced by the relative complementizer suggests that they are DPs containing a relative clause whose complementizer has been raised to D in the absence of any material in D and N, as illustrated in (37):[33]

(37) [$_{DP}$ [$_{D_0}$ som$_i$] [$_{NP}$ [$_{N_0}$ t_i] [$_{CP}$ Op_j [$_{C_0}$ t_i] [$_{AgrSP}$ t_j har stulit min cykel]]]

The antecedent of the extraposed restrictive relative clause is base generated in its matrix clause position: thus, *den flicka* 'the girl' in (36a) is generated as the subject of *är* 'is', *den man* 'the man' in (36b) as the object of *se* 'see', etc.

Even if the antecedent and the relative clause are generated as distinct DPs in the matrix clause, they must obviously be realizations of the same θ-role. Similar cases where two distinct overt DPs realize the same θ-role are illustrated in (38):

(38) a. Kalle, han är inte dum, han.
K., he is not stupid, he
'As for Kalle, he's not stupid.'
b. Nu kommer han över bron, Smirnov.
Now comes he over bridge-the, Smirnov
'Now Smirnov's crossing the bridge.'
c. Kalle, den djäveln är inte dum.
K. the bastard is not stupid
'As for Kalle, the bastard's not stupid.'

d. Kalle, han är inte dum, den djäveln.
    K.   he is not stupid the bastard.
    'As for Kalle, the bastard, he's not stupid.'

In (38a), where the subject is left dislocated, we even have three overt DPs sharing the same θ-role only one of which can be in an A-position.[34] It is often claimed that the pronouns in examples like (38) are resumptive pronouns, a kind of spelled-out traces. This can hardly be the case in the examples with extraposed relatives, though, and the existence of examples like (38c,d) with epithets instead of pronouns indicates that such an analysis is not correct for the other cases with shared θ-roles either.

In (38), as well as in the cases with extraposed relatives, there must be some kind of relation between the DPs that realize the same θ-role. For cases like (36), where the antecedent consists of a free determiner and a noun without definite ending, i.e. a combination not allowed in the absence of a restrictive relative, it is clear that the relative clause must provide the δ-feature. As in the ordinary cases (cf. the discussion of (7c)), I assume LF-raising of the δ-feature associated with the relative complementizer. Such a raising will succeed only in case the φ-features accompanying δ match the φ-features associated with the D of the separated relative head. Note that DP of the extraposed relative is in a complement-head relation to (the trace of) the matrix verb (the lowest V in a Larsonian shell-structure), hence δ can rise by head to head movement from the D-head of the DP hosting the relative clause to the functional projection of which the antecedent of the extraposed clause is the specifier.[35]

Summarizing this section, I have claimed that the obligatory presence of an overt relative complementizer in non-restrictive relatives and extraposed relatives (restrictive or non-restrictive) has the same explanation, namely the overt raising of the relative complementizer. As a consequence of this analysis, extraposed relatives must be base-generated in the lowest complement of the VP-shell.[36]

6. Stacked relatives

The structural relation between the relative head and the relative clause differs in restrictive and non-restrictive cases. According to my analysis, the relative clause in the non-restrictive case is the complement of an empty noun, to which the relative head is the specifier, whereas the relative clause is the complement of the nominal head of the relative head in the restrictive case. This difference is responsible for the different ordering of restrictive and non-restrictive relatives in the case where a single head takes more than one relative clause. An example with stacked relatives of this kind is given in (39):

(39) Brevet som ligger där, som jag för övrigt läst två
 letter-the that is-lying there, that I by the way (have-)read two
 gånger, kom igår.
 times, came yesterday
 'The letter that is lying there, which by the way I have read twice, came yesterday.'

Restrictive and non-restrictive relatives behave differently when stacked, in English as well as in Swedish — when we have both a restrictive and a non-restrictive relative clause, the restrictive one must precede the non-restrictive one. Hence we cannot reverse the order of relative clauses in (39), as shown by the ungrammaticality of (40):

(40) *Brevet, som jag för övrigt läst två gånger, som ligger
 letter-the that I by the way (have-)read two times that is-lying
 dár kom igår.
 there, came yesterday

The restriction on order follows immediately from the proposed analysis. Given my account of relatives, there is only one possibility to derive a case with a restrictive and a non-restrictive relative. This structure is outlined in (41), which gives the Spell-Out structure of (39):

(41) [$_{DP}$ [$_{DP}$ Brevet som ligger där]$_i$ [$_{D_0}$ som$_j$] [$_{NP}$ t_i [$_{N_0}$ t_j] [$_{CP}$ Op_k [$_{C_0}$ t_j] [$_{AgrSP}$ jag för övrigt läst t_k två gånger]]]]

The DP containing the restrictive relative is generated in SpecNP as the antecedent of a non-restrictive relative clause. Prior to Spell Out the DP containing the restrictive relative clause is raised to SpecDP, and *som* is raised to D^0, giving (41).

It is not possible to derive the order of (40), given my analysis: there is no room for a relative clause when the head-noun of the restrictive relative is generated in N^0 on the head line from D to C. Hence the order of stacked restrictive and non-restrictive relatives is predicted.[37]

It is possible, however, to stack more than one restrictive relative clause:

(42) Den karlen som du pratade med som hade mörkt hår var trevlig.
 the man-the that you talked with that had dark hair was nice
 'The guy you spoke with that had dark hair was nice.'

Teleman et al. (1999) note that in such cases it is always possible to coordinate the relative clauses: (43) is identical to (42) in all respects, with the exception of the presence of the coordinator *och* 'and'.

(43)   Den karlen   som du   pratade med ***och*** som hade mörkt hår var
        the man-the that you talked with and that had dark hair was
        trevlig.
        nice
        'The guy who you spoke with and who had dark hair was nice.'

The structural analysis does not prohibit the coordination of relative clauses, restrictive or non-restrictive. Assuming an account of coordination in line with Kayne (1994: 57), where the coordinated parts are specifier and complement of the coordinator, (42)/(43) will get the following structure after the raising of N to D:

(44)   [$_{DP}$ [$_{D_0}$ karlen$_i$] [$_{NP}$ [$_{N_0}$ t_i] [[$_{CP}$ som du pratade med] (och) [$_{CP}$ som hade mörkt hår]]]]

It is also possible to coordinate two non-restrictive relative clauses:

(45)   Min far, som du   träffade igår,   och som du   gillade, ...
        my father, that you met   yesterday and that you liked,
        'My father, who you met yesterday, and who you liked, ...'

The structural analysis is given in (46):

(46)   [$_{DP}$ min far$_i$ [$_{D_0}$som$_j$] [$_{NP}$ t_i [$_{N_0}$ t_j] [[$_{CP}$ t_j du träffade igår] och [$_{CP}$ som du gillade]]]]

The coordination of non-restrictive relatives differs in one respect from the coordination of restrictive ones: the coordinator *och* cannot be left out in the first case. Presumably this can be related to the fact that the relative complementizer is raised out of the first conjunct; see (46).

Concluding, the ordering restriction pertaining to stacked relatives follows as a consequence of the different structural properties of restrictive and non-restrictive relatives in my account. Kayne (1994: 112 ff.), on the other hand, derives the ordering restriction in a totally different way. As mentioned in Section 4.2. Kayne assumes that IP is raised from the relative clause to SpecDP in non-restrictive relatives; consider (18). Applying this analysis of non-restrictive relatives to cases with stacked relatives, Kayne notes (1994: 114) that a raising of IP from a relative embedded within another relative, as in (47), would involve movement of a right branch out of a left branch. This is illustrated in (47b), which gives the structure of the ungrammatical sequence (47a) under Kayne's raising analysis:

(47) a. *the book, which I've read twice, that's on the table
    b. [$_{DP}$ IP$_i$ D^0 [$_{CP}$ [$_{CP}$ book which [C^0 t_i]]]]

According to Kayne, the movement of a right branch from within a left branch is generally prohibited, as in (48). See Kayne (1994: 114, example (144)):

(48) *Who has the cold weather given the sister of a bad case of the flu?

Since the restriction on the order of stacked relatives is related to a general restriction in Kayne's account, he gets it at no cost. Unfortunately, however, the general restriction is not absolute. In (49) I give a Swedish example with movement of a right branch from within a left branch,[38] which is stiff and formal but does not seem to be ungrammatical:

(49) Vilken båt hade den svåra stormen givit seglen på betydande
     which boat had the heavy storm-the given sails-the on great
     skador?
     damages
     'Which boat's sails had the heavy storm damaged badly?'

See Platzack (1974) for a discussion of such extractions. Since it is never possible to violate the ordering restriction on restrictive and non-restrictive relatives, whereas the observation (49) shows that movement of a right branch from within a left branch is marginally possible, it is not evident that the two restrictions are related, as Kayne claims.

7. Left Dislocation and Relative Clauses

Swedish non-restrictive relatives share a number of properties with left dislocation structures, in particular with contrastive left dislocation, as I will show below. It is well-known, especially from the papers in Anagnostopoulou et al. (1997), that such a similarity exists in all Germanic V2 languages. Given my account of non-restrictive relatives, this similarity is not surprising, since the two constructions are assigned almost identical structures. The main structural difference between contrastive left dislocation and non-restrictive relatives is that the relative clause is embedded within a DP. However, as will be evident, the similarity disguises a difference with respect to how the relation is established between the dislocated/antecedent DP and the following clause. Compare the representations in (50c/d) of the examples in (50a/b):

(50) a. Mannen, honom har du nog träffat.
man-the him have you probably met
'The man, you probably have met him.'
b. Mannen, som du nog har träffat, ...
man-the that you probably have met
'The man who you probably have met'
c. *Contrastive Left Dislocation*[39]

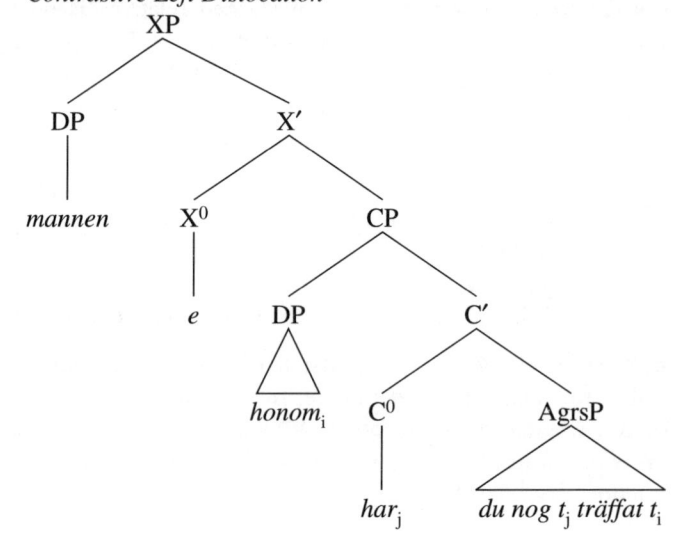

```
                XP
               /  \
             DP    X'
             |    /  \
         mannen  X⁰   CP
                 |   /  \
                 e  DP   C'
                    /\   / \
               honomᵢ  C⁰  AgrsP
                       |    /\
                     harⱼ  du nog tⱼ träffat tᵢ
```

d. *Non-Restrictive Relative*

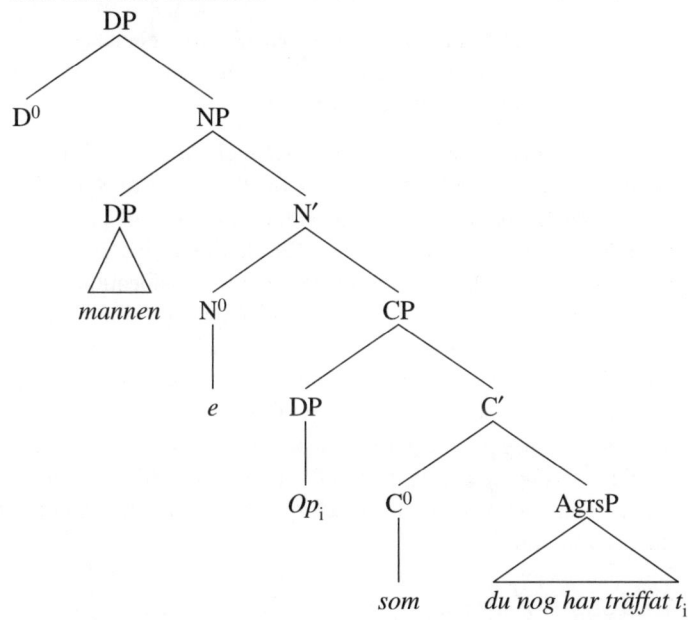

```
              DP
            /    \
          D⁰      NP
                /    \
              DP      N'
              △     /   \
           mannen  N⁰    CP
                   |    /  \
                   e   DP   C'
                       |   /  \
                      Opᵢ C⁰   AgrsP
                           |    △
                          som  du nog har träffat tᵢ
```

In the first part of this section, I will present cases where contrastive left dislocation and non-restrictive relatives display similar properties, saving the discussion of the differences to the second part.

7.1 Shared properties

7.1.1 The prosodic break

Non-restrictive relatives share a prosodic property with contrastive left dislocations: both constructions are associated with an intonational break between the antecedent / dislocated phrase and the rest. If prosodic breaks can be related to structural properties, my account predicts that the break associated with non-restrictive relatives and the break associated with contrastive left dislocation structures are of a common origin. It should furthermore be obvious that my account does not predict a similar break associated with restrictive relatives; see the structure given in (7c) above.

It is not obvious that the account in Kayne (1994) describes the similar prosodic properties of non-restrictive relatives and contrastive left dislocation. Kayne suggests (p.155) that contrastive left dislocation is derived in the same way as relatives. Consider the German sentence in (51):

(51) Den Mann, den haben wir nicht gesehen.
 the man him have we not seen
 'The man we haven't seen.'

In Kayne's account, the complex *den den Mann* is raised from the object position to SpecCP, followed by the raising of *den Mann* to Spec-*den*, which gives the result [*den Mann*$_i$ [*den* [*e*$_i$]]]. This is the same type of process as Kayne proposes for relative clauses. See also Vat (1981), where this analysis is suggested as an account both of relatives and contrastive left dislocation.

At this point we may recall that Kayne (1994) assumes that there is an LF-raising of IP from the relative clause to SpecDP in non-restrictive relatives; see the discussion around (18) above. Kayne suggests that this fronting of IP is triggered by a syntactic feature present in the overt syntax, a feature that is supposed to trigger the intonational break as well. However, since there is no similar raising in contrastive left dislocation, this account fails to relate the intonational break in non-restrictive relatives to the intonational break in left dislocation constructions.

7.1.2 *Scope phenomena*
An element within the left dislocated phrase does not c-command material within the following CP, as is obvious from (50c). Similarly, there is no c-command relation between an element within the antecedent of a non-restrictive relative and the relative clause.

As mentioned in 4.2 a polarity item in the non-restrictive relative clause is not licensed by a potential licenser in the antecedent; this was explained as a result of the lack of a c-command relation between the licenser and the polarity item, i.e. a direct consequence of the geometry of the structure (7d)/(50d). Consequently, it should not be possible to license a polarity item from the left dislocated phrase. The correctness of this prediction is shown by the examples in (52):

(52) *Den största staden, den besökte han någonsin.
 the biggest city-the it visited he ever

[compare (20b)]

Due to the geometry of structure, only the left dislocated element as a whole can be in relation to an element in the following clause. This is illustrated by the examples in (53):

(53) a. Mannen och kvinnan, de blev arresterade.
man-the and woman-the, they were arrested.PL
'As for the man and the woman, they were arrested.'
[compare (28a)]
b. *Mannen och kvinnan, han/hon blev arresterad.
man-the and woman-the he/she was arrested.SG

That the same is true of the relative head of a non-restrictive relative was mentioned in 4.3.

Another case where my account predicts a similarity between left dislocation and non-restrictive relatives concerns fronted DPs that can be given either a countable or an uncountable reading. Consider (21) above. As was shown in (23) it is possible to combine a non-restrictive relative with both readings. Since this possibility was claimed to be a function of the geometry of structure, is is expected that a left dislocated DP displays the same ambiguity. This is also the case, as shown in (54):

(54) a. Blommor, de är vackra.
flowers they are beautiful.PL
'As for flowers, they are beautiful.'
b. Blommor, det är vackert.
flowers it is beautiful.SG
'As for flowers, they are beautiful.'

The countable reading is triggered when the pronoun in SpecCP agrees in number and gender with the dislocated phrase (54a), whereas the uncountable reading is triggered when the pronoun is in its default form (3rd sg. neuter), as in (54b).

7.2 *Differences*

According to my analysis in (50c/d), the relative clause is embedded in a higher DP, whereas the dislocated construction is not embedded. This difference is responsible for the following lack of resemblance between the two constructions. In Section 3.1 I discussed the fact that the relative head does not necessarily have the same Case as the operator in SpecCP: the DP containing the relative clause has case according to its role in the matrix clause, whereas the operator has case according to its role in the relative clause. No such Case discrepancy is expected with contrastive left dislocation, especially not if we assume a raising analysis, as Vat (1981) and Kayne (1994) do (see above). Judging from languages with morphological Case, like German and Icelandic, it is evident that the prediction is correct: in these languages, there is Case agreement between the left dislocated DP and the pronoun in SpecCP (the German example is inspired by an example in Vat (1981), the Icelandic one is taken from Zaenen (1997)):

(55) a. Den   Bismark, den   bewundern manche Deutsche
        the-ACC B.   him-ACC admire   some   Germans
        immer noch.
        still yet
        'Some Germans still admire Bismark.'
    b. Þessum hring, honum   hefur Ólafur lofað   Maríu.
        this-DAT ring him-DAT has   O.   promised M.
        'This ring Olaf promised to Maria'

My account of non-restrictive relatives and contrastive left dislocation also implies a difference concerning the way the relative head and the dislocated phrase are connected to the following clause. According to my discussion in Section 2, in the relative case this connection is mediated by the features of the complementizer: being in spec-head relation to the empty operator in SpecCP, the relative complementizer carries agreement features and the definiteness feature δ, and when attracted by the topmost D these features are brought in spec-head relation to the relative head DP. It is not obvious that a similar mechanism is available in the case of contrastive left dislocation. On the contrary, I have already indicated that a raising analysis seems attractive in this case; this is also the outcome of most of the studies in Anagnostopoulou et al (1997).

I have argued above that φ-feature identification is a necessary condition for linking a relative head to a non-restrictive relative clause. If it is correct, furthermore, that the features of the relative operator must be matched with the features of the relative head via the relative complementizer, we predict it to be impossible to form non-restrictive relatives where no such matching is available. This prediction is supported by examples of the following kind, where we have a match in (56a), but not in (56b).

(56) a. Lisa har en ny   klänning, som Anna f.ö.   har sytt.
        L.   has a new dress   that A. by the way has sewed
        'Lisa has a new dress, which by the way Anna sewed.'
    b. *Lisa har en ny klänning, som Anna f.ö.   också har.
        L.   has a new dress   that A. by the way also has

In (56a), but not in (56b), the relative head and the operator refer to the same dress.[40]

Consider now the fact that idiom chunks sometimes may be left dislocated in Swedish, illustrated in (57):

(57) a. Framsteg det hade han verkligen gjort.
progress it had he really made
'He had really made progress.'
b. En kvarnsten det har han fått om halsen.
a millstone it has he got around neck-the
'He has got a millstone around his neck.'

Since the fronted phrase is part of an idiomatic expression, it is not supposed to have reference of its own. This means that it lacks φ-featues, according to Bouchard (1984). If this is correct, my account predicts that idiom chunks do not occur in non-restrictive relatives, since the relation between the relative clause and the relative head is mediated via the φ-features of the relative complementizer. This prediction seems to be correct, as the examples in (58) show:

(58) a. *Jag blir alltid imponerad av framsteg, som mina barn
I am always impressed by progress that my children
f.ö. gör.[41]
by the way make
b. *Hon var en kvarnsten, som han f.ö. hade fått om
she was a millstone that he by-the-way had got around
halsen.
neck-the

Thus my analysis automatically accounts for the different behavior of idiom chunks in contrastive left dislocation cases and in non-restrictive relatives.

8. Conclusion

In this article I have argued in favor of a representational account of Swedish relatives, taking as my point of departure the fact that a raising analysis is not supported by reconstruction arguments. I suggest an analysis where the relative clause is a complement of N. This N is the nominal head of a restrictive relative clause, but not of a non-restrictive one. In the latter case, the relative head is a DP in the specifier of this N. The proposed structures are outlined in (59a/b) (=7c/d):

298   CHRISTER PLATZACK

(59)   a.   Restrictive interpretation

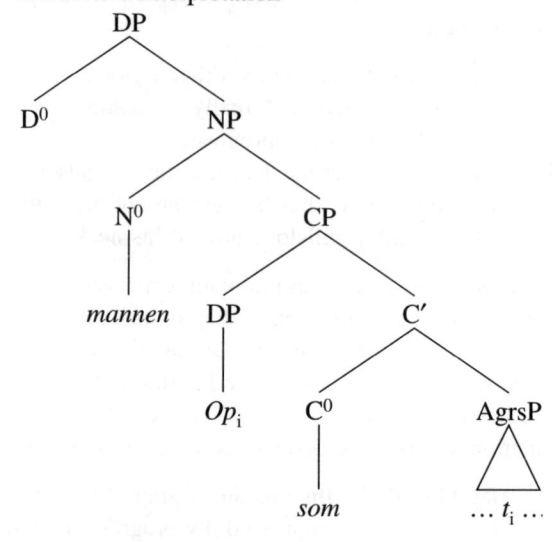

```
                DP
               /  \
             D⁰    NP
                  /  \
                N⁰    CP
                |    /  \
             mannen DP    C'
                    |    /  \
                   Opᵢ  C⁰   AgrsP
                         |    △
                        som  ... tᵢ ...
```

   b.   Non-restrictive interpretation

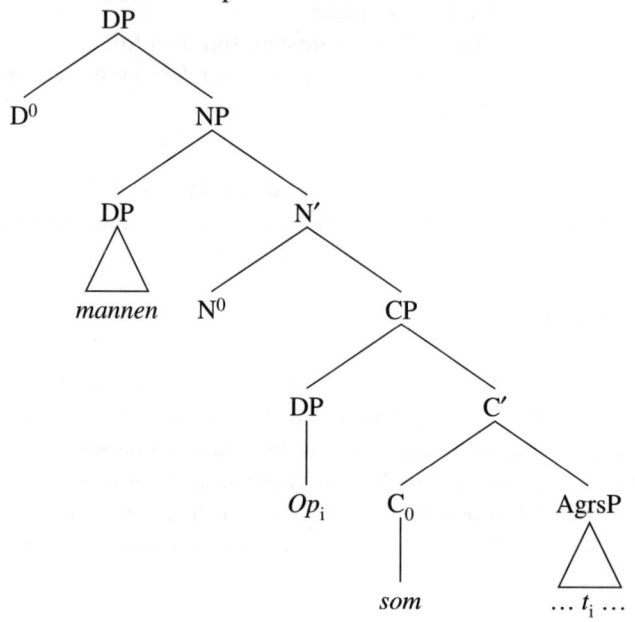

```
                DP
               /  \
             D⁰    NP
                  /  \
                DP    N'
                △    /  \
              mannen N⁰   CP
                         /  \
                        DP    C'
                        |    /  \
                       Opᵢ  C₀   AgrsP
                             |    △
                            som  ... tᵢ ...
```

In the main part of my paper I consider a number of arguments for the proposed account, including predictions about the differences between restrictive and non-restrictive relatives, extraposed relatives, similarities and differences between relative clauses and contrastive left dislocation, and cases where more than one relative clause is attached to a single relative head. In several respects the proposed analysis is shown to be superior to the raising analysis of Kayne (1994); it preserves the virtues of Kayne's approach, e.g. its compatability with the antisymmetric hypothesis, without having its drawbacks.

Notes

1. As pointed out by the anonymous reviewer, many of the problems I address in my paper are also addressed and accounted for by the 'standard' theory of relative clauses developed by Jackendoff (1977), the main difference being, obviously, that Jackendoff's approach is not compatible with Kayne's antisymmetric phrase structure theory. In particular, my account of restrictive and non-restrictive (or appositive) relatives shares with Jackendoff's approach the conviction that it is the structural relation between the head and the relative CP that distinguishes these two types of relatives syntactically.
2. See Åfarli (1994) for a raising analysis of restrictive *som*-relatives in Norwegian.
3. The well-formedness of cases like (4a) seems to depend partly on the relation between the head noun and the PP containing the anaphor. Consider (i), which is (almost) well-formed:

    (i) $^{(?)}$Var la du boken om sitt liv som Russell skrev?
    where put you book-the about his.REFL life that Russell wrote
    'Where did you put the book about his life that Russell wrote?'

    An investigation of the circumstances under which an anaphor in the relative head may or may not be bound by an element of the relative clause would take us too far away from the main theme of this article.
4. Carlson (1977) argues that English contains a third type of relatives, called *Amount Relatives*. On the surface these relatives are similar to restrictive ones, but their syntax and semantics have more in common with comparatives. (i) is a typical example of an amount relative:

    (i) Every man there was on the life-raft died.

    Relatives of this kind are marginally possible in spoken substandard Swedish (Gunlög Josefsson, p.c.):

    (ii) Alla där var på flotten dog.
    all there were on liferaft-the died
    'Everyone there was on the liferaft died.'

5. The complementizer *som* also appears in embedded *wh*-questions and in comparatives; in the last function it translates to English *as*. Consider the following examples:

    (i) a. Han frågade vem som hade kommit.
    he asked who that had arrived
    'He asked who had arrived.'

b. Han är lika glad som du   (är).
    he is as glad as   you (are)
    'He is as glad as you are.'

The complementizer *som* is associated with different grammatical features in its three main uses. In this paper I will suggest that relative *som* contains φ-features and a feature δ, ranging over the definite/indefinite distinction. Interrogative *som* presumably contains a *wh*-feature that must agree with a corresponding *wh*-feature in SpecCP. Comparative *som*, finally, contains at least comparative features.

6. Chomsky (1981: 102) tentatively defines "operator" to include "quantifiers, *wh*-phrases, or a binding NP in COMP; or definite or indefinite operators as in relative clauses". Consider also van Riemsdijk (1997: 10 fn. 11), who reveals uncertainty with respect to the exact nature of the empty category in SpecCP: "it has never been entirely clear to me to what extent assuming null-operators constitutes an improvement over the assumption of a local deletion process applying to wh-like elements under recoverability".

7. Presumably, *som* carries the feature δ as a result of being in spec-head relation with the operator in SpecCP. Note that Morgan (1972) has shown that this operator does not have to have the same value for ±definite as the relative head. E.g., intensive reflexives can only appear with definites as shown in (i) and (ii); however, as (iii) demonstrates, an intensive reflexive is possible even when the head of the relative is indefinite:
   (i)   The plumber himself reads Sartre.
   (ii) *A plumber himself reads Sartre.
   (iii) A plumber who himself reads Sartre said that I should take a look at it.
   Swedish behaves like English in this respect.

8. See Delsing (1993: 30 ff.) for a discussion of the correlation between the D-projection and the presence of an overt article (definite or indefinite).

9. Note that the δ-feature is a feature visible at LF and hence, according to Chomsky (1995: 279), accessible to the computation throughout, whether checked or not. Thus in an example like (i), where there are δ-features in the definite noun phrase as well as in the relative complementizer, both instances of δ are checked in D at LF.
   (i)   Mannen som står   där   är min bror.
         man-the that is-standing there is my brother
         'The man who is standing there is my brother.'

10. In this case, the relative clause is merged as complement to an empty N^0, an option forced upon us by Kayne's framework. See e.g. Cinque (1997) who makes an abundant use of empty heads to derive the underlying order of sentence adverbials.

11. In the examples I will often use the short hand *f.ö.* for *för övrigt* 'by the way'.

12. This requirement may explain why non-restrictive relatives cannot have a negated antecedent: when the head of the relative contains a negated pronoun, the relative clause is always interpreted as restrictive:
    (i) a. Inga spelare som har   gula   kort   får   vara med.   [Restrictive]
                no   players that have yellow cards may take part
                'No players that have yellow cards may take part.'
            b. *Inga spelare, som f.ö.   har   gula   kort, får   vara med. [Non-restrictive]
                 no   players that by-the-way have yellow cards may take part

It is clear from the structure in (7d) that a non-restrictive relative clause is not in the scope of a negation in its head (a negative element within the head of a non-restrictive relative maximally has scope over the relative head). As a consequence the head and *som* does not share all features, presumably blocking (ib). In the restrictive case there is no problem, though, since *som* does not have to agree with the entire relative head.

13. This analysis is also intended to provide an answer to a question raised by the anonymous reviewer: assuming the DP hosting a non-restrictive relative clause is the object of the matrix verb, what exactly is selected by this verb? The answer is that this verb selects for the information in D^0, which is the feature bundle associated with the raised *som*, i.e. features shared with the operator in SpecCP. As mentioned in the text, these features are congruent with the features present in the relative head in the non-restrictive case.

14. Without a free determiner, we get combinations like (i), which have functions similar to proper names:

    (i)   Vita huset   Höga Visan
          white house-the,   high song-the
          'The White House'   'The Song of Songs'

15. A free determiner can occur with a noun lacking the definite ending if and only if the noun is followed by a restrictive relative, as in (i); see Section 4.1. below.

    (i)   Det röda hus   vi just körde förbi ägs   av min syster.
          the red house we just drove by   is-owned by my sister
          'The red house that we just drove past is owned by my sister.'

16. Compare the well-formed correspondences in (i)–(ii):

    (i)   Det röda hus**et**   brann.
          the red house-the was-burning
          'The red house was burning.'
    (ii) Den lille man**nen** skrattade.
          the little man-the laughed
          'The little man laughed.'

17. See Delsing (1993: 5 ff.) for an overview of the gender system in Swedish, and Källström (1993) for a more detailed study. At this point it might be relevant to know that the masculine and the feminine genders are collapsed into one gender in Danish and Swedish, called *uter* in Swedish grammatical tradition and *fælleskøn* 'common gender' in Danish. Norwegian and Icelandic have retained the Old Scandinavian three-gender system with masculine, feminine and neuter.

18. Example (8c) can be compared with cases with other demonstratives, which optionally or obligatory, depending on which demonstrative we choose, may bear the feature δ. Thus, the noun following the demonstrative *denne* 'this' optionally takes the definite ending (*denne man / denne mannen* 'this man' / 'this man-the'), whereas the noun following the demonstratives *den här* (lit. this here) 'this' and *den där* (lit. this there) 'that' must have the definite suffix: *den här mannen* 'this man-the', *den här man 'this man'; etc. I will assume without argument that a demonstrative like *denne* 'this' is in SpecDP at PF, when it is followed by a definite noun, but in D^0, carrying a δ-feature of its own, in the case the noun lacks a definite ending. With regard to demonstratives with a locative, like *den här* 'this here', I follow Schmitt (1996: 241) in assuming that *här* 'here' is an overt locative element which ends up in an Agr-head below D (*den* is presumably in D^0).

19. I follow Platzack (1996a) in assuming that a strong feature must be checked overtly, and that

PF-deletion of the accompanying phonological feature bundle does not occur. Given this assumption, the analysis correctly predicts that the complementizer must be present in non-restrictive relatives, whereas it may be left out in restrictive ones, where the strong feature in D is checked by some instance of δ raised from a head above CP, or there is a free determiner, postponing checking until covert syntax. The difference between restrictive and non-restrictive relatives in this respect is illustrated in (i).

(i)   a.   Den bil (som) vi mötte på vägen   var svart.
           the car that we met   on road-the was black
           'The car that we encountered on the road was black.'
     b.   Den bilen, *(som) vi för övrigt   mötte på vägen,   var svart.
           the car-the that we by the-way met   on road-the was black
           'The car, which by the way we encountered on the road, was black.'

As in English, the complementizer may be left out only if the relative head corresponds to something else than the subject of the relative clause.

20. Note that the complementizer must be left out in the presence of a *wh*-relative.

(i)   Den här boken,   vilken (*som) för övrigt   är mycket bra,   har jag köpt   till
      this here book-the, which   that by the way is very   good, have I   bought to
      min bror.
      my brother
      'This book, which by the way is very good, I have bought for my brother.'

In modern Swedish relatives the *wh*-word and the complementizer cannot occur together, whereas this is possible and sometimes necessary in *wh*-questions:

(ii)   Jag undrar vilken bok *(som) är bäst.
       I wonder which book   that is best
       'I wonder which book is the best one.'

I will have virtually nothing to say about the relation between relative clauses introduced by *som* 'that' and relatives introduced by a *wh*-word in this paper. It should be noted, though, that the use of *wh*-relatives is restricted in Swedish compared to English.

21. According to Holmberg & Sandström (1995), the different order of possessor and head in (ia,b) indicates the structural difference in (ii), where AgrP is a phrase for checking possessive agreement:

(i)   a.   bilen   Jons (Northen Swedish dialects)   b.   Jons bil [Standard Swedish]
          car-the J.'s   J.'s car
(ii)   a.   [$_{DP}$ [$_{D^0}$bilen$_i$ [$_{AgrP}$ Jon [$_{Agr^0}$-s] [..t_i...   b.   [$_{DP}$ Jon$_i$ [$_{D^0}$s$_j$ [$_{AgrP}$ t_i [$_{Agr^{00}}$ t_j]
                                                                               [....bil ...

The genitive -*s* is assumed to originate in Agr^0, being raised to D^0 to check the strong feature of this head (iib). To get the right order, DP in SpecAgrP must move to SpecDP, maybe for the same reason as in (7d).

22. I have to assume a Split-CP of some kind, maybe as in Rizzi (1997), to be able to describe extraction out of relative clauses; in the structures given in this paper, the potential escape hatch SpecCP is occupied by an operator, preventing extraction. Although I do not want to offer any speculations, it has not escaped me that the fact that extraction out of relative clauses is available only in some languages but not in others might be accounted for with reference to different positions of the operator, which perhaps is in a lower specifier within the C-domain

in languages allowing extraction, but in a higher specifier in languages where extraction out of relative clauses is impossible.

23. The anonymous reviewer observes that no explanation is offered for the possibility to extract part of the relative head in non-restrictive clauses. Such extraction is possible in German as well as Swedish:

(i) Über die Liebe$_i$ habe ich [$_{DP}$ ein interessantes Buch t_i [$_{CP}$ das ich dir im übrigen
    about the love have I   an interesting book   that I you by the way
    auch mal empfehlen würde]] gelesen.
    also once recommend would read
    'I read an interesting book about love, which I would recommend you to read some time, by the way.'

(ii) Om kärleken$_i$ har jag läst [$_{DP}$ en intressant bok t_i [$_{CO}$ som jag för övrigt vill
    about love-the has I read   an interesting book   that I by the way want
    rekommendera dig]].
    recommend you
    [Same meaning]

According to my analysis, this is extraction of a PP out of a DP-specifier of a D-head. It is not clear to me if there are any principles blocking such an extraction.

24. Both the Case problem and the DP/NP problem are extensively discussed in Borsley (1997).

25. Remember that the determiner is base-generated in the highest D, according to Kayne's analysis.

26. See Cardinaletti (1990) and Platzack (1996b) for different accounts of Topic Drop.

27. In his careful study of this phenomenon, Källström (1993: 277) notes that the agreeing predicate adjective "serves to delimit the reference of the subject, while the non-agreeing adjective has the opposite effect". Structural attempts to account for the non-agreeing case have been proposed by Cooper (1986), Hellan (1986) and Delsing (1988); they all suggest that the relative head in these cases should be analyzed with an (invisible) neuter head. If they are correct there is agreement between DP and the predicate adjective also in this case.

28. An object expanded with a relative clause is preferably placed after VP adverbs, presumably due to some heaviness condition.

29. This effect is dependent on the content of the restrictive relative as well. Consider (i), where the restrictive relative clause does not evoke an unbounded reading:

(i) Han målade (*i flera år) / på tre veckor tavlorna jag har i
    he painted   for several years / in three weeks paintings-the I have in
    mitt hem.
    my home
    'He painted in three weeks (/*for several years) the paintings I have in my home'

30. Note that if we do not select any SQ-feature for a definite noun in the absence of a relative clause, there is no δ available to check the strong feature in D, hence the structure is blocked. Alternatively we must insert a free determiner in D which carries the δ-feature as in (8c) above. In this case the free determiner is interpreted as a demonstrative.

31. But see Ferguson (1997) for an attempt to describe other cases where the object of a preposition seems to c-command out of PP.

32. The movement of DP involves raising from an A-bar position (Spec-DP) to an A-position, a

kind of movement that we might want to preclude. An alternative analysis, not involving such movement, would be to assume the presence of an invisible pronoun (*pro*) in SpecDP/NP, which gets its interpretation from the antecedent.

33. Note that my theory predicts overt raising of *som* to D as soon as D or N are empty.
34. If the right dislocation position is a DP-position within VP, it is obviously L-related, and I would hesitate to call it an A-bar position.
35. My description is further supported by the observation in Taraldsen (1981) that extractions out of a restrictive relative clause presupposes extraposition. Compare (ia) without extraposition with the extraposed case (ib):

(i) a. *Her er en bok$_i$ som ingen   som leser e_i blir   lykkelig.
       here is a   book that nobody that reads   become happy
       [Norwegian, Taraldsen 1981: ex. (52)]
    b. Her er en bok$_i$ som ingen   blir   lykkelig som leser e_i.
       here is a   book that nobody becomes happy   that reads
       'Here is a book that nobody becomes happy who reads (it).'

According to my description, there is nothing within the DP hosting the restrictive relative clause that can block extraction in extraposition cases, whereas there might be a blocking element in non-extraposition cases, e.g., a DP possessor within the DP hosting the relative clause.

36. This is a simplification. As Haider (1994) points out, an extraposed relative can be followed by an extraposed *that*-clause both in OV and in VO-languages. The following examples are taken from Haider's paper:

(i) a. daß es keinen überrascht, der darüber   nachdenkt, daß dies so ist
       that it noone surprises   who thereover thinks   that this so is
       'that it does not surprise anyone who thinks about it that this should be so'
    b. Någon   berättade som just hade lyssnat på nyheterna att Roy hade
       someone said   who just had listened to news-the that R.   had
       fängslats.
       been-imprisoned
       'Someone who had just listened to the news said that Roy had been imprisoned.'

Interestingly, also a full DP sharing θ-role with another DP in the clause may be followed by an *att*-clause:

(ii) Kalle berättade, den djäveln, att han hade lurat   mig.
     K.   said,   the bastard, that he had cheated me
     'Kalle, the bastard, said that he had cheated me.'

37. As remarked by the anonymous reviewer, this description predicts that the aspectual effect of a restrictive relative discussed in Section 4.4., will disappear when a non-restrictive relative clause is attached after the restrictive one, since the restrictive relative now is in a SpecNP position. This prediction seems to be correct, as the following examples show:

(i) a. Han skrev i flera år   / på tre veckor de böcker jag ville läsa.
       he wrote for several years / in three weeks the books I   wanted to-read
       'He wrote for several years (/in three weeks) the books I wanted to read.'

b. Han skrev (*i flera år) / på tre veckor de böcker jag ville läsa, som
    he wrote for several years / in three weeks the books I wanted to-read that
    f.ö.   ligger där på bordet.
    by the way are-lying there on table-the
    'He wrote for several years (/in three weeks) the books I wanted to read, which by
    the way are lying there on the table.'

38. Within a Larsonian shell structure, the indirect object (*seglen på vilken båt* 'sails-the on which boat') must merge in a SpecVP position.

39. The anonymous reviewer claims that there is no evidence for an empty head (X^0) in Contrastive Left Dislocation. Still, since adjunction to a phrase with a specifier is impossible in Kayne's phrase structure theory, there is no alternative to the analysis in (50c).

40. To express the meaning in (56b), Swedish must use a *wh*-relative with a *wh*-word in the default 3rd person sg. neuter:
    (i) Lisa har en ny klänning, vilket Anna också har.
         L. has a new dress which A. also has
         'Lisa has a new dress, which Anna also does.'

41. In this case the corresponding restrictive relative is well-formed:
    (i) Jag blir alltid imponerad av de framsteg som mina barn gör.
         I am always impressed by the progress that my children make
         'I am always impressed by the progress that my children make.'

References

Anagnostopoulou, E., H. van Riemsdijk, & F. Zwarts (1997). *Materials on Left Dislocation.* Amsterdam/Philadelphia: John Benjamins.

Allwood, J. (1976). The complex NP constraint as a non-universal rule and some semantic factors influencing the acceptability of Swedish sentences which violate the CNPC. *University of Massachusetts Occasional Papers in Linguistics* II: Edited by J. Stilling, Amherst, Mass. [Reprinted as The complex NP contraint in Swedish. *Readings on Unbounded Dependencies in Scandinavian Languages.* Edited by Engdahl & Ejerhed, 15–32. Stockholm: Almquist & Wiksell International. 1982.]

Åfarli, T. (1994). A Promotion Analysis of Restrictive Relative Clauses. *The Linguistic Review* 11: 81–100.

Andersson, L.-G. (1974). Topicalization and relative clause formation. *Gothenburg Papers in Theoretical Linguistics* 25.

Bayer, J. (1984). COMP in Bavarian Syntax. *The Linguistic Review* 3: 209–274.

Borsley, R. (1997). Relative Clauses and the Theory of Phrase Structure. *Linguistic Inquiry* 28: 629–647.

Bouchard, D. (1984). *On the Concept of Empty Categories.* Dordrecht: Foris.

Browning, M. (1987). *Null Operator Constructions.* Doctoral dissertation, MIT, Cambridge, Mass. [New York: Garland, 1991]

Cardinaletti, A. (1990). Subject/object asymmetries in German null-topic constructions and the status of SpecCP. *Grammar in Progress. Glow Essays for Henk van Riemsdijk.* Edited by J. Mascaró & M. Nespor, 75–84. Dordrecht: Foris.
Carlson, G. (1977). Amount relatives. *Language* 53: 520–542.
Chomsky, N. (1981). *Lectures on Government and Binding.* Dordrecht: Foris.
Chomsky, N. (1982). *Some Concepts and Consequences of the Theory of Government and Binding.* Cambridge, Mass.: MIT Press.
Chomsky, N. (1995). *The Minimalist Program.* Cambridge, Mass.: MIT Press.
Chomsky, N. & H. Lasnik (1993). The Theory of Principles and Parameters. *Syntax: An International Handbook of Contemporary Research*, Edited by J. Jacobs, A. von Stechow, W. Sternefeld, & T. Vennemann, Berlin/New York: Walter de Gruyter. [Reprinted in Chomsky (1995), Chapter 1]
Cinque, G. (1999). *Adverbs and Functional Heads. A Cross-Linguistic Perspective.* New York, Oxford: Oxford University Press.
Cooper, R. (1986). Swedish and the Head Feature Convention. *Topics in Scandinavian Syntax.* Edited by L. Hellan & K. K. Christensen, 31–52. Dordrecht: Reidel.
Delsing, L.-O. (1988). The Scandinavian Noun Phrase. *Working Papers in Scandinavian Syntax* 42: 57–79.
Delsing, L.-O. (1993). *The Internal Structure of Noun Phrases in the Scandinavian Languages. A Comparative Study.* Doctoral Dissertation, Department of Scandinavian Languages, Lund.
Emonds, J. (1979). Appositive Relatives Have No Properties. *Linguistic Inquiry* 10: 211–243.
Engdahl, E. (1997). Relative Clause Extractions in Context. *Working Papers in Scandinavian Syntax* 60: 50–79.
Erteschik-Shir, N. (1973). *On the nature of island constraints.* Doctoral dissertation, MIT, Cambridge, Mass.
Ferguson, K. S. (1997). Deducing the Invisibility of PP Nodes from Case Checking and Full Interpretation. An Argument for Agr, LF, Full Interpretation, and Post-LF Binding Conditions. *Glow Newsletter* 38: 22–23.
Groat, E. (1995). English Expletives: A Minimalist Approach. *Linguistic Inquiry* 26: 354–365.
Haider, H. (1994). *All's well that ends well: Order and Licensing of Extraposed CPs.* Talk presented at the Tilburg Conference on Rightward Movement, October 1994.
Hellan, L. (1986). The Headedness of NPs in Norwegian. *Features and Projections.* Edited by H. van Riemsdijk & P. Muysken, 89–122. Dordrecht: Foris.
Holmberg, A, & G. Sandström (1995). Scandinavian possessive constructions from a Northern Swedish viewpoint. *Working Papers in Scandinavian Syntax* 55: 29–49.
Jackendoff, R. (1977). *X-bar Syntax: A Study of Phrase Structure.* Cambridge, Mass.: MIT Press.
Kayne, R. S. (1994). *The Antisymmetry of Syntax.* Cambridge, Mass.: MIT Press.
Källström, R. (1993). *Kongruens i svenskan.* Göteborg: Acta Universitatis Gothoburgensis.

Link, G. (1984). The Logical Analysis of Plurals and Mass Terms: a Lattice Theoretic Approach. *Meaning, Use and Interpretation of Language.* Edited by R. Bäuerle, C. Schwarze & A. von Stechow, 302–323. Berlin: Walter de Gruyter.
Longobardi, G. (1994). Reference and proper names. *Linguistic Inquiry* 25: 609–665.
Morgan, J. (1972). Some aspects of relative clauses in English and Albanian. *The Chicago Which Hunt. Papers from the Relative Clause Festival*, Edited by P.M. Peranteau, J.N. Levi & G.C. Phares, 63–72. Chicago: Chicago Linguistic Society.
Platzack C. (1974). An Exception to the Complex NP Constraint. *Papers from the First Scandinavian Conference of Linguistics.* Edited by Ö. Dahl, 241–254. Göteborg: Department of Linguistics.
Platzack, C. (1996a). Null Subjects, Weak Agr and Syntactic Differences in Scandinavian. *Studies in Comparative Germanic syntax II.* Edited by H. Thráinsson, S.D. Epstein & S. Peter, 180–196. Dordrecht: Kluwer.
Platzack, C. (1996b). Germanic Verb Second Languages. Attract vs. Repel: On optionality, A-bar Movement and the Symmetrical/Asymmetrical Verb Second Hypothesis. *Deutsch-typologisch.* Edited by E. Lang & G. Zifonun, 92–120. Berlin: Walter de Gruyter.
Riemsdijk, H. van (1997). Left Dislocation. *Materials on Left Dislocation.* Edited by E. Anagnostopoulou, H. van Riemsdijk, & F. Zwarts, 1–10. Amsterdam: John Benjamins.
Rizzi. L. (1997). The fine structure of the left periphery. *Elements of Grammar. Handbook in Generative Syntax* 1, 281–337. Edited by L. Haegeman. Dordrecht: Kluwer.
Ross, J.R. (1967). *Constraints on Variables in syntax.* Doctoral dissertation, MIT, Cambridge, Mass.
Schmitt, C. (1996). *Aspect and the Syntax of Noun Phrases.* Doctoral dissertation, University of Maryland, College Park.
Smith, C. (1969). Determiners and Relative Clausaes in a Generative Grammar of English. *Modern Studies in English.* Edited by D. Reibel & S. Schane, 247–263. Englewood Cliffs: Prentice-Hall.
Stowell, T. (1991). Determiners in NP and DP. *Views on phrase structure.* Edited by K. Leffel & D. Bouchard, 37–56. Dordrecht: Kluwer.
Taraldsen, T. (1981). On the Theoretical Interpretation of a Class of "Marked" Extractions. *The Theory of Markedness in Generative Grammar.* Edited by A. Belletti, L. Brandi & L. Rizzi, 475–516. Scuola Normale Superiore Pisa.
Teleman, U., S. Hellberg & E. Andersson (1999). *Svenska Akademiens Grammatik.* Norstedt, Stockholm.
Vat, J. (1981). Left Dislocation, Connectedness and Reconstruction. *Groninger Arbeiten zur Germanistischen Linguistic* (GAGL) 20: 80–103. Reprinted in Anagnostopoulou et al., 67–92.
Vergnaud, J.R. (1974). *French Relative Clauses.* Doctoral dissertation, MIT, Cambridge, Mass.

Wilder, C. (1995). *Die Syntax nichtkanonischer Komplementation: Variation und Komplexität.* Manucript, Arbeitsgruppe Strukturelle Grammatik der Max-Planck-Gesellschaft an der Humboldt-Universität Berlin.

Xu, D. (1997). *Functional Categories in Mandarin Chinese.* Leiden: Holland Institute of Generative Linguistics.

Zaenen, A. (1997). Contrastive Dislocation in Dutch and Icelandic. *Materials on Left Dislocation.* Edited by E. Anagnostopoulou, H. van Riemsdijk, & F. Zwarts, 119–148. Amsterdam: John Benjamins.

Some Consequences of the Complement Analysis for Relative Clauses, Demonstratives and the Wrong Adjectives[*]

Cristina Schmitt
Michigan State University

Introduction

Two main structures have been proposed for relative clauses. In the adjunct analysis (1a), the relative clause (XP) is treated as an adjunct to the nominal head (YP). In the complement analysis, illustrated in (1b), the relative clause is taken to be the complement of the determiner, and the head of the relative clause (YP) is in some specifier position of XP. The latter analysis was first proposed by Vergnaud (1985) based on Kuroda (1968) and more recently has been revitalized by Kayne (1994) who argues that the complement analysis is the only way relative clauses can conform to the Linear Correspondence Axiom.

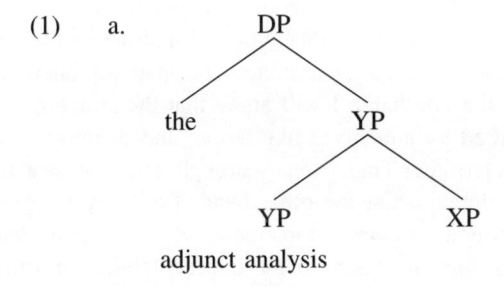

(1) a.

```
          DP
         /  \
       the   YP
            /  \
          YP    XP
```
adjunct analysis

---

[*] I am indebted to Alan Munn for the many comments on previous versions of this paper and to the audience of the Relative Clauses Workshop, especially Christer Platzack and Jamal Ouhalla for comments and encouragement. I also thank the reviewers. The paper profited a lot from their comments.

b. 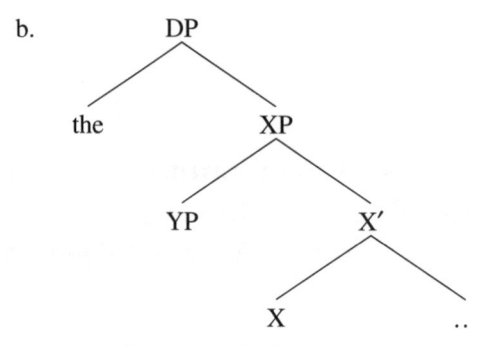
```
         DP
        /  \
      the   XP
           /  \
          YP   X'
              /  \
             X    ..
```
complement analysis
XP = CP
YP = nominal projection

The basic motivation for the complement analysis were facts like (2), which show a tight relation between the definite determiner and the relative clause. (2) also illustrates what I will call Determiner Transparency.

(2)   a.   John made headway.
        b.   *John made the headway.
        c.   John made the headway Bill made.

If we compare (2b) and (2c), we can see that whatever the restriction against the definite in (2b) is, it is overcome by the addition of a relative clause. If *headway* must be indefinite, than the definite in (2c) appears as if it were not there, namely as being transparent. Determiner Transparency is then the ability of (1b) to appear in contexts where definites are not generally acceptable.

The purpose of this paper is to provide further support for structure (1b) and to provide a principled explanation for the Determiner Transparency phenomenon. The goal is two-fold: on the one hand, I will argue that the structure (1b) can be extended to DPs modified by adjectives like *wrong* and demonstratives and that the phenomenon of Determiner Transparency brought about by structure (1b) extends to the aspectual domain. On the other hand, I will try to give a clearer account of why certain non-nominal complements of the definite determiner are allowed and explain how it relates to the unacceptability of simple definites in certain contexts.

This paper is divided as follows: in Section 1 I present the classical data that support the complement analysis for relative clauses and discuss the issues it raises. I also discard some alternative analyses and outline the basic intuition I will be pursuing. In Section 2 I expand the complement analysis to certain adjective modifiers and to demonstratives. In Section 3 I discuss the inability of certain nouns to appear as complements of definites, which constitutes the core data in favour of structure (1b). In Section 4 I discuss some details of the complement analysis I adopt and in Section 5 I show that the complement analysis can explain certain aspectual interpretations which would otherwise be quite unexpected. In Section 6 I summarize the main points.

1. Definite and indefinite behavior of definite relative clauses

1.1 *The puzzles brought about by the data*

Cases in which the definite determiner with a simple nominal is unacceptable but becomes acceptable if a relative clause is added were used by Vergnaud to support the idea that at some level there is a very close connection between the relative clause and the definite determiner, rather than the head noun and the definite determiner.

(3) a. John made (some) headway.   [idioms]
    b. *John made the headway.
    c. The headway John made was amazing.

(4) a. I bought one type of bread.   [type expressions]
    b. *I bought the type of bread.
    c. I bought the type of bread you like.

In (3) the idiom *headway* cannot appear with a definite determiner unless a relative clause is added. The same is true for *type*-expressions in (4) and for measure phrases, illustrated in (5) below.

(5) a. Maria weighs forty-five kilos.   [measures]
    b. *Maria weighs the forty-five kilos.
    c. Maria weighs the forty-five kilos Susana would love to weigh.

Other cases can be added to the classic cases. Consider first example (6):

(6) a. John painted the house a nice color.   [Resultatives]
    b. *John painted the house the nice color.
    c. John painted the house the color his girlfriend liked.

(6b) is unacceptable in contrast with (6a). A similar effect can be found with possessive *with* (from Heim 1987; de Jong 1987). In (7), the definite relative clause is as acceptable as an indefinite:

(7) a. Mary bought a house with windows. [*With*-constructions]
    b. *Mary bought a house with the windows.
    c. Mary bought a house with the windows that she liked.

All of the cases above illustrate the acceptability of definite relative clauses in positions where simple definites are unacceptable. The definite relative clauses above seem to be behaving like the indefinites, i.e., as if the definite determiner were not present.

The examples above pose a number of questions:

I. if relative clauses allow an indefinite behavior, is the definite determiner not a definite?
II. why is the simple nominal unacceptable with the definite in these contexts?
III. why can a definite relative clause appear in contexts that do not allow simple definites?
IV. what else besides relative clauses make the definite element acceptable in these contexts? Is it the case that any element can occupy the XP position in (1) or are there restrictions on what can be the complement of a definite determiner?

In the rest of this section 1 answer (I) and outline what I consider to be the solution for (II) and (III) which will be further discussed in Section 3. Section 2 will deal with (IV).

1.2 *Definite relative clauses are definite*

There are two ways of dealing with the 'indefinite' behavior of the definite relative clauses exemplified above. One is to say that definites in these contexts are all acceptable and that the odd behavior of the simple definite is due to some pragmatic reason. Since the phenomenon covers a wide range of syntactic constructions, however, this seems an unlikely hypothesis, and I will not pursue it further.

Another way of dealing with the 'indefinite' behavior is to deny the definiteness of the definite with a relative clause. In fact such a hypothesis has been suggested by Bianchi (1994/5). She argues that the definite is not really a definite in relative clauses but rather a 'disguised' indefinite.

Clearly, however, a more sophisticated version of such an indefinite behavior has to be at stake since we cannot say that the whole definite relative clause is an indefinite. There are at least three pieces of evidence that show that definite relative clauses actually behave as definites. First, consider partitives as in (8), a context that Barwise & Cooper (1981) used to test definiteness. In partitives, a definite is generally required, as the contrast between (8a) and (8b) illustrates. If the definite were not really a definite with relative clauses, (8c) should be unacceptable, contrary to fact. If the work of making (8c) acceptable had nothing to do with the definite but rather with the relative clause then (8d) should be acceptable. It is not, however. Thus the definite in the relative clause behaves like a definite in partitives.

(8) a. *Two of men
 b. Two of the men
 c. Two of the men we met
 d. *Two of men we met

A second piece of evidence comes from the behavior of the quantifier *todo* 'all' in Brazilian Portuguese. The quantifier *todo* cannot be followed by a plural indefinite (whether followed or not by a relative clause), as illustrated in (9a,d). The definite is, on the other hand, acceptable (9b,c), independently of the relative clause, thus showing that a definite relative clause is not indefinite in this context either.[1]

(9) a. *todos   homens
        all-MASC.PL man-MASC.PL
        'all men'
 b. todos   os   homens
        all-MASC.PL the-MASC.PL man-MASC.PL
        'all the men'
 c. todos   os   homens   que eu conheço
        all.MASC.PL the-MASC.PL man-MASC.PL that I know
        'all the men that I know'
 d. *todos   homens   que eu conheço
        all-MASC.PL man.MASC.PL that I know
        'all men that I know'

A related fact comes from floated *all* in English. Floated *all* is impossible with indefinites, but perfectly acceptable with definites. Definite relative clauses pattern with simple definites, being perfectly acceptable.

(10) a. *(Some) books were *all* on sale
 b. The books were *all* on sale
 c. *Books we bought were *all* on sale
 d. The books we bought were *all* on sale

The examples below illustrate both the definite and indefinite requirements being fulfilled:

(11) a. Mary made all the headway she could make.
b. Mary bought the house with all the windows that she liked.

All requires a definite, but the idiom *headway* cannot be headed by a definite. Thus the definite is satisfying the requirements of *all* but is not taking *headway* as its complement, otherwise (11a) should be unacceptable. Example (11b) makes the same point but this time with *with*.

1.3 Basic intuitions behind the analysis to be proposed

The examples (8) to (10) show definite relative clauses patterning with other definite DPs. Examples (3) to (7), on the other hand, show an indefinite behavior. Example (11) shows both the indefinite and the definite requirement being fulfilled by the same definite relative clause. This should suffice to illustrate what I call Determiner Transparency phenomenon.

What allows this behavior? For concreteness I will assume the structure in (12) for relative clauses.

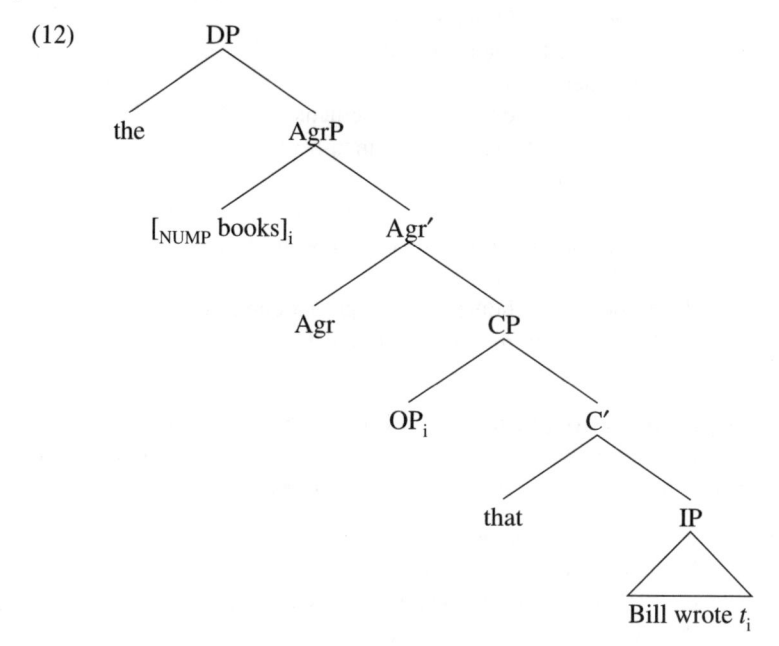

(12)
```
         DP
        /  \
      the   AgrP
           /    \
    [NUMP books]i  Agr'
                  /   \
                Agr    CP
                      /  \
                    OPi   C'
                         /  \
                      that   IP
                            /\
                           Bill wrote ti
```

When we examine this structure, Determiner Transparency is not as mysterious as it may seem at first sight. In the structure above, the definite takes a relative clause as a complement. The head of the relative, which I will assume to be a NumP,[2] is in a sense 'free' from the definite determiner. It is in the specifier of a projection that is part of the extended projection of the CP. Higginbotham (1985) proposed that the determiner enters a theta binding relation with N. In (12), the θ-binding relation holds between the definite and the extended projection of CP, not with the NumP head of the relative clause.

The intuition I would like to pursue here is that the lack of θ-binding between the definite and the NumP allows a definite or an indefinite behavior, depending on what is satisfying the external conditions. In the cases where a definite is required, this requirement is satisfied by the head D. In cases where an indefinite is required, this indefiniteness requirement can be satisfied by the NumP.[3] In a simple DP, we cannot have a definite and an indefinite behavior, because the definite enters a θ-binding relation with the NumP, and the whole phrase will be definite. There is no 'free' NumP in these cases.

With structure (12) and the idea that definite DPs with this structure have both an indefinite and a definite that can satisfy external conditions, we can now extend the data to other types of modification that also display definite and indefinite behavior and can be easily accounted for using a structure like (12).

2. Expanding the domain of the complement analysis: wrong-type adjectives and demonstratives

Definite relative clauses are not the only elements that can appear in contexts where simple definites are disallowed. Demonstratives and certain types of adjectives pattern similarly. In this section I will first show that these elements can be given an analysis like (12), and then I discuss what these elements may have in common so that they can all enter a θ-binding relation with the definite determiner.

2.1 Wrong-*type adjectives*

Consider the following contrasts:

(13) a. *John bought the type of house.
 b. John bought the wrong type of house.
 c. *John bought the big type of house.   [no focus on *big*]
(14) a. *John painted the house the color.   [Resultatives]
 b. John painted the house the wrong color.
 c. *John painted the house the nice color. [no focus on *nice*]

(15) a. *John weighs the weight.
   b. John weighs the wrong weight.
   c. *John weighs the good 45 kilos. [no focus on *good*]

In the examples above, we can see that there is a contrast between the (b) and (c) cases. *Wrong* behaves like the definite relative clause, licensing the definite determiner in contexts where simple definite DPs are not allowed, while *big, nice* and *good* do not (unless contrastive focus is used).

Just as in the relative clause examples, *the wrong NP* still behaves like a definite in partitive and *all* constructions:

(16) a. many of the wrong hypotheses
   b. todos   os   livros   errados
      all-MASC.PL the-MASC.PL   book-MASC.PL   wrong-MASC.PL
      'all the wrong books'
   c. The wrong books were all written by him

If the acceptability of the definite in (13) and (14) is to be associated with a free indefinite, we can explain the distinction between the two classes of adjectives in structural terms. Adjectives like *wrong* will allow the NumP to be free, while adjectives like *big, nice* and *good* will not.

We can think of the distinction between the two classes of adjectives in the following way: while some adjectives are adjuncts to the head noun, not interfering with the θ-binding relation between the noun and the definite determiner, other adjectives take the noun as their complement and are themselves complements of the definite determiner.

For concreteness, I will discuss the minimal pair, given in (17):

(17) a. the long book
   b. the wrong book

Following Higginbotham (1985), we can say that adjectives like *long* are adjoined to NP and enter a θ-identification relation with the noun, as illustrated in (18a); adjectives like *wrong*, on the other hand, take the noun as their complement and θ-mark it, as in (18b).

(18) a.   long ⟨1⟩

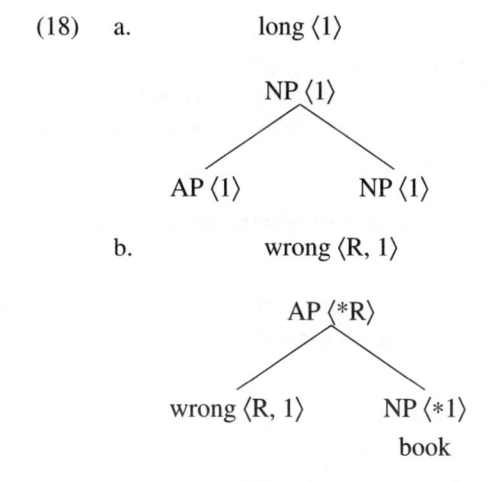

                  NP ⟨1⟩
                 /   \
             AP ⟨1⟩   NP ⟨1⟩

     b.   wrong ⟨R, 1⟩

                    AP ⟨*R⟩
                   /   \
           wrong ⟨R, 1⟩   NP ⟨*1⟩
                           book

If *wrong* takes the nominal as its complement, then *wrong* also has to be able to appear as complement of the definite. This is then another difference between *wrong* and *long*. Higginbotham proposes that definite determiners enter a θ-binding relation with nominals and are able to saturate the open ⟨R⟩ position. Another way of thinking of the same relation is to say that definite determiners select for elements with ⟨R⟩. If this is the case, then relative clauses and *wrong* type of adjectives both have ⟨R⟩.

This will be almost all we need to establish the difference between the two types of adjectives. While the definite determiner will be part of the extended projection of the noun in (18a), this will not be the case in (18b); such a possibility will allow us to obtain, in (18b), but not in (18a), a configuration that is similar to the one proposed for relative clauses. (See (22a) below.)

As for the nominal projection complement of *wrong*, we can assume that it is at least a NumP, given examples such as (19):

(19)   the wrong two books

Two more differences between *long* and *wrong* are important to mention and provide further support for the present proposal. Here I will add data from Brazilian Portuguese, which, like other Romance Languages, generally has post-nominal adjectives which show morphological agreement with the head noun.

The first difference between *long* and *wrong* is that they appear in different orders. *Wrong* is further from the noun than *long*. It is thus the rightmost in Portuguese and the leftmost in English.

(20) a. the wrong long book
 b. *the long wrong book
 c. o   livro   comprido   errado
    the-MASC.SG book-MASC.SG long.MASC.SG wrong.MASC.SG
    'the wrong long book'
 d. *o   livro   errado   comprido
    the-MASC.SG book-MASC.SG wrong.MASC.SG long.MASC.SG
    'the long wrong book'

The second difference is that, while *long* can appear in predicative constructions, *wrong* cannot with the intended reading, as illustrated in (21a, b).

(21) a. O   livro   é   comprido
    the-MASC.SG book.MASC.SG COP long.MASC.SG
    'the book is long'
 b. O   livro   está errado
    the-MASC.SG book.MASC.SG COP wrong.MASC.SG
    'The book is wrong'
 c. Este   livro   é   o   errado
    this-MASC.SG book-MASC.SG COP the-MASC.SG wrong-MASC.SG
    'This book is the wrong one'

The only possible reading of (21b) is that there is something wrong with the book. For example, it has errors.[4] With the intended meaning the only way *errado* 'wrong' can appear in predicative position is if it is preceded by a definite determiner and is followed, in English, by the complement *one*, and in Brazilian Portuguese by a null complement, as illustrated in (21c).

The structure I propose is then the following for English and Brazilian Portuguese:

(22) a.

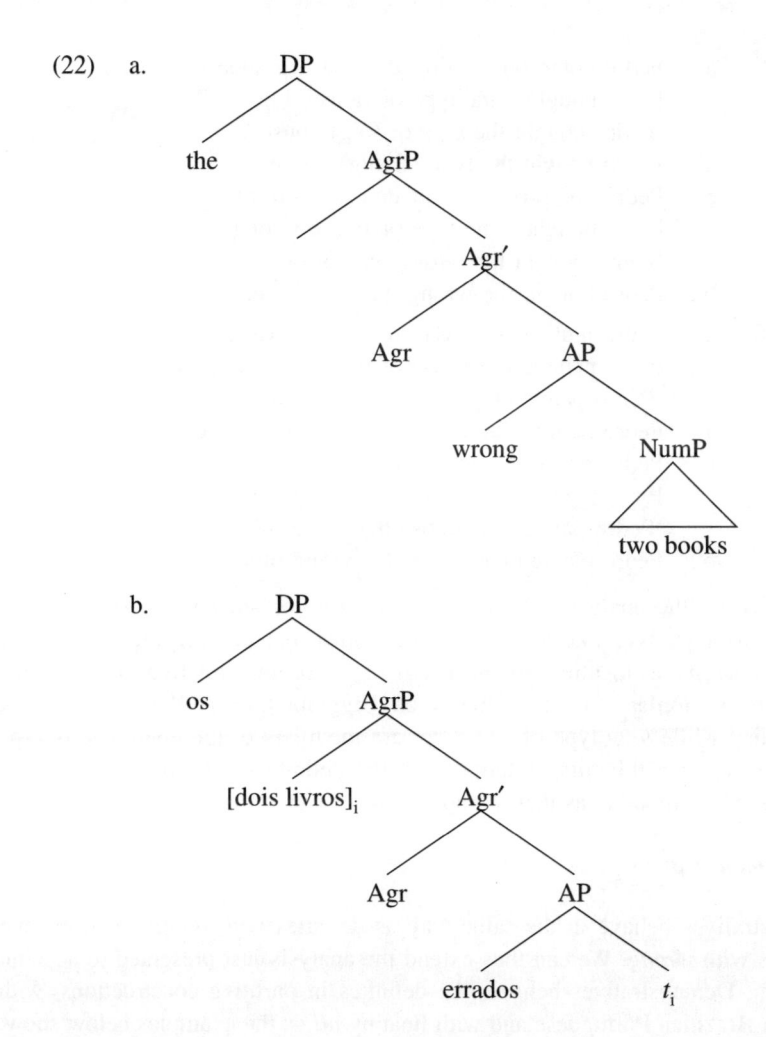

```
         DP
        /  \
      the  AgrP
            \
            Agr'
           /    \
         Agr    AP
              /    \
           wrong   NumP
                   /\
                two books
```

b.

```
         DP
        /  \
       os  AgrP
          /    \
    [dois livros]ᵢ  Agr'
                   /    \
                 Agr    AP
                       /  \
                   errados  tᵢ
```

The only difference between the two languages is that movement to the specifier of Agr is overt in Brazilian Portuguese but not in English, so that the right word-order will obtain.

The structure in (22b) predicts that, in contexts of Determiner Transparency, *errado* will behave in the same way as *wrong*. The examples below show this to be the case.

(23) a. *Pedro comprou o   tipo de casa (grande.)
        P.   bought the type of house big
        'Pedro bought the type of (big) house.'
   a'. *Pedro bought the type of (big) house
   b. Pedro comprou o   tipo de casa errado.
        P.   bought the type of house wrong
        'Pedro bought the wrong type of house.'
   b'. Pedro bought the wrong type of house.
(24) a. *Pedro pintou a   casa   do   azul (lindo.)
        P.   painted the house of-the blue beautiful
        'Pedro painted the house the (beautiful) blue.'
   a'. *Pedro painted the house the (beautiful) blue.
   b. Pedro pintou a   casa   do   azul errado
        P.   painted the house of-the blue wrong
        'Pedro painted the house the wrong blue.'
   b'. Pedro painted the house the wrong blue

Summarizing, the analysis I have presented here for adjectives like *wrong* as opposed to adjectives like *long* rests on the idea that because the behavior of definite + *wrong* is identical to the behavior of definite relative clauses, they should have similar structures. Based on Higginbotham's (1985) proposal, I argued that while *long* type of adjectives are modifiers of the noun, *wrong* type adjectives enter a θ-binding relation with the definite determiner and take the nominals they 'modify' as their complement.[5]

2.2 *Demonstratives*

Demonstratives behave in the same way as definites with relative clauses and definites with *wrong*. We can thus extend the analysis just presented to account for them. Demonstratives behave like definites in partitive constructions, with *todos* in Brazilian Portuguese and with floating *all* as the examples below show:

(25) a. two of {these / the} books
   b. *two of (some) books
(26) a. todos   {esses   / os}   livros
     all.MASC.PL these-MASC.PL / the-MASC.PL books.MASC.PL
     'all {these/ the} books'
   b. *todos   (alguns)   livros
     all-MASC.PL some-MASC.PL book-MASC.PL
     'all (some) books'

(27) a. {Those/the} books were all on the table.
b. *Some books were all on the table.

At the same time they are allowed in all the contexts where regular definites are unacceptable, as illustrated in (28) and (29):

(28) a. John bought that type of house.
b. *John bought the type of house.
(29) a. John painted the house that color.
b. *John painted the house the color.

Since demonstratives show Determiner Transparency effects, then the head noun must be free and the structure must be similar to the relative clauses. If NumP must be free, then the definite must take something else as its complement. There are independent reasons to believe this to be the case.

Bennett (1978) argues that when we say *this house*, we are actually saying *the house here* and *that house* is *the house there*. Demonstratives require demonstration, typically a pointing that makes clear which place is intended. However, according to Bennett, only places can actually be demonstrated. *Here* and *there* are then the only true demonstrative pronouns. The noun *house* that accompanies *this house* is not the element that is providing individual reference for the DP. Rather it is the *here* i.e., the pointing (the demonstratum) that is providing the reference for it. This pointing can be an actual pointing, or it can be made explicit in the discourse by the addition of *here,* as in (30a) and *aqui* in Brazilian Portuguese (30b). Thus, every demonstrative expression has its reference dependent on the context.

(30) a. This here man
b. Esse homem aqui
this man   here
'This here man'

Elements other than discourse anaphora can provide a 'place' for the pointing if there is no explicit *here*. For example, relative clauses can also provide reference. In its restrictive reading, the RC cannot cooccur with *here* as illustrated in (31).

(31) a. ?*This here man we met [*restrictive reading]
b. *?Esse homem aqui que nós encontramos
this man   here that we met
'This here man that we met'

The complementarity between the locative element and the RC suggest that a structure like (32) is on the right track.[6]

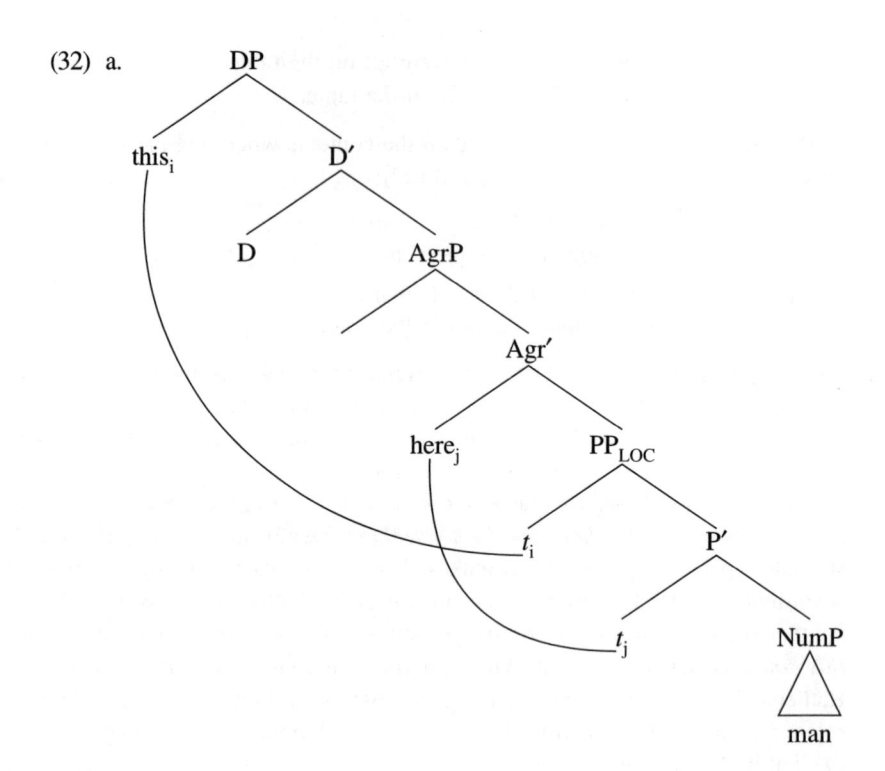

(32) a.
```
            DP
           /  \
       this_i  D'
              /  \
             D    AgrP
                    \
                    Agr'
                   /    \
                here_j   PP_LOC
                        /    \
                      t_i     P'
                             /  \
                           t_j   NumP
                                  △
                                 man
```

b.

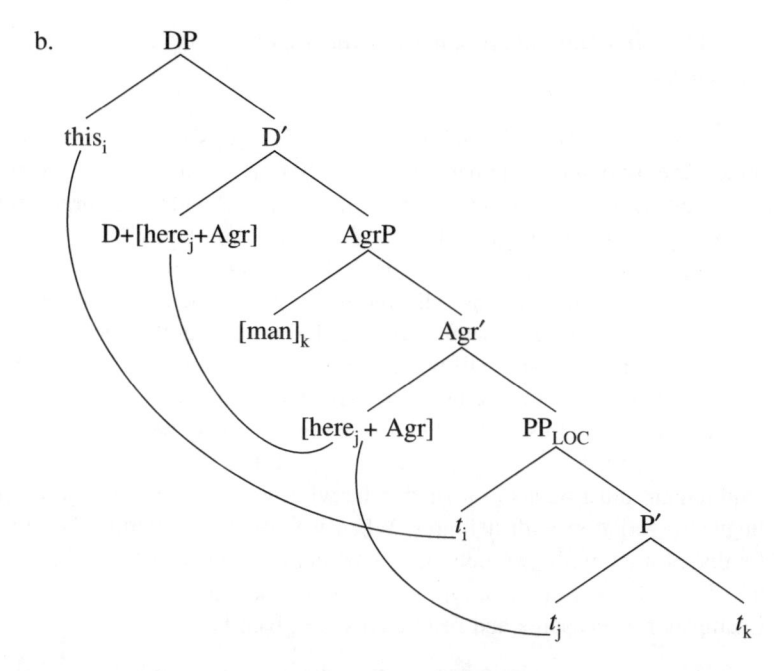

[Tree diagram:
- DP
  - this_i
  - D'
    - D+[here_j+Agr]
    - AgrP
      - [man]_k
      - Agr'
        - [here_j + Agr]
        - PP_LOC
          - t_i
          - P'
            - t_j
            - t_k]

In (32) the locative element can be an overt locative element or a null locative element, which I will notate for the discussion as P_{LOC}. I will assume that it is prepositional since it takes an argument as its complement.[7] The NumP *man* is generated as a complement of a locative phrase, which θ-marks it. The demonstrative, which I will take to be a DP (i.e. a pronoun) is generated in the specifier of the P_{LOC} head and raises to check its D features with the D head where it will agree in proximity and phi features with the P_{LOC}+Agr complex. The structure at Spell-Out for (30a) is given in (32a), and the LF is given in (32b). The P_{LOC} head raises overtly at least to Agr and from there to D to license the D features of the demonstrative. The P_{LOC}+Agr enters a spec head agreement relation with the NumP, being able then to check its phi features. The NumP raises to AgrP to have the agreement features on the P_{LOC}+Agr complex checked. The structure will allow the demonstrative to agree with P_{LOC} in terms of proximity and with the NumP in number.

This structure captures the intuition that the noun phrase is not the complement of the definite head. It is also compatible with Bennett's semantic proposal for demonstratives. Moreover, it also maintains the analysis of Szabolcsi (1994), Campbell (1996) and others that demonstratives are in SpecDP, which would account for the lack of extractability out of Demonstrative phrases.

2.3 What do relative clauses, demonstratives, and wrong-type adjectives have in common?

I have been assuming Higginbotham's (1985) analysis in which definite determiners are θ-bound by elements that have ⟨R⟩. ⟨R⟩ is the nominal counterpart of ⟨E⟩ in the verbal domain and corresponds to the Davidsonian argument. ⟨E⟩ is bound by Tense. In regular definite DPs, the NumP provides the empty ⟨R⟩ position that is saturated by the definite determiner. Now, since relative clauses, P_{LOC}, and some adjectives are allowed to be complements of the definite determiner, they must have something akin to ⟨R⟩, which can then be saturated by the definite. In this section I will present some support for the idea that the crucial property that unifies the elements we have been examining is actually ⟨R⟩.

Before we do this, it should be noted that ⟨R⟩ may be a necessary condition to license definite determiners but not a sufficient condition. Some formal requirement must be also satisfied, otherwise we would not find so much cross-linguistic variation with definites. When we compare Brazilian Portuguese and English, for example, we note that Brazilian Portuguese behaves like English in the classical cases (idioms, type expressions, measure phrases and resultatives). Examples for measures and resultatives are given below:

(33) a. A Maria pesa quarenta e cinco quilos.
         the M. weighs forty and five kilos
         'Maria weighs forty-five kilos.'
     a'. Maria weighs forty-five kilos.
     b. A Maria pesa os quarenta e cinco quilos *(que a
         the M. weighs the forty and five kilos that the
         Susana adoraria pesar).
         S.   would-love to-weigh.
         'Maria weighs the forty five kilos *(Susana would love to weigh)'
     b'. Maria weighs the forty five kilos *(Susana would love to weigh).

(34) a. Pedro pintou a casa de azul.
         P.   painted the house of blue
         'Pedro painted the house blue.'
     b. *Pedro pintou a casa do azul.
         P.   painted the house of-the blue
     c. Pedro pintou a casa do azul que ele gostava.
         P.   painted the house of-the blue that he liked
         'Pedro painted the house the blue he liked.'

However when we examine the case of proper nouns, variation occurs. In English definites with unmodified proper names are ruled out in general as (35a) shows. In Brazilian Portuguese, on the other hand, proper nouns can appear with definite determiners as in (35b) (which means the same as (35c)):

(35) a. *The Pedro likes the Maria.
 b. O Pedro gosta da Maria.
    the P. likes of-the M.
    'Pedro likes Maria.'
 c. Pedro likes Maria.

If the lack or presence of a definite determiner is cross-linguistically variable, it is reasonable to assume that there is also a formal feature distinction (not a semantic distinction) either on the proper noun or on the definite determiner. I will come back to the problem of proper nouns below.

For the moment I would like to concentrate on the cases of *type of* expressions, and nominals in resultatives, possessive *with*, idioms etc., which display the same behavior in both languages.

The ability of a relative clause to license a definite determiner is associated to the fact that relatives clauses are CPs with tense features. Tense can be seen as referential in the sense that it is anchored in the situation and tenses have reference points that relate to event times. Therefore they can provide ⟨R⟩.

If the ability to license definite determiners is to be related to ⟨R⟩ or, more specifically in this case, to Tense, then we would expect that CP tenseless relatives (i.e., infinitival relatives) headed by a definite determiner would be unacceptable.

The hypothesis that Tense is relevant for licensing definite relative clauses encounters some support from two sources: (i) Spanish infinitival relative clauses; (ii) Portuguese relative clauses in the present subjunctive.

Taboas (1995) shows that in Spanish infinitival relatives headed by *que* 'that' are unacceptable with definite determiners but are perfectly acceptable with indefinites. If the licensing of the definite is related to Tense features, and infinitives in Spanish do not have Tense, then we have an explanation for the contrast between (36a) and (36b).

(36) a. *Esta asociación ha encontrado los temas que tratar.
    this association has found the themes that treat.INF
 b. Esta asociación ha encontrado (unos) temas que tratar.
    this association has found (some) themes that treat.INF
    'This association has found (some) themes to discuss.'

A similar case is Portuguese present of subjunctive relative clauses. Consider the following paradigm:

(37) a. *Maria encontrou o homem que fale
 M. found the man that speak-3SG.PRES.SUBJ
 português.
 Portuguese
 b. Maria encontrou o homem que fala
 M. found the man that speak-3SG.PRES.IND
 português.
 Portuguese
 'Maria found the man that speaks Portuguese.'
 c. Maria encontrou um homem que fale
 M. found a man that speak-3SG.PRES.SUBJ
 português.
 Portuguese
 'Maria found a man that would speak Portuguese.'
 d. Maria encontrou um homem que fala
 Maria found a man that speak-3SG.PRES.IND
 português.
 Portuguese
 'Maria found a man that speaks Portuguese.'

If the present of subjunctive is used in the relative clause, then the definite is not acceptable. On the assumption that the present of subjunctive has no reference point because it is tenseless, then we can understand its unacceptability with the definite determiner.[8]

On the assumption that in these cases lack of ⟨R⟩ is the relevant problem, these examples show that it is not any type of relative clause that can license the definite determiner. Rather Tense features must be present.[9]

The idea that some element other than the noun is providing the ⟨R⟩ position can be extended easily to the case of demonstratives, if we adopt Bennet's idea discussed above: the locative element is actually the element that has the ⟨R⟩ position. Thus a definite can take it as its complement.

Although not as intuitive, the case of *wrong*-type adjectives can also be analyzed in the same way. When we say *John bought the wrong book*, we are saying that John bought a book that is the wrong one for that particular event, i.e., for a specific event located in time. If this is correct, then actually ⟨R⟩ is not only an open position in nouns but also in other elements.[10]

We can also conclude that it is not the definite determiner that gives 'reference' to a noun. Rather the complement of the definite has to have an ⟨R⟩ open position in order to be the complement of a definite determiner.

We need now to reexamine the classic cases in order to explain why the nominals in the classic examples were unable to license a definite determiner, why they lack this extra position ⟨R⟩.

3. Why certain nominals cannot be complements of definite determiners

When we examine the classical data in the light of the relative clause proposal in (12), at least two routes can be pursued to explain the acceptability of the definite with a relative cause and the unacceptability of the simple DP in (3) to (7): (a) a DP internal cause, namely something is missing in the nominal; or (b) a DP external cause: if the definite determiner in the simple DP binds the open position of the indefinite, then it can no longer appear in a position where an indefinite is necessary.

3.1 Internal causes

The unacceptability of the definite with simple nouns in (3) to (7) can be related to the idea that something is missing in the nominal. There are two ways of thinking about this lack: as a selection and/or subcategorization problem, or as a feature checking problem, namely something is missing in the noun and the definite does not have its features checked off. At this point I don't know how to decide which approach is more plausible but for the moment all I will hypothesize is that some nouns lack ⟨R⟩.

3.1.1 Lack of ⟨R⟩

There are two cases we can distinguish here: (a) the nominal is intrinsically non-referential, independent of the position it is in; and (b) the nominal must be non-referential because it is not in a referential position, i.e. it is a predicate of some sort.

Of the cases examined, the only clear case that we may argue fit into (a) are the *type of* expressions. *Type* expressions with definite determiners cannot appear in argument positions of eventive verbs, but other nouns can appear with the definite in the same position:

(38) a. John killed the rabbit.
     b. *John killed the type of rabbit.
     c. John killed the type of rabbit we find so cute.

(38) shows that it is *type* that does not take the definite determiner, and not the position it is in that bans the definite determiner.[11] This case leads us to assume that something intrinsic to the nominal *type of rabbit* prevents the definite determiner from being part of the nominal extended projection. It is plausible that this feature is related to ⟨R⟩ in some way, since *type* expressions are sorters and have no reference (see Jackendoff 1985 for a discussion).

Idioms and measures[12] may also belong to the category of inherently ⟨R⟩-less nouns. These nominals have empty positions but the empty position cannot be saturated by the definite determiner.

3.1.2 *Feature checking*
Another kind of internal cause is essentially morphosyntactic.

In proper nouns in English we cannot associate the unacceptability of the definite (in general) to the lack of ⟨R⟩. Here the explanation has to be different. Following Longobardi (1994), we can assume that proper nouns in English are forced to raise to D for morphological reasons. If there is no D for the proper noun to raise to, it has to be generated without the D features, otherwise the derivation would crash. When proper nouns are NumPs and not DPs they can only be interpreted as indefinites. The case of relative clauses with proper nouns illustrates the difference in interpretation between the simple DP proper noun and the NumP proper noun. Sentence (39a) contrasts with (39b), which can be paraphrased with (39c).

(39)   a.   Bill has long hair.
       b.   The Bill that Fred likes has long hair.
       c.   Fred likes a Bill, the one who has long hair.

It is easy to see that the lack of a definite with proper nouns here does not have anything to do with lack of ⟨R⟩. It is not lack of ⟨R⟩ that forces the proper noun to appear without a definite determiner. Here we have an internal cause for the lack of definite and, as we have seen, it is a morphological reason, not a semantic reason. The reason here is very different from the case of *type* expressions. Evidence for this comes from the fact that, in English, singular count nouns are not acceptable without some determiner or a plural marking, but proper nouns are, which indicates that they are different from regular count nouns, including *type* expressions. Moreover, proper nouns are definite even without the determiner, which is not the case of *type* expressions.

3.2 External causes

The case of resultatives and *with* constructions, etc. force an association between the unacceptability of the definite and the position the DP is in. For example, in (40a), *window* does not accept a regular definite determiner. Nevertheless it is clearly impossible to argue that *window* always lacks the ability to be interpreted referentially. Certainly *window* in other contexts is a noun with ⟨R⟩ that can license a definite determiner, as illustrated in (40b).

(40)   a.   *I have a house with the big windows.
           b.   The big windows are open.

In order to preserve the hypothesis that something internal to the head noun is inhibiting the definite determiner to have its features checked, we would have to associate the lack of some feature in the noun to a position. In other words, nouns in certain positions would lack a feature necessary to license the definite determiner. But then it is unclear whether position alone wouldn't be enough and we would not need to invoke anything else.

There are least two routes we can pursue when we try to explain the unacceptability of simple definite DPs in these cases. First, we could argue that all the cases that require an indefinite are predicates in the sense that they do not receive a thematic role, and therefore are incompatible with a definite determiner. Stowell (1989), however, has argued convincingly that definite determiners are not to be barred from predicative position generally. Moreover, if we bar definites from predicative positions, we would in principle have to bar definite relative clauses from the resultative cases, given that we have seen that they are definite as well.

Alternatively we can say that certain contexts require an indefinite, i.e., a nominal projection not headed by a strong quantifier. This indefiniteness requirement has been associated to some sort of 'novelty condition'. For de Jong (1987), for example, possessive *with* and measure complements of *weigh* are all presentational contexts. The unacceptability of the definite is then associated to the fact that we cannot assert what is presupposed. Not all cases will be amenable to this solution, however.

Without entering into the details on how the indefiniteness requirement is to be explained, we can still establish the following generalizations:

(41)   Certain contexts require an indefinite.

(42)   Simple definite DPs are unacceptable in contexts that require an indefinite.

In definite relative clauses, demonstratives and *the wrong* DPs, the nominal is still free from the definite determiner in the sense that the nominal is not the complement of the definite and thus is not part of its extended projection. The indefinite NumP can then act as the indefinite required to form a complex predicate or to provide a variable for some operator.[13]

3.3 *Summary*

So far I have discussed three cases of Determiner Transparency in contexts where a simple definite DP is not acceptable: relative clauses, demonstratives and *wrong* constructions. I attributed the acceptability of the definite or the demonstrative in these cases to the fact that the head noun is not part of the extended projection of the definite determiner, being free from it. In all these cases we have a free indefinite that is able to satisfy external requirements. The definiteness requirement for partitives, *todos* and floated *all* is met by the definite determiner head of the whole DP projection.

In the next section I discuss some details of the complement analysis and make the proposal that the indefinite is still free a bit more precise. Then I discuss a case in which no indefinite is required by the construction, but the free indefinite still has effects.

4. Some details of the complement analysis

In this section I would like to argue that there is another way in which the nominal phrase in a determiner transparency construction is free: because the determiner takes a non-nominal argument, it is the NumP that requires Case and not the DP as a whole.

In this section I will also work out some of the technical issues involved in supporting this claim, and in the next section will provide some empirical evidence that supports it.

Vergnaud's and Kayne's analyses have two independent parts: (a) the noun phrase head of the relative clause is not a constituent with the determiner that heads the whole projection and (b) the head of the relative clause is raised out of the relative clause itself.

For reasons that will become clear shortly I have not assumed the raising analysis for the relative clauses. Instead, I assumed that the head of the relative clause is generated in the specifier of some C-like projection, as illustrated in (43). For the purposes of this paper I will call this projection an Agr projection.

Whether Agr is really Agr or one of the exploded functional projections of CP (cf. Rizzi, 1994) is irrelevant for the moment. This functional projection is necessary if we are to preserve Kayne's antisymmetry hypothesis and not assume the raising analysis.

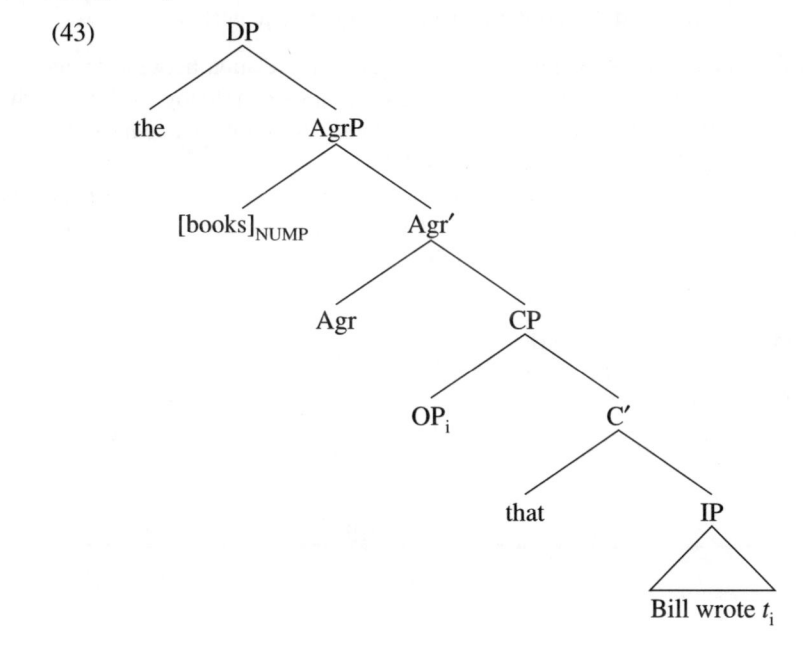

(43)
```
         DP
        /  \
      the   AgrP
           /    \
    [books]_NUMP  Agr'
                 /    \
               Agr     CP
                      /  \
                   OP_i   C'
                         /  \
                       that  IP
                             /\
                         Bill wrote t_i
```

I would like to argue that only nominal projections need to have their Case checked. More specifically only NumPs, QPs or DPs that are part of the extended projection (in the sense of Grimshaw 1991) of nouns need to have their Case checked. The need for Case comes from the head noun that moves into Num^0, Q^0 or D^0 and not from Num, Q or D. If D takes C as its complement, as in (43), then D does not require Case, since C is plausibly [+V] and Cs do not require case in general. If C had Case features it would need a Case that was compatible both with the Case of the head of the relative clause and the Case of the operator. If C has no Case features, Agr cannot have Case features activated by C. It will have the Case features of the head of the relative, with which it is in a Spec–Head relation.

An issue arises here. If D does not have to have its Case features checked, how can we explain the fact that the definite determiner appears in the Case of the nominal head of the relative, as in German (44), for example?

(44) Wir brauchen den Politiker, der unsere Interessen
we need the.ACC politician, who.NOM our interests
vertritt.
represents
'We need the politician who represents our interests.'

This fact raises the following questions: what is the relation between D and the head of the relative that allows D to exhibit the same morphological Case as the head of the relative? Second, if D has Case and D does not raise to have its Case checked, why does the structure not crash?

Consider the case of a language whose nominal modifiers exhibit number and Case agreement. It is assumed that the head noun raises checking off phi features of the adjectives in the checking domain of the adjectives as illustrated below:

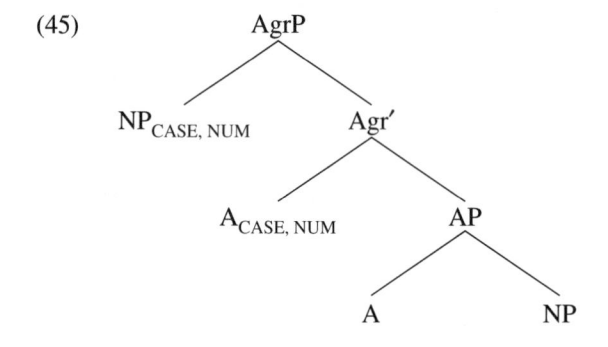

(45)
```
              AgrP
             /    \
    NP_{CASE, NUM}  Agr'
                   /    \
         A_{CASE, NUM}   AP
                        /  \
                       A    NP
```

Number is taken to be interpretable on Nouns and uninterpretable on adjectives (see Chomsky 1995). The noun will check off the number of the adjective. Because number is interpretable in nouns, the features are only eliminated from the adjective. What about Case? Clearly the noun is not a Case checker; otherwise, noun complements would not need to be preceded by a preposition. If nouns cannot be Case checkers for their own complements, then in principle nouns cannot check off the Case of the adjectives either. But then how do we guarantee that the Case of the noun will match the case of the adjectives? Suppose that as the noun moves through the checking domain of the adjective, it checks off number and it looks for matching features, but it does not check its own Case nor the Case of the adjectives. The question is then how Case gets checked on the adjectives. One possibility is that if an NP is modified, this forces pied-piping of the whole DP to a checking position. There the adjective, wherever it is within the nominal projection, gets its Case checked. A problem with this unconstrained checking is to explain how and why noun complements cannot have their Case checked in the same way. Why do we need an extra preposition to do the work in cases like *destruction of the city*?

There is, however, an alternative based on Nunes (1993). He argues that we need to distinguish PF and LF Case. Suppose adjectives do not have LF Case features that are uninterpretable at LF because adjectives only have morphological PF features. PF features have to be matched but not checked. Matching may be still a syntactic process, let's say specifier head agreement or head movement, or it can be a purely PF phenomenon, where some form of feature spreading will be necessary.

I would like to argue that when D has a CP as its complement it has no Case reasons to move, because it only has morphological PF features. It does not need to check off its features. It matches features with C+Agr which has inherited the phi features of the head of the relative but it does not check off its features as illustrated below:

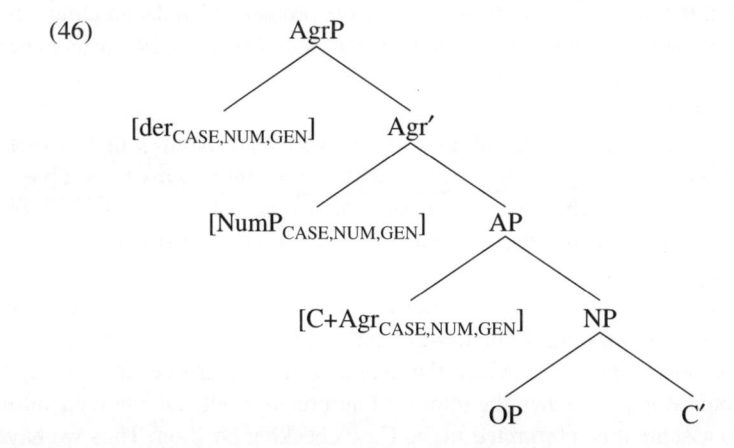

(46)

```
                    AgrP
                   /    \
    [der_CASE,NUM,GEN]   Agr'
                        /    \
        [NumP_CASE,NUM,GEN]   AP
                             /    \
              [C+Agr_CASE,NUM,GEN] NP
                                  /  \
                                 OP   C'
```

The Case of the determiner is purely a PF Case and not an LF Case. In German, there is no determiner without Case morphology, thus determiners can only be seen as chosen with morphological PF Case. There is no option of a morphologically Case-less determiner.

In sum, I am arguing that when the definite determiner takes a non nominal projection as its complement it does not need to check Case features in order to enter LF with unchecked features, because they are part of the extended projection of a non-nominal projection and only nouns need to have their case checked at LF.

The NumP head of the relative clause, demonstrative phrase or the *wrong* DP has to check Case because it is nominal. Thus it will have to move to the closest Case checker. If the DP with the free NumP is the complement of a verb, NumP will check its Case against the verb. If the DP relative clause is within a prepositional phrase, then it will check its Case against the preposition.

Let's consider first the case of idioms, exemplified above. Idioms were an important part of the argument for the raising analysis since it is in general assumed that they must form a unit at the level they are interpreted (see Chomsky 1995, for example).

(47) a. The headway John made was amazing.
 b. John made the headway we expected.
 c. John pulled the fast one that got him a job.

Examples like (47a) showed that the idiom had to reconstruct back to its original position. However, examples like (47b) and (47c), similar to examples discussed first in McCawley (1981), seem to suggest that idioms do not always need to reconstruct back, but can be interpreted in the matrix clause. If the idiom can be interpreted in the matrix clause, then we have the problem of understanding why in general the definite cannot intervene between *headway* and *make* or between *fast one* and *pull*, but the definite can intervene when the structure instantiates determiner transparency.

However, if we argue that idioms like *headway* are NumPs that have to have their Case checked, then we explain why the definite seems to be able to interfere between the verb and *headway* in some cases, but not in others. More specifically, the idea is that the idiomatic interpretation obtains if a spec-head relation obtains between *make* and the NumP *headway*.

This hypothesis has two advantages: by using the checking position for idiom interpretation, instead of the head-complement relation, we do not need to make an exception for cases in which the definite can intervene between the verb and the idiom. Moreover, when the idiom is interpreted inside the relative clause, we can also assume it is interpreted in the Case checking position. Thus we have a unified analysis for both upstairs and downstairs readings of idioms.

Second, by assuming that the idiom *headway* is a NumP, we allow for indefinites (which are probably specifiers of Num) as in (48a), but not for determiners like *the* and *every* to be the head of the extended projection of *headway* as in (48b):

(48) a. John made some headway.
 b. *John made the headway.

The idea that the NumP has to enter a close relation with the selecting verb and that this relation is a specifier head relation can be easily extended to the case of complements of *weigh*. We can easily argue that in order for the right interpretations to obtain with the complement of *weigh*, the verb and the measure have to be in very close relation: namely a checking relation.

What is left to be spelled out in detail is the case of resultatives and possessive *with* but this would lead us too far afield. However, the fact that resultatives in Romance are only possible when preceded by a preposition and in other languages inflect for Case (Finnish for example; see Schmitt 1996 and references there) makes them likely candidates to raise to the closest checking domain so that NumP can check its Case. The same can be said for possessive *with*. The NumP will move out of the relative clause to check Case features against the preposition *with*.

5. Aspectual effects

In this section I will provide further evidence for DT and the need for NumP to raise outside the relative clause, by examining the behavior of DT structures in contexts that do not **require** an indefinite, but where DT structures still behave as if the nominal is free from the definite. More specifically I will explore DPs in object position of verbs that are sensitive to quantity information for aspectual interpretation. In 5.1 I make my assumptions for aspectual interpretations clear. In 5.2 I compare the aspectual interpretations of simple definite DPs with the interpretations of cases of DT; in 5.3 I argue that aspectual effects can be accounted for if the head of the relative clause raises to the checking domain of the verb in order to check Case.

5.1 *Basic observations about aspect*

First consider the following:

(49) a. Pedro matou coelhos {^{ok} por 3 anos / $^{\#}$em duas horas.}
P. killed rabbits for 3 years $^{\#}$in two hours
a'. Pedro killed rabbits { ^{ok} for 3 years / # in two hours.}
b. Pedro matou {o / um} coelho {$^{\#}$por 3 anos / ^{ok} em uma
P. killed the / a rabbit for 3 years / in one
hora.}
hour
b' Pedro killed the rabbit {$^{\#}$for 3 years / ^{ok} in one hour.}

c. Pedro matou os coelhos {#por 3 anos / ok em 2 horas.}
   P.   killed the rabbits   for 3 years /   in 2 hours
c'. Pedro killed the rabbits {#for 3 years/ ok in 2 hours.}
d. Pedro matou dois coelhos {#por 3 anos / ok em 2 horas.}
   P.   killed two rabbits   for 3 years /   in 2 hours
d'. Pedro killed two rabbits {#for 3 years/ okin 2 hours.}

The data above from English and Brazilian Portuguese show the well known fact that aspect is compositional: both nominal properties and verbal properties play a role in the VP aspectual interpretation. In example (49) the verb is kept constant, and the quantity specification of the object is varied. The contrast is discrete: when quantity information is present we obtain a terminative reading. When no quantity information is present the 'VP is interpreted as durative. When the VP is durative, *for many years* is acceptable; when the VP is terminative, *for 3 years* is awkward or unacceptable and *in 3 years* is perfectly acceptable.

In (49a) the bare plural in the complement of *kill* induces a durative reading of the VP predicate, since the bare plural denotes a (potentially) unlimited number of rabbits because in each case the number of rabbits is limited. Only terminative readings are available in (49b,c), as the acceptability (or unacceptability) of the relevant adverbials show. In (49a), the adverbial *for 3 years* is acceptable and establishes an external boundary for the event. Nothing internally establishes a point where the event is considered logically over. In (49b,c,d), on the other hand, the adverbial *for x time* is odd. It forces a stretched reading of the event or an iterated reading, which is pragmatically very odd with *kill,* since we do not tend to kill a rabbit more than once. In these cases, it is necessary to equate the boundary of the event established by the quantity information present in the object and the temporal adverbial. In other words the end of the event has to be equated with the end of the killings. In these cases the adverbial *in x time* is perfectly acceptable.

Verkuyl (1993) has shown that durative readings are the default in the sense that there are various ways to derive a durative reading but only one way to derive a terminative reading, as the examples below show.

(50) a. Mary loved John for 3 years.
     b. Mary pushed the cart for 3 hours.
     c. Mary ran for 3 hours.
     d. #Mary ran a mile for 3 hours.

If the verb is stative, a durative reading will always obtain, independent of the fact that we may have quantity information present in the object, as illustrated in

(50a). In addition, not all verbs are sensitive to quantity information on the object and the result can be a durative VP (50b). Finally, if no quantity information is present, although the verb is of the right type, then a durative reading will be the only possibility, as the contrast between (50c) and (50d) illustrates.

To obtain a terminative reading, not only is an eventive verb necessary but also some indication of quantity. Terminative predicates can be made durative only by forcing iteration of the predicate. Durative predicates, on the other hand, can always be bounded by the addition of an external boundary. In the (49a) above, the adverbial *for many years*, can establish a temporal boundary for the event.

In previous work based on a unified analysis for the VP aspect in Finnish, Czech, English, Spanish, I made the following proposal (Schmitt 1996):

(51) Interpret the VP as terminative, if at the checking domain of the verb there is an eventive verb[14] and quantity information.

In simple DP constructions the whole DP (or its features) will raise for Case checking. If the features are of a bare plural or a mass noun, a durative reading will arise. If an element with quantity information, definite or indefinite, raises to the checking domain of the verb, a terminative reading will arise if the verb is of the right type.

In sum, aspect is a semantic property but dependent on syntactic configurations. If the quantity information is not in the checking domain of the verb, it cannot be used to produce a VP with quantity information, and a durative reading of the VP will obtain.

Evidence for this comes from Finnish. Consider the following example:

(52) a. Tuula rakensi taloa viisi vuotta.
 T. built house-PART five years
 'Tuula was building a/the house for five years.'
 b. #Tuula rakensi talon viisi vuotta.
 T. built house-ACC five years
 'Tuula built a/the house for five years.'

Objects, in Finnish, can appear in accusative or partitive Case. With partitive objects, durative readings will arise even though the complement has quantity information. To explain this I argued that partitive is actually a Case checker, i.e., a null preposition. The evidence for the null prepositional element comes from the fact that partitive is also the Case of certain noun complements. Given that nouns are not considered to be Case checkers, I argued that partitive is checked by a null preposition.

Once partitive objects can be checked by a partitive head, we eliminate the need for the object to raise to the checking domain of the verb. The result will be a durative VP. The relevant configurations for accusative Case checking and partitive Case checking are given below:

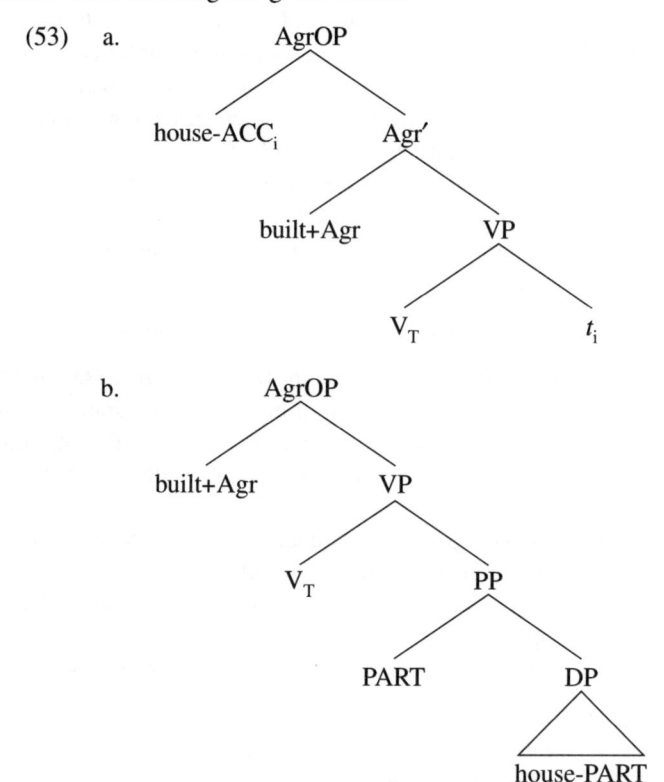

(53) a.
```
         AgrOP
        /     \
   house-ACCᵢ  Agr'
              /    \
        built+Agr   VP
                   /  \
                  Vᴛ   tᵢ
```

b.
```
         AgrOP
        /     \
    built+Agr  VP
              /  \
            Vᴛ    PP
                 /  \
              PART   DP
                     |
                 house-PART
```

Similar cases can be found in Portuguese:

(54) a. Maria comeu o sanduíche em cinco minutos.
M. ate the sandwich in five minutes
'Maria ate the sandwich in five minutes.'
a'. Maria ate the sandwich in five minutes.
b. Maria comeu do sanduíche por 5 minutos. [durative]
M. ate of-the sandwich for 5 minutes.
'Maria ate from the sandwich for 5 minutes.'
b'. Maria ate from the sandwich for 5 minutes

(55) a.

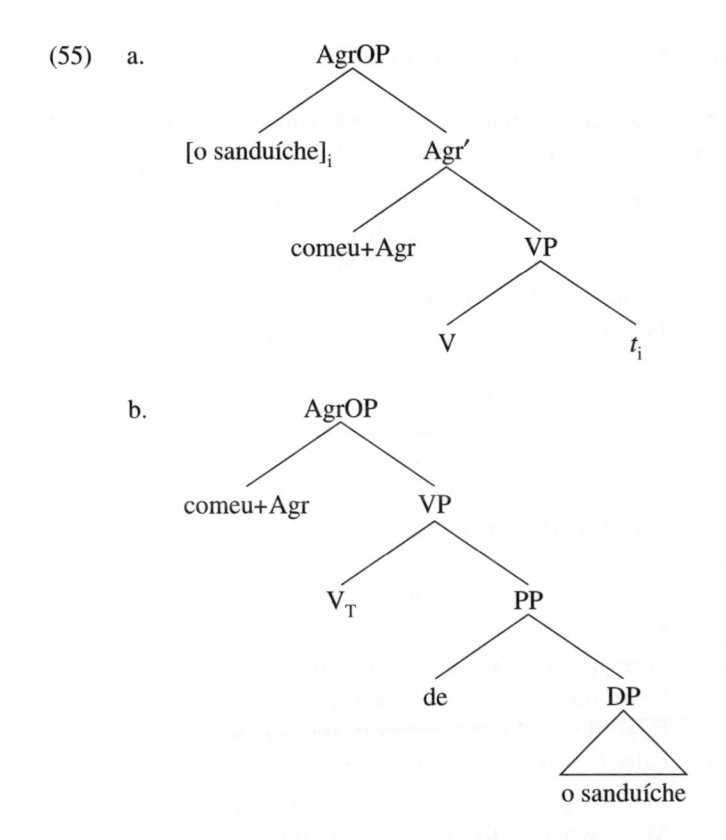

```
          AgrOP
         /     \
  [o sanduíche]_i   Agr'
                   /    \
            comeu+Agr    VP
                        /  \
                       V    t_i
```

b.

```
          AgrOP
         /     \
   comeu+Agr    VP
               /  \
             V_T   PP
                  /  \
                de    DP
                      △
                  o sanduíche
```

In (54a) the DP complement raises to the checking domain of the verb. In (54b), the preposition *de* is a closer Case checker and therefore the DP *o sanduíche* will check its Case against it, and therefore the DP does not need to raise to the checking domain of the verb and the VP will be interpreted as durative.[15]

The proposal that aspect is calculated at the checking domain of the verb amounts to establishing a parallel between aspectual interpretations and wh-scope. In wh-constructions, while the thematic role is interpreted in the base position, the wh-operator is interpreted higher. I would like to argue that the same is true for aspect. While the thematic role is interpreted at the base position, the aspectual interpretation is done at the checking domain of the verb. Note that I am not saying that the movement happens in order to force a particular interpretation. Rather the motivation for movement, just like the motivation for movement in questions is to satisfy a morphological condition. In the case of the VP aspect, Case is the relevant property.

5.2 Determiner transparency and VP aspectual interpretations

With these observations in mind, we can now consider the cases of DT in complement position both in English and Brazilian Portuguese:[16]

(56) a. Pedro [matou [o coelho que comia suas plantas]]
P. [killed [the rabbit that ate his plants]]
{#por 2 anos / ok em duas horas.}
for 2 years / in two hours

a'. Pedro [killed [the rabbit that ate his plants]] {#for 2 years / ok in two hours.}

b. Pedro [matou [os coelhos que comiam suas plantas]]
P. [killed [the rabbits that ate his plants]]
{por 2 anos / em um hora.}
for 2 years in one hour.

b'. Pedro [killed [the rabbits that ate his plants]] {for 2 years / in one hour.}

(57) a. #Pedro dirigiu aquele filme por 3 anos.
P. directed that movie for 3 years
a'. #Peter directed that movie for 3 years.
b. Pedro dirigiu aqueles filmes por 3 anos
P. directed those movies for 3 years.
b'. Peter directed those movies for 3 years.

(58) a. #Maria escreveu o artigo errado por 3 anos
M. wrote the article wrong for 3 years.
a'. #Maria wrote the wrong article for 3 years.
b. Maria escreveu os artigos errados por 3 anos
M. wrote the articles wrong for 3 years.
b'. Maria wrote the wrong articles for 3 years.

In the cases above, a singular definite with a relative clause, a demonstrative and *the wrong* produces terminative readings, as predicted. However, with plurals a durative reading is also available. It is as if the definite determiner can be present or absent in the plural cases for aspectual interpretation.[17]

I would like to argue that the matrix verb in (56) is taking the NumP head of the relative clause as its 'measure'. The DP *the rabbits that ate his plants*, as we have seen, is not *the rabbits*, i.e., a DP with its quantity defined by the definite, but rather *rabbits, the ones that ate his plants*. What the matrix verb 'sees' and uses as a measure for the VP is the NumP *rabbits*; consequently, durative readings will obtain since there is no specified quantity. The definite is not being taken into account. A singular count NumP, on the other hand, will be interpreted as quantized, namely *a rabbit, the one that ate the plants*. Thus the result is a terminative reading. The same is true for the demonstrative case *a rabbit, that one* or *rabbits' those ones*, and for the *wrong* type of adjectives: *a rabbit, the wrong one*; *rabbits' the wrong ones*.

This proposal makes a prediction that, if the NumP nominal head is plural but has quantity information, a terminative reading will obtain and, if mass, a durative reading will obtain.

The data below show this prediction to be borne out:

(59) a. Pedro [matou [os 2 coelhos que comiam as plantas]]
P. killed the 2 rabbits that ate the plants
{#por 2 anos /ok em uma hora.}
for 2 years in one hour
a'. Pedro killed the 2 rabbits that ate the plants {#for 2 years/okin one hour.}

(60) a. #Pedro dirigiu aqueles dois filmes por 3 anos.
P. directed those two movies for 3 years
a'. #Peter directed those two movies for 3 years.
b. Pedro dirigiu aquele lixo {por 3 anos / em 3 anos.}
P. directed that trash for 3 years / in 3 years
b'. Peter directed that trash {for 3 years/in 3 years.}

In sum what we have seen so far is that the indefinite can act as the measure for the VP. The differences in aspectual interpretation between definite DPs and definites with relative clauses, *wrong* or demonstratives arise from the fact that the verb uses the NumP rather than the whole definite DP as a measure for the event. This explains the durative readings of plurals and mass nouns in the examples above, and the terminative readings with singular count and other quantifiers.

5.3 *Where is NumP interpreted*

If we combine the proposal made in (51), namely that VP is interpreted as terminative if at the checking domain of an eventive verb there is quantity information with the proposal that NumP raises to check its Case features, then the facts above are easily explainable.

In cases of DT, the interpretation will depend on the NumP. If it is a singular count or a quantized NumP, terminative readings will arise, otherwise the result will be durative. Assuming that the NumP raises to the checking domain of the verb, nothing extra has to be proposed to account for the transparency of the determiner. We do not need to stipulate that, in some cases, the determiner is not to be taken as relevant and what counts is the NumP inside the DP complement of the relative clause, or even worse, that what counts is the specifier of the specifier in the checking domain of the verb. The reason for the transparency of the determiner in these cases is very simple: the definite cannot be taken as a boundary for the VP because it does not reach the checking domain of the verb.

A tree illustrates the structure that is used for the interpretation of the VP aspect:

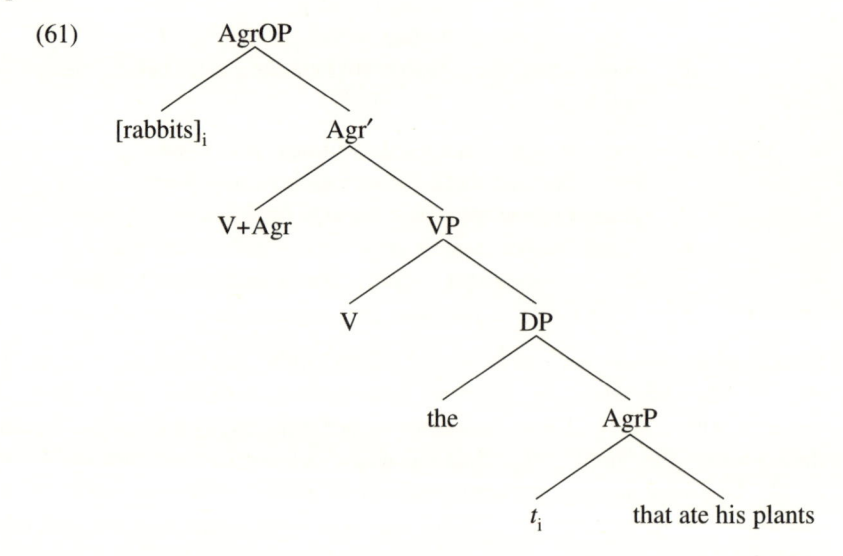

(61)
```
              AgrOP
             /     \
      [rabbits]_i   Agr'
                   /    \
                V+Agr    VP
                        /  \
                       V    DP
                           /  \
                         the   AgrP
                              /    \
                            t_i   that ate his plants
```

What is still left to be explained is the terminative readings that we can obtain with mass terms and bare plural NumPs, as the acceptability of *in x time* adverbials in (56b) and (60) show.

The acceptability of the *in x time* adverbial in cases where the NumP is a mass noun or a non quantized plural is to be related to the fact that the relative clause is able to impose an external boundary on the durative reading. This possibility is predicted, given that durative readings are always the default (i.e. unmarked) case for aspect. The external boundary can be provided by the relative clause itself and is strongly dependent on internal properties of the CP.

We have already seen that durative predicates can be bounded by external boundaries. For example, if we add to (62a) the adverb *for two hours,* the result is a terminative predicate (62b), as the addition of *repeatedly* (which as we have seen requires discrete subevents) shows in (62c):

(62) a. Mary ran.
b. Mary ran for an hour.
c. Mary ran for an hour repeatedly.

To put it simply, it is always possible to bound a durative event, but in order to 'unbound' a terminative event, it is necessary to force iteration of the predicate. To a durative predicate we can add an external boundary. To a terminative predicate we need to force the repetition of the subevent in order to force duration. This fact is easily derivable from a theory that takes durative predicates as the default case and terminative predicates as the marked case.

The durative interpretations of the VP whose verb has a relative clause as its complement are not the result of iteration. This is important, because it shows that, in contrast to (62c), the durative readings are not derived by 'unbounding' a terminative event, i.e. by multiplying bounded subevents, but rather the terminative reading is the result of applying an external boundary to a durative predicate. If we assumed the opposite, i.e. that the derived reading is the durative reading, we would expect durativity to be the result of iteration.

Tense, mood and focus affect the ability of the relative clause to be used as an external boundary. However, it is beyond the scope of this paper to address the internal properties of RCs and their relation to the aspectual interpretations of the matrix. What is important here is that I am not saying there is a structural difference between the terminative readings and the durative readings here with respect to the relative clause. Rather I am saying that the relative clause can be included as an external boundary within the scope of *in x time* adverbials.

In fact, there is evidence that adverbials like *in x time* can be interpreted in various positions and take scope over different parts of the clause, as illustrated below:

(63) a. John will run the race in 20 minutes.
b. He will start running in 20 minutes.
c. John ran the race in 20 minutes.

In (63a, b) the adverbial is related to the starting point of the running or the duration of the running. In (63c) the adverbial modifies its duration.

6. Concluding remarks

In this paper I have shown first that the complement analysis can be extended to other cases besides relative clauses that display the same definite/indefinite behavior. Also the complement analysis helped us make sense of the fact that while simple definite DPs are unacceptable in certain contexts, definites with relative clauses, *wrong* modifiers and demonstratives are acceptable. By assuming the complement analysis we have both a definite and a free indefinite and thus we predict the hybrid behavior. In cases were the definite is required, no problem arises. In cases where an indefinite is required the free indefinite will be able to fulfill the necessary requirements. The hybrid behavior does not need to be associated to some mysterious pragmatic property of definites with *wrong* type adjectives or relative clauses but rather to a structural configuration that allows for a definite and an indefinite behavior. The aspectual interpretations provide further support for the hypothesis that there is a free indefinite, and also support the idea that the NumP head of the relative clause actually moves out of the relative clause for Case reasons. This allows the NumP to enter a checking relation with the verb or to whatever is the closest Case checker.

What is left to be made precise is why some contexts require an indefinite, although they do not force selection of an indefinite.

Notes

1. The same is true for *all* in English with the exception of subjects in generic contexts:
    (i)   a.   *John ate all apples / all apples he bought
          b.   John ate all the apples / all the apples he bought
2. See Section 4 and 5 for arguments in favor of the hypothesis that the head of the relative clause is base generated in this position.
3. Cases where no requirement is being imposed externally will be discussed in Section 4.
4. The fact that the copula verbs in (21a) and (21b) are different (*ser* Vs *estar*) is an independent fact related to the adjective. If we replace *comprido* with *molhado* 'wet', we get the minimal pair with (21b). See Schmitt (1996) for discussion of *ser* and *estar*.
5. Other adjectives that display the same behavior as *wrong* are *same* and *other*.
    (i)   Peter bought the {same/other} type of house.
    (ii) Peter painted the house the { same/other} color.

    Notice that both *same* and *other* in Portuguese are prenominal adjectives, as illustrated below:
    (i)   a.   o   mesmo livro   (ii)   a.   o   outro livro
               the same   book   the other book

b.	*o livro mesmo	b.	*o livro outro
	the book same		the book other

Unfortunately we cannot say that all adjectives that are prenominal in Portuguese exhibit Determiner Transparency effects. But it seems that adjectives that are in a sense modifiers of the event (see Carlson 1987 for an analysis of *same*) are the adjectives that display DT effects with definite determiners. These adjectives, which have the effect of contrasting events (*right* and *wrong, same, different* etc.) can take nominals as complements as well. The idea that these adjectives contrast events suggest a link between their behavior and the behavior of other adjectives with contrastive focus, which seem to allow the same behavior. Other adjectives that also display Determiner Transparency effects are ordinals. The exact characteristics that distinguish both types of adjectives and the role of focus is an issue that deserves further investigation and is beyond the scope of this paper.

6. A reviewer asks why it is impossible to stack relative clauses with demonstratives, when simple relative clauses seem stackable. I believe that the reason lies on the proper analysis of stacked relative clauses. If we take an approach that stacked relative clauses are like parasitic gap constructions, then it becomes clear why (31b) does not behave in the same way. We know that parasitic gaps are only licensed when there is overt A'-movement, which is not the case in (31b).

    Cases like the *this here man with the red beard* are probably cases of appositive modification, as suggested by the reviewers.

7. Alternatively we could assume that the loc element is pronominal. However, since pronominals usually do not take arguments, I will not consider this hypothesis.

8. The subjunctive present has a very narrow distribution in adverbial clauses, unlike the future and past subjunctives. Particularly it is unacceptable in adverbial clauses with *if* and *when*. The present subjunctive is only possible in adverbial clauses when the conjunction is temporal or when it has a concessive meaning. I believe that this narrow distribution has to do with its lack of temporal features.

9. English infinitival relatives, which are headed by *to*, seem to allow definites. One possibility is that the infinitive headed by *to* actually has Tense (see Stowell 1982 for arguments in favor of this hypothesis). Another possibility is that infinitival relatives in English are not structures like (1b). It is beyond the scope of this paper to explore the exact nature of infinitival relatives in English.

10. Note that this case is very different from the following case, frequently discussed in the literature (see Higginbotham 1985, for example):

    (i) a big ant

    Here the adjective can be interpreted in two ways. The ant can be big or big for an ant. Here we are not discussing the appropriateness of the size of the ant with respect to some particular event.

11. *Ones* is also unacceptable with a definite determiner (56a), but become acceptable if a relative clause is added (56b). And again we cannot attribute the unacceptability of *one* with the definite to the position the DP is in the clause. It is tempting to assimilate *one* to this set as well, but *one* has a different distribution (see Campbell 1996).

12. In cases where a measure can appear with a definite determiner, it seems that there is an implicit partitive licensing it, as illustrated below:

    (i) John bought 30 kilos of apples. *The thirty kilos* were enough to make all the pies they needed.

13. It is important to note that the indefinite requirement is not a requirement that there be an indefinite anywhere inside the resultative, as the examples below show. In (ia) there is an indefinite inside the resultative but this is not enough to render the sentence acceptable. The indefinite has to be in a particular position, as (ib) shows. (ia) and (ic) also show that increasing the length of the resultative (in order to increase the amount of information provided by the resultative) does not improve its acceptability.

    (i)   a.   *Mary dyed the dress the nice color for a wedding.
          b.   Mary dyed the dress a nice color for the wedding.
          c.   *Mary dyed the dress the nice color for the wedding.

14. For the more exact formal semantic properties of verbs that force terminative readings when quantity is in the checking domain of the verb see Verkuyl (1993).

15. Two issues arise here: first what happens to the Case features of the verb in cases like (54b). There are two possible routes to take here: either the verb can be generated with or without Case features, with no import for interpretation, since Case is a formal feature. Alternatively we can argue that accusative Case is an inherent property of transitive verbs, i.e., it is a category feature and as such does not need to be checked off of the verb. For the purpose of this paper either possibility can be adopted. In Schmitt (1996) I argue that the second possibility is in fact the correct one.

    A second issue arises with verbs that never assign accusative Case and therefore do not seem to have features that would attract an element to its checking domain. Two cases come to mind: passives and unaccusatives.

    Here we have to remember that aspect is layered: there is VP aspect but there is also IP aspect. In IP aspect it seems that properties of the subject interfere and interact with higher tense/aspect morphology. In the case of Unaccusatives and passives the subject will play a role similar to the role played by objects in regular transitive structures. Thus, the same distinction between a bare plural and a nominal with quantity information that we find with VPs can also be established at the level where the subject enters a checking relation with the complex V+T: bare plurals will be compatible with *for x time adverbs* and subjects with quantity information will force terminative readings of the IP, as illustrated in (i) and (ii) below (see Schmitt 1996 for more evidence of the role of subjects in the aspectual composition):

    (i)   The man arrived in five minutes/ #for five minutes.
    (ii)   Men arrived for 2 hours/ #in 2 hours.
    (iii) #The men that eat a lot arrived for 2 hours.

    As for (iii), my informants tell me it is odd with *for x time* adverbials. This follows from the fact that due to the EPP, raising of the whole Relative Clause is forced. Once the whole DP is raised, the verb + tense has a definite in its checking domain and durative readings become unavailable. The same holds for definite relative clauses subject of passives, illustrated by the contrast between (iv) and (v) below. While a durative reading is possible in (iv), a durative reading in which the only boundary is the one given by the adverbial is awkward in (v).

    (iv)   Men were arrested yesterday for 2 hours.
    (v)   #The men that wore blue were arrested for 2 hours.

16. *For x time* is to interpreted as a modifier of the matrix VP in all these cases.

17. Durative readings of the VP should be separated from quantificational readings

    (i)   a.   John ate apples for 2 minutes.
          b.   Every day John ate apples for 2 minutes.
          c.   John hit the ball for 2 hours.

In (i-a) whatever the number of apples John ate, he only took two minutes doing it. We do not get a reading such that for each apple, it took 2 minutes to eat it. In this case the adverb takes scope over the whole VP. Now consider (i-b). In (i-b) the reading we obtain is that for every day there is an event of eating apples for 2 minutes. Thus in a week the events of apple eating take 14 minutes. *Every* is quantifying over the whole situation. The same is true in (i-c). No matter how many times John hit the ball, the event lasts two hours. Only quantification over the situation can actually multiply the amount of time specified by the adverbial. In other words a bare plural or a definite plural in object position can never scope over *for x time* adverbials. This observation is important because one can always think of a context where the definite can apparently produce durative readings, either because a generic operator is added or because some adverbial multiplies the number of situations. Take (39b): *Bill killed the rabbit for three years*. We can think of a situation in which every year Bill receives a rabbit for his birthday from his grandfather. He kills the rabbit every year and makes a nice dinner for his friends. In this situation some speakers accept (iia):

(ii) a.   For years Bill killed the rabbit on his birthday.
     b.   After the rabbit, the friends would enjoy themselves.

Notice first that *on his birthday* and *for years* are the key elements which allow a quantificational reading. Here we are iterating the whole situation of Bill killing a rabbit, the one he gets for his birthday every year. Notice also that it is in these cases that a simple DP can appear as the name of an event after the preposition *after*, as illustrated in (ii-b). A similar example can be constructed in case there is a hunting competition and Bill always ends up winning and killing the competition's rabbit. Again here what is being iterated is the competition and the rabbit killing event and not the VP. The sentence in which *Bill killed the rabbit for years* is again acceptable. Notice that the sentence becomes unacceptable if we substitute *for years* for *for 2 hours*. Here only a stretched reading is possible. For the remainder of this paper I will not use an unbounded *for x time* expression such as *for years* to test for durative readings but rather a quantized *for x time* expression of shorter duration. In sum, when we deal with aspectual interpretations it is crucial to keep contexts constant and to be sure that we are not introducing elements at the sentential level that can force a quantificational reading of the whole situation.

References

Barwise, J & R. Cooper. (1981). Generalized quantifiers and natural language. *Linguistics and Philosophy* 4: 159–219.
Bennett, M. (1978). Demonstratives and indexicals in Montague grammars. *Synthese* 39: 1–80.
Bianchi, V. (1994/5). *Consequences of Antisymmetry for the syntax of headed relative clauses*. Dissertation, Scuola Normale Superiore Pisa.
Campbell, R. (1996). Specificity operators in SpecDP. *Studia Linguistica* 50–2: 161–188.
Carlson, G. (1987). *Same* and *different:* some consequences for syntax and semantics. *Linguistics and Philosophy* 10: 531:565.
Chomsky, N. (1995). *The minimalist program*. Cambridge, Mass.: MIT Press.

Jong, F. de. (1987). The compositional nature of (in)definiteness. *The representation of (in)definiteness*, Edited by E.J. Reuland & A.G.B. ter Meulen, 270–285. Cambridge, Mass.: MIT Press.
Grimshaw, J. (1991). *Extended projections*. Manuscript, Brandeis University.
Heim, I. (1987). Where does the definiteness restriction apply? Evidence from the definiteness of variables. *The representation of (in)definiteness*, Edited E.J. Reuland & A.G.B. ter Meulen, 21–42. Cambridge, Mass.: MIT Press.
Higginbotham, J. (1985). On semantics. *Linguistic Inquiry* 16: 547–593.
Jackendoff, R. (1985). *Semantics and Cognition*. Cambridge, Mass.: MIT Press.
Kayne, R.S. (1994). *The Antisymmetry of syntax*. Cambridge, Mass.: MIT Press.
Kuroda, S.Y. (1968). English relativization and certain related problems. *Language* 44: 244–266.
Longobardi, G. (1994). Reference and Proper Names: a theory of N-movement in Syntax and Logical Form. *Linguistic Inquiry* 25: 609–665.
McCawley, J.D. (1981). English relative clauses. *Lingua* 53: 99–149.
Nunes, J. (1993). English participle constructions: evidence for [+PF, -LF] Case. *University of Maryland Working Papers* 1: 66–79.
Platzack, C. (this volume). *A complement-of-N^0 account of restrictive and non-restrictive relatives: the case of Swedish*.
Rizzi, L. (1994). *The fine structure of the left periphery*. Manuscript, University of Geneva.
Schmitt, C. (1996). *Aspect and the syntax of noun phrases*. Doctoral Dissertation, University of Maryland, College Park.
Stowell, T. (1982). The tense of infinitives. *Linguistic Inquiry* 13: 561–570.
Stowell, T. (1989). Subjects, specifiers, and X-bar Theory. *Alternative Conceptions of Phrase Structure*. Edited by M. Baltin & A. Kroch, 232–261 Cambridge University Press.
Szabolcsi, A. (1994). The noun phrase. *The syntactic structure of Hungarian*, Edited by F. Kiefer & K. É.-Kiss, 179–274. San Diego: Academic Press.
Táboas, S. (1995). Spanish infinitival relatives: a proposal about their indefiniteness requirement. *Probus* 7: 197–219.
Vergnaud, J.-R. (1985). *Dépendances et niveaux de répresentation en syntax*. Amsterdam: John Benjamins.
Verkuyl, H.J. (1993). *A theory of aspectuality*. Cambridge: Cambridge University Press.

A Head Raising Analysis of Relative Clauses in Dutch[*]

Jan-Wouter Zwart
NWO/University of Groningen

1. Introduction

In this paper, I would like to discuss the properties of relative clauses in Dutch and dialects of Dutch in the light of the *head raising analysis* proposed in Kayne (1994) (based on earlier proposals by Vergnaud 1974).

In the head raising analysis, the head noun of the relative clause (*man* in (1)) is taken to originate inside the relative clause (2):

(1) the man I love

(2) the [$_{CP}$ I love man]

The relative construction in (1) is derived from (2) by raising the noun phrase *man* to the specifier position of CP:

(3) the [$_{CP}$ man$_i$ I love t_i]

This analysis differs from the traditional *adjunction* analysis entertained in Chomsky (1977: 98), in which the relative clause is adjoined to the noun phrase headed by *man*:

(4) the man [$_{CP}$ I love]

---

[*] I would like to thank Artemis Alexiadou, Valentina Bianchi, Veneeta Dayal, Eric Hoekstra, Jan Koster, Gertjan Postma, Hotze Rullmann, Chris Wilder, and the participants of the Berlin Workshop on Relative Clauses. The consequences of the head raising analysis for relative clauses in Dutch were first explored in De Vries (1996), whose input is gratefully acknowledged. The author's research is funded by the Netherlands Organization for Scientific Research, grant 300-75-002.

The complement of *love* in (4) is taken to be an operator element, which moves to the specifier position of CP in a way comparable to the head noun in (3):

(5)   the man [$_{CP}$ OP$_i$ I love t_i]

This paper discusses in more detail the morphology and syntax of the elements appearing in the left periphery of the relative clause in Dutch. Following recent research on the structure of CP in Germanic (esp. Hoekstra 1993), I assume that CP consists of three layers of complementizer phrases, as illustrated in (6):

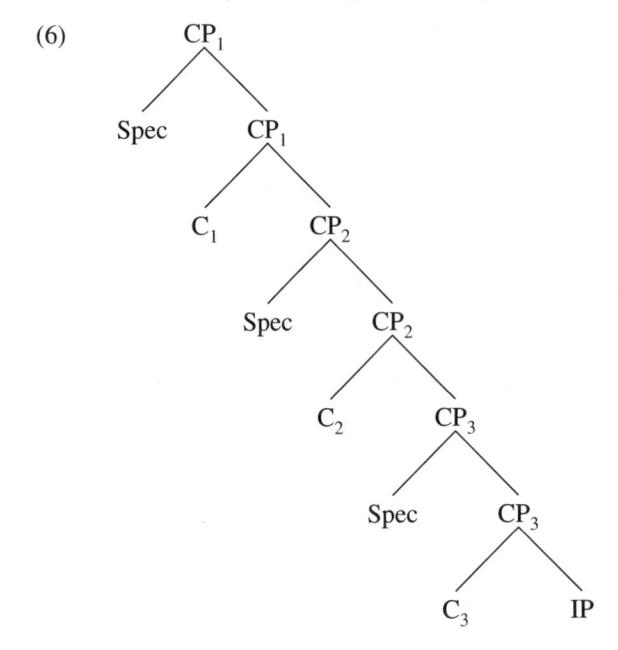

(6)
```
          CP₁
         /   \
      Spec    CP₁
             /   \
           C₁    CP₂
                /   \
             Spec    CP₂
                    /   \
                  C₂    CP₃
                       /   \
                    Spec    CP₃
                           /   \
                         C₃    IP
```

In Hoekstra's (1993) analysis, the three heads C$_1$, C$_2$, and C$_3$ in Dutch are occupied by the complementizers *als* 'if', *of* 'whether', and *dat* 'that', respectively. I will show that these three elements also show up in relative constructions in (dialects of) Dutch, albeit that *als* is represented by a related element, *zo* 'thus'. These observations will allow us to lay out the structure of the relative clause in Dutch in more detail.

Relative pronouns in Dutch can be of a (morphologically) interrogative type (built on the root *w-*, as in (7a)), or of a demonstrative type (built on the root *d-*, as in (7b)):

(7) a. de straat *waar* jij woont
 the street where you live
 'the street where you live'
 b. de man *die* ik bemin
 the man that I love
 'the man that I love'

I propose that CP$_2$ and CP$_3$ provide designated landing sites for the interrogative and demonstrative relative pronouns, respectively. These pronouns are actually determiner elements heading a DP, referred to as DP$_{REL}$. The DP$_{REL}$ is generated in an argument position inside the relative clause, and contains the head noun. The head noun moves along with the DP$_{REL}$ to one of the designated specifier positions in CP, as in the analysis of Kayne (1994) (cf. (7b)):

(8) [$_{DP}$ de [$_{CP1}$ [$_{CP3}$ [$_{IP}$ ik bemin [$_{DP_{rel}}$ die [$_{NP}$ man]]]]]]

In addition, following Bianchi (1999), I propose that the head noun ultimately moves out of the DP$_{REL}$ to the specifier position of a higher phrase, CP$_1$. One of the objectives of this paper is to corroborate this analysis of relative clauses, building on work by Kayne and Bianchi, by providing a semantic motivation for the movement of the head noun to the highest specifier position in the relative clause:

(9) [$_{DP}$ de [$_{CP1}$ [$_{CP3}$ [$_{DP_{rel}}$ die [$_{NP}$ man]]$_i$ [$_{IP}$ ik bemin t_i]]]]

The discussion in what follows is exploratory, and in no way intends to present a fair case for either the traditional or the head raising analysis. Its objective is to describe the phenomena of Dutch in terms of the head raising analysis, and to propose certain modifications of the head raising analysis as far as they may be required in order to make sense of the morphological and syntactic properties of relative clauses in Dutch.

2. An initial problem

Let me start off by presenting a problem from the domain of relative clause constructions of Dutch which favors the head raising analysis of Kayne (1994).

In Dutch, there are two expressions for 'everything' (Latin *omnia*), namely *al* and *alles*. Historically, *alles* is the genetive Case form of *al*. *Al* is a noun, which in present day Dutch is used only in the expression *het Al* 'the Universe', and in certain idiomatic expressions (such as *al met al* 'all in all'). The common form for *omnia* in Dutch is *alles*, and *al* cannot be used as an autonomous argument expression:

(10) a. Ik heb alles/*al
       I have everything
       'I have everything'
    b. Alles/*al is vergeefs
       all   is in-vain
       'Everything is in vain'

However, *al* may appear as an argument expression if modified by an amount relative clause:

(11) a. Ik heb alles/al wat ik wil
       I have all   REL I want
       'I have everything I want'
    b. Alles/al wat ik doe is vergeefs
       all   REL I do is in-vain
       'Everything I do is in vain'

This is only possible if *al* and the relative pronoun are adjacent:

(12) a. ... dat ik alles/*al heb wat ik wil
          that I all   have REL I want
       '... that I have everything I want'
    b. Alles/*al is vergeefs wat ik doe
       all   is in-vain REL I do
       'Everything I do is in vain'

If we adopt the adjunction analysis of relative clauses (cf. (4)), it remains unclear why the presence of an adjunct clause licenses *al* as an autonomous argument expression. Adjuncts are generally optional, and are not expected to have this licensing effect. Moreover, the ungrammaticality of (12a) with *al* suggests that the explanation cannot be semantic. The range of *al/alles* is delimited in the same way in (11) and (12).

The adjacency of *al* and the relative particle *wat* suggests that *al* and *wat* form some kind of collocation. Let us first try to understand why *al* requires an element like *wat* in its immediate vicinity in order to be licit. It will then turn out that only the head raising analysis provides a structure in which *al* and *wat* may form the required collocation.

Consider first *alles* 'everything'. *Alles* consists of two morphemes, the element *al* and a genitive ending. Both morphemes have in common that they are not autonomously referring expressions. *Al* is a grammaticalized element that can only refer in the petrified expression *het Al* 'the Universe'. The genitive ending obviously cannot refer.

Postma (1995) describes these grammatical and grammaticalized elements as being "in zero semantics". Core cases of zero semantics (ZS) elements are determiners and inflectional affixes. Postma makes the interesting observation that elements of universal quantification always require a collocation of two zero semantics morphemes. For example, *everyone* consists of *every* and *one*, both elements in zero semantics. Another, more spectacular example is given in (13), from Dutch:

(13) Ik zag geen kip
      I saw no chicken
      'I didn't see any chickens/anything.'

As the translation of (13) indicates, *geen kip* may have a literal interpretation 'no chicken' or a universal quantification interpretation 'nothing'. In the latter case, *kip* has lost its referential meaning, and is in zero semantics. Since the determiner *geen* is also in zero semantics, it is again the collocation of two zero semantics morphemes that makes the universal quantification interpretation possible.

From this point of view it is understandable that *al* by itself cannot mean 'everything'. In order to make the universal quantification interpretation available, it needs a second zero semantics morpheme in its immediate environment. The genitive suffix in *alles* provides this second zero semantics morpheme. The grammaticality of (14) suggests that the relative determiner *wat* serves the same purpose:

(14) al wat ik wil
      all REL I want
      'Everything I want'

Wat provides the second zero semantics morpheme needed to generate the interpretation of universal quantification. The structure of universal quantifiers is illustrated in (15):

(15) a. *al*   ZS   (no interpretation)
      b. *al-les*   ZS + ZS   'everything'
      c. *al-le*   ZS + ZS   'all'
      d. *al-len*   ZS + ZS   'everyone'
      e. *al-wat*   ZS + ZS   'everything'
      f. *ieder-een* ZS + ZS   'everyone'

The contrast between (10a) and (11a) can now be explained. *Al* can only be used in combination with a relative clause, because the relative clause brings in the determiner needed to create the ZS+ZS configuration that is required for universal quantification. (*Alles* does not require a relative clause, since it is already a ZS+ZS structure, cf. (15).) Similarly, we understand why extraposition of the *wat*-clause (cf. (12)) is impossible with *al* but not with *alles*.

Consider how the two analyses of relative clauses, the adjunction analysis and the head raising analysis, allow us to describe *al wat* as a ZS+ZS collocation. We expect the analysis of relative clauses to provide us with a structural configuration in which the elements *al* and *wat* can interact. The relation between *al* and *wat* should be of a well-known type, ideally a specifier-head relation or a sisterhood relation (where 'sisterhood' is understood in structural terms, not in linear terms).

In the adjunction analysis, *wat* should probably be analyzed as an overt counterpart to the empty operator in (5). Assuming *al* to be the head noun, this yields the following structure:

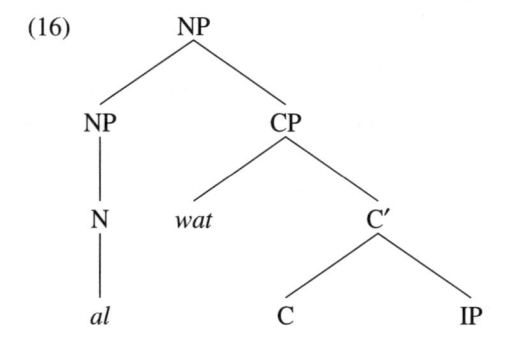

(16)
```
        NP
       /  \
      NP   CP
      |   /  \
      N  wat  C'
      |      /  \
      al    C    IP
```

The relation between *al* and *wat* in (16) is not one of the well-defined syntactic relations *sisterhood, specifier-head agreement, dominance, c-command,* or even *government*. This means that the adjunction analysis does not yield a structure that makes us understand how *al* and *wat* can combine to yield the interpretation of universal quantification.

Consider next the head raising analysis of relative clauses of the type in (14). As will be discussed in more detail below, *wat* is not a complementizer but a relative determiner, comparable to English *which*. Let us continue to assume that *al* is the head noun of the relative construction. In the head raising analysis, then, the head noun *al* is generated inside a DP_{REL}, which is itself generated as an argument inside the relative clause:

(17)   [$_{CP}$ [$_{IP}$ ik wil [$_{DP_{rel}}$ wat [$_{NP}$ al]]]]

The DP_{REL} is raised to a designated specifier position in the layered CP system in the left periphery of the relative clause (cf. (6)). As we will see below, the licensing position for a DP_{REL} headed by a relative pronoun with interrogative morphology is the specifier position of CP_2:

(18)   [$_{CP_2}$ [$_{DP_{rel}}$ wat [$_{NP}$ al]]$_i$ [$_{IP}$ ik wil t_i]]

Except for the labeling of the CP_2, this analysis is exactly the one proposed by Kayne for relative constructions with interrogative relative pronouns in English of the type in (19):

(19)   the man who I love

Kayne proposes that the order of the head noun *man* and the relative pronoun *who* is derived by moving the head noun to the specifier position of the DP_{REL}. Applying this final step to the structure in (18) yields the correct word order in the Dutch example (14) as well:

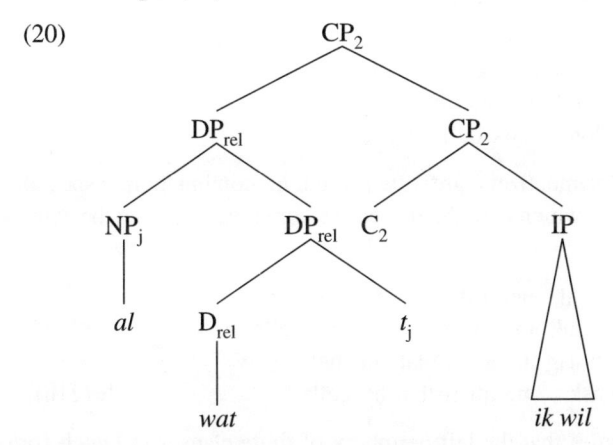

(20)

```
                      CP₂
                     /   \
                  DP_rel   CP₂
                  /   \    /  \
                NP_j  DP_rel  C₂   IP
                 |    /   \
                 al  D_rel  t_j
                      |
                     wat           ik wil
```

In the resulting configuration (20), *al* and *wat* are in a specifier-head relation. This is a well-established structural relation allowing elements to interact. We may hypothesize that this specifier-head relation makes it possible for the two zero semantics elements *al* and *wat* to combine, yielding the interpretation of universal quantification.

Thus, the head raising analysis of relative clauses allows us to understand why the elements *al* and *wat* may 'click', whereas the adjunction analysis leaves the collocational character of *al wat* a complete mystery.

In the remainder of this article, I will assume that the head raising analysis is essentially correct. We will return to the extraposition possibilities in the *al(les) wat*-construction (cf. (12)) in Section 4. In the next section, I will turn to a more detailed analysis of the structure of the left periphery of relative clauses in Dutch.

3. The three layers of CP

Dutch has three complementizers introducing finite clauses, *als*, *of*, and *dat* (see De Rooy 1965; Hoekstra 1993). In their core meanings, *als*, *of*, and *dat* are conditional/temporal, interrogative, and declarative, respectively:

(21) a. Ik ben weg *als* hij belt
I am away if/when he calls
'If/when he calls, I'm gone.'
b. Ik vraag me af *of* hij belt
I ask me off if he calls
'I wonder if he'll call.'
c. Ik denk niet *dat* hij belt
I think not that he calls
'I don't think he'll call.'

However, the complementizers are often used in combination, especially in substandard Dutch, in which case the respective core meanings may be somewhat bleached:

(22) a. Ik denk niet asdat[<alsdat] hij belt
I think not as-that he calls [=(21c)]
b. Ik vraag me af ofdat hij belt
I ask me off if-that he calls [=(21b)]

Hoekstra (1993) argues that the left periphery of finite clauses in Dutch consists of three "CP-layers" headed by *als*, *of*, and *dat*, respectively:

(23)

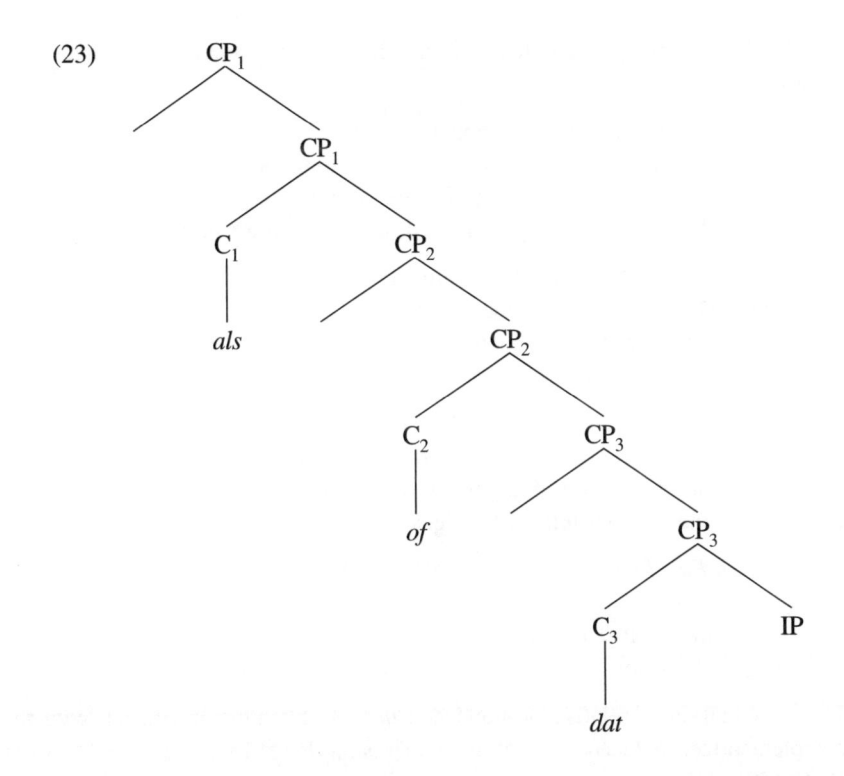

```
         CP₁
        /    \
             CP₁
            /    \
          C₁      CP₂
          |      /    \
         als          CP₂
                    /    \
                   C₂     CP₃
                   |     /    \
                  of          CP₃
                            /    \
                          C₃      IP
                          |
                         dat
```

Part of this structure has been argued for at various places in the recent literature (Müller & Sternefeld 1993; Zwart 1993; Hoekstra & Zwart 1994; Bianchi 1995; among others). Here, I merely intend to discuss whether a case can be made that the structure in (23) is (or may be) present in Dutch relative clauses in full fledged form.

I will discuss the three heads *als*, *of*, and *dat* one by one, starting with *dat*.

3.1 *Dat*

Dutch does not have the *that*-relative construction of English (*the man that I love*). That is, the relative pronoun is never fully replaced by the complementizer *dat*. However, there is abundant evidence of the presence of a complementizer *dat* in relative constructions in Dutch dialects. Unlike present day English, but like in earlier stages of English (cf. Mustanoja 1960: 197; Maling 1978), the complementizer *dat* cooccurs with a relative pronoun.

In the following examples, certain phonological peculiarities have been glossed over:

– *Aalsters* (South Brabant, Vanacker 1948: 143)
(24) Wie *dat* er   nou trouwt zijn stommerike
      REL that there now marries are stupid-ones
      'People who still get married these days are stupid.'

– *Twents* (East Netherlands, Wanink 1948: 33)
(25) D'n heer den *t*   doa geet
      the man REL that there goes
      'the gentlemen who goes over there'

– *Kruinings* (Zeeland, Dek 1934: 14)
(26) 't jongsje dat *à*   histeren van 't dek evalen is
      the kid   REL that yesterday of the deck fallen is
      'the kid that fell off the deck yesterday'

– *South East Flemish* (Teirlinck 1924: 186)
(27) al wa dad ek doe
      all REL that I do
      'All I do.'

The combination of relative pronoun and *that* is obligatory in Frisian, with the complementizer reduced to a clitic *'t* (Tiersma 1985: 132, see also De Boer 1950: 130–134):

(28) in frou   dy *'t* ik ken   [Frisian]
      a woman REL that I know

The complementizer *dat* always follows the relative pronoun, as well as all other complementizers that may appear in the relative construction. This confirms the hypothesis that the phrase headed by *dat* is lowest in the CP-system (24).

3.2 *Of*

Relative clauses with *of* in the dialects of Dutch are not nearly as common as relative clauses with *dat*. Still, a number of examples can be supplied:

– *Maastreechs* (Limburg, Dumoulin & Coumans 1986: 113)
(29) de vrouw die wad of iech gezeen had
      the woman REL what if I   seen had
      'the woman I had seen'

– *Katwijks* (Coast of Holland, Overdiep 1940: 230)
(30) wie of tie vis kóft, die   skreef tat óp
      REL if that fish bought that-one wrote that up
      'whoever bought that fish made a note of that'

– *Amsterdams* (North Holland, Hoekstra 1994: 316)
(31) de vrouw of die ik gezien heb
      the woman if REL I seen have
      'the woman I saw'

Hoekstra (1994: 316) notes that (29) appears to be the only example in the literature where *of* is preceded by a demonstrative relative pronoun. Thus, the following is not attested:

(32) *de vrouw die of ik gezien heb
       the woman REL if I seen have

I would like to propose that *diewad* in (29) is a single complex relative pronoun, headed by the *wh*-element *wat*. (A similar analysis is presumably correct for the Bavarian relative pronoun complex *derwo* (Bayer 1984).)

If so, we can make the generalization that *of* can only have *wh*-elements in its specifier position. This ties in with the use of *of* as interrogative complementizer in (21b).

If relative pronouns in Dutch are generally demonstrative, as seems to be the case, we may understand why the complementizer *of* is relatively rare in relative constructions. A potential exception is free relatives, which are introduced by *wh*-pronouns:

(33) Wie/*die dit leest is gek
      REL   this reads is crazy
      'Who reads this is crazy.'

The example from Katwijks (30) suggests that in this context we may find more instances of *of* in relative constructions.

The Amsterdams example in (31) is apparently extremely rare, perhaps because the relative particles (the complementizer *of* and the relative pronoun *die*) are distributed over two CP-projections (CP_2 and CP_3 in (23)).

We can also make the generalization that C_2 and C_3 provide designated landing sites for *wh*-words and demonstrative words (*d*-words), respectively. A similar conclusion was also reached in Hoekstra & Zwart (1994), where it is shown that long distance interrogatives allow the semantically anomalous appearance of a *wh*-complementizer in the embedded clause, and long distance topicalization constructions do not:

(34) a. Wie$_i$ denk je t_i (of) dat ik t_i gezien heb
    who think you   if that I   seen have
    'Who do you think I saw?'
  b. Dat$_i$ denk ik t_i (*of) dat ik t_i gezien heb
    that think I   if that I   seen have
    'I think I saw that.'

Of in (34b) is excluded because *dat* is a *d*-word rather than a *wh*-word, which uses the specifier position associated with *dat* (C$_3$) as its intermediate landing site. In (34a), on the other hand, *of* is allowed, suggesting that CP$_2$ is present, making available an intermediate landing site for the *wh*-element *wie*.

3.3 *Als*

As far as I have been able to ascertain, *als* is not used as a relative complementizer in the dialects of Dutch, nor in older stages of Dutch.[1] However, if Vercoullie (1925: 11) is correct in deriving *als* from *alzo*, where *al* is an intensifying prefix attached to *zo* 'so', it may be that we have to look for cases of *zo* rather than cases of *als*.

It turns out that *zo* is used as a relative complementizer in Middle Dutch, "semantically identical to the relative particle *dat*" (Verdam 1911: 553), apparently under High German influence (Stoett 1977: 33, see Paul 1920: 238 for High German):

– *Middle Dutch* (Stoett 1977: 33)
(35) die rike   so ontreet
   the rich-one REL rode off
   'the rich man who rode off'

– *High German* (Paul 1920: 238)
(36) bittet für den so euch beleidigen
   pray for those REL you insult
   'pray for those who insult you'

According to all sources, the use of *zo* as a relative complementizer in Middle Dutch is rare. Still, if we link *zo* via *als* to C$_1$, these few occurrences (and the more frequent High German ones) cease to be mysterious.

In Section 4, I will argue that C_1 is the head that hosts the head noun in its specifier position in restrictive relative clauses.

3.4 *Zero complementizers*

Even if none of the complementizers *als/zo*, *of*, and *dat* are present, it can be argued that at least part of the structure in (32) is there. In particular, certain effects of the presence of complementizers are felt, even if no overt complementizer is visible.

First, relative clauses with or without overt complementizers show the word order of embedded clauses:

(37) a. de man die ons *niet kon zien*
        the man REL us   not could see
        'the man who couldn't see us'
    b. ...dat die man ons *niet kon   zien*
        ...that that man us not could see
        '...that that man couldn't see us.'

(38) a. *de man die *kon   ons *niet zien*
        the man REL could us not see
    b. *...dat die man *kon   ons *niet zien*
        ...that that man could us not see

(39) a. De man *kon   ons *niet zien*
        the man could us not see
        'The man could not see us.'
    b. Die man die   *kon   ons *niet zien*
        the man that-one could us not see
        'The man could not see us.'

In (37), the finite verb *kon* 'could' follows the negation element *niet*, and is part of a verb cluster with the infinitive *zien* 'see' ((37a), relative clause, (37b), embedded complement clause). The examples in (38) show that the finite verb cannot move to the left in relative clauses (38a) and embedded clauses (38b). As can be seen, relative clauses and embedded clauses pattern alike, and differ from subject initial main clauses (39a) and left dislocation constructions (39b).

In this respect, relative clauses are comparable to embedded questions, which often do not have an overt complementizer:

(40) a. Ik vroeg me af wie (of dat) ons niet *kon*   zien
        I asked me off who if that us not could see
        'I wondered who couldn't see us.'

b. *Ik vroeg me af wie (of dat) *kon*   ons niet zien
   I asked me off who if that could us not see

In (40a), the finite verb *kon* 'could' appears to the right of the negation element *niet*, and is part of a verb cluster with the infinitive *zien* 'see'. In (40b) the finite verb has been moved out of the verb cluster to a position to the left of the negation element. The result is ungrammatical.

It has been a common notion of Germanic generative syntax since Koster (1975) and Den Besten (1977) that the absence of finite verb movement to the left is related to the presence of a complementizer. A complementizer blocks movement of the finite verb. I will not here discuss the various implementations of this idea (see Vikner 1995 and Zwart 1993, 1997 for recent discussion). But assuming the generalization to be correct, the embedded clause word order in relative clauses and embedded interrogatives suggests that a genuine complementizer is always present, even though the complementizer may be phonetically empty.

A second indication that relative clauses without overt complementizer feature an empty complementizer is the presence of complementizer agreement effects in relative clauses without overt complementizer. The following are three examples of complementizer agreement in relative clauses in Dutch dialects, one with (41) and two without overt complementizer (42)–(43) (*dast* in (42) is an inflected neuter relative pronoun, not a complementizer):

– *Kruinings* (Zeeland, Dek 1934: 15)
(41) a. die à   flink werkt
         REL that-SG hard works-SG
         'who works hard'
     b. die an   flink werken
         REL that-PL hard work-PL
         'who work hard'

– *Gronings* (North East Netherlands, Ter Laan 1953: 57)
(42) a. 't kind dat dood is
         the child REL dead is
         'the child that is dead'
     b. 't klaid dast   doar aan hest
         the clothes REL-2SG there on have-2SG
         'the clothes that you're wearing'

– *South Hollandic* (Van Haeringen 1939)
(43) a. een jonge die werke wil
       a   boy REL-SG work wants-SG
       'a guy who wants to work'
    b. jonges die-e werke wille
       boys REL-PL work want-PL
       'guys who want to work'

Hoekstra & Marácz (1989) and Zwart (1993, 1997) have argued that complementizer agreement is a morphological reflex of movement to C of a lower functional head, associated with subject-verb agreement (INFL of Chomsky 1986, AgrS of Chomsky 1991):

(44)   [$_{CP}$ C [$_{AgrSP}$ AgrS ...]]

If so, the complementizer agreement in (42)–(43) suggests that the relevant C-positions must be present, even if the complementizers themselves are not phonetically present. (See Zwart 1997: 256f for more discussion.)

Note that the situation where C is occupied by a phonetically empty complementizer appears to be the unmarked situation in relative clauses in Dutch and dialects of Dutch.

3.5 *Conclusion*

In this section I have discussed the three-layered CP hypothesis of Hoekstra (1993). It turns out that there is reason to believe that relative clauses in Dutch potentially involve all three complementizers *als (zo)*, *of*, and *dat*. This is clearest with *of* and *dat*, which appear regularly in the left periphery of relative clauses in dialects of Dutch. *Als/zo* does not occur overtly in relative clauses in (dialects of) present day Dutch, but possibly the element *so* appearing in relative clauses in Middle Dutch must be equated with the C$_1$ complementizer *als*.

The complementizers *als/zo*, *of*, and *dat* are morphologically easily distinguished from the various relative pronouns appearing in relative constructions. These are all either demonstrative (*die* nonneuter and plural, *dat* neuter singular, *daar* locative) or interrogative (*wie, wat, waar*). These demonstrative and interrogative pronouns appear in topicalizations/left dislocations (cf. (39b)) and *wh*-questions as well, and are considered to occupy the specifier position of a [+d] CP and a [+wh] CP, respectively (Hoekstra & Zwart 1994; Zwart 1997;

Zwart, 1998). We therefore get a clear picture of the status of the various elements appearing in relative constructions in Dutch:

(45)   [$_{DP}$ D [$_{CP_1}$ C$_1$ [$_{CP_2}$ *wie/wat/waar of* [$_{CP_3}$ *die/dat/daar dat* [$_{IP}$ ...]]]]]

The only part of (45) that is not as clear is the status of CP_1. We will turn to a discussion of this highest CP-level next.

4. The position of the head noun

4.1 *Recapitulation*

Let us recapitulate the various steps in the derivation of relative constructions in Dutch, according to the head raising analysis.

- Step 1: The relative clause is generated as the sister of the determiner which is intuitively associated with the head noun:

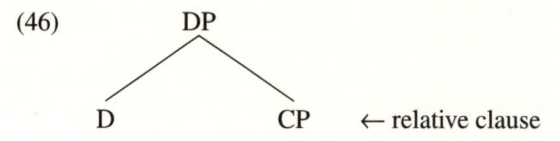

(46)   DP
       / \
      D   CP   ← relative clause

- Step 2: The head noun is generated inside a DP$_{REL}$ which is itself generated as an argument of the verb in the relative clause:

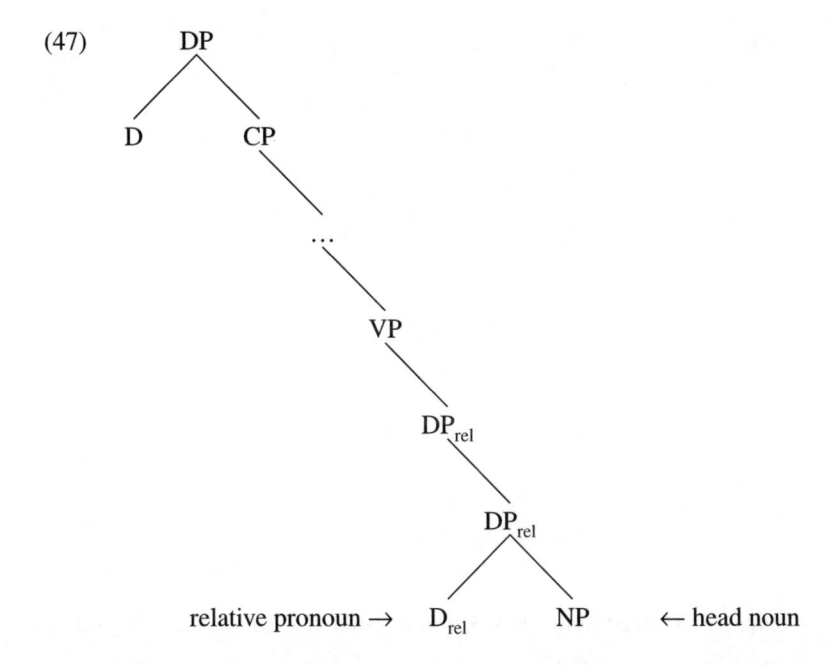

(47)
```
         DP
        /  \
       D    CP
             \
             ...
               \
                VP
                 \
                  DP_rel
                    \
                    DP_rel
                   /    \
                  D_rel   NP
```
relative pronoun →   D_rel   NP   ← head noun

- Step 3: The relative determiner (relative pronoun) can be either of the interrogative type [carrying the feature [+wh]) or of the demonstrative type (carrying the feature [+d]). These features trigger movement to the specifier position of either a [+wh] CP (CP_2 in (23)) or a [+d] CP (CP_3 in (23)):

(48)

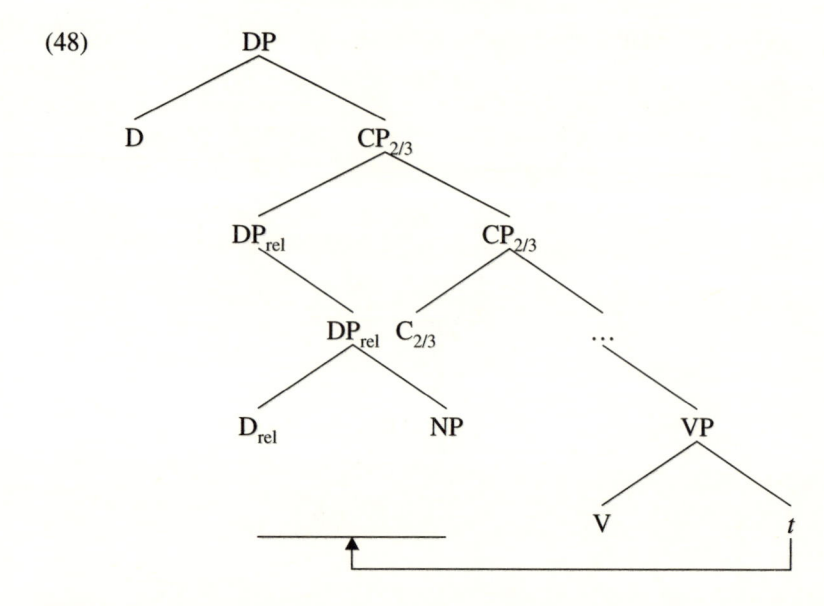

```
              DP
             /  \
            D    CP_{2/3}
                /      \
            DP_rel      CP_{2/3}
            /    \      /     \
        DP_rel  C_{2/3}        ...
        /   \                   |
     D_rel   NP                 VP
                               /  \
                              V    t
```

— Step 4: The head noun moves to the specifier position of DP_{REL} (cf. (20)):

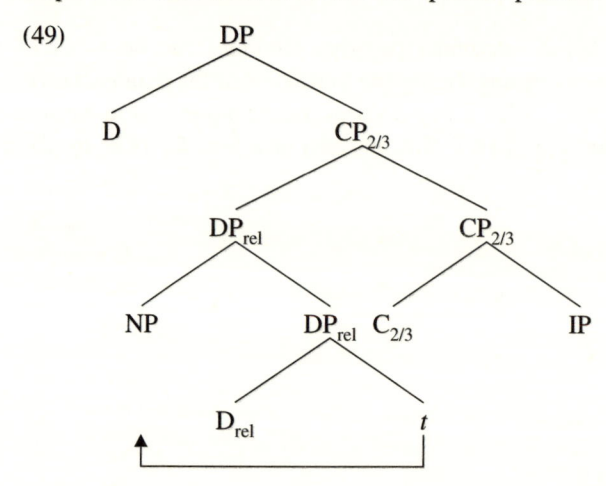

(49)

```
              DP
             /  \
            D    CP_{2/3}
                /      \
            DP_rel      CP_{2/3}
            /    \      /     \
          NP   DP_rel C_{2/3}  IP
                /  \
             D_rel  t
```

These steps yield the correct order of elements in the relative construction:

(50) a. det. < noun < rel.pron. < comp. < rest
     b. *de*   *man* *die*   *(dat)* *ik zag*
        the   man   who   that   I saw

So far, the analysis follows Kayne (1994), with the exception of the further articulation of the CP-system.

However, as also argued in Bianchi (1999), there is reason to believe that a final step must be added to the derivation. This step takes the head noun out of the DP_{REL} into the specifier of a higher functional projection. I will argue here and in the next section that this functional projection is CP_1 of the structure in (23):

– Step 5: The head noun moves to the specifier position of CP_1:

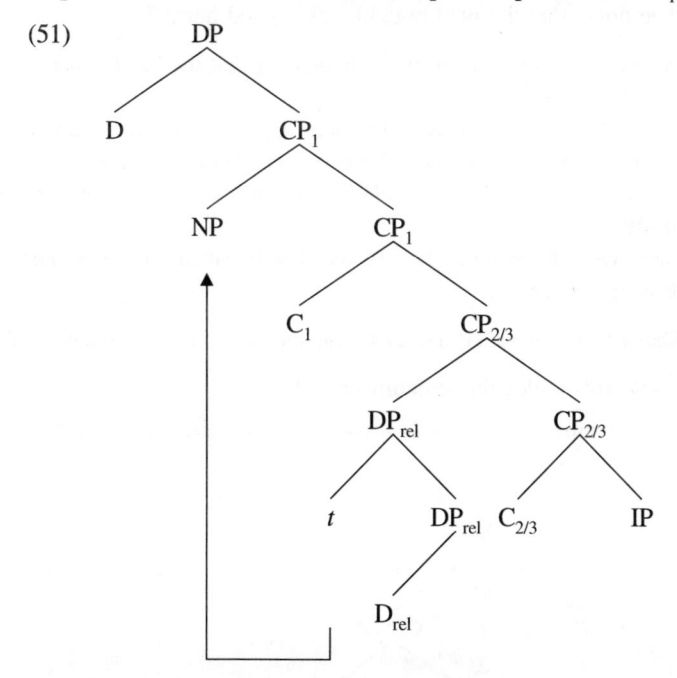

(51)

[Tree diagram: DP dominates D and CP_1; CP_1 dominates NP and CP_1; inner CP_1 dominates C_1 and $CP_{2/3}$; $CP_{2/3}$ dominates DP_{rel} and $CP_{2/3}$; DP_{rel} dominates t and DP_{rel}; inner DP_{rel} dominates D_{rel}; inner $CP_{2/3}$ dominates $C_{2/3}$ and IP. Arrow shows movement from inside DP_{rel} to NP.]

The following subsection lists three arguments in support of the additional movement of the head noun to $SpecCP_1$.

4.2 Arguments for movement of the head noun to SpecCP₁

4.2.1 Head final relative clauses in Latin

This argument is due to Bianchi (1999: 193).

One of the key assets of the head raising analysis is that it allows for a unified description of head initial and head final relative clauses. Head initial relative clauses are of the familiar type discussed so far: the head noun occupies a left peripheral position inside the relative clause (or, in the adjunction analysis, precedes the relative clause). In head final relative clauses, the head noun occupies a right peripheral position in the relative clause (or follows the relative clause, cf. Cole 1987 and Basilico 1996 for discussion). The following is an example from Quechua (Cole 1987):

(52) nuna ranti-shaq-n bestya alli bestya-m ka-rqo-n
man buy-PERFECT-3 horse-NOM good horse-EVID be-PST-3
'The horse that the man bought was a good horse.'

Clauses in Quechua are strictly verb final, suggesting that the head noun *bestya* 'horse' has been displaced.[2]

Kayne (1994: 96) proposes to describe head final relative constructions as involving the same derivational steps as head initial relative constructions, with an additional step moving the IP of the relative clause into the specifier position of the topmost DP.

For reasons that will become clear below, I will list this IP-movement as step 6, i.e. following step 5:

– Step 6: The relative clause IP moves to the specifier position of the top DP.

Starting from (49), this yields the structure in (53):

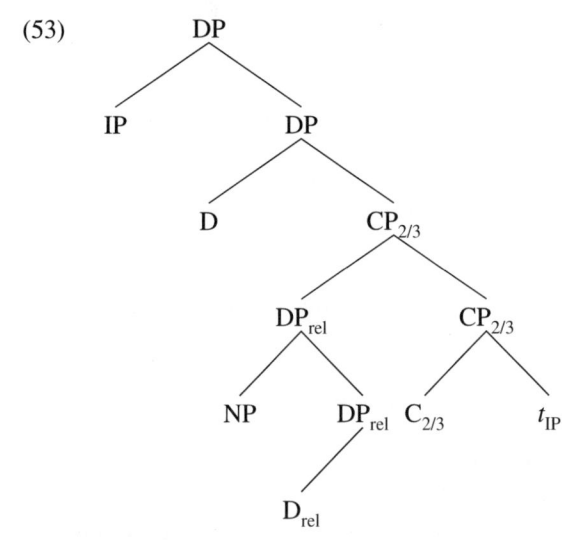

(53)

[tree diagram: DP dominating IP and DP; lower DP dominates D and CP$_{2/3}$; CP$_{2/3}$ dominates DP$_{rel}$ and CP$_{2/3}$; DP$_{rel}$ dominates NP and DP$_{rel}$; lower DP$_{rel}$ dominates D$_{rel}$; lower CP$_{2/3}$ dominates C$_{2/3}$ and t_{IP}]

This changes the order of elements from (50) to (54):

(54) a. rest < det. < noun < rel.pron. < comp.
     b. ik zag   de   man   die   dat
        I saw   the   man   who   that

The determiner, the relative pronoun (D_{REL}), and the complementizer are not expressed in the Quechua construction. Apart from that, the Quechua word order matches the word order in (54):

(55) a. rest   < (det) < noun   < (rel.pron) < (comp)
     b. nuna rantishaqn   bestya
        man bought   horse

This analysis predicts, though, that in languages where the relative pronoun is overtly expressed, it will follow the head noun in a head final relative construction. This can be tested in Latin, which has both head initial (56a) and head final (56b) relative constructions:[3]

(56) a. odorare   hanc   pallam   quam   ego habeo
        smell-IMP   this-ACC   mantle-ACC   which-ACC   I   hold
        'Smell this mantle which I am holding here.'
     b. odorare   hanc   quam   ego habeo   pallam
        smell-IMP   this-ACC   which-ACC   I   hold   mantle-ACC
        'Smell this mantle which I am holding here.'

Let us ignore the demonstrative pronoun *hanc* 'this', which must be generated higher than DP if this analysis of head final relative clauses is to be successful.

In the analysis proposed by Kayne (1994), (56b) must be derived from (56a) by moving what we have indicated as the 'rest' of the relative clause to SpecDP, stranding the head noun in SpecCP (as illustrated in (53)):

(57) a. rest < (det)   < noun   < rel.pron. < (comp)
     b. ego habeo   pallam   quam
        I hold   mantle   which

However, if the rest of the relative clause equals IP, we predict the word order in (57), which is ungrammatical, and we fail to derive the correct word order of (56a).

This suggests that the 'rest' of the relative clause comprises more than IP, and includes at least the relative pronoun (D_{REL}) *quam*. But in the structure in (53), *quam* sits in the specifier position of CP_2 (*quam* being a determiner of the [+wh] type), together with the head noun *pallam*. In other words, *quam* does not form a constituent with the IP to the exclusion of the head noun.

The additional movement of the head noun to a higher specifier position proposed as step 5 above (following Bianchi 1999) overcomes this problem. If step 6 applies to the structure in (51), the constituent moving to SpecDP to yield the head final relative construction could be $CP_{2/3}$, stranding the head noun in the specifier position of CP_1:

(58) *hanc* [$_{DP}$ [$_{CP_2}$ [$_{DP_{rel}}$ t_i *quam*]$_j$ C_2 [$_{IP}$ *ego habeo* t_j]]$_k$ D [$_{CP_1}$ *pallam* C_1 t_k]]

This forms the first argument supporting movement of the head noun out of DP_{REL} to the specifier position of CP_1.

4.2.2 *Extraposition in Dutch*

A second argument supporting additional movement of the head noun derives from the possibility or impossibility of relative clause extraposition in Dutch.

Recall from the discussion of relative clauses headed by *al* versus *alles* (both meaning 'everything', see Section 2), that relative clause extraposition is allowed only with *alles*, not with *al*:

(59) a. Ik heb alles/al wat ik wil
         I have all   what I want
         'I have everything I want.'
     b. ...dat ik alles/*al heb wat ik wil
         ...that I all   have what I want
         '...that I have everything I want.'

In Section 2, I have described *al wat* as sitting in a specifier-head configuration inside the DP_{REL}, which has itself moved to the specifier position of CP_2. See the structure in (20), repeated here as (60):

(60)

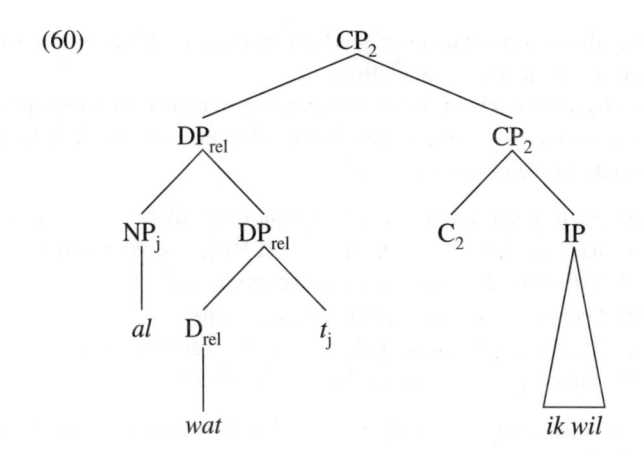

```
                    CP₂
                   /   \
              DP_rel    CP₂
             /    \    /   \
          NP_j  DP_rel C₂   IP
           |    /   \       /\
           al D_rel  t_j   ik wil
              |
              wat
```

It is clear from this structure that the sequence *wat ik wil* 'what I want' does not form a constituent to the exclusion of the head noun *al* 'all'. This immediately explains the impossibility of extraposition with *al* in (59b).

At the same time, this conclusion implies that (60) does not correctly describe the structure of the variant of (59) with *alles*, since the construction with *alles* does allow extraposition of the string *wat ik wil*.

The proposed additional movement of the head noun *alles* to the specifier position of CP₁ again overcomes the problem:

(61) [$_{DP}$ [$_{CP_1}$ [$_{NP}$ *alles*]$_i$ C$_1$ [$_{CP_2}$ [$_{DP_{rel}}$ t_i *wat*]$_j$ C$_2$ [$_{IP}$ *ik wil* t_j]]]]

Starting from the structure in (61), extraposition can be derived by moving CP₂, stranding the head noun *alles* in SpecCP₁.

As before, this derivation is excluded with *al* because *al* and *wat* must be in a specifier-head agreement configuration in order for *al* to be interpretable as contributing to universal quantification.

The status of extraposition in the framework of Kayne (1994) is somewhat unclear. For reasons that do not concern us here, the framework disallows rightward movement. Kayne (1994) proposes to describe extraposition as involving leftward movement of the head noun, stranding the 'extraposed' clause:

(62) dat ik *alles*   heb [*t* wat ik wil]
      that I everything have   what I want
      'that I have everything I want'

This analysis differs from the one proposed here, in that extraposition is derived by the additional movement of the head noun itself, whereas in the analysis proposed here, the additional movement of the head noun takes place within the relative clause, and merely feeds extraposition.

As Koster (1996) shows, Dutch offers compelling evidence that extraposition is not derived by leftward movement of the head noun. This is clear from constructions in which the head noun is in a PP:

(63) a. Hij heeft gesproken [met [de [[man die] alles wist]]]
he has spoken with the man REL everything knew
'He talked to the man who knew everything.'
b. Hij heeft met de man gesproken die alles wist
he has with the man spoken REL everything knew
'He talked to the man who knew everything.'

The brackets in (63a) reflect Kayne's analysis. It is clear that leftward movement of *met de man* 'with the man' in order to derive (63b) involves movement of a non-constituent. The analysis proposed here, in which the head noun has been moved out of the DP$_{REL}$ headed by the relative pronoun *die*, does not affect this conclusion: movement of *met de man* would still involve movement of a non-constituent.

If extraposition is to be derived via leftward movement, the only possibility seems to be that the relative clause, including the relative pronoun, moves to the left, skipping the head noun and the top determiner (as well as the preposition in (63)), followed again by another leftward movement of the PP just skipped by the relative clause (see Barbiers 1995 for discussion of the various possibilities):

(64) a. [CP$_{2/3}$ [PP P [DP D [CP1 NP t]]]]

b. [PP P [DP D [CP1 NP t]]] [CP$_{2/3}$ t]

Such a derivation can only succeed if the head noun has been moved out of the DP$_{REL}$ before 'extraposition' applies. The additional movement of the head noun to SpecCP$_1$ proposed here achieves just that.

4.2.3 *Relative constructions with* amba *in Kiswahili*
A third argument supporting the proposed movement of the head noun out of DP$_{REL}$ to SpecCP$_1$ is provided by the order of elements in the Kiswahili relative construction with *amba* (cf. Barrett-Keach 1985).

In Kiswahili (a Bantu language spoken in Tanzania, and in large parts of

East Africa as a *lingua franca*), relative clauses contain a pronominal element consisting of a subject marker and a suffix -*o*. The subject marker is a gender/number marker also used on the verb to mark (noun class) agreement with the subject. In relative clauses, the subject marker agrees with the head noun. The -*o* ending appears to have a deictic, referential function (cf. Polomé 1967: 60).

The following are examples of these pronominal elements taken from various noun classes:

(65)   class   subject marker   relative element
     a.   2   wa   o   < wa+o
     b.   4   i   yo < i+o
     c.   7   ki   cho < ki+o

I will refer to the relative element as 'relative pronoun' (pace Barrett-Keach 1985: 43f).

The relative pronoun is suffixed to what appears to be a relative complementizer *amba*:[4]

(66)   kitabu amba cho wa-li-ki-som-a
        book$_7$ COMP REL$_7$ SM$_2$-PST-OM$_7$-read-IND
        'the book they read'

In (66), the head noun *kitabu* 'book' agrees with the relative pronoun *cho* and with the object marker *ki* on the verb.

Amba is taken to derive from the root *amb* 'say'. It is apparently morphologically related to *kwamba*, which is used as a complementizer, and may actually surface in relative clauses:

(67)   kitabu amba cho kwamba wa-li-ki-som-a
        book$_7$ COMP REL$_7$ COMP   SM$_2$-PST-OM$_7$-read-IND
        'the book they read'

Barrett-Keach (1985) proposes that *amba* still functions as a verb for phrase structure purposes, projecting a VP and selecting an embedded clause complement. But in the absence of *morphological* evidence that *amba* functions as a verb, I prefer to treat it on a par with *kwamba*, as one of the complementizers in the CP system.

Applying the head raising analysis to the Kiswahili *amba* relative construction leads to the following description. The relative determiner D$_{REL}$ is probably best represented by the relative pronoun. The various steps in the derivation listed in Section 4.1 can then be illustrated as follows:

(68) a. D *amba kwamba walikisoma cho kitabu*   [steps 1 and 2]
      b. D *amba [cho kitabu]$_i$ kwamba walikisoma t$_i$*   [step 3]
      c. D *amba [[kitabu]$_j$ cho t$_j$] kwamba walikisoma*   [step 4]

These four steps taken from Kayne (1994) do not yield the correct order of elements, as *amba* and the relative pronoun *cho* are still separated by the head noun *kitabu*. The proposed fifth step takes the head noun to the specifier of *amba*, yielding the correct order of elements:

(68) D *[kitabu]$_k$ amba [t$_k$ cho] kwamba walikisoma*   [step 5]

This suggests that the derivation of relative clauses involves a step moving the head noun to the left of the complementizer.

In the description proposed here, *kwamba* and *amba* are both complementizers, *kwamba* presumably comparable to the Dutch [+d] C$_3$ complementizer *dat* (in view of the deictic/referential nature of the relative pronoun in its specifier position), and *amba* comparable to the Dutch C$_1$ complementizer *als/zo*. I have no evidence that *amba* should be located in C$_1$, but the only alternative would seem to be that *amba* is in C$_2$. Then if DP$_{REL}$ (including the head noun and the relative pronoun) is moved to SpecCP$_3$ in step 3 (cf. (68)), we would still have to conclude that some movement takes the head noun out of DP$_{REL}$ across *amba*.

Alternatively, still pursuing the idea that *amba* is not in C$_1$ but in C$_2$, DP$_{REL}$ could be moved to SpecCP$_2$, i.e. to the specifier of *amba* itself. This would make it very difficult to derive the correct order *amba-cho*. The required movements are illustrated in (69), neither of them very attractive:

(69)

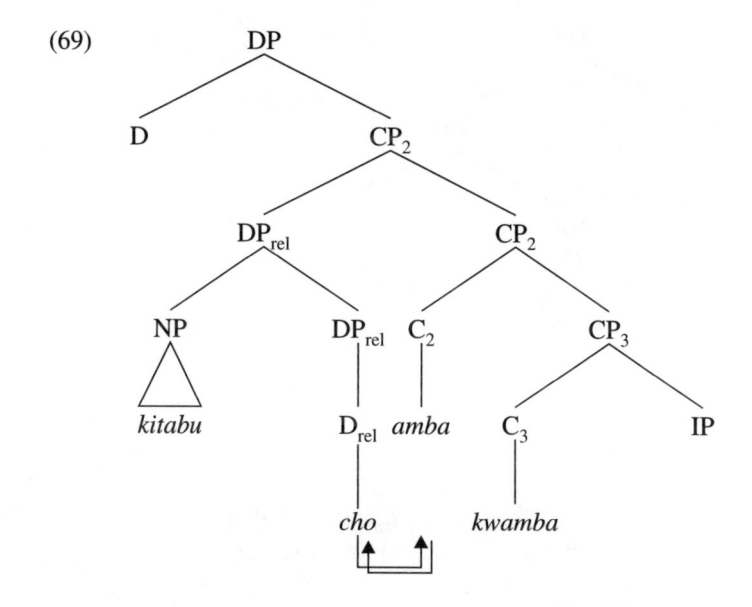

```
              DP
             /  \
            D    CP₂
                /    \
             DP_rel    CP₂
             /   \     /   \
           NP   DP_rel C₂   CP₃
           |    |      |    /  \
         kitabu D_rel amba C₃   IP
                |          |
                cho      kwamba
```

In (69), either the head C_2 moves and adjoins to the head D_{REL} of the element in its specifier position, or vice versa. In both cases, the moved element fails to c-command its trace.

In the analysis proposed here, the required movement of *cho* to *amba* does not incur such problems:

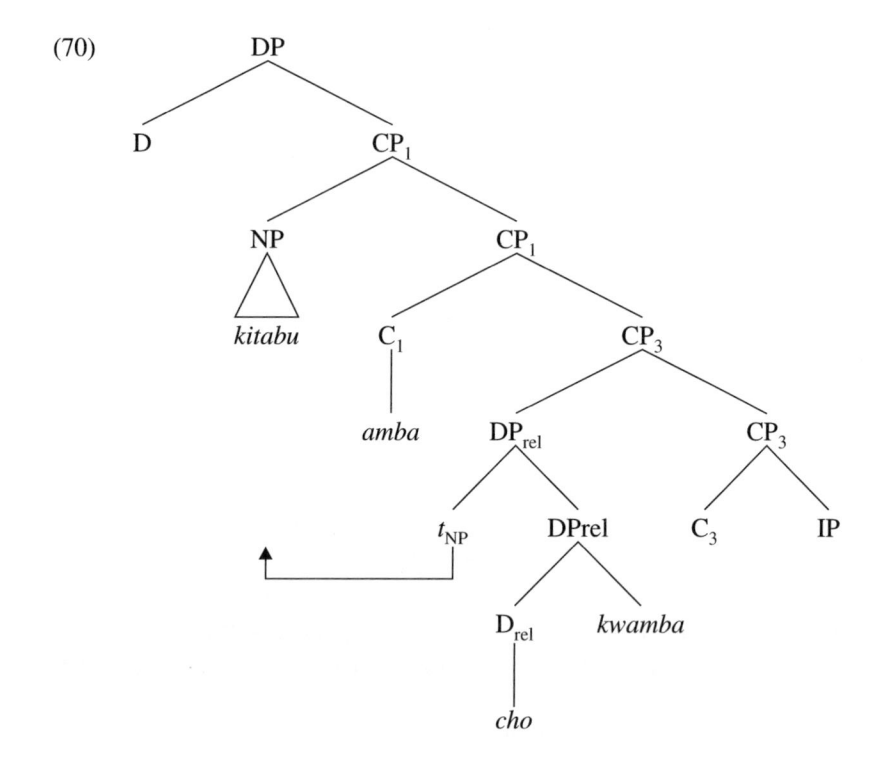

```
                    DP
                   /  \
                  D    CP₁
                      /   \
                    NP     CP₁
                    △    /   \
                  kitabu C₁    CP₃
                         |    /  \
                        amba DPrel  CP₃
                            /  \   /  \
                          tNP  DPrel C₃  IP
                               /  \
                             Drel  kwamba
                              |
                             cho
```

In (70), *cho* adjoins to *amba*, the moved category c-commanding its trace along the lines of Baker (1988). Alternatively, *cho* and *amba* are combined through cliticization.

Thus, the *amba* relative clause construction of Kiswahili is readily described in terms of the head raising analysis of Kayne (1994), provided the analysis is supplemented with the additional movement of the head noun to the highest SpecCP proposed by Bianchi (1999) and here.[5]

4.3 Conclusion

In this section I have argued, following Bianchi (1999), that the head noun in relative constructions occupies the specifier position of the highest CP in the relative clause, and has been moved out of the DP_REL in which it was generated.

In the final section, I would like to discuss the semantic contribution of the CP₁ projection proposed here.

5. CP₁ as a 'Restriction Phrase'

5.1 *A semantic trigger for movement of the head noun to CP₁*

So far, we have been reasonably successful in describing the elements appearing in relative clause constructions in Dutch in terms of their morphological properties.

As we have seen above, relative pronouns in Dutch can be of the *wh*-type (*wie-wat-waar*) or of the *d*-type (*die-dat-daar*). Likewise, the complementizers appearing in relative clauses can be of the *wh*-type (*of*) or of the *d*-type (*dat*). In Dutch, *wh*-elements and *d*-elements move to a position in the CP-system obligatorily (see Zwart, 1998, for the obligatory movement of *d*-elements in so-called topicalization constructions). As argued in Hoekstra & Zwart (1994), these elements target designated positions in the CP-system: *wh*-elements move to the specifier position of a *wh*-CP, and *d*-elements move to the specifier position of a *d*-CP. We have seen above that the same is presumably true in relative clauses, in which a DP (the DP$_{REL}$) headed by a *wh*-relative pronoun or a *d*-relative pronoun moves to the specifier position of a *wh*-CP (CP$_2$) or a *d*-CP (CP$_3$), respectively.

Note that relative clauses in Dutch never show *wh*-relative pronouns and *d*-relative pronouns appearing at the same time:

(71) *wie die dit leest is gek
 REL REL this reads is crazy

The only exception is, again, the Maastreechs combination *diewat*, which I have suggested above is a complex *wh*-relative pronoun.

The proposed analysis is a straightforward implementation of the "split CP hypothesis" as discussed in Zwart (1993), Hoekstra & Zwart (1994), Müller & Sternefeld (1993), and elsewhere.

The semantic effects of the movement of the DP$_{REL}$ to CP are familiar from *wh*-movement and left dislocation/topicalization. The movement is a standard procedure for turning a proposition into a property (*lambda abstraction*). In the traditional adjunction analysis, movement of the empty operator serves the same semantic purpose (cf. (5)). Being a property, the relative clause denotes a set which intersects with the set denoted by the head noun (cf. Partee 1975: 229, Larson & Segal 1995: 256).

There is, however, an important difference between the traditional adjunction analysis and the head raising analysis. In the adjunction analysis, the head noun is outside the relative clause, so that the head noun and the relative clause are independent constituents. As a result, the mapping from syntactic structure to semantic interpretation is straightforward, two independent constituents combining to yield the required intersection of sets.

In the head raising analysis, the head noun is a proper part of the relative clause, sitting in the specifier position of the extracted category DP_{REL}. Moreover, what is intuitively regarded as the relative clause, the combination of the relative pronoun (D_{REL}) and the relative clause IP, is not a constituent excluding the head noun. This makes it impossible to straightforwardly derive the interpretation of the relative construction as involving an intersection of two sets. The syntactic structure does not provide a situation in which the relative clause modifies the head noun.

I would like to propose that the additional movement of the head noun out of DP_{REL} to the specifier position of CP_1, argued for in Section 4, serves to create a configuration in which the relative clause and the head noun can again be interpreted as two independent constituents, one restricting the interpretation of the other via set intersection, just like in the traditional adjunction analysis. In other words, movement of the head noun sets up a situation in which the head noun and the relative clause are independent constituents, each representing a set, and in which the interpretation of the relative construction involves the intersection of these two sets.

I will argue in the next subsection that CP_1, headed by *als/zo* in Dutch, is the typical functional projection for expressing the relation of restriction that is characteristic of restrictive relative clauses. If this is correct, we may conjecture that C_1 attracts the head noun for semantic reasons: it needs an element in its specifier position in order to perform its function as a 'restrictor'. In this respect, C_1 differs from $C_{2/3}$, which appear to attract elements to their specifier positions for purely morphological reasons.

5.2 C_1 *as a Restrictor*

We have assumed that CP_1 in Dutch is headed by the complementizers *als* 'if' and/or *zo* 'so'. Consider how *als* and *zo* are employed outside relative constructions.

Als is used in comparisons (72) and in conditional/temporal clauses (73):

(72) a. groen *als* gras
       green as grass
       'green as grass'
   b. Amerika *als* vredestichter
       America as peace maker
       'America as peace maker'

(73) a. *Als* hij belt (dan) ben ik weg
      if he calls then am I away
      'If he calls, I'm out.'
   b. *Als* ik in Phoenix ben (dan) is zij al wakker
      if I in Phoenix am then is she already awake
      'By the time I get to Phoenix she'll be awake already.'

Zo is used as a manner demonstrative (74), as a (deictic) extent marker (75) and, again, in conditional clauses (76):

(74) *Zo* moet je dat doen
    so must you that do
    'That is the way to do it.'

(75) a. *zo* groen
      so green
      'that green'
   b. *zo* groen dat het pijn doet aan je ogen
      so green that it pain does to your eyes
      'so green that it hurts your eyes'

(76) *Zo* je wilt kun je langskomen
    so you want can you along-come
    'In case you want, you can stop by.'

Distal demonstratives in Dutch are generally characterized by an initial *d-*:

(77) a. person   *die*
   b. thing   *dat*
   c. time   *dan*
   d. place   *daar*

The original distal manner demonstrative was *dus* 'thus'. This leads me to believe that the demonstrative use of *zo* in (74) is a later development. I will ignore it here.

In its other uses, *zo*, in combination with its complement, measures out an extent. In (75) the unnamed subject of *groen* is only green to a certain extent (usually given by deixis or information available in the discourse, or, in the case of (75b), supplied by the result clause). In (76) the proper paraphrase is that the person addressed by the speaker may stop by 'to the extent that (the situation is such that) he wants to'.

More generally, a conditional clause specifies a crucial point at which a consequence starts to apply. This is also true of the conditional clauses with *als* in (73). As indicated, the consequence may be introduced by the temporal demonstrative element *dan*, lending the construction the appearance of a correlative construction (cf. (78)):

(78) Wie dit leest die is gek
      who this reads DEM is crazy
      'Who reads this is crazy.'

Finally, *als* in (72) also acts as an extent delimitor. For instance, (72b) can be paraphrased as 'America in its role of peace maker, to the extent that it is a peace maker'.

Let us therefore assume that the head of CP_1 serves to indicate the extent to which whatever is in its complement (the relative clause) applies to whatever is in its specifier (the head noun). Thus, (79a) is paraphrased as (79b):

(79) a. the man I saw
      b. the [man to the extent that I saw him]

This is very close to the *such that* paraphrase of restrictive relative clauses employed by Montague (1973) and Partee (1975).[6]

The semantic properties of *als/zo* suggest that CP_1 is a 'Restrictor Phrase', illustrated in (80), where β restricts the interpretation of α (in a pretheoretical sense):

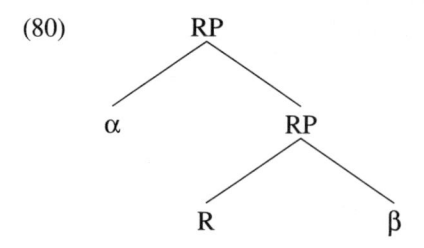

(80)
```
        RP
       /  \
      α    RP
          /  \
         R    β
```

I will assume that restrictive relative clauses are defined by a the configuration in (80), where α = the head noun and β = the relative clause. This provides the trigger for extraction of α, the head noun, out of DP_{REL}, which occupies the specifier position of β.[7]

5.3 Conclusion

In this section I have argued that the semantic interpretation of restrictive relative constructions provides an additional argument in support of the movement of the head noun to $SpecCP_1$ proposed by Bianchi (1999).

The interpretation of restrictive relative constructions requires that the top determiner, the head noun, and the relative clause enter into the semantic computation as independent constituents. In the head raising analysis of Kayne (1994), the head noun is entangled with the remainder of the relative clause, making a straightforward semantic interpretation seemingly impossible. Sub-extraction of out the $CP_{2/3}$ restores the head noun as an independent constituent, ready to contribute to the interpretation of the relative construction via interaction with the relative clause, and, ultimately, the outer determiner.

6. Conclusion

In this paper, I have proposed a description of restrictive relative constructions in Dutch in terms of the head raising analysis of Kayne (1994).

In the analysis proposed here, the head noun is generated inside the relative clause, as part of a DP headed by a demonstrative or interrogative determiner (the D_{REL}, traditionally known as the relative pronoun). The relative clause as a whole is a sister to a determiner (referred to as the top determiner or the outer determiner), as proposed by Kayne (1994). The head noun ends up in a position right adjacent to the outer determiner as an accidental consequence of two crucial derivational steps. First, the DP_{REL} moves to the specifier position of a projection in the CP-system matching its morphological features. Thus, if the D_{REL} is of the *wh*-type, the DP_{REL} is attracted by a [+wh] complementizer, and if the D_{REL} is of the *d*-type, the DP_{REL} is attracted by a [+d] complementizer. We have seen that the corresponding *wh*-complementizer and *d*-complementizer do show up in (dialects of) Dutch, always immediately following the [+wh] or [+d] DP_{REL}. Secondly, the head noun moves out of the DP_{REL} to the specifier position of a higher CP, the highest projection inside the relative clause. I have argued that this is the CP identified by Hoekstra (1993) as the highest layer of the Dutch CP-system, headed by *als* (and, in relative clauses, by *zo*).

I have presented several arguments for this movement of the head noun to $SpecCP_1$, which was already proposed by Bianchi (1999). The arguments all hinge on the circumstance that the movement of the head noun allows us to treat the relative clause as a constituent excluding the head noun. Syntactically, this makes it possible to describe various movement processes in a more satisfactory way (for example in the derivation of head final relative constructions and in the analysis of extraposition). Semantically, the separation of the head noun and the relative clause allows for the various elements of the relative construction (the outer determiner, the head noun, and the relative clause) to interact as independent constituents, yielding a straightforward semantic interpretation.

Relative constructions in (dialects of) Dutch have many fascinating properties, most of which I have not been able to address in this paper. However, I hope that the discussion presented here contributes to illuminating one aspect of the relative clause construction in Dutch, namely the morphology of the relative pronominals and complementizers, and the order in which these elements appear.

Notes

1. Bob de Jong (p.c.) suggests that the *à* element in the Krunings complementizer *dat à* in (26) is really *als* rather than *dat*, as I have assumed. The data in Dek (1934) suggest that *à* stands for both *dat* and *als* (as well as for *al* 'already', in fact). However, Dek (1934: 14) consistently glosses *à* in relative clauses as 'dat'.
2. In the glosses, EVID = evidential, NOM = nominative. Quechua also has a head internal relative construction in which the head noun precedes *ranti-shaq-n* 'bought', albeit in accusative rather than nominative case. I will not discuss head internal relative clauses here, which Kayne (1994: 96) analyzes as a subcase of head final relative clauses.
3. In the glosses, IMP = imperative, ACC = accusative.
4. Kiswahili has two other ways of constructing relative clauses, which do not involve the element *amba*. These constructions involve either infixation or suffixation of the relative pronoun to the verb. I will not discuss these constructions here.

    The following abbreviations are used in the glosses: SM = subject marker, OM = object marker, IND = indicative mood. The noun classes of the various elements are indicated in subscript.
5. The relative clause constructions without *amba* can be described along similar lines. The difference with the *amba* construction is that now a verbal element must be assumed to move to C_1, either an auxiliary verb (in the so-called tensed relative), consisting of a subject marker, a tense/aspect marker, and suffixed with the relative pronoun (*kitabu wa-li-cho ki-som-a* 'book SM-PST-REL OM-read-IND'), or a main verb without tense markers (in the so-called general relative), consisting of subject and object agreement markers and a verbal root, and again suffixed with the relative pronoun (*kitabu wa-ki-som-a-cho* 'book SM-OM-read-IND-REL'. This analysis presupposes that tensed verbs in Kiswahili are actually combinations of an auxiliary and a main verb, only the former moving to C_1 in tensed relative clauses. There is some evidence of a prosodic nature in Barrett-Keach (1985: 37f) that this is correct, but the position overall appears to be highly contentious. Evidence for verb movement to C in tensed relative clauses is provided by the obligatory subject-verb inversion in these constructions (Bokamba 1976; Vitale 1981: 98), but the circumstance that both the auxiliary part and the main verb part precede the subject in this case may be a problem for the analysis suggested in this note.
6. Partee (1975: 230) notes that the *such that* paraphrase "can be defended linguistically on the grounds that precisely analogous forms are perfectly colloquial in some languages," referring to Nadkarni (1970). If we are correct, the restrictive relative constructions with *so* in older stages of Dutch and High German (cf. (35)–(36)) illustrate the same point. Note that none of the High German examples given by Paul (1920: 238f) appear to be appositives, suggesting that the *so*-construction is indeed restricted to restrictive relative clauses. Another language

employing an overt extent delimitor as a relative complementizer is Norwegian (*som* 'like', cf. Taraldsen 1978).

7. It is tempting to propose for amount relatives (Carlson 1977; Heim 1987; Grosu & Landman 1998) the same syntactic analysis as for restrictive relatives, namely involving a head noun in the specifier position of an RP. The difference with restrictive relatives appears to be that the restrictor (C_1) adds to the extent delimitation an element of cardinality or degree (presumably through some interaction with the top determiner (cf. Grosu & Landman 1998)). However, certain properties of amount relatives (notably the absence of an indefiniteness effect inside the relative clause) suggest that the status of the gap in the relative clause is different in amount relatives, which should be ascribed to the status of DP_{REL} rather than to the status of C_1. I will leave this aspect of the analysis for further study.

Appositive relative constructions should lack CP_1. As a result, appositives should not allow extraposition, apparently a correct prediction.

References

Baker, M.C. (1988). *Incorporation; A Theory of Grammatical Function Changing*. University of Chicago Press.
Barbiers, S. (1995). *The Syntax of Interpretation*. Dissertation, University of Leiden.
Barrett-Keach, C. (1985). *The Syntax and Interpretation of the Relative Clause Construction in Swahili*. New York: Garland.
Basilico, D. (1996). Head Position and Internally Headed Relative Clauses. *Language* 72: 498–532.
Bayer, J. (1984). COMP in Bavarian Syntax. *The Linguistic Review* 3: 209–274.
Besten, H. den. (1977). *On the Interaction of Root Transformations and Lexical Deletive Rules*. Manuscript. MIT/University of Amsterdam.
Bianchi, V. (1999). *Consequences of Antisymmetry: headed relative clauses*. Berlin: Mouton de Gruyter.
Boer, B. de. (1950). *Studie over het dialect van Hindeloopen*. Van Gorcum, Assen.
Bokamba, E.G. (1976). Relativization in Bantu Languages Revisited. *The Second LACUS Forum 1975*, Edited by P.A. Reich. 292–310. Hornbeam Press: Columbia,.
Carlson, G. (1977). Amount Relatives. *Language* 53: 520–542.
Chomsky, N. (1977). On Wh-Movement. *Formal Syntax*, Edited by P.W. Culicover, T. Wasow, & A. Akmajian, 71–132. Academic Press, New York,
Chomsky, N. (1986). *Barriers*. Cambridge: MIT Press.
Chomsky, N. (1991). Some Notes on Economy of Derivation and Representation. *Principles and Parameters in Comparative Grammar*, Edited by R. Freidin. 417–454. Cambridge: MIT Press.
Cole, P. (1987). The structure of internally headed relative clauses. *Natural Language and Linguistic Theory* 5: 277–302.
Dek, J. (1934). *Het Kruiningsch dialekt II*. Middelburg.
Dumoulin, P. & J. Coumans. (1986). *Sjöd miech nog eint in. Het dialect van Maastricht*. BZZTôH, The Hague.

Grosu, A. & F. Landman. (1998). Strange Relatives of the Third Kind. *Natural Language Semantics* 6, 125–170.
Haeringen, C B.van (1939). Congruerende voegwoorden. *Tijdschrift voor Nederlandse Taal- en Letterkunde* 58: 161–176.
Heim, I. (1987). Where Does the Indefiniteness Restriction Apply?. *The Representation of (In)definiteness*, Edited by E.J. Reuland & A.G.B. ter Meulen. Cambridge: MIT Press.
Hoekstra, E. (1993). Dialectal Variation inside CP as Parametric Variation. *Dialektsyntax*, [*Linguistische Berichte* Sonderheft 5], Edited by W. Abraham & J. Bayer, 161–179.
Hoekstra, E. (1994). Overtollige voegwoorden en de volgorde *of + interrogativum/ relativum*. *De nieuwe taalgids* 87: 314–321.
Hoekstra, E. & J.-W. Zwart (1994). De struktuur van CP: Functionele projecties voor topics en vraagwoorden in het Nederlands. *Spektator* 23, 191–212.
Hoekstra, J. & L. Marácz (1989). On the Position of Inflection in West Germanic. *Working Papers in Scandinavian Syntax* 44: 75–88.
Kayne, R.S. (1994). *The Antisymmetry of Syntax*. Cambridge: MIT Press.
Koster, J. (1975). Dutch as an SOV Language. *Linguistic Analysis* 1: 111–136.
Koster, J. (1996). *Left-Right Asymmetries in Dutch*. Paper presented at the Workshop on Relative Clauses, Berlin, November 1996.
Laan, K. ter. (1953). *Proeve van een Groninger Spraakkunst*. Winschoten: Van der Veen.
Larson, R. & G. Segal (1996). *Knowledge of Meaning. An Introduction to Semantic Theory*. Cambridge: MIT Press.
Maling, J. (1978). The Complementizer in Middle English Appositives. *Linguistic Inquiry* 9: 719–725.
Montague, R. (1973). The Proper Treatment of Quantification in Ordinary English. *Approaches to Natural Language*, Edited by J. Hintikka, J.M.E. Moravcsik, & P. Suppes. Dordrecht: Reidel.
Müller, G. & W. Sternefeld. (1993). Improper Movement and Unambiguous Binding. *Linguistic Inquiry* 24: 461–507.
Mustanoja, T.F. (1960). *Middle English Syntax I.*, Helsinki: Société néophilologique.
Nadkarni, M. (1970). *NP-Embedded Structures in Kannada and Konkani*. Doctoral Dissertation, UCLA. [reference in Partee 1975]
Overdiep, G.S. (1940). *De Volkstaal van Katwijk aan Zee*. Antwerp: Standaard Boekhandel.
Partee, B. (1975). Montague Grammar and Transformational Grammar. *Linguistic Inquiry* 6: 203–300.
Paul, H. (1920). *Deutsche Grammatik IV*. Halle: Max Niemeyer.
Polomé, E.C. (1967). *Swahili Language Handbook*. Washington: Center for Applied Linguistics.
Postma, G. (1995). *Zero Semantics*. Doctoral Dissertation University of Leiden.
Rooy, J.de. (1965). *Als-Of-Dat*. Van Gorcum, Assen.
Stoett, F.A. (1977). *Middelnederlandsche Spraakkunst. Syntaxis*. The Hague: Martinus Nijhoff.

Taraldsen, K. T. (1978). The Scope of Wh-Movement in Norwegian. *Linguistic Inquiry* 9: 623–640.
Teirlinck, I. (1924). *Klank- en vormleer van het Zuid-Oostvlaandersch dialect*. Gent: W. Siffer.
Tiersma, P. M. (1985). *Frisian Reference Grammar*. Dordrecht: Foris.
Vanacker, V. F. (1948). *Syntaxis van het Aalsters dialect*. Gent.
Vercoullie, J. (1925). *Beknopt Etymologisch Woordenboek*. [Third Impression]. Gent: Van Rysselberghe & Rombout.
Verdam, J. (1911). *Middelnederlandsch Handwoordenboek*. The Hague: Martinus Nijhoff.
Vergnaud, J.-R. (1974). *French Relative Clauses*. Doctoral Dissertation, MIT.
Vikner, S. (1995). *Verb Movement and Expletive Subjects in the Germanic Languages*. New York: Oxford University Press.
Vitale, A. J. (1981). *Swahili Syntax*. Dordrecht: Foris.
Vries, M. de. (1996). *Relatieve bijzinnen in de zinsstructuur van Kayne*. MA-thesis, University of Groningen.
Wanink, G. H. (1948). *Twents-Achterhoeks Woordenboek met grammatica*. Thieme, Zutphen.
Zwart, C. J. W. (1993). *Dutch Syntax, A Minimalist Approach*. Doctoral Dissertation, University of Groningen.
Zwart, C. J. W. (1997). *Morphosyntax of Verb Movement; A Minimalist Approach to the Syntax of Dutch*. Dordrecht: Kluwer Academic Publishers.
Zwart, C. J. W. (1998). Where Is Syntax? Syntactic properties of left dislocation in Dutch and English. *The Limits of Syntax*, Edited by P. Culicover & L. McNally. [Syntax and Semantics Series]. San Diego: Academic Press.

Name Index

A

Abney, S.   153, 197
Åfarli, T.   299
Akmajian, A.   177
Alexiadou, A.   25, 44, 154
Allen, C. L.   55
Allwood, J.   275
Anagnostopoulou, E.   291, 296
Andersson, L.-G.   275
Andrews, A.   14, 21, 44
Aoun, J.   128

B

Babby, L.   64
Baker, M. C.   376
Baltin, M.   206
Barbiers, S.   372
Barker, C.   155
Barrett-Keach, C.   372f., 382
Barss, A.   7, 9f.
Barwise, J.   193, 312
Basilico, D.   368
Bayer, J.   148, 276, 359
Besten, H. d.   362
Bianchi, V.   9, 18f., 31f., 35–37, 43, 77, 79, 98–102, 105–109, 111f., 114, 143, 194, 312, 351, 357, 367, 370, 376, 380f.
Boer, B. de   358
Bokamba, E. G.   382
Borer, H.   128

Borsley, R.   16, 32, 44, 105f., 114, 153, 194, 266, 303
Boskovic, Z.   10
Bouchard, D.   297
Bresnan, J.   6, 23, 45, 155f.
Browning, M.   3, 5–7, 10, 44, 59, 76, 190

C

Campbell, R.   323, 345
Cardinaletti, A.   303
Carlson, G.   10–12, 21, 28–30, 88f., 96, 105, 109, 112f., 116, 299, 345, 383
Chomsky, N.   2f., 5–7, 9, 17f., 23, 36, 44, 59, 62f., 69, 77, 83f., 99, 106, 111, 122, 125, 128, 139, 148f., 161, 163, 167, 169f., 172, 174, 178, 180f., 183f., 186f., 189–192, 194, 196, 202, 225, 269, 284, 300, 332, 334, 349, 363
Cinque, G.   125, 154, 184f., 300
Cole, P.   20, 27, 29, 241–244, 246, 261, 368
Collins, C.   155
Comrie, B.   45, 153
Cooper, R.   193, 282, 312
Corver, N.   5
Csató, E.   155

D

Dasgupta, P. 205f.
Dayal, V. 45f., 54, 76f., 89, 100, 102, 104, 110, 113
Dek, J. 358, 362, 382
Delsing, L.-O. 266, 269f., 272f., 276, 282, 300f.
Demirdache, H. 5
Den Dikken, M. 10, 45
Donaldson, S. 201, 205
Downing, B.T. 27, 45, 54
Dumoulin, P. 358

E

Emonds, J. 34, 37f., 96, 98, 101, 103, 116f., 161, 163–167, 170–172, 177, 182f., 196, 280
Enç, M. 94
Engdahl, E. 275
Ernout, A. 78
Erteschik-Shir, N. 275

F

Fabb, N. 34, 46, 98, 101
Ferguson, K. S. 303
Fiengo, R. 237
Franks, S. 64
Friedemann, M.-A. 114

G

Gärtner, H.-M. 46f.
Giusti, G. 64
Grimshaw, J. 23, 45, 331
Groos, A. 23
Grosu, A. 15, 21, 23–26, 28–30, 33f., 36f., 39, 45f., 76f., 83, 86, 90, 93f., 383

H

Haeringen, C. B. v. 363
Haider, H. 304
Hale, K. 248
Halle, M. 36, 64

Hankamer, J. 134, 137, 139, 144, 155
Harada, S. I. 248f., 251f.
Harbert, W. 55, 58, 60, 69, 74, 78f.
Haudry, J. 54, 56f., 66, 74, 77, 79
Heim, I. 10, 28, 311, 383
Hellan, L. 282
Heycock, C. 10
Higginbotham, J. 315–317, 320, 324, 345
Higgins, F. R. 7, 45
Hock, H. H. 54
Hoekstra, E. 43, 350, 356f., 359, 363, 377, 381
Hoji, H. 40, 232f., 235
Holmberg, A. 272, 273, 302
Honda, K. K. 260
Horvath, J. 101, 140
Hoshi, K. 253, 260
Huang, C.-T. J. 13, 99, 153f., 179–181, 183

I

Iatridou, S. 45
Ishii, Y. 253, 259
Ito, J. 246f., 261
Izvorski, R. 25, 37

J

Jackendoff, R. 5, 34, 37, 98, 101, 114, 176, 177, 196f., 280, 299, 328
Jacobson, P. 24, 29, 45
Jaeggli, O. 38, 130, 134, 139
Jones, C. 44
Jong, F. de 311, 329, 382

K

Kachru, Y. 201, 205
Källström, R. 282, 301
Kamp, H. 34
Kanerva, J. 155f.

NAME INDEX

Kayne, R. 1, 4, 14f., 17–20, 24f., 27f., 31, 33, 35–37, 40f., 43–46, 54, 60f., 69, 74, 77, 79, 97–99, 101f., 105f., 111f., 114, 122, 129, 152, 155, 192, 194, 201, 207, 212f., 216, 225–227, 231f., 236–238, 240f., 243–245, 254f., 258, 260, 265f., 276f., 280f., 286f., 290f., 293–295, 299f., 303, 305, 309, 330f., 349, 351, 355, 367–369, 371f., 374, 376, 381f.
Keenan, E. 27, 31, 45, 54, 193, 231, 238f.
Kenesei, I. 79
Kennelly, S. 153
Keyser, S.J. 191
Kiparsky, P. 67, 78
Kitagawa, Y. 191, 248
Knecht, L. 134, 137, 139, 144
Koopman, H. 149, 191
Kornfilt, J. 28, 38, 127f., 130, 133, 137f., 140, 152–156
Koster, J. 143, 188, 362, 372
Kroch, A. 10
Kroll, W. 78f.
Kuno, S. 40, 141, 146, 153, 232, 258, 260
Kuroda, S.-Y. 191, 232, 241, 246f., 253, 258, 309

L

Ladusaw, W. 92
Landman, F. 15, 21, 24, 26, 28–30, 34, 37, 39, 46, 76f., 83, 92, 94f., 383
Lappin, S. 89
Larson, R. 24f., 377
Lasnik, H. 18, 161, 163, 169f., 172, 183, 191f., 260, 269
Law, P. 18, 38, 172, 191
Lehmann, C. 21, 45, 100
Li, A. 128

Link, G. 13, 28, 37, 114, 283
Longobardi, G. 276, 328

M

Mahajan, A. 20, 26, 39f., 45, 204, 206, 213, 216, 218, 223, 226, 239f.
Manzini, R. 36, 63, 106, 108
Marantz, A. 36, 64
May, R. 9, 172
McCawley, J. 12, 34, 37, 98, 101, 191, 205f., 227, 334
McCloskey, J. 128, 153f.
Mihara, K.-I. 232, 241, 245, 248
Milsark, G. 28, 94
Mitchell, B. 58
Moltmann, F. 44
Morgan, J. 300
Müller, G. 43, 357, 377
Muller, C. 85
Munn, A. 8
Murasugi, K. 29, 40, 231f., 235, 241, 245, 247f., 255–257, 259f.
Mustanoja, T.F. 357

N

Nadkarni, M. 382
Nepesova, R.G. 154
Nishigauchi, T. 153
Nunes, J. 333

O

Ortiz de Urbina, J. 140
Ouhalla, J. 128, 154f.
Overdiep, G.S. 359
Özsoy, S. 153

P

Panhuis, D.H. 78
Partee, B. 132, 193, 377, 380, 382
Paul, H. 360, 382
Peranteau, P.M. 44

Perlmutter, D.   13, 14, 40, 232, 238
Pesetsky, D.   148, 156
Pittner, K.   58, 60, 77, 78
Platzack, C.   9, 31, 41f., 291, 301, 303
Pollock, J.-Y.   177
Polomé, E. C.   373
Postma, G.   353
Pullum, G.   173, 175–177
Pustejovsky, J.   153

R
Raposo, E.   154
Reinhart, T.   83, 99, 169, 242
Riemsdijk, H. v.   23, 155, 300
Rizzi, L.   36, 63, 72, 77, 84f., 129f., 142f., 156, 178, 187, 195, 302, 331
Rooryck, J.   45
Rooy, J. de   356
Ross, J. R.   13f., 125, 139, 152, 181, 184, 194, 280
Rothstein, S.   30
Rouveret, A.   186
Rudin, C.   25
Rullmann, H.   24, 29, 46, 89

S
Safir, Kenneth   3, 34, 37, 76, 100f., 130
Sag, I.   191
Saito, M.   234, 237, 240, 243, 260
Schachter, P.   11, 61, 105, 192f.
Schmalz, J. H.   78
Schmitt, C.   11, 30, 42f., 283f., 301, 335, 337, 344, 346
Sells, P.   33f.
Sjoberg, A. F.   154
Smith, C.   3f., 8, 193, 265
Smits, R.   45
Srivastav, V.   21, 25f., 39, 45, 54f., 74–77, 79, 89, 100, 102, 104, 110, 113, 205–212, 224, 226f.

Stechow, A. v.   9, 46, 89
Sternefeld, W.   43, 357, 377
Stockwell, R.   8, 193
Stoett, F. A.   360
Stowell, T.   191, 236, 276, 329, 345
Subbarao, K. V.   201, 205–207, 210, 223
Suñer, M.   154
Szabolcsi, A.   323

T
Tanaka, H.   153
Taraldsen, K. T.   304, 383
Teirlinck, I.   358
Teleman, U.   289
Thomas, F.   78
Tiersma, P. M.   358
Trask, R. L.   151
Truckenbrodt, H.   216, 227
Tsubomoto, A.   260

U
Underhill, R.   134, 137, 144

V
Vanacker, V. F.   358
Varlokosta, S.   25, 45
Vat, J.   294–296
Vercoullie, J.   360
Verdam, J.   360
Vergnaud, R.   3f., 8, 11, 61, 152, 186, 192, 212, 265, 280, 309, 311, 330, 349
Verkuyl, H.   43, 336, 346
Vikner, S.   362
Vitale, A. J.   382

W
Wali, K.   205
Wanink, G. H.   358
Watanabe, A.   29
Webelhuth, G.   240

Wilder, C. 20, 44–46, 85, 97, 186, 194, 218f., 221, 227, 266, 286
Williams, E. 44f., 115
Williamson, J. 13, 20, 30
Wiltschko, M. 47

X
Xu, D. 274

Z
Zaenen, A. 296
Zagona, K. 177
Zimmer, K. 155
Zushi, M. 255
Zwart, C.J.-W. 18, 36, 43, 357, 359, 362–364, 377

Subject Index

A
acquisition   163, 172, 189, 231f., 235, 237, 255, 259
antisymmetry   15, 60f., 63, 74, 98f., 111f., 114, 207, 231f., 237, 255, 260, 331

C
Case attraction   35, 58–60, 68–70, 74, 77–79
Case theory   39, 186–189
checking (checking theory, checking configuration)   36, 59, 63, 66, 72, 77, 107f., 145, 187, 194, 196, 273, 276, 279, 302, 327f., 332–335, 337–339, 341f., 344, 346
complementizer   14, 27, 30f., 41, 43, 72, 105, 123, 164, 166, 168, 173f., 178, 191f., 236, 245–247, 255, 259, 269, 273, 279, 284f., 287f., 290, 296f., 299f., 302, 350, 355, 357–363, 369, 373f., 381–383

Copy theory   7, 16, 28, 202, 204, 207, 218, 225

D
deletion   27, 39f., 106, 165–167, 171, 205, 214–216, 218f., 226f., 244f., 248, 300, 302

demonstrative   43, 67f., 73, 78, 201, 211, 224, 226, 272, 301, 303, 321, 323, 330, 333, 340f., 350f., 359, 363, 365, 369, 379–381
determiner
    determiner complementation   1, 11, 14, 16, 24, 28, 42, 44
    determiner transparency   42, 310, 314, 319, 321, 330, 345
    relative determiner   32, 36, 43, 56, 66, 69, 70–73, 75, 79

E
extraposition   5f., 18–20, 42f., 85, 139, 205–207, 212, 216, 218f., 222, 286, 304, 354, 356, 370–372, 381, 383

G
generalized binding   38, 122, 137, 146

I
idiom (idiom chunk)   11f., 42, 44, 166, 168, 297, 311, 314, 334

L
languages
    Ancient Greek   35, 53, 58, 60, 67, 72, 74, 78
    Basque   140
    Bavarian   148, 276, 359

Brazilian Portuguese 43, 313, 317–321, 324f., 336, 340
Bulgarian 22, 25
Chinese 154, 179–181, 194, 274
Danish 275, 301
Dutch 43, 90, 94, 115, 143, 349–353, 355–360, 362–364, 370, 372, 374, 377–379, 381f.
English 6, 14–18, 25, 27, 30, 38, 41, 45f., 90–94, 100, 109, 123–127, 132, 148f., 152, 155, 163f., 170, 179–181, 191, 193–195, 197, 203, 219, 233–236, 245, 258, 266, 273, 279f., 283, 289–300, 302, 313, 317–319, 324f., 328, 336f., 340, 344f., 355, 357
French 17, 28, 85, 90, 94, 103, 148f., 151
Frisian 358
German 2f., 8, 18, 46f., 78, 90, 115f., 143, 155f., 194, 197, 219, 237, 276, 294–296, 303, 331, 333, 360, 382
Greek 22, 25, 31, 90, 194
(Modern) Hebrew 90, 92
Hindi 20f., 25–27, 29, 35, 39f., 45, 47, 54f., 60, 65, 74, 113, 201–207, 210, 212–214, 216–219, 223, 225–227, 239
Hungarian 79, 140
Icelandic 296, 301
Indonesian 100
Italian 17, 31, 130, 195
Japanese 12, 20, 29, 40, 46, 112, 115f., 141, 153–155, 231–241, 243–248, 253–261
Lakhota 12f., 20, 30
Latin 35f., 53–55, 58–60, 62, 65, 67, 71–74, 78, 352, 367, 369
Norwegian 275, 297, 301, 304, 383

Old English 35, 53–55, 58, 60, 65, 74, 77
Old High German 35, 53, 58–60, 77
Persian 152
Quechua 12, 20, 29, 368f., 382
Romanian 90–93, 95, 113
Russian 64, 92
Spanish 130, 325, 337
Swedish 31, 41f., 265–269, 272f., 275, 277–280, 282f., 289, 291, 297, 300–303, 305
Turkish 28, 38, 112, 115, 121–125, 127–130, 132, 135, 139, 141, 143f., 148f., 151–156
Turkmen 154
Yiddish 156
Yucatec Mayan 100
Linear Correspondence Axiom (LCA) 15f., 20, 27, 41, 46, 309

M
maximalization 21, 24, 28f., 76, 90, 92, 102f.

N
nominalization 121–123, 125, 128f., 134–137, 140, 143f., 151f.
null operator (empty operator) 3, 6–8, 16, 44, 189f., 300

P
pied-piping 15, 17, 19, 25, 42, 45, 105, 108, 332
promotion (head-raising) analysis
 head movement analysis 4, 7f., 13–15, 27, 41f., 349, 351, 353–356, 364, 367, 373, 376–378, 381
 raising analysis 7–9, 11f., 14, 16, 28, 31f., 35f., 42f., 60f., 64f., 74f., 77–79, 100, 105, 111f., 114f., 126, 192, 266f., 290,

SUBJECT INDEX

295–297, 299, 331, 334, 349, 351, 353–356, 364, 367, 373, 376–378, 381

R

reconstruction   7–9, 12, 16, 31f., 40f., 98, 106, 111f., 233, 238, 240, 265–267, 297

relative clause types
  appositive   5, 21, 30–34, 37, 41, 44, 46, 77, 85, 96–100, 102, 109, 112, 114–116 265f., 268, 270–291, 293–297, 299–304, 345
  correlative   20f., 25–27, 29, 35–37, 39, 45f., 54–57, 65–68, 74–78, 85f., 88f., 92, 96, 99f., 102, 104, 110, 113, 115, 201–205, 207, 225, 380
  degree relative 5f., 8, 21, 28f., 37, 44, 112f.
  existential relative   85f., 91, 103, 111

free relative   20f., 29, 44, 79, 91–96, 110, 359
hydra   13, 37, 114, 280, 282
internally headed (head internal) relative   12f., 20f., 27, 40, 46, 231f., 241–248, 250–255, 261, 382
maximalizing relative   21, 28–30, 37, 87–90, 96, 100, 102f., 105, 109–112, 116
multiple relative   40, 75, 212
prenominal (head final, N-final) relative   27f., 40, 46, 202, 231, 237–244, 255, 367–370, 381

S

stacking   15, 30, 42, 345

W

wh-in-situ   204, 213
wh-movement   2f., 5–8, 10, 13, 25, 29, 108, 139, 153, 377
wh-pronoun   3, 6, 30, 45, 105f., 108

In the series LINGUISTIK AKTUELL/LINGUISTICS TODAY (LA) the following titles have been published thus far, or are scheduled for publication:

1. KLAPPENBACH, Ruth (1911-1977): *Studien zur Modernen Deutschen Lexikographie. Auswahl aus den Lexikographischen Arbeiten von Ruth Klappenbach, erweitert um drei Beiträge von Helene Malige-Klappenbach.* 1980.
2. EHLICH, Konrad & Jochen REHBEIN: *Augenkommunikation. Methodenreflexion und Beispielanalyse.* 1982.
3. ABRAHAM, Werner (ed.): *On the Formal Syntax of the Westgermania. Papers from the 3rd Groningen Grammar Talks (3e Groninger Grammatikgespräche), Groningen, January 1981.* 1983.
4. ABRAHAM, Werner & Sjaak De MEIJ (eds): *Topic, Focus and Configurationality. Papers from the 6th Groningen Grammar Talks, Groningen, 1984.* 1986.
5. GREWENDORF, Günther and Wolfgang STERNEFELD (eds): *Scrambling and Barriers.* 1990.
6. BHATT, Christa, Elisabeth LÖBEL and Claudia SCHMIDT (eds): *Syntactic Phrase Structure Phenomena in Noun Phrases and Sentences.* 1989.
7. ÅFARLI, Tor A.: *The Syntax of Norwegian Passive Constructions.* 1992.
8. FANSELOW, Gisbert (ed.): *The Parametrization of Universal Grammar.* 1993.
9. GELDEREN, Elly van: *The Rise of Functional Categories.* 1993.
10. CINQUE, Guglielmo and Guiliana GIUSTI (eds): *Advances in Roumanian Linguistics.* 1995.
11. LUTZ, Uli and Jürgen PAFEL (eds): *On Extraction and Extraposition in German.* 1995.
12. ABRAHAM, W., S. EPSTEIN, H. THRÁINSSON and C.J.W. ZWART (eds): *Minimal Ideas. Linguistic studies in the minimalist framework.* 1996.
13. ALEXIADOU Artemis and T. Alan HALL (eds): *Studies on Universal Grammar and Typological Variation.* 1997.
14. ANAGNOSTOPOULOU, Elena, Henk VAN RIEMSDIJK and Frans ZWARTS (eds): *Materials on Left Dislocation.* 1997.
15. ROHRBACHER, Bernhard Wolfgang: *Morphology-Driven Syntax. A theory of V to I raising and pro-drop.* 1999.
16. LIU, FENG-HSI: *Scope and Specificity.* 1997.
17. BEERMAN, Dorothee, David LEBLANC and Henk van RIEMSDIJK (eds): *Rightward Movement.* 1997.
18. ALEXIADOU, Artemis: *Adverb Placement. A case study in antisymmetric syntax.* 1997.
19. JOSEFSSON, Gunlög: *Minimal Words in a Minimal Syntax. Word formation in Swedish.* 1998.
20. LAENZLINGER, Christopher: *Comparative Studies in Word Order Variation. Adverbs, pronouns, and clause structure in Romance and Germanic.* 1998.
21. KLEIN, Henny: *Adverbs of Degree in Dutch and Related Languages.* 1998.
22. ALEXIADOU, Artemis and Chris WILDER (eds): *Possessors, Predicates and Movement in the Determiner Phrase.* 1998.
23. GIANNAKIDOU, Anastasia: *Polarity Sensitivity as (Non)Veridical Dependency.* 1998.
24. REBUSCHI, Georges and Laurice TULLER (eds): *The Grammar of Focus.* 1999.
25. FELSER, Claudia: *Verbal Complement Clauses. A minimalist study of direct perception constructions.* 1999.
26. ACKEMA, Peter: *Issues in Morphosyntax.* 1999.

27. RŮŽIČKA, Rudolf: *Control in Grammar and Pragmatics. A cross-linguistic study.* 1999.
28. HERMANS, Ben and Marc van OOSTENDORP (eds.): *The Derivational Residue in Phonological Optimality Theory.* 1999.
29. MIYAMOTO, Tadao: *The Light Verb Construction in Japanese. The role of the verbal noun.* 1999.
30. BEUKEMA, Frits and Marcel den DIKKEN (eds.): *Clitic Phenomena in European Languages.* 2000.
31. SVENONIUS, Peter (ed.): *The Derivation of VO and OV.* n.y.p.
32. ALEXIADOU, Artemis, Paul LAW, André MEINUNGER and Chris WILDER (eds.): *The Syntax of Relative Clauses.* 2000.
33. PUSKÁS, Genoveva: *Word Order in Hungarian. The syntax of $\bar{A}$-positions.* n.y.p.
34. REULAND, Eric (ed.): *Arguments and Case. Explaining Burzio's Generalization.* n.y.p.
35. HRÓARSDÓTTIR, Thorbjörg. *Word Order Change in Icelandic. From OV to VO.* n.y.p.
36. GRIJZENHOUT, Janet and Birgit GERLACH (eds.): *Clitics in Phonology, Morphology and Syntax.* n.y.p.
37. LUTZ, Uli, Gereon MÜLLER and Arnim von STECHOW (eds.): *Wh-Scope Marking.* n.y.p.
38. MEINUNGER, André: *Syntactic Aspects of Topic and Comment.* n.y.p.
39. GELDEREN, Elly van: *A History of English Reflexive Pronouns. Person, "Self", and Interpretability.* n.y.p.
40. HOEKSEMA, Jack, Hotze RULLMANN, Victor SANCHEZ-VALENCIA and Ton van der WOUDEN (eds.): *Perspectives on Negation and Polarity Items.* n.y.p.